MICROSOFT
Access 97
Complete Concepts and Techniques

Gary B. Shelly
Thomas J. Cashman
Philip J. Pratt

SHELLY
CASHMAN
SERIES®

COURSE TECHNOLOGY
ONE MAIN STREET
CAMBRIDGE MA 02142

an International Thomson Publishing company I(T)P®

CAMBRIDGE ALBANY BONN CINCINNATI LONDON MADRID MELBOURNE

MEXICO CITY NEW YORK PARIS SAN FRANCISCO TOKYO TORONTO WASHINGTON

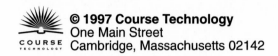

© **1997 Course Technology**
One Main Street
Cambridge, Massachusetts 02142

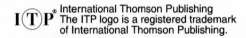

International Thomson Publishing
The ITP logo is a registered trademark
of International Thomson Publishing.

Printed in the United States of America

For more information, contact Course Technology:

Course Technology
One Main Street
Cambridge, Massachusetts 02142, USA

International Thomson Publishing Europe
Berkshire House
168-173 High Holborn
London, WC1V 7AA, United Kingdom

Thomas Nelson Australia
102 Dodds Street
South Melbourne
Victoria 3205 Australia

Nelson Canada
1120 Birchmont Road
Scarborough, Ontario
Canada M1K 5G4

International Thomson Editores
Campos Eliseos 385, Piso 7
Colonia Polanco
11560 Mexico D.F. Mexico

International Thomson Publishing GmbH
Konigswinterer Strasse 418
53227 Bonn, Germany

International Thomson Publishing Asia
Block 211, Henderson Road #08-03
Henderson Industrial Park
Singapore 0315

International Thomson Publishing Japan
Hirakawa-cho Kyowa Building, 3F
2-2-1 Hirakawa-cho, Chiyoda-ku
Tokyo 102, Japan

ISBN 0-7895-1344-7

PHOTO CREDITS: *Project 1, pages A 1.4-5*, James Smithson, Courtesy of Smithsonian Institute; American flag, © Metatools, created by PhotoSpin; *Project 2, pages A 2.2-3*, Credit card and mail sign, Courtesy of Corel Professional Photos CD-ROM Image usage; David Janssen, provided by Motion Picture & Television Photo Archive, sign post and path, © Metatools, created by PhotoSpin; *Project 3, pages A 3.2-3*, Dr. Thaddeus S. C. Lowe, provided by NorthWind Archives; Goodyear blimp photo, Courtesy of Goodyear Rubber and Tire Company; *Project 4, page A 4.4* Pelicans, Courtesy of Corel Professional Photos CD-ROM Image usage; *Project 5, pages A 5.2-3* Medieval man and Roman ruins, Courtesy of Corel Professional Photos CD-ROM Image usage; *Project 6, pages A 6.2-3* Indian, Indian painting, Brahman, and dragon Courtesy of Corel Professional Photos CD-ROM Image usage.

3 4 5 6 7 8 9 10   BC   10 9 8 7

MICROSOFT
Access 97

Complete Concepts and Techniques

▶ **PROJECT FIVE**
ENHANCING FORMS WITH OLE FIELDS,
HYPERLINKS, AND SUBFORMS

▶ **PROJECT SIX**
CREATING AN APPLICATION SYSTEM USING
MACROS, VBA, AND THE SWITCHBOARD
MANAGER

▶ INTEGRATION FEATURE
LINKING EXCEL WORKSHEETS
TO AN ACCESS DATABASE

Preface

The Shelly Cashman Series® offers the finest textbooks in computer education. The Microsoft Office 97 books continue with the innovation, quality, and reliability that you have come to expect from this series. We are proud that both our Office 95 and Office 4.3 books are best-sellers, and we are confident that our Office 97 books will join their predecessors.

With Office 97, Microsoft has raised the stakes by adding a number of new features, especially the power of the Internet. The Shelly Cashman Series team has responded with Office 97 books that present the core application concepts required in any introductory application software course, as well as new features such as the Office 97 Internet tools.

In our Office 97 books, you will find an educationally sound and easy-to-follow pedagogy that combines a step-by-step approach with corresponding screens. Every project and exercise in the books are new and designed to take full advantage of the Office 97 features. The popular Other Ways and More About features have been amended to offer in-depth knowledge of Office 97. The all-new project openers provide a fascinating perspective on the subject covered in the project. The Shelly Cashman Series Office 97 books will make your computer application software class an exciting and dynamic one that your students will remember as one of their better educational experiences.

Objectives of This Textbook

Microsoft Access 97: Complete Concepts and Techniques is intended for a two-unit course that presents Microsoft Access 97. No experience with a computer is assumed, and no mathematics beyond the high school freshman level is required. The objectives of this book are:

▶ To teach the fundamentals of Microsoft Access 97

▶ To help students demonstrate their proficiency in Microsoft Access 97 and prepare them to pass the Expert level Microsoft Office User Specialist Exam for Microsoft Access 97

▶ To foster an appreciation of databases as a useful tool in the workplace

▶ To give students an in-depth understanding of database design; creating a database; querying a database; maintaining a database; importing an Excel worksheet into an Access database; creating reports and forms; publishing reports to the Web; enhancing forms by using OLE fields, hyperlinks, and subforms; and using macros, VBA, and the Switchboard Manager to create an application system

▶ To expose students to examples of the computer as a useful tool

▶ To develop an exercise-oriented approach that allows students to learn by example

▶ To encourage independent study and help those who are working on their own in a distance education environment

Approved by Microsoft as Courseware for the Microsoft Office User Specialist Program — Expert Level

This book has been approved by Microsoft as courseware for the Microsoft Office User Specialist program. After completing the projects and exercises in this book, the student will be prepared to take the Expert level Microsoft Office User Specialist Exam for Microsoft Access 97. By passing the certification exam for a Microsoft software program students demonstrate their proficiency in that program to employers. This exam is offered at participating test centers, participating corporations, and participating employment agencies. For more information about certification, please visit Microsoft's World Wide Web site at http://microsoft.com/office/train_cert/.

The Shelly Cashman Approach

Features of the Shelly Cashman Series Office 97 books include:

▶ Project Orientation: Each project in the book uses the unique Shelly Cashman Series screen-by-screen, step-by-step approach.

▶ Screen-by-Screen, Step-by-Step Instructions: Each of the tasks required to complete a project is identified throughout the development of the project. Then, steps to accomplish the task are specified. The steps are accompanied by screens. Hence, students learn from this book the same as if they were using a computer.

▶ Thoroughly Tested Projects: The computer screens in the Shelly Cashman Series Office 97 books are captured from the author's computer. The screen is captured immediately after the author performs the step specified in the text. Therefore, every screen in the book is correct because it is produced only after performing a step, resulting in unprecedented quality in a computer textbook.

▶ Multiple Ways to Use the Book: This book can be used in a variety of ways, including: (a) Lecture and textbook approach — The instructor lectures on the material in the book. Students read and study the material and then apply the knowledge to an application on the computer; (b) Tutorial approach — Students perform each specified step on a computer. At the end of the project, students have solved the problem and are ready to solve comparable student assignments; (c) Other approaches — Many instructors lecture on the material and then require their students to perform each step in the project, reinforcing the material lectured. Students then complete one or more of the In the Lab exercises at the end of the project; and (d) Reference — Each task in a project is clearly identified. Therefore, the material serves as a complete reference.

▶ Other Ways Boxes for Reference: Microsoft Access 97 provides a variety of ways to carry out a given task. The Other Ways boxes included at the end of most of the step-by-step sequences specify the other ways to execute the task completed in the steps. Together, the steps and the Other Ways box make a comprehensive and convenient reference unit; you no longer have to reference tables at the end of a project or at the end of a book.

> **OtherWays**
> 1. Click Reports tab, select report, click Print button on toolbar
> 2. Click Reports tab, select report, on File menu click Print
> 3. Click Reports tab, select report, press CTRL+P

More *About* **Switchboards**

An application system is simply an easy-to-use collection of forms, reports, and/or queries designed to satisfy the needs of some specific user or groups of users, like the users at Pilotech Services. A switchboard system is one type of application system that is very popular in the Windows environment.

◗ More About Feature: The More About Features in the margins provide background information that complements the topics covered, adding interest and depth to the learning process.

Organization of This Textbook

Microsoft Access 97: Complete Concepts and Techniques provides detailed instruction on how to use Access 97. The material is divided into six projects and two integration features as follows:

Project 1 – Creating a Database Using Design and Datasheet Views   In Project 1, students are introduced to the concept of a database and shown how to use Access to create a database. Topics include creating a database; creating a table; defining the fields in a table; opening a table; adding records to a table; closing a table; and previewing and printing the contents of a table. Other topics in this project include using a form to view data; using the Report Wizard to create a report; and using Access Help. Students also learn how to design a database to eliminate redundancy.

Project 2 – Querying a Database Using the Select Query Window   In Project 2, students learn to use queries to obtain information from the data in their databases. Topics include creating queries, running queries, and printing the results. Specific query topics include displaying only selected fields; using character data in criteria; using wildcards; using numeric data in criteria; using various comparison operators; and creating compound criteria. Other related topics include sorting, joining tables, and restricting records in a join. Students also use computed fields, statistics, and grouping.

Project 3 – Maintaining a Database Using the Design and Update Features of Access
In Project 3, students learn the crucial skills involved in maintaining a database. Topics include using Datasheet view and Form view to add new records, to change existing records, and to delete records; and searching for a record. Students learn to change the structure of a table; add additional fields; change characteristics of existing fields; create a variety of validation rules; and specify referential integrity. Students perform mass changes and deletions using queries and create single-field and multiple-field indexes.

Integration Feature – Integrating Excel Worksheet Data into an Access Database   In this section, students learn how to create an Access table based on data stored in an Excel worksheet by using the Import Spreadsheet Wizard. Topics include creating a database and converting an Excel worksheet to an Access database.

Project 4 – Reports, Forms, and Publishing Reports on the Web   In Project 4, students learn to create custom reports and forms. Topics include creating queries for reports; using the Report Wizard; modifying a report design; saving a report; printing a report; creating a report with grouping and subtotals; removing totals from a report; and changing the characteristics of items on a report. They also learn how to publish the report they have created to the World Wide Web using the Publish to the Web Wizard. Other topics include creating an initial form using the Form Wizard; modifying a form design; moving fields; and adding calculated fields and combo boxes. Students learn how to change a variety of field characteristics such as font styles, formats, and colors.

Project 5 – Enhancing Forms with OLE Fields, Hyperlinks, and Subforms   In Project 5, students learn to use date, memo, OLE, and hyperlink fields. Topics include incorporating these fields in the structure of a database; updating the data in these fields and changing the table properties; creating a form that uses a subform to incorporate a one-to-many relationship between tables; manipulating subforms on a main form; incorporating date, memo, OLE, and hyperlink fields in forms; and incorporating various visual effects in forms. Students also learn to use the hyperlink fields to access Web pages and to use date and memo fields in a query.

Project 6 – Creating an Application System Using Macros, VBA, and the Switchboard Manager   In Project 6, students learn how to create a switchboard system, a system that allows users to easily access tables, forms, and reports simply by clicking buttons. Topics include creating and running macros; adding command buttons to a form; adding a combo box for finding records to a form; modifying VBA code associated with an object on a form; and creating and using a switchboard system.

Integration Feature 2 – Linking Excel Worksheets to an Access Database   In this section, students learn how to link Excel worksheets to an Access database. Topics include creating the Access database, linking the individual worksheets in a workbook to tables in the database, and using the linked worksheets.

End-of-Project Student Activities

A notable strength of the Shelly Cashman Series Office 97 books is the extensive student activities at the end of each project. Well-structured student activities can make the difference between students merely participating in a class and students retaining the information they learn. The activities in the Office 97 books include:

▶ **What You Should Know** A listing of the tasks completed within a project together with the pages where the step-by-step, screen-by-screen explanations appear. This section provides a perfect study review for students.

▶ **Test Your Knowledge** Four pencil-and-paper activities designed to determine students' understanding of the material in the project. Included are true/false questions, multiple-choice questions, and two short-answer activities.

▶ **Use Help** Any user of Access 97 must know how to use Help, including the Office Assistant. Therefore, this book contains two Use Help exercises per project. These exercises alone distinguish the Shelly Cashman Series from any other set of Office 97 instructional materials.

▶ **Apply Your Knowledge** This exercise requires students to open and manipulate a file on the Data Disk that accompanies the Office 97 books.

▶ **In the Lab** Three in-depth assignments per project require students to apply the knowledge gained in the project to solve problems on a computer.

▶ **Cases and Places** Seven unique case studies require students to apply their knowledge to real-world situations.

Instructor's Resource Kit

A comprehensive Instructor's Resource Kit (IRK) accompanies this textbook in the form of a CD-ROM. The CD-ROM includes an electronic Instructor's Manual (called ElecMan) and teaching and testing aids. The CD-ROM (ISBN 0-7895-1334-X) is available through your Course Technology representative or by calling one of the following telephone numbers: Colleges and Universities, 1-800-648-7450; High Schools, 1-800-824-5179; and Career Colleges, 1-800-477-3692. The contents of the CD-ROM are listed below.

▶ **ElecMan (*Electronic Instructor's Manual*)** ElecMan is made up of Microsoft Word files. The files include lecture notes, solutions to laboratory assignments, and a large test bank. The files allow you to modify the lecture notes or generate quizzes and exams from the test bank using your own word processor. Where appropriate, solutions to laboratory assignments are embedded as icons in the files. When an icon appears, double-click it; the application will start and the solution will display on the screen. ElecMan includes the following for each project: project objectives; project overview; detailed lesson plans with page number references; teacher notes and activities; answers to the end-of-project exercises; test bank of 110 questions for every project (50 true/false, 25 multiple choice, and 35 fill-in-the-blank) with page number references; and transparency references. The transparencies are available through the Figures on CD-ROM described below.

▶ **Figures on CD-ROM** Illustrations for every screen in the textbook are available. Use this ancillary to create a slide show from the illustrations for lecture or to print transparencies for use in lecture with an overhead projector.

▶ **Course Test Manager** This cutting-edge Windows-based testing software helps instructors design and administer tests and pretests. The full-featured online program permits students to take tests at the computer where their grades are computed immediately. Automatic statistics collection, student guides customized to the student's performance, and printed tests are only a few of the features.

▶ **Lecture Success System** Lecture Success System files are designed for use with the application software package, a personal computer, and a projection device. The files allow you to explain and illustrate the step-by-step, screen-by-screen development of a project in the textbook without entering large amounts of data.

▶ **Instructor's Lab Solutions** Solutions and required files for all the In the Lab assignments at the end of each project are available.

▶ **Lab Tests/Test Outs** Tests that parallel the In the Lab assignments are supplied for the purpose of testing students in the laboratory on the material covered in the project or testing students out of the course.

▶ **Student Files** All the files that are required by students to complete the Apply Your Knowledge and a few of the In the Lab exercises are included.

▶ **Interactive Labs** Eighteen hands-on interactive labs that take students from ten to fifteen minutes each to step through help solidify and reinforce mouse and keyboard usage and computer concepts.

Shelly Cashman Online

Shelly Cashman Online is a World Wide Web service available to instructors and students of computer education. Visit Shelly Cashman Online at www.scseries.com. Shelly Cashman Online is divided into four areas:

▶ **Series Information** Information on the Shelly Cashman Series products.

▶ **The Community** Opportunities to discuss your course and your ideas with instructors in your field and with the Shelly Cashman Series team.

▶ **Teaching Resources** Designed for instructors teaching from and using Shelly Cashman Series textbooks and software. This area includes password-protected instructor materials that can be downloaded, course outlines, teaching tips, and much more.

▶ **Student Center** Dedicated to students learning about computers with Shelly Cashman Series textbooks and software. This area includes cool links, data from Data Disks that can be downloaded, and much more.

Acknowledgments

The Shelly Cashman Series would not be the leading computer education series without the contributions of outstanding publishing professionals. First, and foremost, among them is Becky Herrington, director of production and designer. She is the heart and soul of the Shelly Cashman Series, and it is only through her leadership, dedication, and tireless efforts that superior products are made possible. Becky created and produced the award-winning Windows 95 series of books.

Under Becky's direction, the following individuals made significant contributions to these books: Peter Schiller, production manager; Ginny Harvey, series specialist and developmental editor; Ken Russo, Mike Bodnar, Stephanie Nance, Greg Herrington, and Dave Bonnewitz, graphic artists; Jeanne Black, Quark expert; Patti Koosed, editorial assistant; Nancy Lamm, Lyn Markowicz, Cherilyn King, Marilyn Martin, and Steve Marconi, proofreaders; Cristina Haley, indexer; Sarah Evertson of Image Quest, photo researcher; and Peggy Wyman and Jerry Orton, Susan Sebok, and Nancy Lamm, contributing writers.

Special thanks go to Jim Quasney, our dedicated series editor; Lisa Strite, senior product manager; Lora Wade, associate product manager; Scott MacDonald and Tonia Grafakos, editorial assistants; and Sarah McLean, product marketing manager. Special mention must go to Suzanne Biron, Becky Herrington, and Michael Gregson for the outstanding book design; Becky Herrington for the cover design; and Ken Russo for the cover illustrations.

Gary B. Shelly
Thomas J. Cashman
Philip J. Pratt

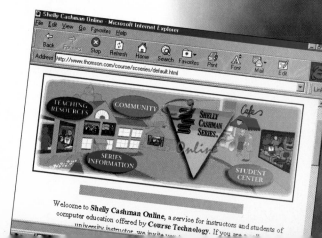

Shelly Cashman Series – Traditionally Bound Textbooks

The Shelly Cashman Series presents the following computer subjects in a variety of traditionally bound textbooks as shown in the table below. For more information, see your Course Technology representative or call one of the following telephone numbers: Colleges and Universities, 1-800-648-7450; High Schools, 1-800-824-5179; and Career Colleges, 1-800-477-3692.

COMPUTERS	
Computers	Discovering Computers: A Link to the Future, World Wide Web Enhanced
	Discovering Computers: A Link to the Future, World Wide Web Enhanced Brief Edition
	Using Computers: A Gateway to Information, World Wide Web Edition
	Using Computers: A Gateway to Information, World Wide Web Brief Edition
	Exploring Computers: A Record of Discovery 2e with CD-ROM
	A Record of Discovery for Exploring Computers 2e
	Study Guide for Discovering Computers: A Link to the Future, World Wide Web Enhanced
	Study Guide for Using Computers: A Gateway to Information, World Wide Web Edition
	Brief Introduction to Computers 2e (32-page)
WINDOWS APPLICATIONS	
Integrated Packages	Brief Introduction to Microsoft Office 97 (4 projects)
	Microsoft Office 97 Essentials (8 projects)
	Microsoft Office 97: Introductory Concepts and Techniques (15 projects)
	Microsoft Office 97: Advanced Concepts and Techniques
	Microsoft Office 95: Introductory Concepts and Techniques (15 projects)
	Microsoft Office 95: Advanced Concepts and Techniques
	Microsoft Office 4.3 running under Windows 95: Introductory Concepts and Techniques
	Microsoft Office for Windows 3.1 Introductory Concepts and Techniques Enhanced Edition
	Microsoft Office: Introductory Concepts and Techniques
	Microsoft Office: Advanced Concepts and Techniques
	Microsoft Works 4* • Microsoft Works 3.0*
Windows	Introduction to Microsoft Windows NT Workstation 4
	Microsoft Windows 95: Introductory Concepts and Techniques (96-page)
	Introduction to Microsoft Windows 95 (224-page)
	Microsoft Windows 95: Complete Concepts and Techniques
	Microsoft Windows 3.1 Introductory Concepts and Techniques
	Microsoft Windows 3.1 Complete Concepts and Techniques
Word Processing	Microsoft Word 97* • Microsoft Word 7* • Microsoft Word 6* • Microsoft Word 2.0
	Corel WordPerfect 7 • WordPerfect 6.1* • WordPerfect 6* • WordPerfect 5.2
Spreadsheets	Microsoft Excel 97* • Microsoft Excel 7* • Microsoft Excel 5* • Microsoft Excel 4
	Lotus 1-2-3 97* • Lotus 1-2-3 Release 5* • Lotus 1-2-3 Release 4* • Quattro Pro 6
Database Management	Microsoft Access 97* • Microsoft Access 7* • Microsoft Access 2
	Paradox 5 • Paradox 4.5 • Paradox 1.0 • Visual dBASE 5/5.5
Presentation Graphics	Microsoft PowerPoint 97* • Microsoft PowerPoint 7* • Microsoft PowerPoint 4*
DOS APPLICATIONS	
Operating Systems	DOS 6 Introductory Concepts and Techniques
	DOS 6 and Microsoft Windows 3.1 Introductory Concepts and Techniques
Word Processing	WordPerfect 6.1 • WordPerfect 6.0 • WordPerfect 5.1
Spreadsheets	Lotus 1-2-3 Release 4 • Lotus 1-2-3 Release 2.4 • Lotus 1-2-3 Release 2.3
Database Management	dBASE 5 • dBASE IV Version 1.1 • dBASE III PLUS • Paradox 4.5
PROGRAMMING AND NETWORKING	
Programming	Microsoft Visual Basic 5
	Microsoft Visual Basic 4 for Windows 95* (available with Student version software)
	Microsoft Visual Basic 3.0 for Windows*
	QBasic • QBasic: An Introduction to Programming • Microsoft BASIC
	Structured COBOL Programming (Micro Focus COBOL also available)
Networking	Novell NetWare for Users
	Business Data Communications: Introductory Concepts and Techniques
Internet	The Internet: Introductory Concepts and Techniques (UNIX)
	Netscape Navigator 4: An Introduction
	Netscape Navigator 3: An Introduction • Netscape Navigator 2 running under Windows 3.1
	Netscape Navigator: An Introduction (Version 1.1)
	Netscape Composer
	Microsoft Internet Explorer 3: An Introduction
SYSTEMS ANALYSIS	
Systems Analysis	Systems Analysis and Design, Second Edition

*Also available as a Double Diamond Edition, which is a shortened version of the complete book

Shelly Cashman Series – Custom Edition® Program

If you do not find a Shelly Cashman Series traditionally bound textbook to fit your needs, the Shelly Cashman Series unique **Custom Edition** program allows you to choose from a number of options and create a textbook perfectly suited to your course. Features of the **Custom Edition** program are:

▶ Textbooks that match the content of your course

▶ Windows- and DOS-based materials for the latest versions of personal computer applications software

▶ Shelly Cashman Series quality, with the same full-color materials and Shelly Cashman Series pedagogy found in the traditionally bound books

▶ Affordable pricing so your students receive the **Custom Edition** at a cost similar to that of traditionally bound books

The table on the right summarizes the available materials.

For more information, see your Course Technology representative or call one of the following telephone numbers: Colleges and Universities, 1-800-648-7450; High Schools, 1-800-824-5179; and Career Colleges, 1-800-477-3692.

For Shelly Cashman Series information, visit Shelly Cashman Online at **www.scseries.com**

COMPUTERS	
Computers	Discovering Computers: A Link to the Future, World Wide Web Enhanced
	Discovering Computers: A Link to the Future, World Wide Web Enhanced Brief Edition
	Using Computers: A Gateway to Information, World Wide Web Edition
	Using Computers: A Gateway to Information, World Wide Web Brief Edition
	A Record of Discovery for Exploring Computers 2e (available with CD-ROM)
	Study Guide for Discovering Computers: A Link to the Future, World Wide Web Enhanced
	Study Guide for Using Computers: A Gateway to Information, World Wide Web Edition
	Introduction to Computers (32-page)

OPERATING SYSTEMS	
Windows	Microsoft Windows 95: Introductory Concepts and Techniques (96-page)
	Introduction to Microsoft Windows NT Workstation 4
	Introduction to Microsoft Windows 95 (224-page)
	Microsoft Windows 95: Complete Concepts and Techniques
	Microsoft Windows 3.1 Introductory Concepts and Techniques
	Microsoft Windows 3.1 Complete Concepts and Techniques
DOS	Introduction to DOS 6 (using DOS prompt)
	Introduction to DOS 5.0 or earlier (using DOS prompt)

WINDOWS APPLICATIONS	
Integrated Packages	Microsoft Works 4*
	Microsoft Works 3.0*
Microsoft Office	Using Microsoft Office 97 (16-page)
	Using Microsoft Office 95 (16-page)
	Brief Introduction to Microsoft Office 97 (300-page)
	Microsoft Office 97 Essentials (576-page)
	Object Linking and Embedding (OLE) (32-page)
	Microsoft Outlook 97 • Microsoft Schedule+ 7
	Introduction to Integrating Office 97 Applications (48-page)
	Introduction to Integrating Office 95 Applications (80-page)
Word Processing	Microsoft Word 97* • Microsoft Word 7* • Microsoft Word 6* • Microsoft Word 2.0
	Corel WordPerfect 7 • WordPerfect 6.1* • WordPerfect 6* • WordPerfect 5.2
Spreadsheets	Microsoft Excel 97* • Microsoft Excel 7* • Microsoft Excel 5* • Microsoft Excel 4
	Lotus 1-2-3 97* • Lotus 1-2-3 Release 5* • Lotus 1-2-3 Release 4* Quattro Pro 6
Database Management	Microsoft Access 97* • Microsoft Access 7* • Microsoft Access 2*
	Paradox 5 • Paradox 4.5 • Paradox 1.0 • Visual dBASE 5/5.5
Presentation Graphics	Microsoft PowerPoint 97* • Microsoft PowerPoint 7* • Microsoft PowerPoint 4*

DOS APPLICATIONS	
Word Processing	WordPerfect 6.1 • WordPerfect 6.0 • WordPerfect 5.1
Spreadsheets	Lotus 1-2-3 Release 4 • Lotus 1-2-3 Release 2.4 • Lotus 1-2-3 Release 2.3
	Quattro Pro 3.0 • Quattro with 1-2-3 Menus
Database Management	dBASE 5 • dBASE IV Version 1.1 • dBASE III PLUS
	Paradox 4.5 • Paradox 3.5

PROGRAMMING AND NETWORKING	
Programming	Microsoft Visual Basic 5 • Microsoft Visual Basic 4 for Windows 95* (available with Student version software) • Microsoft Visual Basic 3.0 for Windows*
	Microsoft BASIC • QBasic
Networking	Novell NetWare for Users
Internet	The Internet: Introductory Concepts and Techniques (UNIX)
	Netscape Navigator 4: An Introduction
	Netscape Navigator 3: An Introduction
	Netscape Navigator 2 running under Windows 3.1
	Netscape Navigator: An Introduction (Version 1.1)
	Netscape Composer
	Microsoft Internet Explorer 3: An Introduction

*Also available as a mini-module

Microsoft *Access 97*

Microsoft Access 97

Creating a Database Using Design and Datasheet Views

Objectives:

You will have mastered the material in this project when you can:

▶ Describe databases and database management systems
▶ Start Access
▶ Describe the features of the Access screen
▶ Create a database
▶ Create a table
▶ Define the fields in a table
▶ Open a table
▶ Add records to an empty table
▶ Close a table
▶ Close a database and quit Access
▶ Open a database
▶ Add records to a nonempty table
▶ Print the contents of a table
▶ Use a form to view data
▶ Create a custom report
▶ Use Microsoft Access Help
▶ Design a database to eliminate redundancy

Selections
Collections
One of a Kind

*Anthology of Data
and Other Priceless
Keepsakes*

S eventy-four years after his
death, the skeleton of an
obscure, but wealthy English
scientist was disinterred and taken
across the Atlantic to lie with
honor in the institution his money
had founded — in a nation he had
never seen! His final resting place,
known as the "nation's attic," is
now home to a fabulous array of
artifacts that number in excess of
140 million. When James Smithson
left his fortune to the United
States to found the Smithsonian
Institution, he doubtless never
imagined how successful his
eccentric bequest would become.

Among its incredible collections, the Smithsonian displays
such rarities as the 45.5-karat Hope
Diamond, Judy Garland's ruby
slippers from *The Wizard of Oz*,
Charles Lindbergh's *Spirit of Saint
Louis*, the original Star-Spangled
Banner, and the wood-encased
prototype of the first Apple

DATABASE

ITEM	LOCATION
Ruby slippers	1st floor/rm.5
Spirit of St.	hanging
Apple comp.	2nd. floor/rm.3
Star banner	2nd. floor/rm.2

computer. Managing so many objects is no easy matter for the Smithsonian, which relies on computer databases to inventory and categorize its priceless collections and track the constant stream of donated articles.

Millions flock to see this eclectic display every year, partly from curiosity but also because collecting seems to be a common human fascination. Bootjacks, tintypes, inkwells, Elvis memorabilia, snuffboxes, ceramic dragons, tea cozies, and meerschaum pipes are among the thousands of articles that people collect. At the Southern California Exposition in Del Mar, California, even a collection of "Shoes without Mates — Found Beside the Freeway" was exhibited one year.

Compared to the Smithsonian's needs, most private collections do not require extensive databases. Yet, even in a modest book or music library, databases are convenient for locating an item or providing backup for tax purposes. As a collection expands, however, the need for a sophisticated database management system (DBMS), such as Microsoft Access 97, becomes increasingly important.

One of the more extensive applications of databases in today's world is that of gathering collections of names, addresses, and individual data, that then are used for such purposes as companies selling to or servicing clients, charities soliciting donations, politicians seeking support, or the U.S. government keeping tabs on Medicare benefits.

Whether you collect Pickard China or priceless paintings or just need to keep track of your friends and clients, Microsoft Access 97 provides the means to create your own information collection that can organize data on any subject quickly and easily. The Access Table Wizard helps you choose fields from a variety of predefined tables such as business contacts, household inventory, or medical records. If you want to create your own table, Access guides you each step of the process With its graphical user interface (GUI), you will find it easy to store, retrieve, and change data.

How favorable for the world that James Smithson did not squander his fortune collecting echoes like the hapless millionaire in Mark Twain's story, "The Canvasser's Tale." Even Access 97, with all its power, might have trouble managing echoes that talk back for fifteen minutes or others that speak only German.

Microsoft

Access 97

Creating a Database Using Design and Datasheet Views

Case Perspective

Pilotech Services is a new company offering a variety of technical services to its clients. Such services can include assistance with hardware and software problems, special backup services, archiving services, and so on. Each client is assigned to a specific technician at Pilotech. Services are billed at the technician's hourly billing rate. The management of Pilotech Services needs to maintain data on its technicians as well as its clients. By placing the data in a database, managed by a database management system such as Access, Pilotech ensures that its data is current and accurate. Using Access, managers are able to produce a variety of useful reports. In addition, they need to be able to ask questions concerning the data in the database and obtain answers to these questions easily and rapidly.

Introduction

Creating, storing, sorting, and retrieving data are important tasks. In their personal lives, many people keep a variety of records such as names, addresses, and telephone numbers of friends and business associates, records of investments, records of expenses for tax purposes, and so on. These records must be arranged for quick access. Businesses also must be able to store and access information quickly and easily. Personnel and inventory records, payroll information, client records, order data, and accounts receivable information all are crucial and must be available readily.

The term **database** describes a collection of data organized in a manner that allows access, retrieval, and use of that data. A database management system, such as Access, allows you to use a computer to create a database; add, change, and delete data in the database; sort the data in the database; retrieve data in the database; and create forms and reports using the data in the database.

In Access, a database consists of a collection of tables. Figure 1-1 shows a sample database for Pilotech Services. It consists of two tables. The Client table contains information about Pilotech's clients. The Technician table contains information about the technicians to whom these clients are assigned.

The rows in the tables are called **records**. A record contains information about a given person, product, or event. A row in the Client table, for example, contains information about a specific client.

fields

clients of
technician
Joanna Levin

Client table

CLIENT NUMBER	NAME	ADDRESS	CITY	STATE	ZIP CODE	BILLED	PAID	TECH NUMBER
AM53	Ashton-Mills	216 Rivard	Grattan	MA	58120	$215.50	$155.00	11
AS62	Alton-Scripps	722 Fisher	Empire	MA	58216	$425.00	$435.00	12
BL26	Blake Suppliers	5752 Maumee	Grattan	MA	58120	$129.50	$0.00	12
DE76	D & E Grocery	464 Linnell	Marshall	VT	52018	$385.75	$300.00	17
GR56	Grant Cleaners	737 Allard	Portage	NH	59130	$215.00	$165.00	11
GU21	Grand Union	247 Fuller	Grattan	MA	58120	$128.50	$0.00	12
JE77	Jones Electric	57 Giddings	Marshall	VT	52018	$0.00	$0.00	12
MI26	Morland Int.	665 Whittier	Frankfort	MA	56152	$212.50	$223.25	11
SA56	Sawyer Inc.	31 Lafayette	Empire	MA	58216	$352.50	$250.00	17
SI82	Simpson Ind.	752 Cadieux	Fernwood	MA	57412	$154.00	$0.00	12

records

Technician table

TECH NUMBER	LAST NAME	FIRST NAME	ADDRESS	CITY	STATE	ZIP CODE	HOURLY RATE	YTD EARNINGS
11	Levin	Joanna	26 Cottonwood	Carlton	MA	59712	$25.00	$6,245.00
12	Rogers	Brad	7972 Marsden	Kaleva	VT	57253	$30.00	$7,143.30
17	Rodriguez	Maria	263 Topsfield	Hudson	MA	57240	$35.00	$7,745.50

technician
Joanna Levin

FIGURE 1-1

The columns in the tables are called fields. A **field** contains a specific piece of information within a record. In the Client table, for example, the fourth field, City, contains the city where the client is located.

The first field in the Client table is the Client Number. This is a code assigned by Pilotech to each client. Like many organizations, Pilotech calls it a *number* although it actually contains letters. The client numbers have a special format. They consist of two uppercase letters followed by a two-digit number.

These numbers are unique; that is, no two clients will be assigned the same number. Such a field can be used as a **unique identifier**. This simply means that a given client number will appear only in a single record in the table. Only one record exists, for example, in which the client number is BL26. A unique identifier also is called a **primary key**. Thus, the Client Number field is the primary key for the Client table.

The next eight fields in the Client table include the Name, Address, City, State, Zip Code, Billed, Paid, and Tech Number. The Billed field contains the amount billed to the client. The Paid field contains the amount the client already has paid.

For example, Client AM53 is Ashton-Mills. It is located at 216 Rivard in Grattan, Massachusetts. The zip code is 58120. The client has been billed $215.50 and already has paid $155.00 of this amount.

Each client is assigned to a single technician. The last field in the Client table, Tech Number, gives the number of the client's technician.

The first field in the Technician table, Tech Number, is the number assigned by Pilotech to each technician. These numbers are unique, so Tech Number is the primary key of the Technician table.

The other fields in the Technician table are Last Name, First Name, Address, City, State, Zip Code, Hourly Rate, and YTD Earnings. The Hourly Rate field gives the technician's hourly billing rate, and the YTD Earnings field contains the total amount that has been billed by the technician for the technician's services so far this year.

For example, Technician 11 is Joanna Levin. She lives at 26 Cottonwood in Carlton, Massachusetts. Her zip code is 59712. Her hourly billing rate is $25.00 and her YTD earnings are $6,245.00.

The tech number appears in both the Client table and the Technician table. It is used to relate clients and technicians. For example, in the Client table, you see that the tech number for client AM53 is 11. To find the name of this technician, look for the row in the Technician table that contains 11 in the Tech Number field. Once you have found it, you know the client is assigned to Joanna Levin. To find all the clients assigned to Joanna Levin, look through the Client table for all the clients that contain 11 in the Tech Number field. Her clients are AM53 (Ashton-Mills), GR56 (Grant Cleaners), and MI26 (Morland, Int.).

Project One — Pilotech Services Database

Together with the management of Pilotech Services, you have determined that the data that must be maintained in the database is the data shown in Figure 1-1 on page A 1.7. You first must create the database and the tables it contains. In the process, you must define the fields included in the two tables, as well as the type of data each field will contain. You then must add the appropriate records to the tables. You also must print the contents of the tables. Finally, you must create a report with the Client Number, Name, Billed, and Paid fields for each client of Pilotech Services. Other reports and requirements for the database at Pilotech Services will be addressed with the Pilotech Services management in the future.

What Is Microsoft Access?

Microsoft Access is a powerful database management system (DBMS) that functions in the Windows environment and allows you to create and process data in a database. To illustrate the use of Access, this book presents a series of projects.

The projects use the Client and Technician tables. In Project 1, the two tables that comprise the database are created and the appropriate records are added to them. The project also uses a form to display the data in the tables. In addition, the project presents steps and techniques to prepare and print a custom report that represents the data in the database.

Overview of Project Steps

The database preparation steps give you an overview of how the database consisting of the Client table and the Technician table shown in Figure 1-1 on page A 1.7 will be constructed. The following tasks will be completed in this project.

1. Start Access.
2. Create a database called Pilotech Services.
3. Create the Client table by defining its fields.
4. Save the Client table in the database called Pilotech Services.
5. Add data records to the Client table.
6. Print the contents of the Client table.
7. Create the Technician table, save it, and add data records to it.
8. Create a form to display data in the Client table.
9. Create and print a report that presents the data in the Client table.

The following pages contain a detailed explanation of each of these steps.

Mouse Usage

In this book, the mouse is the primary way to communicate with Access. You can perform six operations with a mouse: point, click, right-click, double-click, drag, and right-drag. If you have a **Microsoft IntelliMouse™** , then you also have a wheel between the left and right buttons. This wheel can be used to perform three additional operations: rotate wheel, click wheel, or drag wheel.

Point means you move the mouse across a flat surface until the mouse pointer rests on the item of choice on the screen. As you move the mouse, the mouse pointer moves across the screen in the same direction. **Click** means you press and release the left mouse button. The terminology used in this book to direct you to point to a particular item and then click is, click the particular item. For example, click the Primary Key button on the toolbar, means point to the Primary Key button on the toolbar and then click.

Right-click means you press and release the right mouse button. As with the left mouse button, you normally will point to an item on the screen prior to right-clicking. Right-clicking produces a **shortcut menu**, which is a menu of the more frequently used commands that relate to the portion of the screen to which you are pointing. You then can select one of these commands by pointing to it and clicking the left mouse button.

Double-click means you quickly press and release the left mouse button twice without moving the mouse. In most cases, you must point to an item before double-clicking. **Drag** means you point to an item, hold down the left mouse button, move the item to the desired location on the screen and then release the left mouse button. **Right-drag** means you point to an item, hold down the right mouse button, move the item to the desired location and then release the right mouse button.

If you have a Microsoft IntelliMouse™ , then you can use **rotate wheel** to view parts of a table that are not visible. The wheel also can serve as a third button. When the wheel is used as a button, it is referred to as the **wheel button**. For example, dragging the wheel button causes some applications to scroll in the direction you drag.

The use of the mouse is an important skill when working with Microsoft Access 97.

More *About* **Creating a Database**

In some DBMSs, every table, query, form, or report is stored in a separate file. This is not the case in Access, in which a database is stored in a single file on disk. The file contains all the tables, queries, forms, reports, and programs that you create for this database.

Starting Access and Creating a New Database

To start Access, Windows 95 must be running. Perform the following steps to start Access and create a new database.

Steps To Start Access

1 Place a formatted floppy disk in drive A, click the Start button, and point to New Office Document near the top of the Start menu.

The Start menu displays (Figure 1-2).

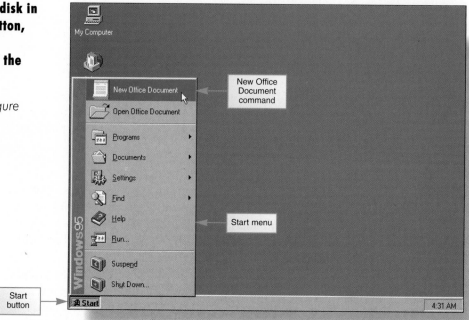

FIGURE 1-2

2 Click New Office Document. If the General tab is not selected, that is, if it does not display in front of the other tabs, click the General tab. Make sure the Blank Database icon is selected and then point to the OK button.

The New Office Document dialog box displays (Figure 1-3). The Blank Database icon is selected.

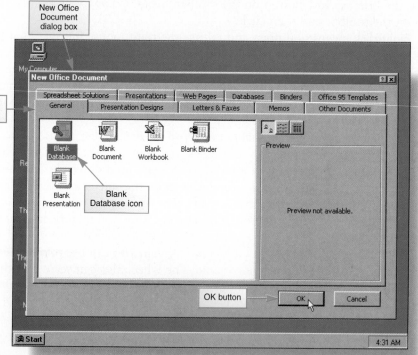

FIGURE 1-3

3 Click the OK button and then point to the Save in box arrow.

The File New Database dialog box displays (Figure 1-4).

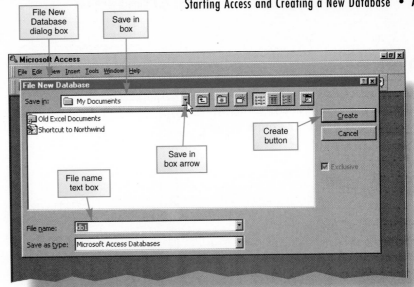

FIGURE 1-4

4 Click the Save in box arrow and then point to 3½ Floppy (A:).

The Save in list box displays (Figure 1-5).

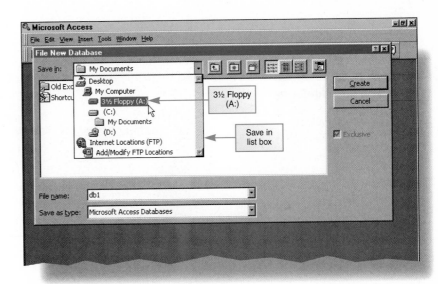

FIGURE 1-5

5 Click 3½ Floppy (A:).

The Save in box contains 3½ Floppy (A:) (Figure 1-6).

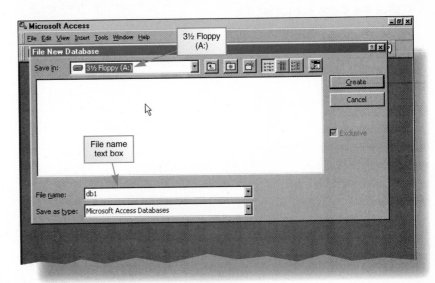

FIGURE 1-6

6 **Click in the File name text box. Repeatedly press the BACKSPACE key to delete db1 and then type** Pilotech Services **as the file name. Point to the Create button.**

The file name is changed to Pilotech Services (Figure 1-7).

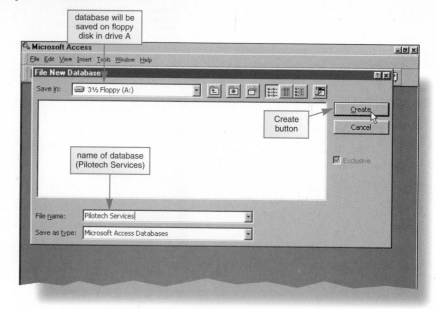

FIGURE 1-7

7 **Click the Create button to create the database.**

The Pilotech Services database is created. The Pilotech Services : Database window displays on the desktop (Figure 1-8). The Office Assistant, a tool you can use to obtain help while working with Microsoft Access may display. (You will see how to use the Office Assistant later in this project.)

8 **If the Office Assistant displays, click the Close button for the Office Assistant.**

The Office Assistant no longer displays.

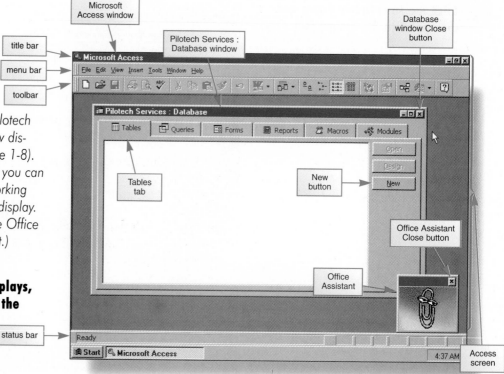

FIGURE 1-8

Other Ways

1. Right-click Start button, click Open, double-click New Office Document
2. On Office shortcut bar click Start a New Document button
3. On the Start menu click Programs, click Microsoft Access

The Access Desktop and the Database Window

The first bar on the desktop (Figure 1-8) is the **title bar**. It displays the title of the product, Microsoft Access. The button on the right is the **Close button**. Clicking the Close button closes the window.

The second bar is the **menu bar**. It contains a list of menus. You select a menu from the menu bar by clicking the menu name.

The third bar is the **toolbar**. The toolbar contains buttons that allow you to perform certain tasks more quickly than using the menu bar. Each button contains a picture, or **icon**, depicting its function. The specific buttons on the toolbar will vary, depending on the task on which you are working.

The **taskbar** at the bottom of the screen displays the Start button, any active windows, and the current time.

Immediately above the Windows 95 taskbar is the **status bar** (Figure 1-8). It contains special information that is appropriate for the task on which you are working. Currently, it contains the word, Ready, which means Access is ready to accept commands.

The **Database window**, referred to in Figure 1-8 as the Pilotech Services : Database window, is a special window that allows you to access easily and rapidly a variety of objects such as tables, queries, forms, and reports. To do so, you will use the various components of the window.

Creating a Table

An Access database consists of a collection of tables. Once you have created the database, you must create each of the tables within it. In this project, for example, you must create both the Client and Technician tables shown in Figure 1-1 on page A 1.7.

To create a table, you describe the **structure** of the table to Access by describing the fields within the table. For each field, you indicate the following:

1. **Field name** — Each field in the table must have a unique name. In the Client table (Figure 1-9 on page A 1.14), for example, the field names are Client Number, Name, Address, City, State, Zip Code, Billed, Paid, and Tech Number.
2. **Data type** — Data type indicates to Access the type of data the field will contain. Some fields can contain only numbers. Others, such as Billed and Paid, can contain numbers and dollar signs. Still others, such as Name, and Address, can contain letters.
3. **Description** — Access allows you to enter a detailed description of the field.

You also can assign field widths to text fields (fields whose data type is Text). This indicates the maximum number of characters that can be stored in the field. If you do not assign a width to such a field, Access assumes the width is 50.

You also must indicate which field or fields make up the **primary key**; that is, the unique identifier, for the table. In the sample database, the Client Number field is the primary key of the Client table and the Tech Number field is the primary key of the Technician table.

The rules for field names are:

1. Names can be up to 64 characters in length.
2. Names can contain letters, digits, and spaces, as well as most of the punctuation symbols.
3. Names cannot contain periods, exclamation points (!), or square brackets ([ ]).
4. The same name cannot be used for two different fields in the same table.

More *About*
Toolbars

Normally, the correct Access toolbar automatically will display. If it does not, click View on the menu bar, and then click Toolbars. Select the toolbar for the activity in which you are engaged and then click the Close button.

More *About*
Creating a Table

Access includes **Table Wizards** that can guide you through the table-creation process by suggesting some commonly used tables and fields. If you already know the fields you need, however, it usually is easier to simply create the table yourself.

Structure of Client table

FIELD NAME	DATA TYPE	FIELD SIZE	PRIMARY KEY?	DESCRIPTION
Client Number	Text	4	Yes	Client Number (Primary Key)
Name	Text	20		Client Name
Address	Text	15		Street Address
City	Text	15		City
State	Text	2		State (Two-Character Abbreviation)
Zip Code	Text	5		Zip Code (Five-Character Version)
Billed	Currency			Current Billed Amount
Paid	Currency			Current Paid Amount
Tech Number	Text	2		Number of Client's Technician

Data for Client table

CLIENT NUMBER	NAME	ADDRESS	CITY	STATE	ZIP CODE	BILLED	PAID	TECH NUMBER
AM53	Ashton-Mills	216 Rivard	Grattan	MA	58120	$215.50	$155.00	11
AS62	Alton-Scripps	722 Fisher	Empire	MA	58216	$425.00	$435.00	12
BL26	Blake Suppliers	5752 Maumee	Grattan	MA	58120	$129.50	$0.00	12
DE76	D & E Grocery	464 Linnell	Marshall	VT	52018	$385.75	$300.00	17
GR56	Grant Cleaners	737 Allard	Portage	NH	59130	$215.00	$165.00	11
GU21	Grand Union	247 Fuller	Grattan	MA	58120	$128.50	$0.00	12
JE77	Jones Electric	57 Giddings	Marshall	VT	52018	$0.00	$0.00	12
MI26	Morland Int.	665 Whittier	Frankfort	MA	56152	$212.50	$223.25	11
SA56	Sawyer Inc.	31 Lafayette	Empire	MA	58216	$352.50	$250.00	17
SI82	Simpson Ind.	752 Cadieux	Fernwood	MA	57412	$154.00	$0.00	12

FIGURE 1-9

More *About* Data Types

Different database management systems have different available data types. Even data types that are essentially the same can have different names. The Access Text data type, for example, is referred to as Character in some systems and Alpha in others.

Each field has a **data type**. This indicates the type of data that can be stored in the field. The data types you will use in this project are:

1. **Text** — The field can contain any characters.
2. **Number** — The field can contain only numbers. The numbers can be either positive or negative. Fields are assigned this type so they can be used in arithmetic operations. Fields that contain numbers but will not be used for arithmetic operations usually are assigned a data type of Text. The Tech Number field, for example, is a text field because the Tech Numbers will not be involved in any arithmetic.
3. **Currency** — The field can contain only dollar amounts. The values will be displayed with dollar signs, commas, decimal points, and with two digits following the decimal point. Like numeric fields, you can use currency fields in arithmetic operations. Access assigns a size to currency fields automatically.

The field names, data types, field widths, primary key information, and descriptions for the Client table are shown in Figure 1-9. With this information, you are ready to begin creating the table. To create the table, use the following steps.

Steps **To Create a Table**

1 **Click the New button in the Pilotech Services : Database window (see Figure 1-8 on page A 1.12). Point to Design View.**

The New Table dialog box displays (Figure 1-10).

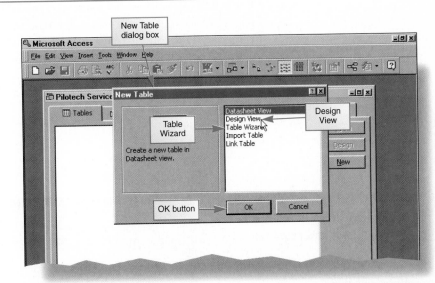

FIGURE 1-10

2 **Click Design View and then click the OK button.**

The Table1 : Table window displays (Figure 1-11).

3 **Click the Maximize button for the Table1 : Table window.**

A maximized Table1 : Table window displays.

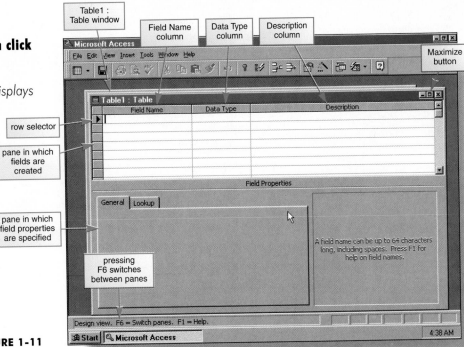

FIGURE 1-11

Other Ways

1. Click New Object button arrow on toolbar, click Table
2. On Insert menu click Table
3. Press ALT+N

Defining the Fields

The next step in creating the table is to define the fields by specifying the required details in the Table window. To do so, make entries in the Field Name, Data Type, and Description columns. Enter additional information in the Field Properties box in the lower portion of the Table window. To do so, press the F6 key to move from the upper **pane** (portion of the screen), the one where you define the fields, to the lower pane, the one where you define field properties. Enter the appropriate field size and then press the F6 key to return to the upper pane. As you define the fields, the **row selector** (Figure 1-11 on page A 1.15) indicates the field you currently are describing. It is positioned on the first field, indicating Access is ready for you to enter the name of the first field in the Field Name column.

Perform the following steps to define the fields in the table.

Steps

To Define the Fields in a Table

1 **Type** Client Number **(the name of the first field) in the Field Name column and press the TAB key.**

The words, Client Number, display in the Field Name column and the insertion point advances to the Data Type column, indicating you can enter the data type (Figure 1-12). The word, Text, one of the possible data types, currently displays. The arrow indicates a list of data types is available by clicking the arrow.

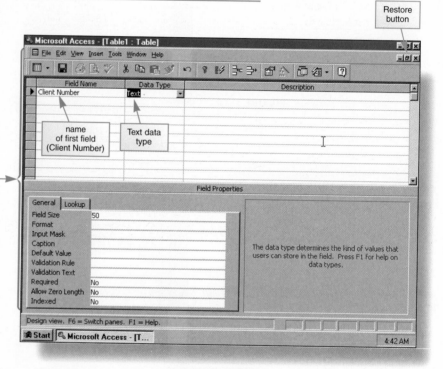

FIGURE 1-12

2 Because Text is the correct data type, press the TAB key to move the insertion point to the Description column, type Client Number (Primary Key) as the description and then point to the Primary Key button on the toolbar.

A ScreenTip, which is a description of the button, displays partially obscuring the description of the first field (Figure 1-13).

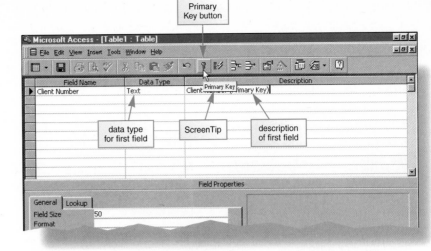

FIGURE 1-13

3 Click the Primary Key button to make Client Number the primary key and then press the F6 key to move the insertion point to the Field Size text box.

*The Client Number field is the primary key as indicated by the key symbol that displays in the row selector (Figure 1-14). The **row selector** is a small box or bar that, when clicked, selects the entire row. The current entry in the Field Size text box (50) is selected.*

FIGURE 1-14

4 Type 4 as the size of the Client Number field. Press the F6 key to return to the Description column for the Client Number field and then press the TAB key to move to the Field Name column in the second row.

The row selector moves to the second row just below the field name Client Number (Figure 1-15).

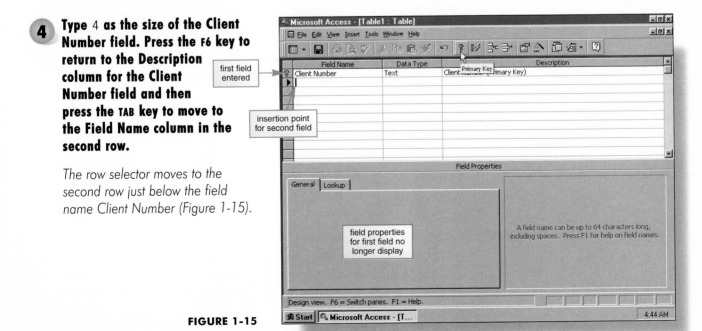

FIGURE 1-15

5 Use the techniques illustrated in Steps 1 through 4 to make the entries from the Client table structure shown in Figure 1-9 on page A 1.14 up through and including the name of the Billed field. You will not need to click the Primary Key button for any of these fields. Click the Data Type column arrow and then point to the Currency data type.

The additional fields are entered (Figure 1-16). A list of available data types displays in the Data Type column for the Billed field.

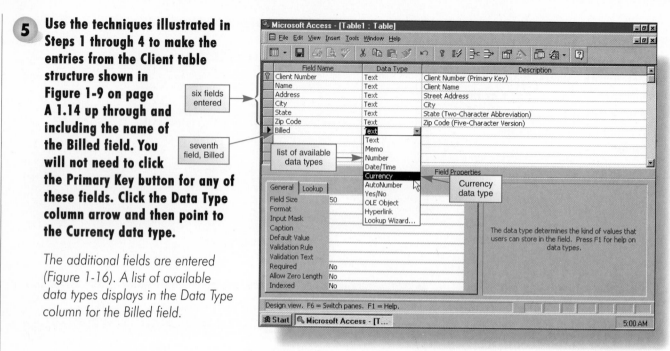

FIGURE 1-16

6 Click the Currency data type and then press the TAB key. Make the remaining entries from the Client table structure shown in Figure 1-9.

The fields are all entered (Figure 1-17)

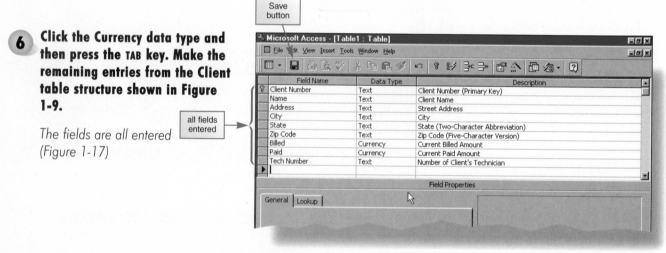

FIGURE 1-17

Correcting Errors in the Structure

When creating a table, check the entries carefully to ensure they are correct. If you make a mistake and discover it before you press the TAB key, you can correct the error by repeatedly pressing the BACKSPACE key until the incorrect characters are removed. Then, type the correct characters. If you do not discover a mistake until later, you can click the entry, type the correct value and then press the ENTER key.

If you accidentally add an extra field to the structure, select the field, by clicking the leftmost column on the row that contains the field to be deleted. Once you have selected the field, press the DELETE key. This will remove the field from the structure.

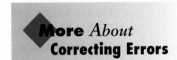

If you forget a field, select the field that will follow the field you wish to add, click Insert on the menu bar and then click Rows. The remaining fields move down one row, making room for the missing field. Make the entries for the new field in the usual manner.

If you made the wrong field a primary key field, click the correct primary key entry for the field and then click the Primary Key button on the toolbar.

As an alternative to these steps, you may want to start over. To do so, click the Close button for the Table1 : Table window and then click No. The original desktop displays and you can repeat the process you used earlier.

Saving a Table

The Client table structure now is complete. The final step is to **save the table** within the database. At this time, you should give the table a name.

Table names are from one to 64 characters in length and can contain letters, numbers, and spaces. The two table names in this project are Client and Technician.

To save the table, complete the following steps.

Steps To Save a Table

1 **Click the Save button on the toolbar (see Figure 1-17). Type** Client **as the name of the table in the Table Name text box and then point to the OK button.**

The Save As dialog box displays (Figure 1-18). The name of the table displays in the Table Name text box.

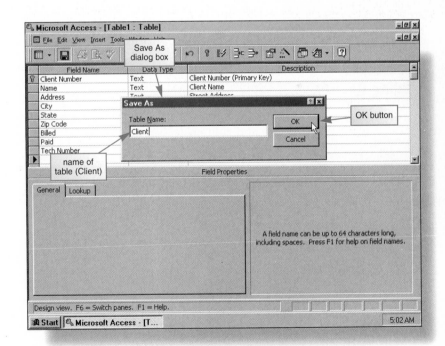

FIGURE 1-18

2 Click the OK button and then point to the Close button for the Client : Table window.

The Table is saved on the floppy disk in drive A. The name of the table is now Client as indicated in the title bar (Figure 1-19).

3 Click the Close button for the Client : Table window. (Be sure not to click the Close button on the first line, because this would close Microsoft Access.)

The Client : Table window no longer displays.

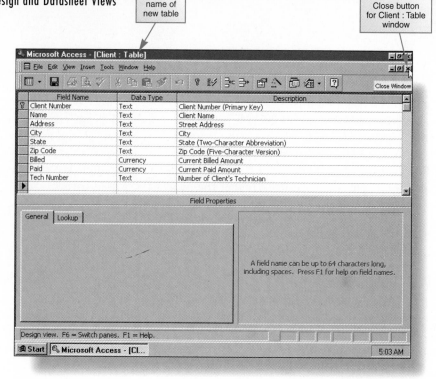

name of new table

Close button for Client : Table window

FIGURE 1-19

More *About*
Adding Records

As soon as you have entered or modified a record and moved to another record, the original record is saved. This is different from other tools. The rows entered in a spreadsheet, for example, are not saved until the entire spreadsheet is saved.

Adding Records to a Table

Creating a table by building the structure and saving the table is the first step in a two-step process. The second step is to **add records** to the table. To add records to a table, the table must be open. To **open a table**, right-click the table in the Database window and then click Open on the shortcut menu. The table displays in Datasheet view. In **Datasheet view**, the table is represented as a collection of rows and columns called a **datasheet**. It looks very much like the tables shown in Figure 1-1 on page A 1.7.

You often add records in phases. You may, for example, not have enough time to add all the records in one session. To illustrate this process, this project begins by adding the first two records in the Client table (Figure 1-20). The remaining records are added later.

Client table (first 2 records)

CLIENT NUMBER	NAME	ADDRESS	CITY	STATE	ZIP CODE	BILLED	PAID	TECH NUMBER
AM53	Ashton-Mills	216 Rivard	Grattan	MA	58120	$215.50	$155.00	11
AS62	Alton-Scripps	722 Fisher	Empire	MA	58216	$425.00	$435.00	12

FIGURE 1-20

To open the Client table and then add records, use the following steps.

Steps To Add Records to a Table

1 **Right-click the Client table in the Pilotech Services : Database window and then point to Open on the shortcut menu.**

The shortcut menu for the Client table displays (Figure 1-21). The Pilotech Services : Database window is maximized because the previous window, the Client : Table window, was maximized. (If you wanted to restore the Database window to its original size, you would click the window's Restore button.)

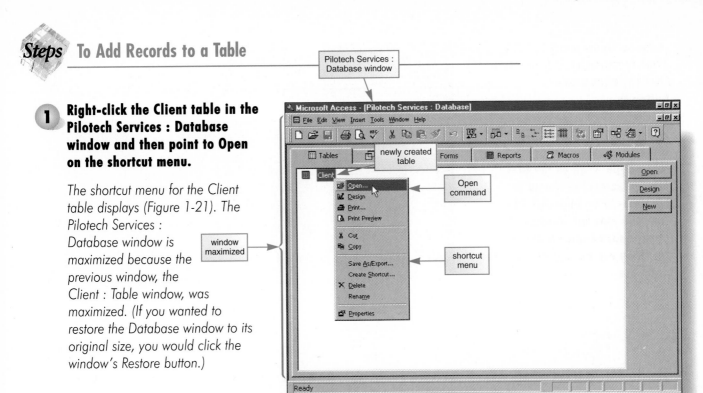

FIGURE 1-21

2 **Click Open on the shortcut menu.**

*The Client : Table window displays (Figure 1-22). The window contains the Datasheet view for the Client table. The **record selector** is positioned on the first record. The status bar at the bottom of the window also indicates that the record selector is positioned on record 1.*

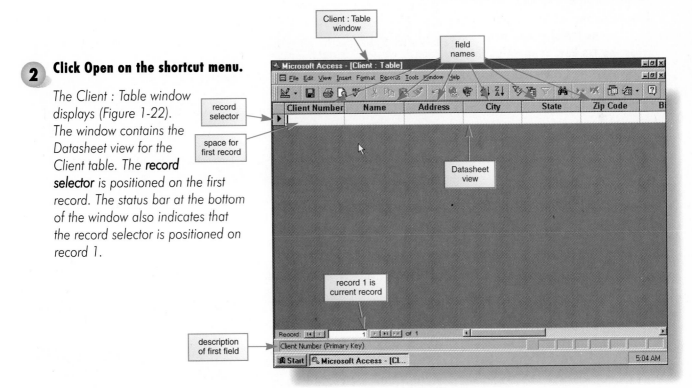

FIGURE 1-22

3 If your window is not already maximized, click the Maximize button to maximize the window containing the table. Type AM53 as the first Client Number, as shown in Figure 1-20 on page A 1.20. Be sure you type the letters in uppercase, because that is the way they are to be entered in the database.

The Client Number is entered, but the insertion point is still in the Client Number field (Figure 1-23).

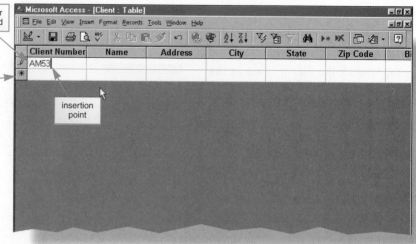

FIGURE 1-23

4 Press the TAB key to complete the entry for the Client Number field. Type Ashton-Mills as the name and then press the TAB key. Type 216 Rivard as the address and then press the TAB key. Type Grattan as the city and then press the TAB key. Type MA as the state name and then press the TAB key. Type 58120 as the zip code.

The Name, Address, City, and State fields are entered. The data for the Zip Code field displays on the screen (Figure 1-24), but the entry is not complete because you have not yet pressed the TAB key.

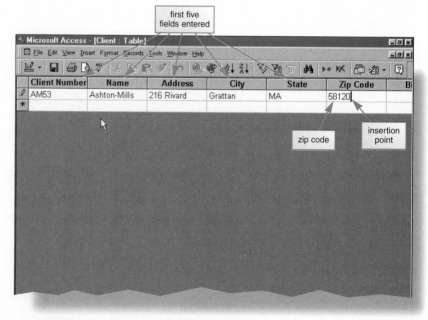

FIGURE 1-24

5 Press the TAB key.

The fields shift to the left (Figure 1-25). The Billed field displays.

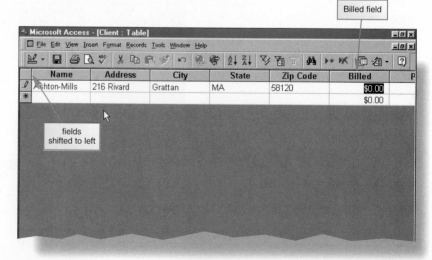

FIGURE 1-25

6 Type 215.50 **as the billed amount and then press the TAB key. (You do not need to type dollar signs or commas. In addition, if the digits to the right of the decimal point were both zeros, you would not need to type the decimal point.) Type** 155 **as the paid amount and then press the TAB key. Type** 11 **as the Tech Number to complete the record.**

The fields have shifted to the left (Figure 1-26). The Billed and Paid values display with dollar signs and decimal points. The value for the Tech Number has been entered, but the insertion point still is positioned on the field.

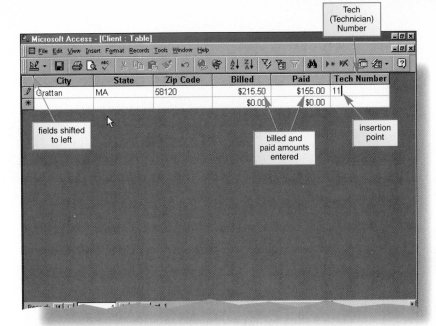

FIGURE 1-26

7 **Press the TAB key.**

The fields shift back to the right, the record is saved, and the insertion point moves to the Client Number on the second row (Figure 1-27).

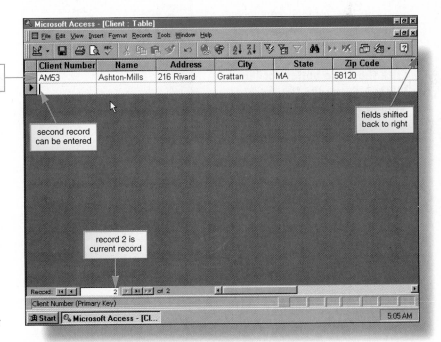

FIGURE 1-27

8 **Use the techniques shown in Steps 3 through 7 to add the data for the second record in Figure 1-20 on page A 1.20.**

The second record is added and the insertion point moves to the Client Number on the third row (Figure 1-28).

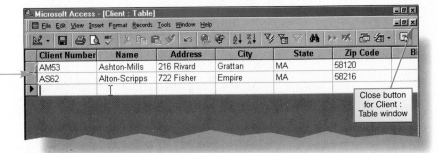

FIGURE 1-28

Closing a Table and a Database and Quitting Access

It is a good idea to close a table as soon as you have finished working with it. It keeps the screen from getting cluttered and prevents you from making accidental changes to the data in the table. If you no longer will work with the database, you should close the database as well. With the creation of the Client table complete, you can quit Access at this point.

Perform the following steps to close the table and the database and then quit Access.

Steps | To Close a Table and Database and Quit Access

1 Click the Close button for the Client : Table window (see Figure 1-28 on page A 1.23).

The datasheet for the Client table no longer displays (Figure 1-29).

2 Click the Close button for the Pilotech Services : Database window (see Figure 1-29).

The Pilotech Services : Database window no longer displays.

3 Click the Close button for the Microsoft Access window.

The Microsoft Access window no longer displays.

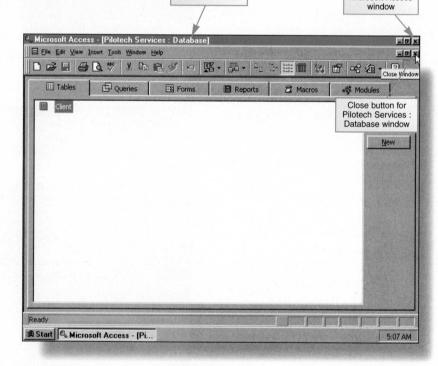

FIGURE 1-29

OtherWays

1. Double-click Control-menu icon on title bar for window
2. On File menu click Close

Opening a Database

To work with any of the tables, reports, or forms in a database, the database must be open. To open a database from the Windows 95 desktop, click Open Office Document on the Start menu by performing the following steps. (The Other Ways box indicates ways to open a database from within Access.)

Steps To Open a Database

1 Click the Start button and then point to Open Office Document on the Start menu (Figure 1-30).

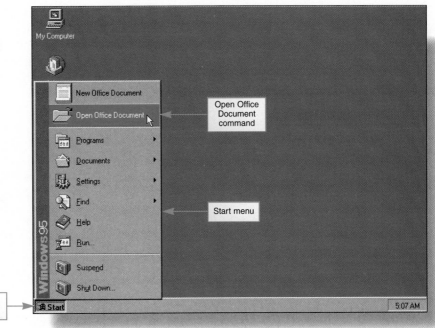

FIGURE 1-30

2 Click Open Office Document. If necessary, click the Look in box arrow and then click 3½ Floppy (A:) in the Look in list box. If it is not already selected, click the Pilotech Services database name. Point to the Open button.

The Open Office Document dialog box displays (Figure 1-31). The 3½ Floppy (A:) folder displays in the Look in box and the files on the floppy disk in drive A display. Your list may be different.

3 Click the Open button.

The database opens and the Pilotech Services : Database window displays.

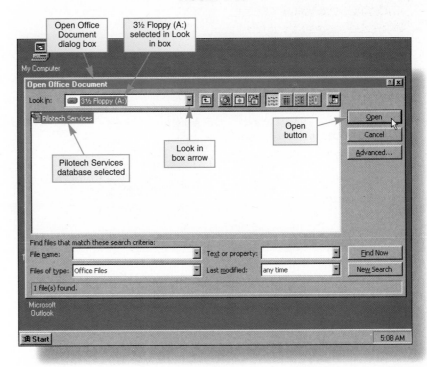

FIGURE 1-31

*Other*Ways

1. Click Open Database button on toolbar
2. On File menu click Open Database
3. Press CTRL+O

Adding Additional Records

You can add records to a table that already contains data using a process almost identical to that used to add records to an empty table. The only difference is that you place the insertion point after the last data record before you enter the additional data. To do so, use the **Navigation buttons** found near the lower-left corner of the screen. The purpose of each of the Navigation buttons is described in Table 1-1.

Table 1-1	
BUTTON	PURPOSE
First Record	Moves to the first record in the table
Previous Record	Moves to the previous record
Next Record	Moves to the next record
Last Record	Moves to the last record in the table
New Record	Moves past the last record in the table to a position for a new record

Complete the following steps to add the remaining records (Figure 1-32) to the Client table.

Client table (last 8 records)								
CLIENT NUMBER	NAME	ADDRESS	CITY	STATE	ZIP CODE	BILLED	PAID	TECH NUMBER
BL26	Blake Suppliers	5752 Maumee	Grattan	MA	58120	$129.50	$0.00	12
DE76	D & E Grocery	464 Linnell	Marshall	VT	52018	$385.75	$300.00	17
GR56	Grant Cleaners	737 Allard	Portage	NH	59130	$215.00	$165.00	11
GU21	Grand Union	247 Fuller	Grattan	MA	58120	$128.50	$0.00	12
JE77	Jones Electric	57 Giddings	Marshall	VT	52018	$0.00	$0.00	12
MI26	Morland Int.	665 Whittier	Frankfort	MA	56152	$212.50	$223.25	11
SA56	Sawyer Inc.	31 Lafayette	Empire	MA	58216	$352.50	$250.00	17
SI82	Simpson Ind.	752 Cadieux	Fernwood	MA	57412	$154.00	$0.00	12

FIGURE 1-32

Steps To Add Additional Records to a Table

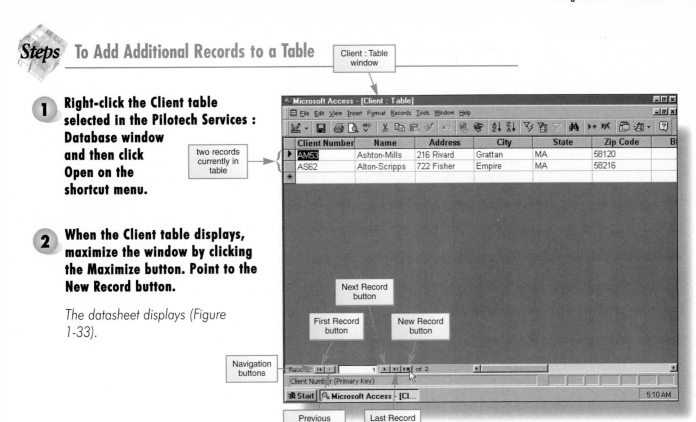

1 Right-click the Client table selected in the Pilotech Services : Database window and then click Open on the shortcut menu.

2 When the Client table displays, maximize the window by clicking the Maximize button. Point to the New Record button.

The datasheet displays (Figure 1-33).

FIGURE 1-33

3 Click the New Record button.

Access places the insertion point in position to enter a new record (Figure 1-34).

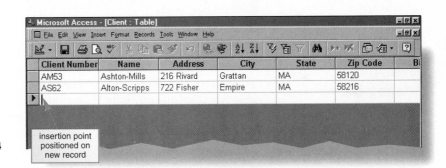

FIGURE 1-34

4 Add the remaining records from Figure 1-32 using the same techniques you used to add the first two records. Point to the Close button.

The additional records are added (Figure 1-35).

5 Close the window containing the table by clicking its Close button.

FIGURE 1-35

*Other***Ways**

1. Click New Record button on toolbar
2. On Insert menu click New Record

Correcting Errors in the Data

Check your entries carefully to ensure they are correct. If you make a mistake and discover it before you press the TAB key, correct it by pressing the BACKSPACE key until the incorrect characters are removed and then typing the correct characters.

If you discover an incorrect entry later, correct the error by clicking the incorrect entry and then making the appropriate correction. If the record you must correct is not on the screen, use the Navigation buttons (Next Record, Previous Record, and so on) to move to it. If the field you want to correct is not visible on the screen, use the horizontal scroll bar along the bottom of the screen to shift all the fields until the one you want displays. Then make the correction.

If you add an extra record accidentally, select the record by clicking the **record selector** that immediately precedes the record. Then, press the DELETE key. This will remove the record from the table. If you forget a record, add it using the same procedure as for all the other records. Access will place it in the correct location in the table automatically.

If you cannot determine how to correct the data, you are, in effect, stuck on the record. Access neither allows you to move to any other record until you have made the correction, nor allows you to close the table. If you encounter this situation, simply press the ESC key. Pressing the ESC key will remove from the screen the record you are trying to add. You then can move to any other record, close the table, or take any other action you desire.

Previewing and Printing the Contents of a Table

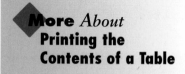

More *About*
Printing the
Contents of a Table

You can change the paper size, paper source, or the printer that will be used to print the report. To change any of these, select the Page sheet of the Page Setup dialog box, click the appropriate down arrow, and then select the desired option.

When working with a database, you often will need to **print** a copy of the table contents. Figure 1-36 shows a printed copy of the contents of the Client table. (Yours may look slightly different, depending on your printer.) Because the Client table is wider substantially than the screen, it also will be wider than the normal printed page in portrait orientation. **Portrait orientation** means the printout is across the width of the page. **Landscape orientation** means the printout is across the length of the page. Thus, to print the wide database table, use landscape orientation. If you are printing the contents of a table that fits on the screen, you will not need landscape orientation. A convenient way to change to landscape orientation is to **preview** what the printed copy will look like by using Print Preview. This allows you to determine whether landscape orientation is necessary and, if it is, to change easily the orientation to landscape. In addition, you also can use Print Preview to determine whether any adjustments are necessary to the page margins.

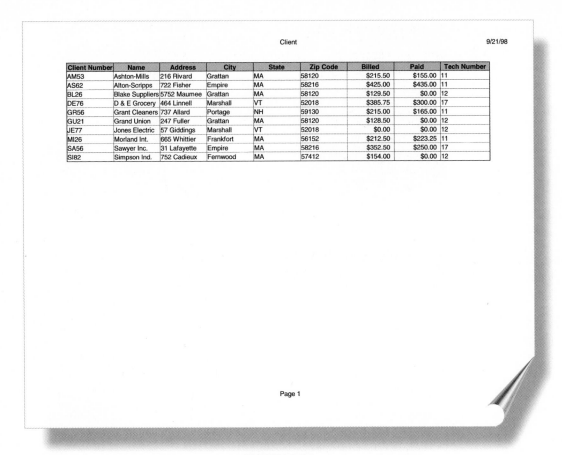

| | | | | | | | | |
| Client | | | | | | | | 9/21/98 |

Client Number	Name	Address	City	State	Zip Code	Billed	Paid	Tech Number
AM53	Ashton-Mills	216 Rivard	Grattan	MA	58120	$215.50	$155.00	11
AS62	Alton-Scripps	722 Fisher	Empire	MA	58216	$425.00	$435.00	11
BL26	Blake Suppliers	5752 Maumee	Grattan	MA	58120	$129.50	$0.00	12
DE76	D & E Grocery	464 Linnell	Marshall	VT	52018	$385.75	$300.00	17
GR56	Grant Cleaners	737 Allard	Portage	NH	59130	$215.00	$165.00	11
GU21	Grand Union	247 Fuller	Grattan	MA	58120	$128.50	$0.00	12
JE77	Jones Electric	57 Giddings	Marshall	VT	52018	$0.00	$0.00	12
MI26	Morland Int.	665 Whittier	Frankfort	MA	56152	$212.50	$223.25	11
SA56	Sawyer Inc.	31 Lafayette	Empire	MA	58216	$352.50	$250.00	17
SI82	Simpson Ind.	752 Cadieux	Fernwood	MA	57412	$154.00	$0.00	12

Page 1

FIGURE 1-36

Perform the following steps to use Print Preview to preview and then print the Client table.

 Steps **To Preview and Print the Contents of a Table**

① **Right-click the Client table and then point to Print Preview on the shortcut menu.**

The shortcut menu for the Client table displays (Figure 1-37).

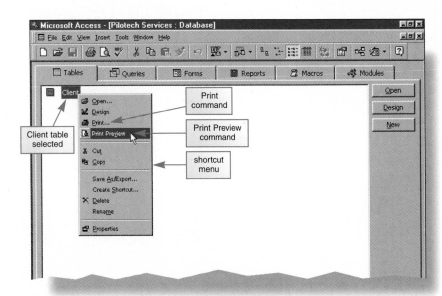

FIGURE 1-37

2 Click Print Preview on the shortcut menu. Point anywhere in the upper-right portion of the report.

The preview of the report displays (Figure 1-38).

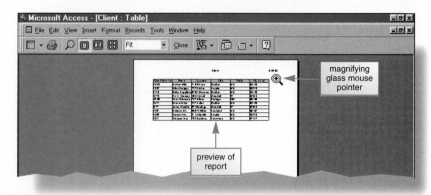

FIGURE 1-38

3 Click the magnifying glass mouse pointer in the approximate position shown in Figure 1-38.

The portion surrounding the mouse pointer is magnified (Figure 1-39). The last field that displays is the Zip Code field. The Billed, Paid, and Tech Number fields do not display. To display the additional fields, you will need to switch to landscape orientation.

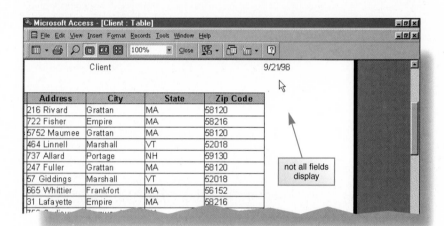

FIGURE 1-39

4 Click File on the menu bar and then point to Page Setup.

The File menu displays (Figure 1-40).

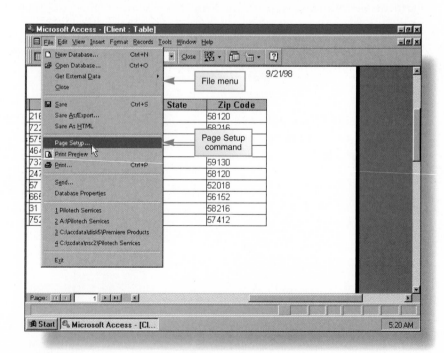

FIGURE 1-40

5 **Click Page Setup and then point to the Page tab.**

The Page Setup dialog box displays (Figure 1-41).

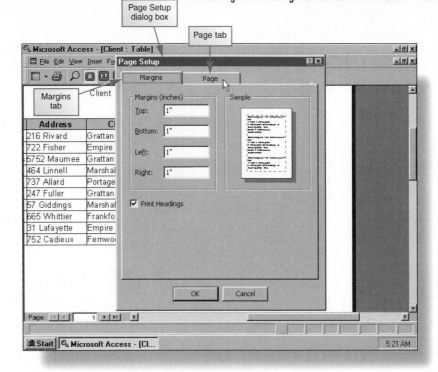

FIGURE 1-41

6 **Click the Page tab and then point to Landscape.**

The Page sheet displays (Figure 1-42). The Portrait option button currently is selected. (Option button refers to the round button that indicates choices in a dialog box. When the corresponding option is selected, the button contains within it a solid circle. Clicking an option button selects it, and deselects all others.)

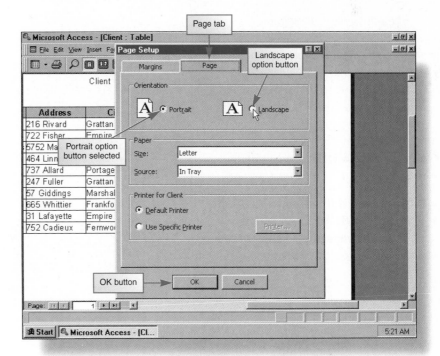

FIGURE 1-42

7 Click Landscape and then click the OK button. Click the mouse pointer to view the entire report.

The orientation is changed to landscape as shown by the report that displays on the screen (Figure 1-43). The characters in the report are so small that it is difficult to determine whether all fields currently display. To zoom in on a portion of the report, click the desired portion of the report.

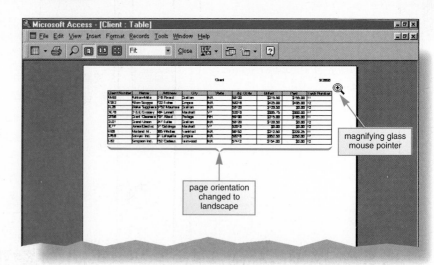

FIGURE 1-43

8 Click the magnifying glass mouse pointer in the approximate position shown in Figure 1-43.

The portion surrounding the mouse pointer is magnified (Figure 1-44). The last field that displays is the Tech Number field, so all fields currently display. If they did not, you could decrease the left and right margins, the amount of space left by Access on the left and right edges of the report.

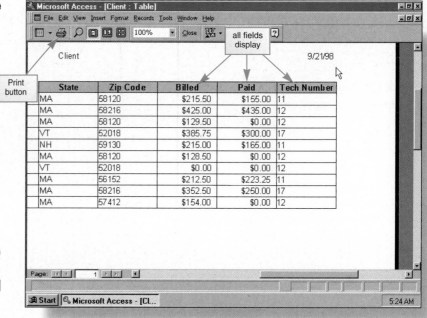

FIGURE 1-44

9 Click the Print button to print the report. Click the Close button when the report has been printed to close the Print Preview window.

The Preview window no longer displays.

Other Ways

1. On File menu click Print Preview to preview
2. On File menu click Print to print
3. Press CTRL+P to print

Creating Additional Tables

A database typically consists of more than one table. The sample database contains two, the Client table and the Technician table. You need to repeat the process of creating a table and adding records for each table in the database. In the sample database, you need to create and add records to the Technician table. The structure and data for the table are given in Figure 1-45. The steps to create the table follow.

Structure of Technician table

FIELD NAME	DATA TYPE	FIELD SIZE	PRIMARY KEY?	DESCRIPTION
Tech Number	Text	2	Yes	Technician Number (Primary Key)
Last Name	Text	10		Last Name of Technician
First Name	Text	8		First Name of Technician
Address	Text	15		Street Address
City	Text	15		City
State	Text	2		State (Two-Character Abbreviation)
Zip Code	Text	5		Zip Code (Five-Character Version)
Hourly Rate	Currency			Hourly Rate of Technician
YTD Earnings	Currency			YTD Earnings of Technician

Data for Technician table

TECH NUMBER	LAST NAME	FIRST NAME	ADDRESS	CITY	STATE	ZIP CODE	HOURLY RATE	YTD EARNINGS
11	Levin	Joanna	26 Cottonwood	Carlton	MA	59712	$25.00	$6,245.00
12	Rogers	Brad	7972 Marsden	Kaleva	VT	57253	$30.00	$7,143.30
17	Rodriguez	Maria	263 Topsfield	Hudson	MA	57240	$35.00	$7,745.50

FIGURE 1-45

 Steps To Create an Additional Table

1 Make sure the Pilotech Services database is open. Point to the New button.

The Pilotech Services : Database window displays (Figure 1-46). If you recently maximized another window, this window also will be maximized as shown in the figure. If not, it will appear in its normal size.

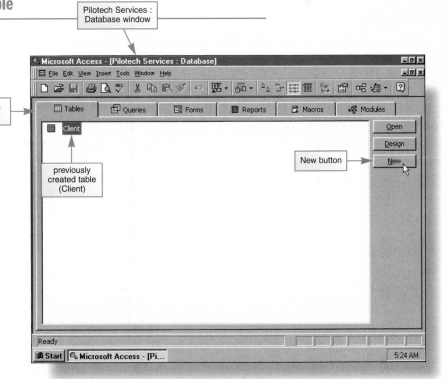

FIGURE 1-46

2 Click the New button, click Design View in the New Table dialog box, click the OK button and then enter the data for the fields for the Technician table from Figure 1-45 on page A 1.33. Be sure to click the Primary Key button when you enter the Tech Number field. Point to the Save button on the toolbar.

The entries display (Figure 1-47).

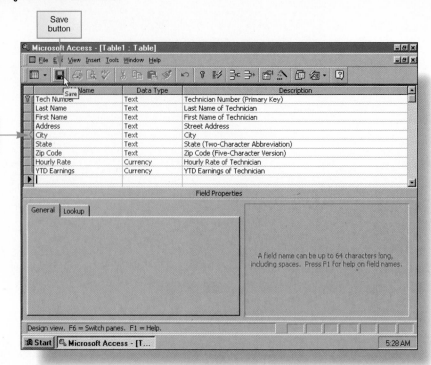

FIGURE 1-47

3 Click the Save button, type Technician as the name of the table, and click the OK button. Click the Close button to close the Table window.

The table is saved in the Pilotech Services database. The Table window no longer displays.

Adding Records to the Additional Table

Now that you have created the Technician table, use the following steps to add records to it.

Steps **To Add Records to an Additional Table**

1 Right-click the Technician table and point to Open on the shortcut menu.

The shortcut menu for the Technician table displays (Figure 1-48).

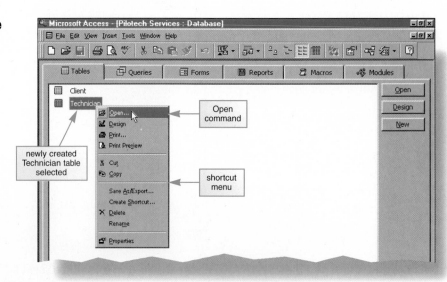

FIGURE 1-48

2 Click Open on the shortcut menu and then enter the Technician data from Figure 1-45 into the Technician table.

The datasheet displays with three records entered (Figure 1-49).

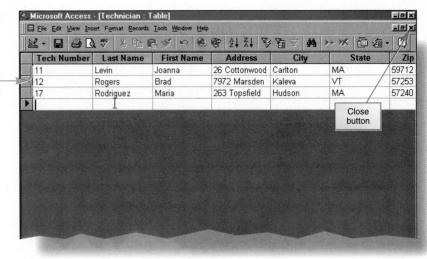

FIGURE 1-49

3 Click the Close button for the Technician : Table window to close the table.

Access closes the table and removes the datasheet from the screen.

Using a Form to View Data

In creating tables, you have used Datasheet view; that is, the data on the screen displayed as a table. You also can use **Form view**, in which you see a single record at a time.

The advantage with Datasheet view is you can see multiple records at once. It has the disadvantage that, unless you have few fields in the table, you cannot see all the fields at the same time. With Form view, you see only a single record, but you can see all the fields in the record. The view you choose is a matter of personal preference.

Creating a Form

To use Form view, you first must **create a form**. The simplest way to create a form is to use the **New Object: AutoForm button** on the toolbar. To do so, first select the table for which the form is to be created in the Database window and then click the New Object: AutoForm button. A list of available objects displays. Select AutoForm from the list by clicking it in the list.

Perform the following steps using the New Object: AutoForm button to create a form for the Client table.

More *About*
Forms

Attractive and functional forms can improve greatly the data entry process. Forms are not restricted to data from a single table, but can incorporate data from multiple tables as well as special types of data like pictures and sounds. A good DBMS like Access furnishes an easy way to create sophisticated forms.

 Steps To Use the New Object: AutoForm Button to Create a Form

1 Make sure the Pilotech Services database is open, the Database window displays, and the Client table is selected. Point to the New Object: AutoForm button arrow on the toolbar (Figure 1-50).

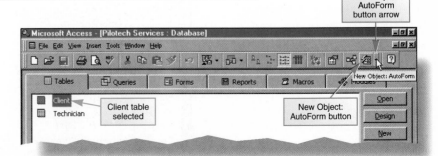

FIGURE 1-50

2 Click the New Object: AutoForm button arrow and then point to AutoForm.

A list of objects that can be created displays (Figure 1-51).

FIGURE 1-51

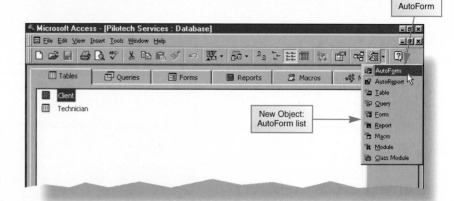

3 Click AutoForm in the New Object: AutoForm list.

The form displays (Figure 1-52).

FIGURE 1-52

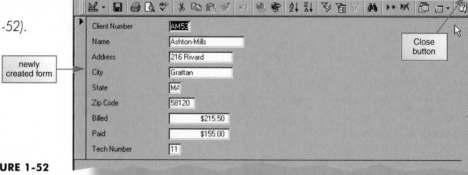

Closing and Saving the Form

Closing a form is similar to closing a table. The only difference is that you will be asked if you want to **save the form** unless you have previously saved it. Perform the following steps to close the form and save it as Client.

Steps **To Close and Save a Form**

1 Click the Close button for the Client window (see Figure 1-52). Point to the Yes button.

The Microsoft Access dialog box displays (Figure 1-53).

FIGURE 1-53

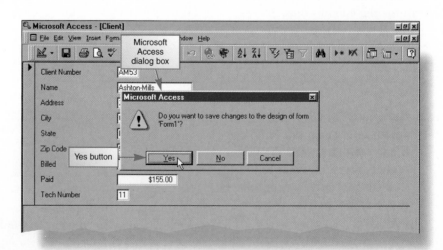

2 Click the Yes button and then point to the OK button.

The Save As dialog box displays (Figure 1-54). The name of the table (Client) becomes the name of the form automatically. This name can be replaced with any name.

3 Click the OK button in the Save As dialog box.

The form is saved as part of the database and is removed from the screen. The Pilotech Services : Database window again displays.

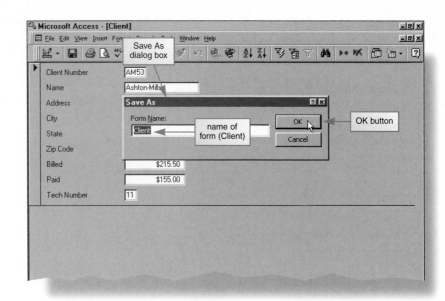

FIGURE 1-54

Opening the Saved Form

Once you have saved a form, you can use it at any time in the future by opening it. **Opening a form** is similar to opening a table; that is, make sure the form to be opened is selected, right-click, and then click Open on the shortcut menu. Before opening the form, however, the Forms tab, rather than the Tables tab, must be selected.

Perform the following steps to open the Client form.

Steps **To Open a Form**

1 With the Pilotech Services database open and the Database window on the screen, point to the Forms tab (Figure 1-55).

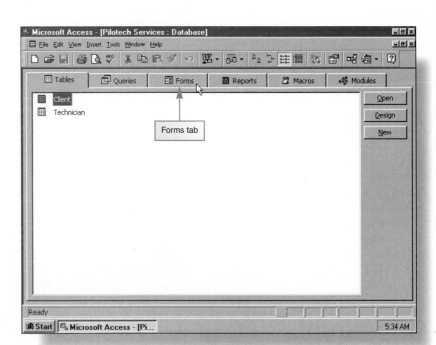

FIGURE 1-55

2 Click the Forms tab, right-click the Client form and then point to Open on the shortcut menu.

The Forms sheet is selected and the list of available forms displays (Figure 1-56). Currently, the Client form is the only form. The shortcut menu for the Client form displays.

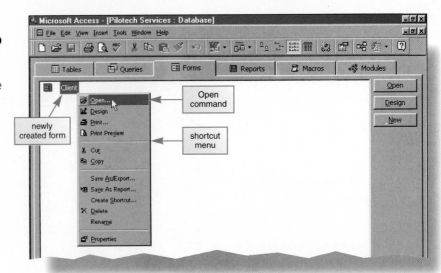

FIGURE 1-56

3 Click Open on the shortcut menu.

The Client form displays (Figure 1-57).

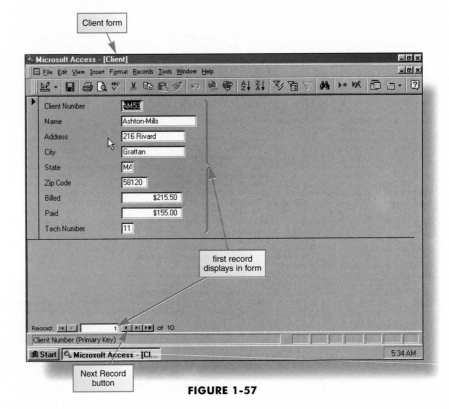

FIGURE 1-57

OtherWays

1. Click Forms tab, double-click desired Form
2. Click desired form, click Open button
3. Press ALT+O

Using the Form

You can **use the form** just as you used Datasheet view. You use the Navigation buttons to move between records. You can add new records or change existing ones. To delete the record displayed on the screen, after selecting the record by clicking its record selector, press the DELETE key. Thus, you can perform database operations using either Form view or Datasheet view.

Because you can see only one record at a time in Form view, to see a different record, such as the fifth record, use the Navigation buttons to move to it. To move from record to record in Form view, perform the following step.

Steps To Use a Form

1 **Click the Next Record button four times.**

The fifth record displays on the form (Figure 1-58).

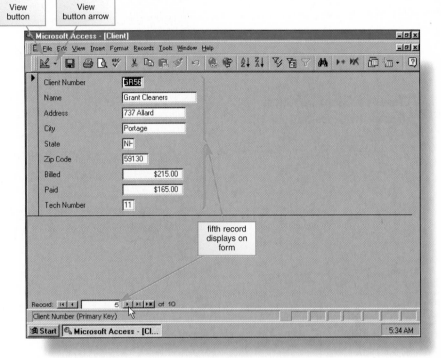

FIGURE 1-58

Switching Between Form View and Datasheet View

In some cases, once you have seen a record in Form view, you will want to move to Datasheet view to again see a collection of records. To do so, click the Form View button arrow on the toolbar and then click Datasheet View in the list that displays.

Perform the following steps to switch from Form view to Datasheet view.

Steps To Switch from Form View to Datasheet View

1 **Click the View button arrow on the toolbar (see Figure 1-58) and then point to Datasheet View.**

The list of available views displays (Figure 1-59).

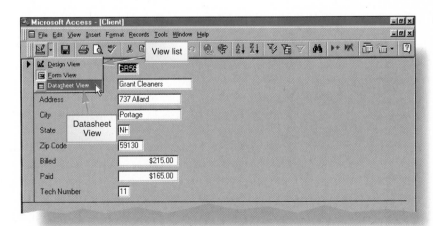

FIGURE 1-59

2 Click Datasheet View.

The table displays in Datasheet view (Figure 1-60). The record selector is positioned on the fifth record.

3 Close the Client window by clicking its Close button.

The datasheet no longer displays.

Close button

Client Number	Name	Address	City	State	Zip Code	B
AM53	Ashton-Mills	216 Rivard	Grattan	MA	58120	
AS62	Alton-Scripps	722 Fisher	Empire	MA	58216	
BL26	Blake Suppliers	5752 Maumee	Grattan	MA	58120	
DE76	D & E Grocery	464 Linnell	Marshall	VT	52018	
GR56	Grant Cleaners	737 Allard	Portage	NH	59130	
GU21	Grand Union	247 Fuller	Grattan	MA	58120	
JE77	Jones Electric	57 Giddings	Marshall	VT	52018	
MI26	Morland Int.	665 Whittier	Frankfort	MA	56152	
SA56	Sawyer Inc.	31 Lafayette	Empire	MA	58216	
SI82	Simpson Ind.	752 Cadieux	Fernwood	MA	57412	

fifth record is current record

Datasheet view

Record: 5 of 10

Client Number (Primary Key)

Start | Microsoft Access - [Cl... 5:35 AM

FIGURE 1-60

Other Ways

1. On View menu click Datasheet View

Creating a Report

Earlier in this project, you printed a table using the Print button. The report you produced was shown in Figure 1-36 on page A 1.29. While this type of report presented the data in an organized manner, it was not very flexible. It included all the fields, but in precisely the same order in which they occurred in the table. A way to change the title was not presented; it remained Client.

In this section, you will **create the report** shown in Figure 1-61. This report features significant differences from the one in Figure 1-36. The portion at the top of the report in Figure 1-61, called a **page header**, contains a custom title. The contents of this page header appear at the top of each page. The **detail lines**, which are the lines that are printed for each record, contain only those fields you specify.

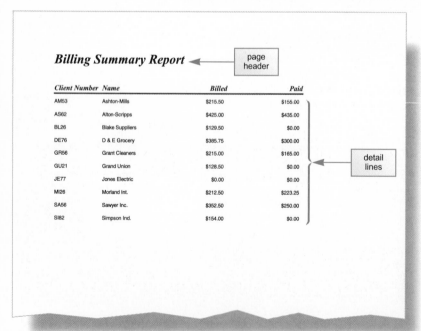

Billing Summary Report ← page header

Client Number	Name	Billed	Paid
AM53	Ashton-Mills	$215.50	$155.00
AS62	Alton-Scripps	$425.00	$435.00
BL26	Blake Suppliers	$129.50	$0.00
DE76	D & E Grocery	$385.75	$300.00
GR56	Grant Cleaners	$215.00	$165.00
GU21	Grand Union	$128.50	$0.00
JE77	Jones Electric	$0.00	$0.00
MI26	Morland Int.	$212.50	$223.25
SA56	Sawyer Inc.	$352.50	$250.00
SI82	Simpson Ind.	$154.00	$0.00

detail lines

FIGURE 1-61

Perform the following steps to create the report in Figure 1-61.

To Create a Report

1 **Click the Tables tab. Make sure the Client table is selected. Click the New Object: AutoForm button arrow on the toolbar.**

The list of available objects displays (Figure 1-62).

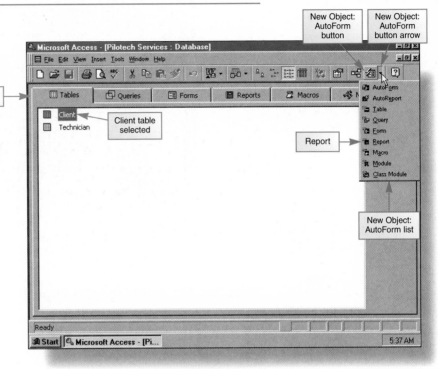

FIGURE 1-62

2 **Click Report and then point to Report Wizard.**

The New Report dialog box displays (Figure 1-63).

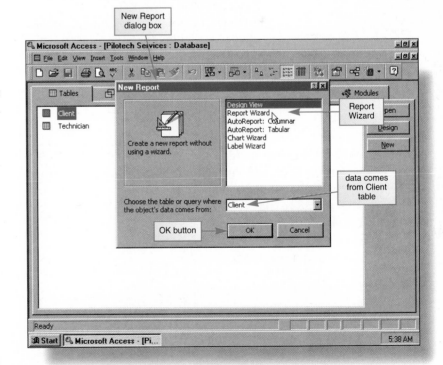

FIGURE 1-63

3 Click Report Wizard and then click the OK button. Point to the Add Field button.

The Report Wizard dialog box displays (Figure 1-64).

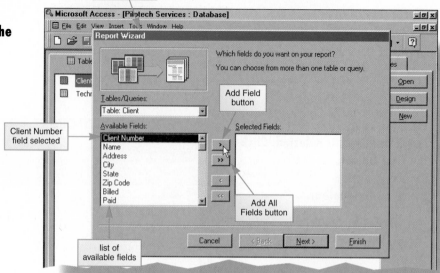

FIGURE 1-64

Selecting the Fields for the Report

To select a field for the report; that is, to indicate the field that is to be included in the report, click the field in the Available Fields list box. Next, click the Add Field button. This will move the field from the Available Fields list box to the Selected Fields list box, thus including the field in the report. If you wanted to select all fields, a shortcut is available simply by clicking the Add All Fields button.

To select the Client Number, Name, Billed, and Paid fields for the report, perform the following steps.

Steps To Select the Fields for a Report

1 Click the Add Field button to add the Client Number field. Add the Name field by clicking it and then clicking the Add Field button. Add the Billed and Paid fields just as you added the Client Number and Name fields.

The fields for the report display in the Selected Fields list box (Figure 1-65).

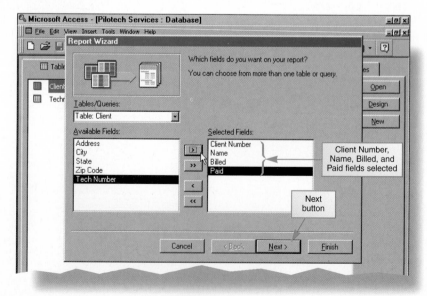

FIGURE 1-65

2 Click the Next button.

The Report Wizard dialog box displays (Figure 1-66).

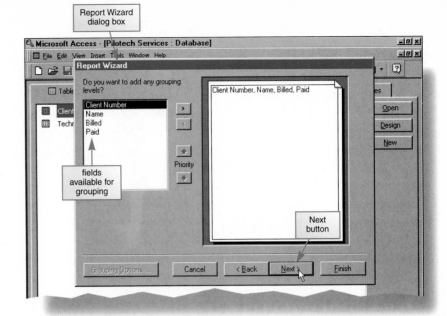

FIGURE 1-66

Completing the Report

Several additional steps are involved in completing the report. With the exception of changing the title, the Access selections are acceptable, so you simply will click the Next button.

Perform the following steps to complete the report.

 To Complete a Report

1 Because you will not specify any grouping, click the Next button in the Report Wizard dialog box (see Figure 1-66). Click the Next button a second time because you will not need to make changes on the screen that follows.

The Report Wizard dialog box displays (Figure 1-67). In this dialog box, you can change the layout or orientation of the report.

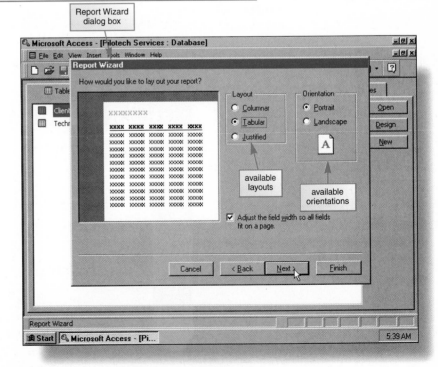

FIGURE 1-67

2 Make sure that Tabular is selected as the layout and Portrait is selected as the orientation and then click the Next button.

The Report Wizard dialog box displays (Figure 1-68). In this dialog box, you can select a style for the report.

FIGURE 1-68

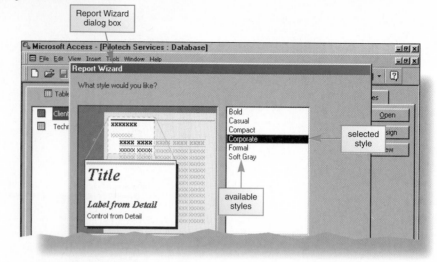

3 Be sure that the Corporate style is selected and then click the Next button.

The Report Wizard dialog box displays (Figure 1-69). In this dialog box, you can specify a title for the report.

FIGURE 1-69

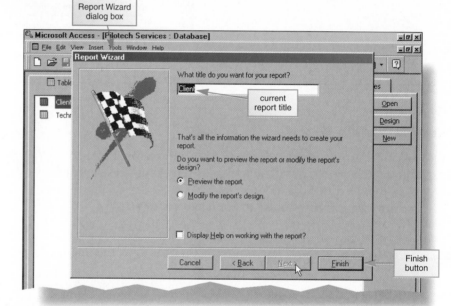

4 Type Billing Summary Report as the new title and then click the Finish button.

A preview of the report displays (Figure 1-70). Yours may look slightly different, depending on your printer.

FIGURE 1-70

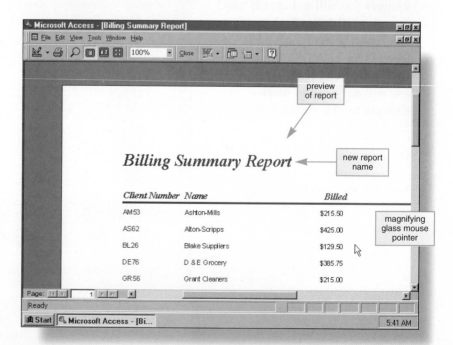

5 Click anywhere within the report to see the entire report.

The entire report displays (Figure 1-71).

6 Close the report by clicking the Close button for the Billing Summary Report window.

The report no longer displays. It has been saved automatically using the name Billing Summary Report.

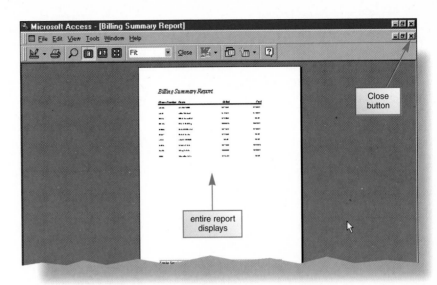

FIGURE 1-71

Printing the Report

To print a report from the Database window, first make sure the report displays. Then, you can click Print on the shortcut menu to print the report or Print Preview on the shortcut menu to see a preview of the report on the screen. Perform the following steps to print the report.

 To Print a Report

1 Click the Reports tab in the Database window, right-click the Billing Summary Report and then point to Print on the shortcut menu.

The shortcut menu for the Billing Summary Report displays (Figure 1-72).

2 Click Print on the shortcut menu.

The report prints. It should look similar to the one shown in Figure 1-61 on page A 1.40.

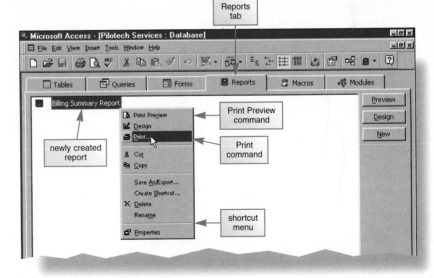

FIGURE 1-72

Closing the Database

Once you have finished working with a database, you should close it. The following step closes the database by closing its Database window.

TO CLOSE A DATABASE

Step 1: Click the Close button for the Pilotech Services : Database window.

Microsoft Access Help

At any time while you are working with Microsoft Access, you can answer your questions by using Access Help. Used properly, this form of online assistance can increase your productivity and reduce your frustrations by minimizing the time you spend learning how to use Access. Table 1-2 summarizes the categories of Access Help available to you.

Table 1-2		
TYPE	DESCRIPTION	ACTIVATE BY
Office Assistant	Answers your questions, offers tips, and provides Help for a variety of Access features	Clicking Office Assistant button on the toolbar
Contents sheet	Groups Help topics by general categories; use when you know only the general category of the topic in question	Clicking Contents and Index on the Help menu, then clicking the Contents tab
Index sheet	Similar to an index in a book; use when you know exactly what you want	Clicking Contents and Index on the Help menu, then clicking the Index tab
Find sheet	Searches the index for all phrases that include the term in question	Clicking Contents and Index on the Help menu, then clicking the Find tab
Question Mark button and What's This? command	Identify unfamiliar items on the screen	Clicking the Question Mark button, then clicking an item in a dialog box; clicking What's This? on the Help menu, then clicking an item on the screen

The following sections show examples of each type of online Help described in Table 1-2.

Using the Office Assistant

The **Office Assistant** answers your questions and suggests more efficient ways to complete a task. With the Office Assistant active, for example, you can type a word or phrase in a text box and the Office Assistant will provide immediate Help on the subject. In addition, as you perform a task, the Office Assistant accumulates tips that suggest more efficient ways to complete the task. This tip feature is part of the **IntelliSense™ technology** built into Access, which understands what you are trying to do and suggests better ways to do it.

The following steps show how to use the Office Assistant to obtain information on creating a table.

Steps To Obtain Help Using the Office Assistant

1 If the Office Assistant is not on the screen, click the Office Assistant button on the toolbar. If the Office Assistant is on the screen, click it. Type create in the What would you like to do? text box and then point to the Search button (Figure 1-73).

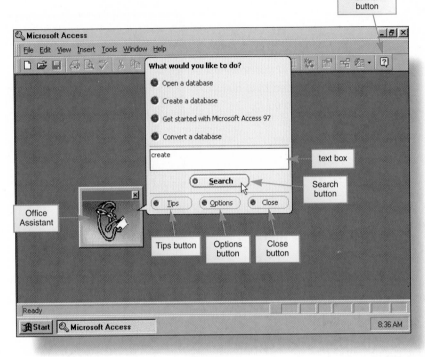

FIGURE 1-73

2 Click the Search button and then point to Create a table.

The Office Assistant displays a list of topics relating to the word create (Figure 1-74).

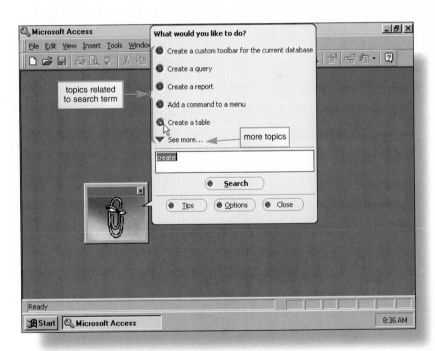

FIGURE 1-74

3 **Click Create a table.**

The Office Assistant displays the Microsoft Access 97 window with Help on creating a table (Figure 1-75). The underlined words in green and the topics at the bottom of the window preceded by a button are **links** to topics related to creating a table. When you move the mouse pointer over a link, it changes to a pointing hand.

4 **Click the Close button on the Microsoft Access 97 title bar.**

The Microsoft Access 97 window disappears and control returns to the desktop.

5 **Click the Close button on the title bar of the Office Assistant window.**

The Office Assistant disappears from the screen.

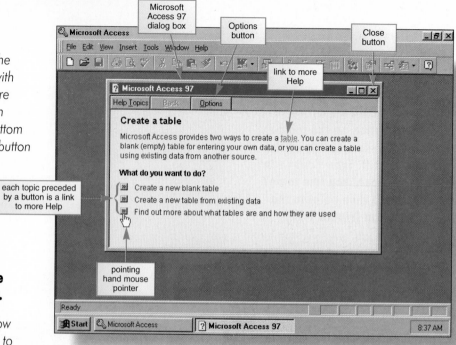

FIGURE 1-75

You can use the Office Assistant to search for Help on any topic concerning Access. Once Help displays, you can read it, print it via the **Options button** or shortcut menu, or click one of the links to display a related topic. If you display a related topic, click the **Back button** to return to the previous screen. You also can click the **Help Topics button** to obtain Help through the Contents, Index, and Find tabs.

When you right-click the Office Assistant window, a shortcut menu displays (Figure 1-76). It allows you to change the look and feel of the Office Assistant. For example, you can hide the Office Assistant, display tips, change the way it works, change the icon representing the Office Assistant, or view animation of the Office Assistant. These options also are available through the Options button that displays when you click the Office Assistant.

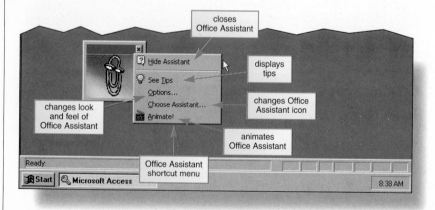

FIGURE 1-76

Using the Contents Sheet to Obtain Help

The Contents sheet in the Help Topics dialog box offers you assistance when you know the general category of the topic in question, but not the specifics. The following steps show how to use the Contents sheet in the Help Topics: Microsoft Access 97 dialog box to obtain information on adding or editing data.

 Steps **To Obtain Help Using the Contents Sheet**

1 **Click Help on the menu bar and then point to Contents and Index.**

The Help menu displays (Figure 1-77).

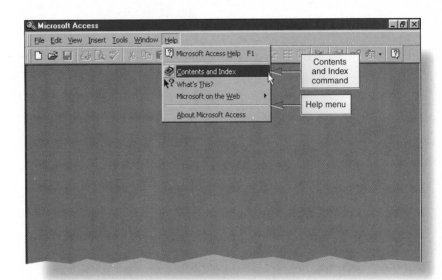

FIGURE 1-77

2 **Click Contents and Index. Click the Contents tab. Double-click the Working with Data book. Point to the Adding or Editing Data book.**

The Help Topics: Microsoft Access 97 dialog box displays (Figure 1-78). The Contents sheet displays with the Working with Data book open.

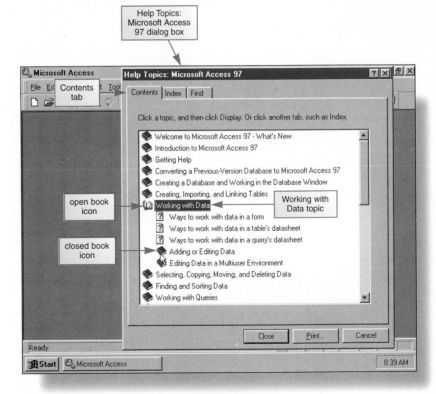

FIGURE 1-78

3 **Double-click the Adding or Editing Data book.**

The Adding or Editing Data book is open with a list of topics (Figure 1-79).

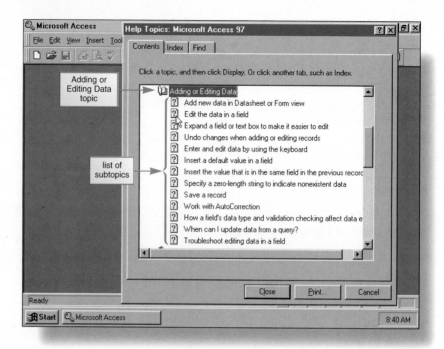

FIGURE 1-79

4 **Double-click the topic, Edit the data in a field, listed below the open book Adding or Editing Data.**

A Microsoft Access 97 window displays describing the steps for editing the data in a field (Figure 1-80).

5 **After reading the information, click the Close button in the Microsoft Access 97 window.**

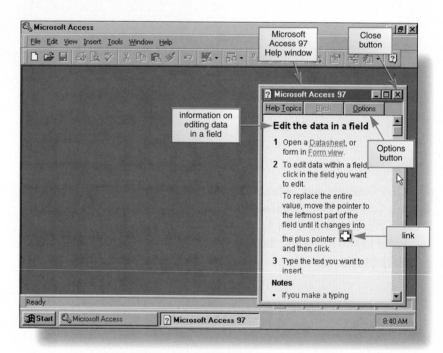

FIGURE 1-80

Instead of closing the Microsoft Access 97 window in Step 5, you can click Help Topics in Figure 1-80 to return to the Contents sheet (Figure 1-79). If you right-click in the Microsoft Access 97 window, a shortcut menu will display with several commands, such as Print Topic and Copy. You can use the Copy command to copy the Help information to a Word document.

Each topic on the Contents sheet (Figure 1-79) is preceded by a book icon or question mark icon. A **book icon** indicates subtopics are available. A **question mark icon** means information will display on the topic if you double-click the title. Notice how the book icon opens when you double-click the book (or its title).

Rather than double-clicking a topic in the list box, you can click it and then use the buttons in the dialog box to open a book, display information on a topic, or print information on a topic.

Using the Index Sheet to Obtain Help

The next sheet in the Help Topics: Microsoft Access 97 dialog box is the Index sheet. Use the Index sheet when you know the term you want to find or at least the first few letters of the term. Use the Index sheet in the same manner you would use an index at the back of a textbook.

The following steps show how to obtain information on primary keys by using the Index sheet and entering the letters, pri, the first three letters of primary.

 Steps To Obtain Help Using the Index Sheet

1 **Click Help on the menu bar and then click Contents and Index. Click the Index tab.**

The Index sheet displays in the Help Topics: Microsoft Access 97 dialog box.

2 **Type** pri **in the top text box labeled 1.**

The words, primary keys, display in the lower list box labeled 2 (Figure 1-81). Several index entries relating to primary keys are in the list.

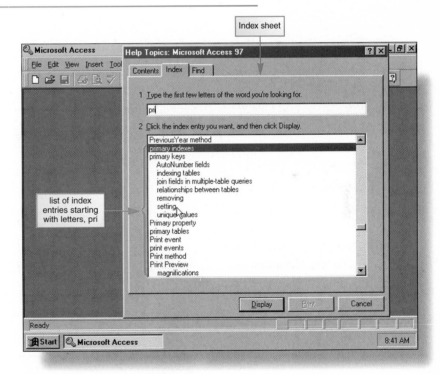

FIGURE 1-81

3 Double-click the index entry, setting, under primary keys. Double-click Set or change the primary key in the Topics Found dialog box.

Information on setting or changing the primary key displays in the Microsoft Access 97 window (Figure 1-82).

4 Click the Close button in the upper-right corner of the Microsoft Access 97 window to close it.

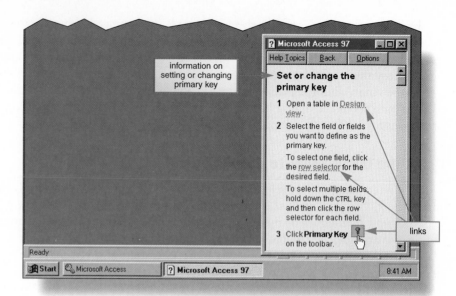

FIGURE 1-82

Using the Find Sheet to Obtain Help

The third sheet in the Help Topics: Microsoft Access 97 dialog box is the Find sheet. The Find sheet will return a list of all topics pertaining to the word or phrase you type in the text box. You then can further select words to narrow your search.

The following steps show how to obtain information on connecting database applications to the Internet.

 Steps **To Obtain Help Using the Find Sheet**

1 Click Help on the menu bar and then click Contents and Index. Click the Find tab.

The Find sheet displays in the Help Topics: Microsoft Access dialog box.

2 Type web in the top text box labeled 1. Click Web in the middle list box labeled 2. Click the down arrow on the scroll bar in the lower list box labeled 3. Point to New Internet Features for Developers.

The message box indicates that 69 topics were found (Figure 1-83).

FIGURE 1-83

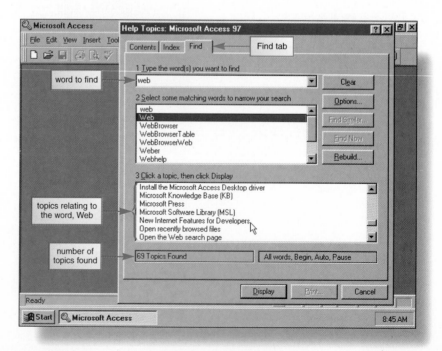

3 **Double-click New Internet Features for Developers.**

Information describing new Internet features displays (Figure 1-84).

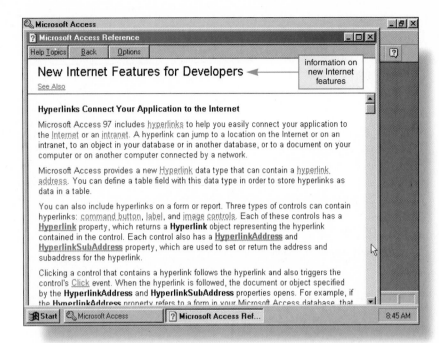

FIGURE 1-84

You can see from the previous steps that the Find sheet allows you to enter a word similarly to the Index sheet, but instead of displaying an alphabetical listing, the Find sheet lists all the words or phrases that include the word you entered. You then can click the appropriate words or phrases to narrow your search.

Obtaining Web Information

To obtain Web-related information, you can use the Microsoft on the Web command on the Help menu. A submenu of Web-related commands displays (Figure 1-85). If you click any command on the submenu, your system will launch your browser and connect to a corresponding page on the World Wide Web. Use the commands on the Microsoft on the Web submenu to obtain up-to-date information on a variety of topics.

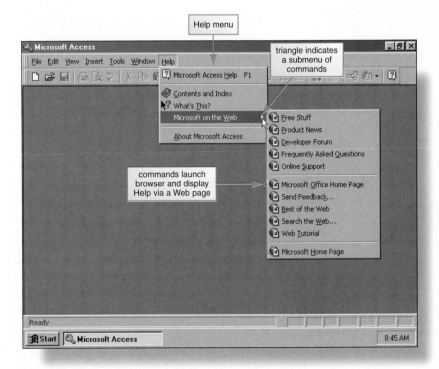

FIGURE 1-85

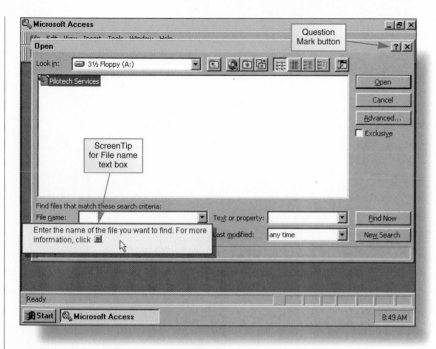

FIGURE 1-86

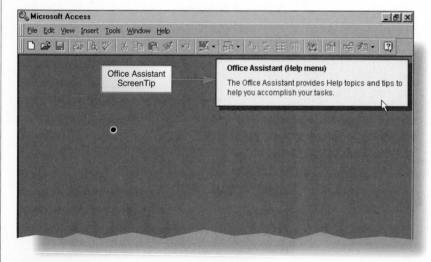

FIGURE 1-87

Using the Question Mark Button or Help Button to Define Items on the Screen

Use the Question Mark button or What's This? command on the Help menu when you are not sure of an item on the screen or its function. Click either button and the mouse pointer changes to an arrow and a question mark. Next, click any item on which you want more information. The information displayed is called a **ScreenTip**.

The **Question Mark button** displays in the upper-right corner of dialog boxes, next to the Close button. For example, in Figure 1-86, the Open dialog box is on the screen. If you click the Question Mark button and then click anywhere in the File name text box, an explanation of the File name text box displays.

Whereas the Question Mark button is used to display ScreenTips concerning items in a dialog box, the **What's This? command** on the Help menu is used to display ScreenTips concerning items on the Access window. Once you click What's This?, you can move the arrow and question mark pointer to any menu name, button, or cell, and click to display a ScreenTip. For example, clicking the Office Assistant button displays the ScreenTip shown in Figure 1-87. Click anywhere in the window to close the ScreenTip.

Designing a Database

Database design refers to the arrangement of data into tables and fields. In the example in this project, the design is specified, but in many cases, you will have to determine the design based on what you want the system to accomplish.

With large, complex databases, the database design process can be extensive. Major sections of advanced database textbooks are devoted to this topic. Often, however, you should be able to design a database effectively by keeping one simple principle in mind: Design to remove redundancy. **Redundancy** means storing the same fact in more than one place.

More *About*
Database Design

There is a special technique for identifying and eliminating redundancy, called **normalization**. For a description and illustration of this technique, see *Concepts of Database Management*, by Pratt and Adamski (CTI, 1997). The text also includes a complete database design method.

To illustrate, you need to maintain the following information shown in Figure 1-88. In the figure, all the data is contained in a single table. Notice that the data for a given Technician (number, name, address, and so on) occurs on more than one record.

Client table

CLIENT NUMBER	NAME	ADDRESS	CITY	STATE	ZIP CODE	BILLED	PAID	TECH NUMBER	LAST NAME	FIRST NAME
AM53	Ashton-Mills	216 Rivard	Grattan	MA	58120	$215.50	$155.00	11	Levin	Joanna
AS62	Alton-Scripps	722 Fisher	Empire	MA	58216	$425.00	$435.00	12	Rogers	Brad
BL26	Blake Suppliers	5752 Maumee	Grattan	MA	58120	$129.50	$5,000.00	12	Rogers	Brad
DE76	D & E Grocery	464 Linnell	Marshall	VT	52018	$385.75	$300.00	17	Rodriguez	Maria
GR56	Grant Cleaners	737 Allard	Portage	NH	59130	$215.00	$165.00	11	Levin	Joanna
GU21	Grand Union	247 Fuller	Grattan	MA	58120	$128.50	$0.00	12	Rogers	Brad
JE77	Jones Electric	57 Giddings	Marshall	VT	52018	$0.00	$0.00	12	Rogers	Brad
MI26	Morland Int.	665 Whittier	Frankfort	MA	56152	$212.50	$223.25	11	Levin	Joanna
SA56	Sawyer Inc.	31 Lafayette	Empire	MA	58216	$352.50	$250.00	17	Rodriguez	Maria
SI82	Simpson Ind.	752 Cadieux	Fernwood	MA	57412	$154.00	$0.00	12	Rogers	Brad

duplicate technician names

ADDRESS	CITY	STATE	ZIP CODE	HOURLY RATE	YTD EARNINGS
26 Cottonwood	Carlton	MA	59712	$25.00	$6,245.00
7972 Marsden	Kaleva	VT	57253	$30.00	$7,143.30
7972 Marsden	Kaleva	VT	57253	$30.00	$7,143.30
263 Topsfield	Hudson	MA	57240	$35.00	$7,745.50
26 Cottonwood	Carlton	MA	59712	$25.00	$6,245.00
7972 Marsden	Kaleva	VT	57253	$30.00	$7,143.30
7972 Marsden	Kaleva	VT	57253	$30.00	$7,143.30
26 Cottonwood	Carlton	MA	59712	$25.00	$6,245.00
263 Topsfield	Hudson	MA	57240	$35.00	$7,745.50
7972 Marsden	Kaleva	VT	57253	$30.00	$7,143.30

FIGURE 1-88

Storing this data on multiple records is an example of redundancy, which causes several problems:

1. Redundancy wastes space on the disk. The address of Technician 11 (Joanna Levin), for example, should be stored only once. Storing this fact several times is wasteful.
2. Redundancy makes updating the database more difficult. If, for example, Joanna Levin moves, her address would need to be changed in several different places.
3. A possibility of inconsistent data exists. Suppose, for example, that you change the address of Joanna Levin on client GR56's record to 146 Valley, but do not change it on client AM53's record. In both cases, the Tech Number is 11, but the addresses are different. In other words, the data is inconsistent.

The solution to the problem is to place the redundant data in a separate table, one in which the data will no longer be redundant. If, for example, you place the data for technicians in a separate table (Figure 1-89), the data for each technician will appear only once.

technician data is in separate table

Technician table

TECH NUMBER	LAST NAME	FIRST NAME	ADDRESS	CITY	STATE	ZIP CODE	HOURLY RATE	YTD EARNINGS
11	Levin	Joanna	26 Cottonwood	Carlton	MA	59712	$25.00	$6,245.00
12	Rogers	Brad	7972 Marsden	Kaleva	VT	57253	$30.00	$7,143.30
17	Rodriguez	Maria	263 Topsfield	Hudson	MA	57240	$35.00	$7,745.50

Client table

CLIENT NUMBER	NAME	ADDRESS	CITY	STATE	ZIP CODE	BILLED	PAID	TECH NUMBER
AM53	Ashton-Mills	216 Rivard	Grattan	MA	58120	$215.50	$155.00	11
AS62	Alton-Scripps	722 Fisher	Empire	MA	58216	$425.00	$435.00	12
BL26	Blake Suppliers	5752 Maumee	Grattan	MA	58120	$129.50	$0.00	12
DE76	D & E Grocery	464 Linnell	Marshall	VT	52018	$385.75	$300.00	17
GR56	Grant Cleaners	737 Allard	Portage	NH	59130	$215.00	$165.00	11
GU21	Grand Union	247 Fuller	Grattan	MA	58120	$128.50	$0.00	12
JE77	Jones Electric	57 Giddings	Marshall	VT	52018	$0.00	$0.00	12
MI26	Morland Int.	665 Whittier	Frankfort	MA	56152	$212.50	$223.25	11
SA56	Sawyer Inc.	31 Lafayette	Empire	MA	58216	$352.50	$250.00	17
SI82	Simpson Ind.	752 Cadieux	Fernwood	MA	57412	$154.00	$0.00	12

FIGURE 1-89

Notice that you need to have the Tech Number in both tables. Without it, no way exists to tell which technician is associated with which client. All the other technician data, however, was removed from the Client table and placed in the Technician table. This new arrangement corrects the problems of redundancy in the following ways:

1. Because the data for each technician is stored only once, space is not wasted.
2. Changing the address of a technician is easy. You have only to change one row in the Technician table.
3. Because the data for a technician is stored only once, inconsistent data cannot occur.

Designing to omit redundancy will help you to produce good and valid database designs.

Project Summary

Project 1 introduced you to starting Access and creating a database. You created the database that will be used by Pilotech Services. Within the Pilotech Services database, you created the Client and Technician tables by defining the fields within them. You then added records to these tables. Once you created the tables, you printed the contents of the tables. You also used a form to view the data in the table. Finally, you used the Report Wizard to create a report containing the Client Number, Name, Billed, and Paid fields for each client of Pilotech Services.

What You Should Know

Having completed this project, you now should be able to perform the following tasks:

▶ Add Additional Records to a Table *(A 1.27)*
▶ Add Records to a Table *(A 1.21)*
▶ Add Records to an Additional Table *(A 1.34)*
▶ Close a Database *(A 1.46)*
▶ Close a Table and Database and Quit Access *(A 1.24)*
▶ Close and Save a Form *(A 1.36)*
▶ Complete a Report *(A 1.43)*
▶ Create a Report *(A 1.41)*
▶ Create a Table *(A 1.15)*
▶ Create an Additional Table *(A 1.33)*
▶ Define the Fields in a Table *(A 1.16)*
▶ Obtain Help Using the Contents Sheet *(A 1.49)*
▶ Obtain Help Using the Find Sheet *(A 1.52)*
▶ Obtain Help Using the Index Sheet *(A 1.51)*

▶ Obtain Help Using the Office Assistant *(A 1.47)*
▶ Open a Database *(A 1.25)*
▶ Open a Form *(A 1.37)*
▶ Preview and Print the Contents of a Table *(A 1.29)*
▶ Print a Report *(A 1.45)*
▶ Save a Table *(A 1.19)*
▶ Select the Fields for a Report *(A 1.42)*
▶ Start Access *(A 1.10)*
▶ Switch from Form View to Datasheet View *(A 1.39)*
▶ Use a Form *(A 1.39)*
▶ Use the New Object: AutoForm Button to Create a Form *(A 1.35)*

A+ Test Your Knowledge

1 True/False

Instructions: Circle T if the statement is true or F if the statement is false.

T F 1. A field contains information about a given person, product, or event.

T F 2. An Access database consists of a collection of tables.

T F 3. If you do not assign a width to a text field, Access assumes the width is 25.

T F 4. You can use the TAB key to move to the next field in a record in Datasheet view.

T F 5. Field names can be no more than 64 characters in length and can include numeric digits.

T F 6. The only field type available for fields that must be used in arithmetic operations is number.

T F 7. To delete a record from a table, select the record and then press the DELETE key.

T F 8. To add a field to a table structure, select the field that will follow the field you want to add, click Insert on the menu bar and then click Rows.

T F 9. To add records to a table that already contains data, open the table and then click the Append Record button.

T F 10. Controlling redundancy results in an increase in consistency.

2 Multiple Choice

Instructions: Circle the correct response.

1. A database is _____.
   a. the same as a file
   b. a collection of data organized in a manner that allows access, retrieval, and use of that data
   c. a software product
   d. none of the above

2. Which of the following is not a benefit of controlling redundancy?
   a. greater consistency is maintained
   b. less space is occupied
   c. update is easier
   d. all of the above are benefits

3. A field that uniquely identifies a particular record in a table is called a _____.
   a. secondary key
   b. foreign key
   c. principal key
   d. primary key

4. Access is a(n) _____.
   a. application software package
   b. DBMS
   c. database
   d. both a and b

 Test Your Knowledge

5. To add a record to a table that already contains data, open the table and click the _____ button.
   a. Add Record
   b. New Record
   c. Append Record
   d. Insert Record

6. A record in Access is composed of a _____.
   a. series of databases
   b. series of files
   c. series of records
   d. series of fields

7. To make a field the primary key for a table, select the field and then click the _____ button on the toolbar.
   a. Unique Key
   b. Single Key
   c. First Key
   d. Primary Key

8. To remove a field from a table structure, select the field and then press the _____ key(s).
   a. DELETE
   b. CTRL+D
   c. CTRL+DELETE
   d. CTRL+Y

9. To change to landscape orientation to print a table, on the File menu, click _____.
   a. Print Preview
   b. Page Setup
   c. Print
   d. Print Settings

10. To move from the upper pane, the one where you define fields, in the Table window to the lower pane, the one where you define field properties, press the _____ key.
    a. F3
    b. F4
    c. F6
    d. F7

 Test Your Knowledge

3 Understanding Access Windows

Instructions: In Figure 1-90, arrows point to the major components of an Access window. In the spaces provided, indicate the purpose of each of these components.

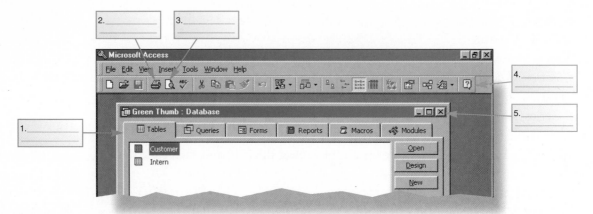

FIGURE 1-90

4 Understanding the Table Window in Datasheet View

Instructions: On the form in Figure 1-91, arrows point to the major components of a Table window in Datasheet view. In the spaces provided, indicate the purpose of each of these components.

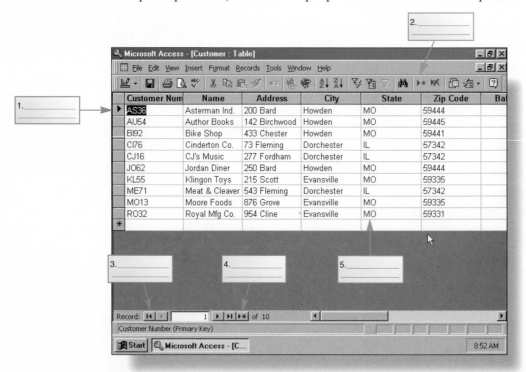

FIGURE 1-91

Use Help

1 Reviewing Project Activities

Instructions: Perform the following tasks using a computer.

1. Start Access.
2. If the Office Assistant is on your screen, then click it to display its balloon. If the Office Assistant is not on your screen, then click the Office Assistant button on the toolbar.
3. Click the Office Assistant and type `data types` in the What would you like to do? text box. Click the Search button.
4. Click What data type should I use for a field in my table?. Read the Help information. Use the shortcut menu or Options button to print the information. Hand in the printout to your instructor.
5. Click the Help Topics button. Click the Index tab. Type `Datasheet` in the top text box labeled 1 and then double-click entering and editing data under Datasheet view in the list box labeled 2. Double-click Delete a record in Datasheet or Form view in the Topics Found dialog box. When the Help information displays, read it. Use the shortcut menu or Options button to print the information. Hand in the printout to your instructor. Click the Help Topics button to return to the Help Topics: Microsoft Access 97 dialog box.
6. Click the Find tab. Type `preview` in the top text box labeled 1. Click Previewing in the list box abeled 2. Double-click Preview a report in the list box labeled 3. When the Microsoft Access 97 window displays, read it and use the shortcut menu or Options button to print the information. Click the Preview all the data in the report page by page button in the Help window. Print the Help information. Hand in the printouts to your instructor. Click the Close button.

2 Expanding on the Basics

Instructions: Use Access Help to better understand the topics listed below. If you are unable to print the Help information, then answer the question on your own paper.

1. Using the Working with Data book on the Contents sheet in the Help Topics: Microsoft Access 97 dialog box, answer the following questions:
   a. When does Access save the data in a record?
   b. How can you save the data in a record while you are editing it?
2. Using the words, shortcut keys, and the Index tab in the Help Topics: Microsoft Access 97 dialog box, display and print the shortcut keys to use in Datasheet view and Form view. Then, answer the following questions:
   a. Which key or combination keys add a new record?
   b. Which key or combination keys delete the current record?
   c. Which key or combination keys save changes to the current record?

(continued)

Use Help

Expanding on the Basics *(continued)*

    d. Which key or combination keys undo changes in the current field?

    e. Which key or combination keys insert the value from the same field in the previous record?

3. Use the Find sheet in the Help Topics: Microsoft Access 97 dialog box to display and print information about automatically correcting two capital letters in a row.

4. Use the Office Assistant to display and print information about backing up a database.

Apply Your Knowledge

CAUTION: To ensure you have enough disk space to save your files, it is recommended that you create a copy of the Data Disk that accompanies this book. Then, delete folders from the copy of the Data Disk that are not needed for the application you are working on. Do the following: (1) Insert the Data Disk in drive A; (2) start Explorer; (3) right-click the 3½ Floppy (A:) folder in the All Folders side of the window; (4) click Copy Disk; (5) click Start and OK as required; (6) insert a floppy disk when requested; (7) delete all folders on the floppy disk you created except the Access folder; (8) remove the floppy disk from drive A and label it Access Data Disk.

1 Changing Data and Creating Reports

Instructions: Start Access and open the Green Thumb document from the Access folder on the Data Disk that accompanies this book. Green Thumb is a small company that was started by two graduates of the horticulture program at the local college. It provides plants and plant care to local businesses. Green Thumb designs indoor landscapes and does regular maintenance, for example, watering, fertilizing, and pruning. The company employs horticulture students who do internships with the company. Green Thumb has a database that keeps track of its interns and customers. The database has two tables. The Customer table contains data on the customers who use Green Thumb's services. The Intern table contains data on the students employed by Green Thumb. The structure and data are shown for the Customer table in Figure 1-92 below and at the top of the next page and for the Intern table in Figure 1-93.

Structure of Customer table

FIELD NAME	DATA TYPE	FIELD SIZE	PRIMARY KEY?	DESCRIPTION
Customer Number	Text	4	Yes	Customer Number (Primary Key)
Name	Text	20		Customer Name
Address	Text	15		Street Address
City	Text	15		City
State	Text	2		State (Two-Character Abbreviation)
Zip Code	Text	5		Zip Code (Five-Character Version)
Balance	Currency			Amount Owed by Customer
Intern Id	Text	3		Id of Customer's Intern

Apply Your Knowledge

Data for Customer table

CUSTOMER NUMBER	NAME	ADDRESS	CITY	STATE	ZIP CODE	BALANCE	INTERN ID
AS36	Asterman Ind.	200 Bard	Howden	MO	59444	$85.00	102
AU54	Author Books	142 Birchwood	Howden	MO	59445	$50.00	109
BI92	Bike Shop	433 Chester	Howden	MO	59441	$40.00	109
CI76	Cinderton Co.	73 Fleming	Dorchester	IL	57342	$0.00	113
CJ16	CJ's Music	277 Fordham	Dorchester	IL	57342	$105.00	102
JO62	Jordan Diner	250 Bard	Howden	MO	59444	$74.00	109
KL55	Klingon Toys	215 Scott	Evansville	MO	59335	$115.00	109
ME71	Meat & Cleaver	543 Fleming	Dorchester	IL	57342	$138.00	102
MO13	Moore Foods	876 Grove	Evansville	MO	59335	$0.00	113
RO32	Royal Mfg Co.	954 Cline	Evansville	MO	59331	$93.00	109

FIGURE 1-92

Structure of Intern table

FIELD NAME	DATA TYPE	FIELD SIZE	PRIMARY KEY?	DESCRIPTION
Intern Id	Text	3	Yes	Intern Identification Number (Primary Key)
Last Name	Text	10		Last Name of Intern
First Name	Text	8		First Name of Intern
Address	Text	15		Street Address
City	Text	15		City
State	Text	2		State (Two-Character Abbreviation)
Zip Code	Text	5		Zip Code (Five-Character Version)
Pay Rate	Currency			Hourly Pay Rate

Data for Intern table

INTERN ID	LAST NAME	FIRST NAME	ADDRESS	CITY	STATE	ZIP CODE	PAY RATE
102	Dang	Chou	764 Clay	Howden	MO	59444	$7.50
109	Hyde	Michelle	65 Parkwood	Dorchester	IL	57342	$7.75
113	Lopez	Javier	345 Norton	Howden	MO	59444	$7.65

FIGURE 1-93

(continued)

Apply Your Knowledge

Changing Data and Creating Reports *(continued)*

Perform the following tasks.

1. Open the Intern table in Datasheet view and add the following record to the table:

| 105 | Eckels | Lois | 24 Riley | Evansville | MO | 59335 | 7.40 |

Close the Intern table.

2. Open the Intern table again. Notice that the record you just added has been moved. It is no longer at the end of the table. The records are in order by the primary key, Intern Id.
3. Print the Intern table.
4. Open the Customer table.
5. Change the Intern Id for customer KL55 to 105.
6. Print the Customer table.
7. Create the report shown in Figure 1-94 for the Customer table.

Balance Due Report

Customer Number	Name	Balance
AS36	Asterman Ind.	$85.00
AU54	Author Books	$50.00
BI92	Bike Shop	$40.00
CI76	Cinderton Co.	$0.00
CJ16	CJ's Music	$105.00
JO82	Jordan Diner	$74.00
KL55	Klingon Toys	$115.00
ME71	Meat & Cleaver	$138.00
MO13	Moore Foods	$0.00
RO32	Royal Mfg Co.	$93.00

FIGURE 1-94

8. Print the report.

In the Lab

1 Creating the Museum Mercantile Database

Problem: The County Museum runs a small gift shop, Museum Mercantile, that is staffed by volunteers. The museum purchases products from vendors that specialize in handcrafted products and vintage merchandise. The director of the museum has asked you to create and update a database that volunteers can use. The database consists of two tables. The Product table contains information on items available for sale. The Vendor table contains information on the vendors.

Instructions: Perform the following tasks.

1. Create a new database in which to store all the objects related to the gift shop data. Call the database Museum Mercantile.
2. Create the Product table using the structure shown in Figure 1-95. Use the name Product for the table.

Structure of Product table

FIELD NAME	DATA TYPE	FIELD SIZE	PRIMARY KEY?	DESCRIPTION
Product Id	Text	4	Yes	Product Id Number (Primary Key)
Description	Text	25		Description of Product
On Hand	Number	Long Integer		Number of Units On Hand
Cost	Currency			Cost of Product
Selling Price	Currency			Selling Price of Product
Vendor Code	Text	2		Code of Product Vendor

Data for Product table

PRODUCT ID	DESCRIPTION	ON HAND	COST	SELLING PRICE	VENDOR CODE
CH04	Chess Set	11	$26.75	$28.90	WW
DI24	Dinosaurs	14	$3.75	$4.95	MS
GL18	Globe	2	$27.50	$29.95	MS
JG01	Jigsaw Puzzle	3	$5.40	$6.95	MS
PC03	Pick Up Sticks	5	$8.50	$10.95	WW
ST23	Stationery	8	$3.95	$5.00	AR
TD05	Tiddly Winks	6	$13.75	$15.95	WW
WI10	Wizard Cards	10	$7.50	$9.95	MS
WL34	Wildlife Posters	15	$2.50	$2.95	AR
YO12	Wooden YoYo	9	$1.60	$1.95	WW

FIGURE 1-95

(continued)

In the Lab

Creating the Museum Mercantile Database (continued)

3. Add the data shown in Figure 1-95 to the Product table.
4. Print the Product table.
5. Create the Vendor table using the structure shown in Figure 1-96. Use the name Vendor for the table.

Structure of Vendor table

FIELD NAME	DATA TYPE	FIELD SIZE	PRIMARY KEY?	DESCRIPTION
Vendor Code	Text	2	Yes	Vendor Code (Primary Key)
Name	Text	20		Name of Vendor
Address	Text	15		Street Address
City	Text	15		City
State	Text	2		State (Two-Character Abbreviation)
Zip Code	Text	5		Zip Code (Five-Character Version)
Telephone Number	Text	12		Telephone Number (999-999-9999 Version)

Data for Vendor table

VENDOR CODE	NAME	ADDRESS	CITY	STATE	ZIP CODE	TELEPHONE NUMBER
AR	Artisan's Co-op	3540 Grand	Hancock	WI	69780	414-555-7865
MS	Museum Stores	134 Union	Delana	SD	41345	605-555-3498
WW	Woodworkers	655 Clive	Great Falls	WV	34567	304-555-4532

FIGURE 1-96

6. Add the data shown in Figure 1-96 to the Vendor table.
7. Print the Vendor table.
8. Create a form for the Product table. Use the name Product for the form.
9. Create and print the report shown in Figure 1-97 for the Product table.

Inventory Report

Product Id	Description	On Hand	Cost
WI10	Wizard Cards	10	$7.50
PC03	Pick Up Sticks	5	$8.50
WL34	Wildlife Posters	15	$2.50
TD05	Tiddly Winks	6	$13.75
ST23	Stationery	8	$3.95
JG01	Jigsaw Puzzle	3	$5.40
YO12	Wooden YoYo	9	$1.60
DI24	Dinosaurs	14	$3.75
GL18	Globe	2	$27.50
CH04	Chess Set	11	$26.75

FIGURE 1-97

In the Lab

2 Creating the City Telephone System Database

Problem: The city government maintains its own internal telephone system. Each user is billed separately for monthly charges and all the bills for a department are sent to the department manager. The telephone manager has asked you to create and update a database that the city government can use as a telephone tracking system. The database consists of two tables. The User table contains information on the individuals with telephone accounts. The Department table contains information on the department in which the individual works.

Instructions: Perform the following tasks.

1. Create a new database in which to store all the objects related to the telephone system data. Call the database City Telephone System.
2. Create the User table using the structure shown in Figure 1-98. Use the name User for the table.

Structure of User table

FIELD NAME	DATA TYPE	FIELD SIZE	PRIMARY KEY?	DESCRIPTION
User Id	Text	4	Yes	User Id Number (Primary Key)
Last Name	Text	14		Last Name of User
First Name	Text	10		First Name of User
Phone Ext	Text	4		Telephone Extension (9999 Version)
Office	Text	3		Office Location (Room Number)
Basic Charge	Currency			Basic Service Charge (per Month)
Extra Charges	Currency			Extra Charges for Special Services and Long Distance Calls (per Month)
Dept Code	Text	3		Code of User's Department

Data for User table

USER ID	LAST NAME	FIRST NAME	PHONE EXT	OFFICE	BASIC CHARGE	EXTRA CHARGES	DEPT CODE
T129	Bishop	Fred	3383	212	$10.00	$22.00	ITD
T238	Chan	Rose	3495	220	$13.00	$29.95	ITD
T347	Febo	Javier	4267	323	$10.00	$7.75	HRS
T451	Ginras	Mary	3156	444	$17.00	$52.85	APV
T536	Hanneman	William	3578	317	$13.00	$18.75	HRS
T645	Johnsen	Paul	4445	234	$21.00	$7.75	ITD
T759	Kim	Lei	3068	310	$10.00	$13.55	ENG
T780	Mentor	Melissa	3418	525	$17.00	$73.95	PLN
T851	Sanchez	Alfredo	3134	438	$11.00	$6.25	APV
T888	TenClink	Brian	3414	521	$10.00	$37.45	PLN

FIGURE 1-98

(continued)

In the Lab

Creating the City Telephone System Database (continued)

3. Add the data shown in Figure 1-98 to the User table.
4. Print the User table.
5. Create the Department table using the structure shown in Figure 1-99. Use the name Department for the table.

Structure of Department table

FIELD NAME	DATA TYPE	FIELD SIZE	PRIMARY KEY?	DESCRIPTION
Dept Code	Text	3	Yes	Department Code (Primary Key)
Dept Name	Text	14		Name of Department
First Name	Text	8		First Name of Department Manager
Last Name	Text	12		Last Name of Department Manager

Data for Department table

DEPT CODE	DEPT NAME	FIRST NAME	LAST NAME
APV	Assessment	Joyce	Murphy
ENG	Engineering	Darnell	James
HRS	Housing	Billie	Buchanan
ITD	Income Tax	Maria	Fuentes
PLN	Planning	Joseph	Lippman

FIGURE 1-99

6. Add the data shown in Figure 1-99 to the Department table.
7. Print the Department table.
8. Create a form for the User table. Use the name User for the form.
9. Use the form you created to add the following two new city employees to the User table.

| T087 | Anders | Jane | 3923 | 531 | $10.00 | $0.00 | PLN |
| T832 | Reison | Jason | 3803 | 312 | $13.00 | $0.00 | ENG |

10. Create and print the report shown in Figure 1-100 for the User table. When the Report Wizard asks, What Sort Order do you want for your records?, click the Last Name field.

Telephone List

Last Name	First Name	Phone Ext	Office	Dept Code
Anders	Jane	3923	531	PLN
Bishop	Fred	3383	212	ITD
Chan	Rose	3495	220	ITD
Febo	Javier	4267	323	HRS
Ginras	Mary	3156	444	APV
Hanneman	William	3578	317	HRS
Johnsen	Paul	4445	234	ITD
Kim	Lei	3068	310	ENG
Mentor	Melissa	3418	525	PLN
Reison	Jason	3803	312	ENG
Sanchez	Alfredo	3134	438	APV
TenClink	Brian	3414	521	PLN

FIGURE 1-100

3 Creating the City Scene Database

Problem: The *City Scene* is a local arts magazine that relies on advertising to help finance its operations. Local firms buy advertising from ad representatives who work for the magazine. Ad representatives receive a commission based on the advertising revenues they generate. The managing editor of the magazine has asked you to create and update a database that will keep track of the advertising accounts and ad representatives. The database consists of two tables. The Advertiser table contains information on the organizations that advertise in the magazine. The Ad Rep table contains information on the representative assigned to the advertising account.

Instructions: Perform the following tasks.

1. Create a new database in which to store all the objects related to the advertising data. Call the database City Scene.
2. Create the Advertiser table using the structure shown in Figure 1-101 on the next page. Use the name Advertiser for the table.
3. Add the data shown in Figure 1-101 to the Advertiser table.

(continued)

In the Lab

Creating the City Scene Database *(continued)*

Structure of Advertiser table

FIELD NAME	DATA TYPE	FIELD SIZE	PRIMARY KEY?	DESCRIPTION
Advertiser Number	Text	4	Yes	Advertiser Number (Primary Key)
Name	Text	20		Name of Advertiser
Address	Text	15		Street Address
City	Text	15		City
State	Text	2		State (Two-Character Abbreviation)
Zip Code	Text	5		Zip Code (Five-Character Version)
Balance	Currency			Amount Currently Owed
Amount Paid	Currency			Amount Paid Year-to-Date
Ad Rep Number	Text	2		Number of Advertising Representative

Data for Advertiser table

ADVERTISER NUMBER	NAME	ADDRESS	CITY	STATE	ZIP CODE	BALANCE	AMOUNT PAID	AD REP NUMBER
A226	Alden Books	74 Benton	Fernwood	WA	91191	$60.00	$535.00	16
B101	Bud's Diner	384 Carter	Crestview	OR	92332	$155.00	$795.00	19
C047	Chip and Putt	1 Golfview	Crestview	OR	92330	$0.00	$345.00	19
C134	Clover Clothes	62 Adams	New Castle	WA	91234	$100.00	$835.00	22
D216	Dogs 'n Draft	3 Riverview	Crestview	OR	92330	$260.00	$485.00	16
F345	Fast Freddie's	507 Oakley	Fernwood	WA	91191	$0.00	$775.00	19
G080	Green Thumb	619 Lincoln	New Castle	WA	91234	$185.00	$825.00	19
L189	Lighthouse Inc.	1 Riverview	Crestview	OR	92330	$35.00	$150.00	16
N034	New Releases	107 Main	Fernwood	WA	91191	$435.00	$500.00	22
S010	Skates R You	67 Adams	New Castle	WA	91234	$85.00	$235.00	16

FIGURE 1-101

4. Print the Advertiser table.
5. Create the Ad Rep table using the structure shown in Figure 1-102. Use the name Ad Rep for the table. Be sure to change the field size for the Comm Rate field to Double.
6. Add the data shown in Figure 1-102 to the Ad Rep table.

In the Lab

Structure of Ad Rep table

FIELD NAME	DATA TYPE	FIELD SIZE	PRIMARY KEY?	DESCRIPTION
Ad Rep Number	Text	2	Yes	Advertising Rep Number (Primary Key)
Last Name	Text	10		Last Name of Advertising Rep
First Name	Text	8		First Name of Advertising Rep
Address	Text	15		Street Address
City	Text	15		City
State	Text	2		State (Two-Character Abbreviation)
Zip Code	Text	5		Zip Code (Five-Character Version)
Comm Rate	Number	Double		Commision Rate on Advertising Sales
Compensation	Currency			Year-to-Date Total Compensation

Data for Ad Rep table

AD REP NUMBER	LAST NAME	FIRST NAME	ADDRESS	CITY	STATE	ZIP CODE	COMM RATE	COMMISSION
16	Hammond	Anne	75 Bartow	New Castle	WA	91234	0.08	$6,000.00
19	Morales	Louis	67 Shawmont	Fernwood	WA	91191	0.07	$5,750.00
22	Rodgers	Elaine	43 Manderly	Crestview	OR	92332	0.08	$6,500.00

FIGURE 1-102

7. Print the Ad Rep table.
8. Create a form for the Advertiser table. Use the name Advertiser for the form.
9. Open the form you created and change the address for Advertiser Number B101 to 384 Gartern.
10. Change to Datasheet view and delete the record for Advertiser Number F345.
11. Print the Advertiser table.
12. Create and print the report shown in Figure 1-103 on the next page for the Advertiser table.

(continued)

In the Lab

Creating the City Scene Database *(continued)*

Status Report

Advertiser Number	Name	Balance	Amount Paid
A226	Alden Books	$60.00	$535.00
B101	Bud's Diner	$155.00	$795.00
C047	Chip and Putt	$0.00	$345.00
C134	Clover Clothes	$100.00	$835.00
D216	Dogs 'n Draft	$260.00	$485.00
G080	Green Thumb	$185.00	$825.00
L189	Lighthouse Inc.	$35.00	$150.00
N034	New Releases	$435.00	$500.00
S010	Skates R You	$85.00	$235.00

Monday, September 21, 1998   *Page 1 of 1*

FIGURE 1-103

Cases and Places

The difficulty of these case studies varies: ❯ are the least difficult; ❯❯ are more difficult; and ❯❯❯ are the most difficult.

1 ❯ For years, the students at your school have complained about the inequities of the book buy-back policy. Student government finally has decided to do something about it by organizing a used textbook cooperative. As a member of student government, you create a system whereby students can locate other students who have used a particular book in a previous semester and want to sell it to another student. Student government advertises the plan on its Web page and receives the responses shown in Figure 1-104.

Create a database to store the file related to the textbooks. Then create a table, enter the data from Figure 1-104, and print the table.

BOOK TITLE	AUTHOR	COURSE USED	PRICE	SELLER'S NAME	TELEPHONE	CONDITION (E=EXCELLENT, G=GOOD, P=POOR)
Sociology Today	Munroe	Soc 101	$14	Joe Van	555-7632	G
Creative Writing	Swan & Shell	Eng 150	$18	Mary Nordman	555-9421	E
Reach for the Stars	Alvarez	Ast 210	$23	John Mott	555-9981	E
Creative Writing	Swan & Shell	Eng 150	$15	Peter Rudd	555-9156	E
Ethics for Today's Society	Garrison & Pierce	Phi 310	$20	Sandi Radle	555-7636	P
Sociology Today	Munroe	Soc 101	$17	Daniel Lewis	555-0873	E
Understanding Psychology	Navarone	Psy 101	$22	Karen Sing	555-9802	P
Electronic Circuitry	Carlson	Egr 255	$37	Karen Sing	555-9802	G
Nutrition for Our Souls	Francis	Nrs 330	$18	Dave Corsi	555-2384	E
Geriatric Nursing	Dyer	Nrs 265	$36	Mary Healy	555-9932	E

FIGURE 1-104

Cases and Places

2 ▶ You have decided to start a meal delivery service. As a first step, you consult the telephone directory for the numbers of local restaurants to make reservations and to order food for carry out and delivery. You have decided to create a database to store these numbers along with other pertinent data about the establishment, such as address, hours of operation, type of food, and days when specials are offered. You gather the information shown in Figure 1-105.

Create a database to store the file related to the restaurants. Then create a table, enter the data from Figure 1-105, and print the table.

NAME	TELEPHONE	ADDRESS	OPEN	CLOSE	FOOD TYPE	SPECIALS	CARRYOUT	DELIVERY
Noto's	(714) 555-2339	223 N. Jackson	11:00 a.m.	11:00 p.m.	Japanese	Wednesday	Yes	No
Ole Taco	(714) 555-5444	3294 E. Devon	4:00 p.m.	10:00 p.m.	Mexican	Monday	Yes	No
Red Rose	(714) 555-8001	1632 W. Clark	3:00 p.m.	1:00 a.m.	Indian	Friday	No	No
Pan Pacific	(714) 555-2470	3140 W. Halsted	11:00 a.m.	4:00 a.m.	Korean	Thursday	Yes	No
New Crete	(714) 555-9337	1805 W. Broadway	3:30 p.m.	10:00 p.m.	Greek	Monday	Yes	No
Texas Diner	(714) 555-1673	2200 E. Lawrence	4:30 p.m.	1:00 a.m.	American	Thursday	Yes	Yes
Little Venice	(714) 555-8632	13 N. Devon	11:30 a.m.	2:00 a.m.	Italian	Wednesday	Yes	No
Curry and More	(714) 555-3377	1027 E. Wells	5:00 p.m.	2:00 a.m.	Indian	Thursday	Yes	No
Napoli's Pizza	(714) 555-6168	787 N. Monroe	10:30 a.m.	3:00 a.m.	Italian	Tuesday	Yes	Yes
House of China	(714) 555-7373	1939 W. Michigan	11:00 a.m.	11:00 p.m.	Chinese	Wednesday	Yes	No

FIGURE 1-105

3 ▶▶ A local nursing home has a variety of classic movies on videocassette. You are a volunteer at the home and the director of volunteers has asked you to create an inventory of the movies. One afternoon, you sort through the boxes and list each movie's name, leading actors, year produced, and original running time. You also assign a rating system of one to four stars. You create the following list: *The Little Princess*, starring Shirley Temple and Richard Greene, 1939, 94 minutes, three stars; *North by Northwest*, Cary Grant and Eva Marie Saint, 1959, 136 minutes, four stars; *Of Mice and Men*, Burgess Meredith and Lon Chaney Jr., 1939, 107 minutes, four stars; *The Quiet Man*, John Wayne and Maureen O'Hara, 1952, 129 minutes, four stars; *On the Waterfront*, Marlon Brando and Eva Marie Saint, 1954, 108 minutes, four stars; *Pardon My Sarong*, Bud Abbott and Lou Costello, 1942, 84 minutes, three stars; *Ride 'em Cowboy*, Bud Abbott and Lou Costello, 1942, 82 minutes, two stars; *You Can't Take It With You*, Jean Arthur and Lionel Barrymore, 1938, 127 minutes, three stars; *The Undefeated*, John Wayne and Rock Hudson, 1969, 119 minutes, two stars; and *Operation Pacific*, John Wayne and Patricia Neal, 1951, 109 minutes, three stars. Using this information, create a database to store the file related to these movies. Then create a table, enter the data, and print the table.

Cases and Places

4 ▶▶ You are taking a nutrition class this semester, and your instructor has assigned you a research project on the relationship between heart disease and meat. Heart disease is one of the leading killers of adults in this country. With this knowledge, the meat industry has aggressively tried to deliver products that are low in fat and yet high in nutrients. The American Heart Association states that lean meat can be part of a healthy diet, as long as the meat is served in moderation. Three cooked ounces of lean cuts of beef have various nutritional contents. Eye of round has 140 calories, top round steak has 150 calories, tip round roast has 160 calories, sirloin steak has 170 calories, and top loin and tenderloin steaks both have 180 calories. Regarding fat content, eye of round and top round steak have four fat grams in three ounces, tip round roast and sirloin both have six grams, top loin steak has eight grams, and tenderloin steak has the most with nine grams. Cholesterol also varies, with eye of round the lowest at 60 milligrams in three ounces, top loin with 65 mg, top round, tip round, and tenderloin with 70 mg, and sirloin the highest with 75 mg. Create a database to store the file related to the nutritional content of meat. Then create a table, enter the data, and print the table.

5 ▶▶▶ As any comparison shopper knows, food and drug store prices can vary dramatically from one store to another. Make a list of six specific items you purchase frequently from area stores in the four categories of dairy (for example, milk, yogurt, butter, sour cream, cottage cheese), snacks (for example, pretzels, soda, granola bars, raisins, rice cakes), cosmetics/toiletries (for example, deodorant, bath soap, toothpaste, shampoo, contact lens solution), and kitchen supplies (for example, paper towels, dish washing detergent, scouring pads, trash bags, sandwich bags). List the size or weight of each item. Then, visit a local convenience store, grocery store, and discount store to compare prices. Be certain you obtain prices on identical products. Then create a table, enter the data you obtained in each category, and print the table.

6 ▶▶▶ Because you do not live on campus, you do not have easy access to a campus directory. When you do locate the book, usually you cannot find the information you need. Consequently, you have decided to create your own database containing the pertinent information. Obtain important names, telephone numbers, and room numbers of campus offices that you frequent. Start by organizing the data in the categories of faculty, administration, and services. In the faculty category, list your adviser and your instructors from this semester. In the administration category, list the registrar, the dean of your area, and the financial aid director. In the services category, list the bookstore, campus police station, daycare services, and library reference desk. Add other pertinent data to any of the categories. Then create a table, enter the data you obtained, and print the table.

Cases and Places

7 ▶▶▶ Your accounting professor has given every student in the class a hypothetical $1,000. Your assignment is to research Individual Retirement Accounts (IRAs). Visit or call a total of five local banks, credit unions, or savings and loan associations. Make a list of the current interest rates for an IRA opened with $1,000, minimum investment amount, total amount earned by the time you turn age 65, annual fees, and amount you would be penalized if you withdrew the money in two years. Using this information, create a database and enter the data showing the types of financial institutions (bank, savings and loan, or credit union), names of the financial institutions, their addresses and telephone numbers, interest rates, annual fees, total values of the IRAs by age 65, amount of interest earned in this time, and amount you would be penalized if you withdrew the money in two years. Print this table, and then create and print a bar graph indicating the amount of interest you would earn and the total value of your IRA at age 65 for each financial institution.

Querying a Database Using the Select Query Window

Objectives:

You will have mastered the material in this project when you can:

▶ State the purpose of queries
▶ Create a new query
▶ Use a query to display all records and all fields
▶ Run a query
▶ Print the answer to a query
▶ Close a query
▶ Clear a query
▶ Use a query to display selected fields
▶ Use character data in criteria in a query
▶ Use wildcards in criteria
▶ Use numeric data in criteria
▶ Use comparison operators
▶ Use compound criteria involving AND
▶ Use compound criteria involving OR
▶ Sort the answer to a query
▶ Join tables in a query
▶ Restrict the records in a join
▶ Use computed fields in a query
▶ Calculate statistics in a query
▶ Use grouping with statistics
▶ Save a query
▶ Use a saved query

Project 2

In Pursuit of the Money Trail

At a bullfight in Madrid during the 1960s, thousands of Spaniards rose from their seats cheering, "El Fugitivo," when they spotted David Janssen in the crowd. Star of the world-popular television series, *The Fugitive*, Janssen portrayed Dr. Richard Kimble, a man unjustly accused of murdering his wife, a crime actually committed by Fred Johnson — a one-armed man. The series aired from 1963 to 1967. Each episode featured Dr. Richard Kimble with his feigned, humble smile and moody, sideways leer engaged in a weekly search to clear his name and escape the clutches of determined, but technologically challenged, Inspector Gerard. In those days before massive worldwide databases shared by law enforcement officials everywhere, the doctor had a much better chance of eluding capture.

Such evasion still is possible in the 1990s, but much more difficult, owing to the fact that virtually all human activity in the modern world creates an economic event of some kind. When a retail clerk swipes your credit card through a reader, not only is the purchase approved according to your credit availability, but the information is recorded and classified for billing purposes and for future research analysis. Similar actions occur when your check shoots around the track of a check verifier.

Credit card and checking account activity have become the two primary sources of information about people. Using these sources to trap tax evaders, the Internal Revenue Service monitors spending activity in order to calculate *imputed* income, and likewise, private and law enforcement investigators routinely use such data to construct personality profiles. Social Security numbers and Driver License numbers, originally based on the economics of pensions and automobile ownership, also aid in collecting data. As we move to so-called *cyberdollars* — money on a debit card — *all* transactions made in the new cash will be recorded.

Usually, if a person tries to disappear it's because of some illegal activity, but occasionally, the law itself needs to hide people, as in the Federal Witness Protection Program. Ironically, this is becoming more difficult because the very tools developed by law enforcement also can be used by the bad guys!

These same databases are used to research new consumer products, stream-line mail delivery, supply better foods and medicines, and improve education, among the dozens of beneficial uses. Without databases, activities that we take for granted — utilities, insurance, airline reservations, food services — and a host of other vital functions would be impossible.

Microsoft Access 97 gives you the power to build your own personal or business databases that are every bit as effective as the gigantic repositories maintained by governments and larger companies. Using Access query capabilities and an extensive set of statistical functions, the tasks of retrieving and analyzing data are simplified substantially.

You may not be an aspiring Charlie Chan or Sherlock Holmes, but when it comes to tracking down answers, Access can be the perfect detective.

Microsoft
Access 97

Querying a Database Using the Select Query Window

Case Perspective

Now that Pilotech Services has created a database with client and technician data, the management and staff of the organization hope to gain the benefits they expected when they set up the database. One of the more important benefits is the capability of easily asking questions concerning the data in the database and rapidly obtaining the answers. Among the questions they want answered are the following:

1. What are the billed and paid amounts for client DE76?

2. Which clients' names begin with Gr?

3. Which clients are located in Grattan?

4. What is the outstanding amount (amount billed minus amount paid) for each client?

5. Which clients of technician 12 have been billed more than $300?

Introduction

A database management system such as Access offers many useful features, among them the capability of answering questions such as those posed by the management of Pilotech Services (Figure 2-1). The answers to these questions, and many more, are found in the database, and Access can find the answers quickly. When you pose a question to Access, or any other database management system, the question is called a query. A **query** is simply a question represented in a way that Access can understand.

Thus, to find the answer to a question, you first create a corresponding query using the techniques illustrated in this project. Once you have created the query, you instruct Access to **run the query**; that is, to perform the steps necessary to obtain the answer. When finished, Access will display the answer to your question in the format shown at the bottom of Figure 2-1.

Project Two — Querying the Pilotech Services Database

You must obtain answers to the questions posed by the management of Pilotech Services. These include the questions shown in Figure 2-1, as well as any other questions that management deems important.

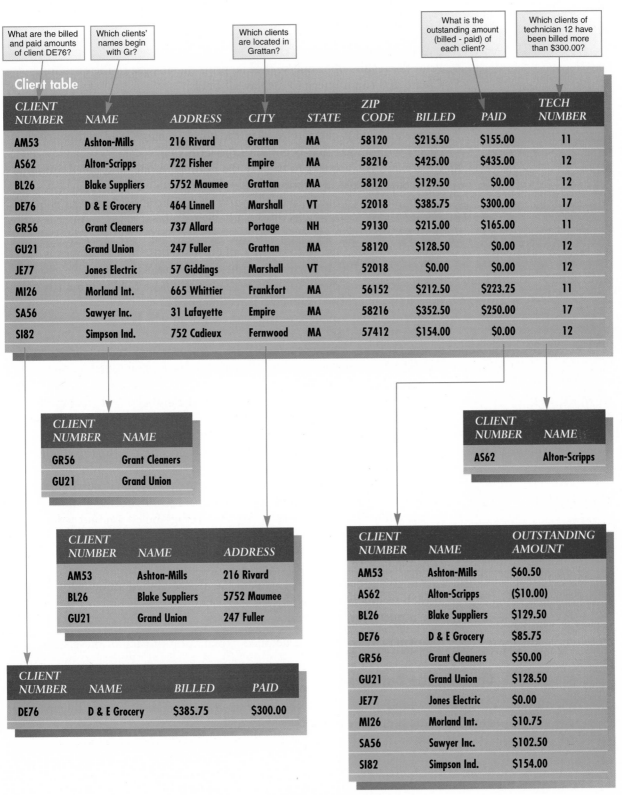

FIGURE 2-1

Overview of Project Steps

The project steps give you an overview of how the Pilotech Services database will be queried. The following tasks will be completed in this project.

1. Start Access and open the Pilotech Services database.
2. Create a new query
3. Create and run a query to display the client number, name, and technician number for all clients.
4. Print the results of a query; that is, print the answer to the question.
5. Create and run a query to display all fields.
6. Create and run a query to display the client number, name, billed amount, and paid amount of client DE76.
7. Create and run a query to display the number, name, and address of those clients with names that begin with the letters Gr.
8. Create and run a query to display the number, name, and billed amounts for clients located in Grattan.
9. Create and run a query to display all clients whose paid amount is $0.00.
10. Create and run a query to display all clients whose billed amount is more than $300.
11. Create and run a query to display all clients whose billed amount is greater than $300 and whose technician is technician 12.
12. Create and run a query to display all clients whose billed amount is more than $300 or whose technician is technician 12.
13. Create and run a query to display the cities in which the clients are located in alphabetical order.
14. Create and run a query to display the number, name, technician number, and billed amount for all clients sorted by descending billed amount within technician number.
15. Create and run a query to display the client number, name, technician number, technician's last name, and technician's first name for all clients.
16. Create and run a query to display the client number, name, technician number, technician's last name, and technician's first name for all clients whose billed amount is more than $300.
17. Create and run a query to display the number, name, and outstanding amount (billed amount minus paid amount) for all clients.
18. Create and run a query to calculate the average billed amount for all clients.
19. Create and run a query to calculate the average billed amount for clients of technician 12.
20. Create and run a query to calculate the average billed amount for clients of each technician.
21. Save a query for future use.

The following pages contain a detailed explanation of each of these steps.

Opening the Database

Before creating queries, first you must open the database. The following steps summarize the procedure to complete this task.

TO OPEN A DATABASE

Step 1: Click the Start button.

Step 2: Click Open Office Document and then click 3½ Floppy (A:) in the Look in list box. Make sure the database called Pilotech Services is selected.

Step 3: Click the Open button. If the Tables tab is not already selected, click the Tables tab.

The database is open and the Pilotech Services : Database window displays.

Creating a New Query

You **create a query** by making entries in a special window called a **Select Query window**. Once the database is open, the first step in creating a query is to select the table for which you are creating a query in the Database window. Next, using the New Object: AutoForm button, you will design the new query. The Select Query window will display. It typically is easier to work with the Select Query window if it is maximized. Thus, as a standard practice, maximize the Select Query window as soon as you have created it.

Perform the following steps to begin the creation of a query.

Steps **To Create a Query**

1 **With the Pilotech Services database open, the Tables tab selected, and the Client table selected, click the New Object: AutoForm button arrow on the toolbar.**

The list of available objects displays (Figure 2-2).

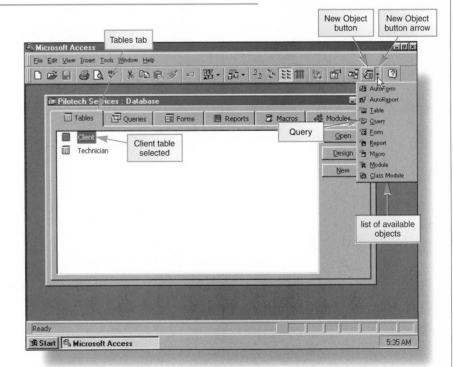

FIGURE 2-2

2 **Click Query.**

The New Query dialog box displays (Figure 2-3).

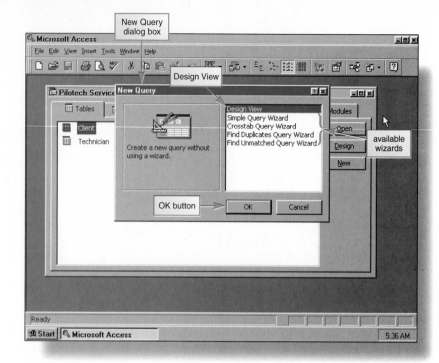

FIGURE 2-3

3 **With Design View selected, click the OK button.**

The Query1 : Select Query window displays (Figure 2-4).

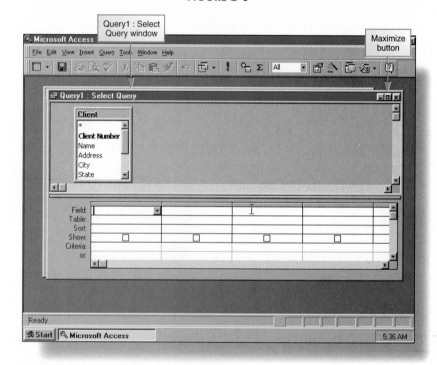

FIGURE 2-4

4 Maximize the Query1 : Select Query window by clicking its Maximize button, and then point to the dividing line that separates the upper and lower panes of the window. The mouse pointer will change shape to a two-headed arrow with a horizontal bar.

*The Query1 : Select Query window is maximized (Figure 2-5). The upper pane of the window contains a field list for the Client table. The lower pane contains the **design grid**, which is the area where you specify fields to be included, sort order, and the criteria the records you are looking for must satisfy.*

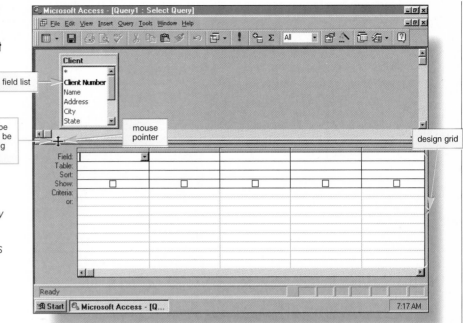

FIGURE 2-5

5 Drag the line down to the approximate position shown in Figure 2-6 and then move the mouse pointer to the lower edge of the field list box so it changes shape to a two-headed arrow as shown in the figure.

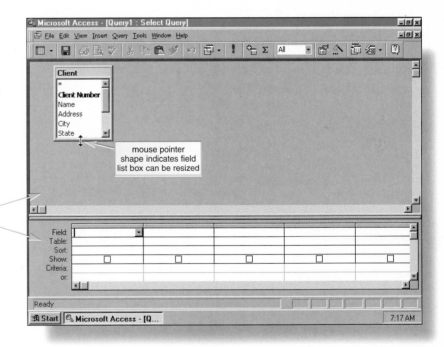

FIGURE 2-6

6 Drag the lower edge of the box down far enough so that all fields in the Client table are visible.

All fields in the Client table display (Figure 2-7).

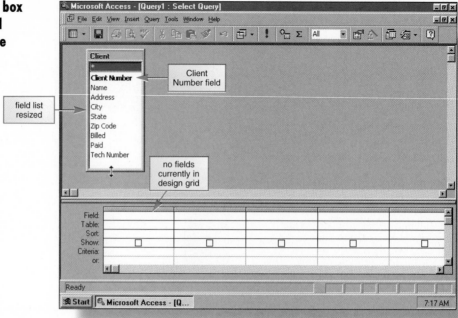

FIGURE 2-7

Using the Select Query Window

Once you have created a new Select Query window, you are ready to create the actual query by making entries in the design grid in the lower pane of the window. You enter the names of the fields you want included in the Field row in the grid. You also can enter criteria, such as, client number must be DE76, in the Criteria row of the grid. When you do so, only the record or records that match the criterion will be included in the answer.

Displaying Selected Fields in a Query

Only the fields that appear in the design grid will be included in the results of the query. Thus, to display only certain fields, place only these fields in the grid, and no others. If you place the wrong field in the grid inadvertently, click Edit on the menu bar and then click Delete to remove it. Alternatively, you could click Clear Grid to clear the entire design grid and then start over.

The following steps create a query to show the client number, name, and technician number for all clients by including only those fields in the design grid.

Steps | To Include Fields in the Design Grid

1 Make sure you have a maximized
Query1 : Select Query window
containing a field list for the
Client table in the upper pane of
the window and an empty
design grid in the lower
pane (see Figure 2-7).

2 Double-click the Client Number
field to include the Client
Number field in the query.

*The Client Number is included as
the first field in the design grid
(Figure 2-8).*

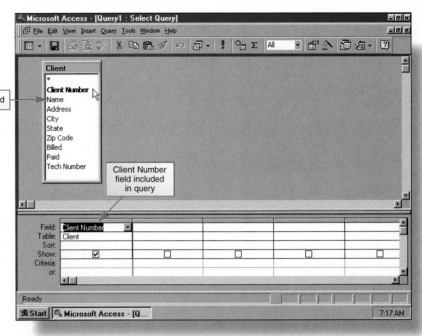

FIGURE 2-8

3 Double-click the Name field to
include it in the query. Include
the Tech Number field using the
same technique.

*The Client Number, Name, and
Tech Number fields are included in
the query (Figure 2-9).*

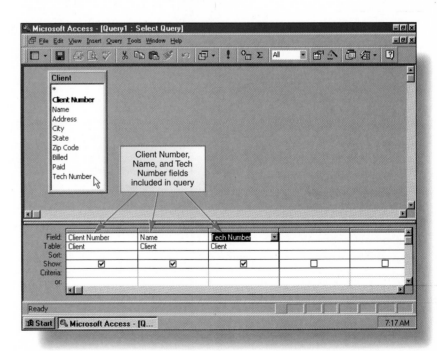

FIGURE 2-9

▶*Other***Ways**

1. Drag field from list box to
   grid

2. Click column in grid, click
   arrow, click field

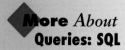

More *About*
Queries: SQL

The most widespread of all the query languages is a language called SQL. In SQL, users type commands like SELECT BILLED FROM CLIENT WHERE CITY = "Marshall" to find the billed amounts of all clients who live in Marshall.

Running a Query

Once you have created the query, you need to **run the query** to produce the results. To do so, click the Run button. Access then will perform the steps necessary to obtain and display the answer. The set of records that makes up the answer will be displayed in Datasheet view. Although it looks like a table that is stored on your disk, it really is not. The records are constructed from data in the existing Client table. If you were to change the data in the Client table and then rerun this same query, the results would reflect the changes.

 To Run the Query

1 **Point to the Run button on the toolbar (Figure 2-10).**

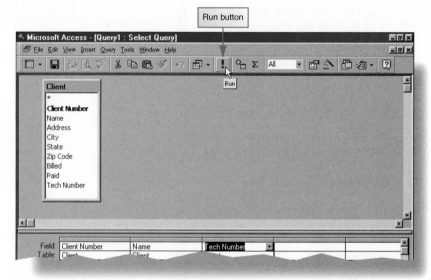

FIGURE 2-10

2 **Click the Run button.**

The query is executed and the results display (Figure 2-11). If you do not move the mouse pointer at all after clicking the Run button, the ScreenTip for the Sort Ascending button will display as shown in the figure. This ScreenTip may obscure a portion of the first record. (Because only three fields exist in this query, the first record is not obscured by a button's ScreenTip.) As a general practice, it is a good idea to move the mouse pointer as soon as you have run a query, so it no longer points to the toolbar.

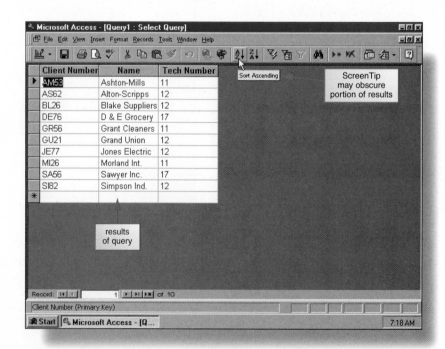

FIGURE 2-11

3 **Move the mouse pointer to a position that is outside of the data and is not on the toolbar.**

The data displays without obstruction (Figure 2-12). Notice that an extra blank row, marking the end of the table, displays at the end of the results.

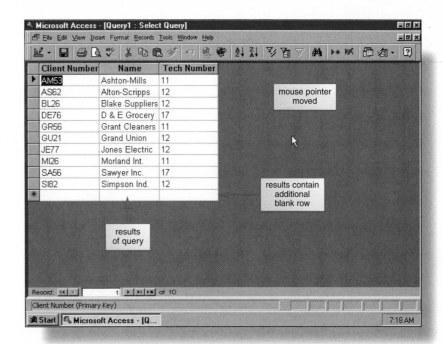

FIGURE 2-12

OtherWays

1. On Query menu click Run

In all future examples, after running a query, move the mouse pointer so the table displays without obstruction.

Printing the Results of a Query

To print the results of a query, use the same techniques you learned in Project 1 to print the data in the table. Complete the following steps to print the query results that currently display on the screen.

TO PRINT THE RESULTS OF A QUERY

Step 1: Ready the printer and then point to the Print button on the toolbar (Figure 2-13).
Step 2: Click the Print button.

The results print.

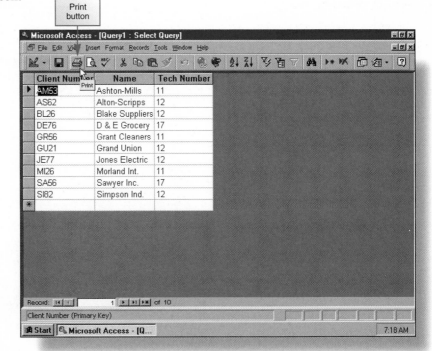

FIGURE 2-13

If the results of a query require landscape orientation, switch to landscape orientation before you click the Print button as indicated in Project 1 on page A 1.29.

Returning to the Select Query Window

You can examine the results of a query on your screen to see the answer to your question. You can scroll through the records, if necessary, just as you scroll through the records of any other table. You also can print a copy of the table. In any case, once you are finished working with the results, you can return to the Select Query window to ask another question. To do so, click the View button arrow on the toolbar as shown in the following steps.

Steps **To Return to the Select Query Window**

1 **Point to the View button arrow on the toolbar (Figure 2-14).**

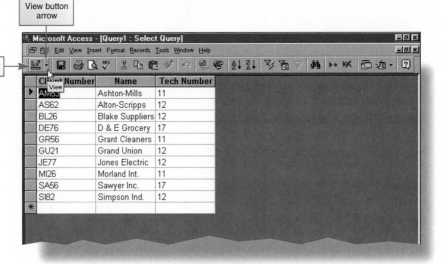

FIGURE 2-14

2 **Click the View button arrow. Point to Design View.**

The Query View list displays (Figure 2-15).

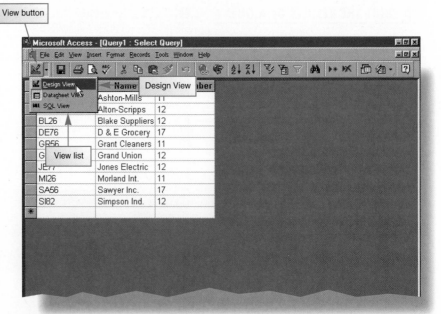

FIGURE 2-15

3 **Click Design View.**

The Query1 : Select Query window displays (Figure 2-16).

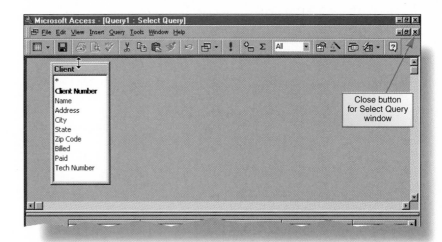

FIGURE 2-16

Closing a Query

To **close a query**, close the Select Query window. When you do so, Access displays the Microsoft dialog box asking if you want to save your query for future use. If you think you will need to create the same exact query often, you should save the query. For now, you will not save any queries. You will see how to save them later in the project. The following steps close a query without saving it.

To Close the Query

1 **Click the Close button for the Query1 : Select Query window (Figure 2-16).**

The Microsoft Access dialog box displays (Figure 2-17). Clicking the Yes button saves the query and clicking the No button closes the query without saving.

2 **Click the No button in the Microsoft Access dialog box.**

The Query1 : Select Query window is removed from the desktop.

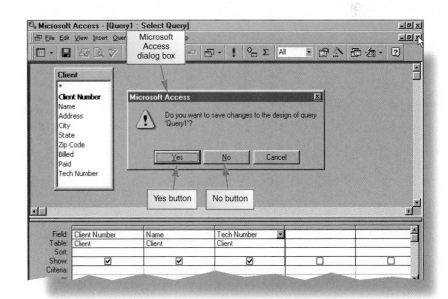

FIGURE 2-17

Including All Fields in a Query

If you want to **include all fields** in a query, you could select each field individually. A more simplified way exists to include fields, however. By selecting the **asterisk (*)** that appears in the field list, you are indicating that all fields are to be included. Complete the following steps to use the asterisk to include all fields.

Steps   To Include All Fields in a Query

1 **Be sure you have a maximized Query1 : Select Query window containing a field list for the Client table in the upper pane of the window and an empty design grid in the lower pane. (See Steps 1 through 6 on pages A 2.7 through A 2.10 to create the query and resize the window.) Point to the asterisk at the top of the field list box.**

A maximized Query1 : Select Query window displays (Figure 2-18). The two panes of the window have been resized.

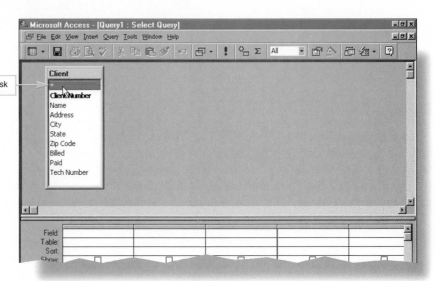

FIGURE 2-18

2 **Double-click the asterisk in the field list box and then point to the Run button on the toolbar.**

The table name, Client, followed by an asterisk is added to the design grid (Figure 2-19), indicating all fields are included.

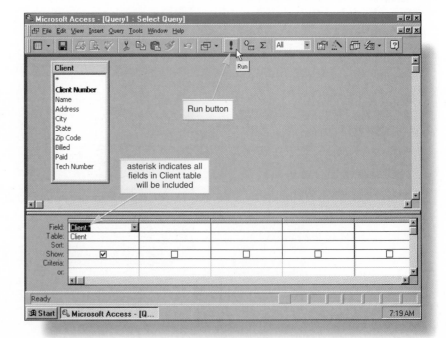

FIGURE 2-19

3 **Click the Run button.**

The results display and all fields in the Client table are included (Figure 2-20).

4 **Click the View button arrow on the toolbar. Click Design View to return to the Query1 : Select Query window.**

The datasheet is replaced by the Query1 : Select Query window.

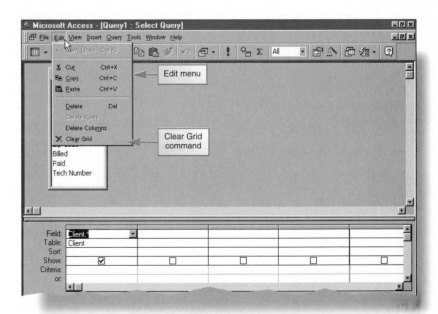

all fields included

View button

Client Number	Name	Address	City	State	Zip Code	B
AM53	Ashton-Mills	216 Rivard	Grattan	MA	58120	
AS62	Alton-Scripps	722 Fisher	Empire	MA	58216	
BL26	Blake Suppliers	5752 Maumee	Grattan	MA	58120	
DE76	D & E Grocery	464 Linnell	Marshall	VT	52018	
GR56	Grant Cleaners	737 Allard	Portage	NH	59130	
GU21	Grand Union	247 Fuller	Grattan	MA	58120	
JE77	Jones Electric	57 Giddings	Marshall	VT	52018	
MI26	Morland Int.	665 Whittier	Frankfort	MA	56152	
SA56	Sawyer Inc.	31 Lafayette	Empire	MA	58216	
SI82	Simpson Ind.	752 Cadieux	Fernwood	MA	57412	

FIGURE 2-20

OtherWays

1. Drag asterisk from list box to grid
2. Click column in grid, click arrow, click asterisk

Clearing the Design Grid

If you make mistakes as you are creating a query, you can fix each one individually. Alternatively, you simply may want to **clear the query**; that is, clear out the entries in the design grid and start over. One way to clear out the entries is to close the Select Query window and then start a new query just as you did earlier. A simpler approach, however, is to click Clear Grid on the Edit menu.

Steps To Clear a Query

1 **Click Edit on the menu bar.**

The Edit menu displays (Figure 2-21).

2 **Click Clear Grid.**

Access clears the design grid so you can enter your next query.

Microsoft Access - [Query1 : Select Query]

File Edit View Insert Query Tools Window Help

	Cut	Ctrl+X
	Copy	Ctrl+C
	Paste	Ctrl+V
	Delete	Del
	Delete Rows	
	Delete Columns	
	Clear Grid	

Edit menu

Clear Grid command

Billed
Paid
Tech Number

Field: Client.*
Table: Client
Sort:
Show: ☑
Criteria:
or:

FIGURE 2-21

Entering Criteria

When you use queries, usually you are looking for those records that satisfy some criterion. You might want the name, billed, and paid amounts of the client whose number is DE76, for example, or of those clients whose names start with the letters, Gr. To **enter criteria**, enter them on the Criteria row in the design grid below the field name to which the criterion applies. For example, to indicate that the client number must be DE76, you would type DE76 in the Criteria row below the Client Number field. You first must add the Client Number field to the design grid before you can enter the criterion.

The next examples illustrate the types of criteria that are available.

More *About*
Using Text Data in Criteria

Some database systems require that text data must be enclosed in quotation marks. For example, to find customers in Michigan, "MI" would be entered as the criterion for the State field. In Access this is not necessary, because Access will insert the quotation marks automatically.

Using Text Data in Criteria

To use **text data** (data in a field whose type is text) in criteria, simply type the text in the Criteria row below the corresponding field name. The following steps query the Client table and display the client number, name, billed amount, and paid amount of client DE76.

Steps | To Use Text Data in a Criterion

1 One by one, double-click the Client Number, Name, Billed, and Paid fields to add them to the query. Point to the Criteria entry for the first field in the design grid.

The Client Number, Name, Billed, and Paid fields are added to the design grid (Figure 2-22). The mouse pointer on the Criteria entry for the first field (Client Number) has changed shape to an I-beam.

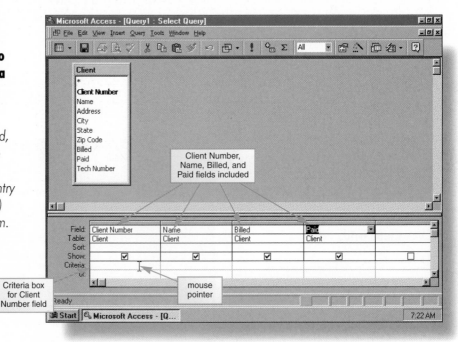

FIGURE 2-22

2 Click the criteria entry, type DE76 **as the criteria for the Client Number field.**

The criteria is entered (Figure 2-23).

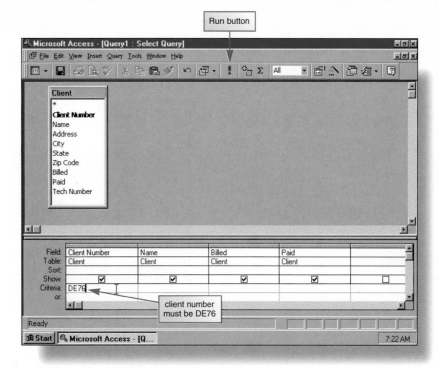

FIGURE 2-23

3 Run the query by clicking the Run **button.**

The results display (Figure 2-24). Only client DE76 is included. (The extra blank row contains $0.00 in the Billed and Paid fields. Unlike text fields, which are left blank, number and currency fields in the extra row contain 0. Because the Billed and Paid fields are currency fields, the values display as $0.00.)

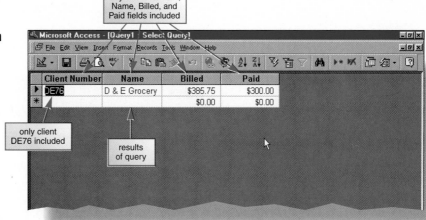

FIGURE 2-24

Using Wildcards

Two special wildcards are available in Microsoft Access. **Wildcards** are symbols that represent any character or combination of characters. The first of the two wildcards, the **asterisk (*)**, represents any collection of characters. Thus Gr* represents the letters, Gr, followed by any collection of characters. The other wildcard symbol is the **question mark (?)**, which represents any individual character. Thus t?m represents the letter, T, followed by any single character followed by the letter, m, such as Tim or Tom.

The steps on the next page use a wildcard to find the number, name, and address of those clients whose names begin with Gr. Because you do not know how many characters will follow the Gr, the asterisk is appropriate.

Steps To Use a Wildcard

1 Click the View button on the toolbar to return to the Query1 : Select Query window. Click the Criteria row under the Client Number field and then use the DELETE or BACKSPACE key to delete the current entry (DE76). Click the Criteria row under the Name field. Type LIKE Gr* as the entry.

The criteria is entered (Figure 2-25).

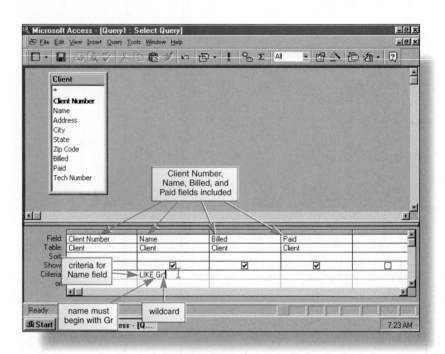

FIGURE 2-25

2 Click the Run button on the toolbar.

The results display (Figure 2-26). Only the clients whose names start with Gr are included.

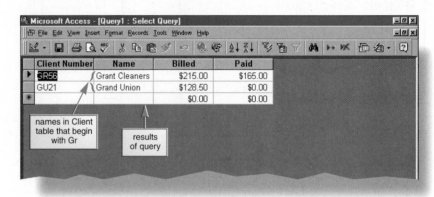

FIGURE 2-26

Criteria for a Field Not in the Result

In some cases, you may have criteria for a particular field that should not appear in the results of the query. For example, you may wish to see the client number, name, address, and billed amounts for all clients located in Grattan. The criteria involves the City field, which is not one of the fields to be included in the results.

To enter a criterion for the City field, it must be included in the design grid. Normally, this also would mean it would appear in the results. To prevent this from happening, remove the check mark from its **Show check box** in the Show row of the grid. The following steps illustrate the process by displaying the client number, name, and billed amounts for clients located in Grattan.

Steps To Use Criteria for a Field Not Included in the Results

1 **Click the View button on the toolbar to return to the Query1 : Select Query window. On the Edit menu, click Clear Grid.**

Access clears the design grid so you can enter the next query.

2 **Include the Client Number, Name, Address, Billed, and City fields in the query. Type** Grattan **as the criteria for the City field and then point to the City field's Show check box.**

The fields are included in the grid, and the criteria for the City field is entered (Figure 2-27). The space between the left scroll arrow and the scroll box indicates that fields are off the leftmost edge of the grid. In this case, the first field, Client Number, currently does not display. Clicking the left scroll arrow would move the scroll box to the left, shift the fields currently in the grid to the right, and cause the Client Number field to display.

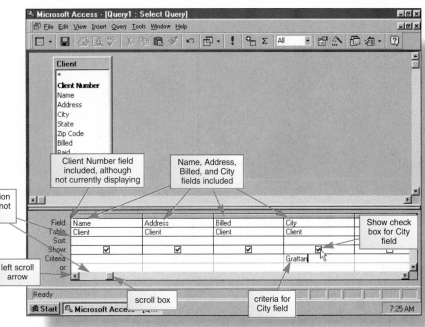

FIGURE 2-27

3 **Click the Show check box to remove the check mark.**

The check mark is removed from the Show check box for the City field (Figure 2-28), indicating it will not show in the result. Access has added quotation marks before and after Grattan automatically.

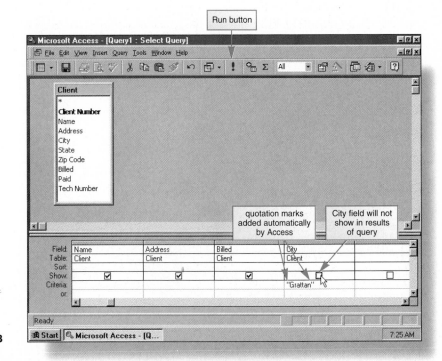

FIGURE 2-28

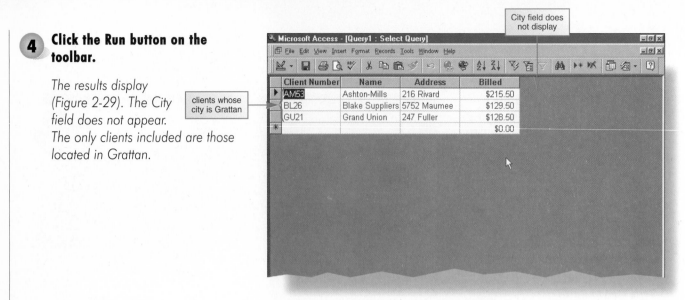

4 **Click the Run button on the toolbar.**

The results display (Figure 2-29). The City field does not appear. The only clients included are those located in Grattan.

clients whose city is Grattan

City field does not display

FIGURE 2-29

Using Numeric Data in Criteria

To enter a number in a criterion, type the number without any dollar signs or commas. Complete the following steps to display all clients whose paid amount is $0.00. To do so, you will need to type a zero as the criterion for the Paid field.

 Steps **To Use a Number in a Criterion**

1 **Click the View button on the toolbar to return to the Query1 : Select Query window. On the Edit menu, click Clear Grid. Click the left scroll arrow so no space exists between the scroll arrow and the scroll box.**

Access clears the design grid so you can enter the next query.

2 **Include the Client Number, Name, Billed, and Paid fields in the query. Type 0 as the criterion for the Paid field. You need not enter a dollar sign or decimal point in the criterion.**

The fields are selected and the criterion is entered (Figure 2-30).

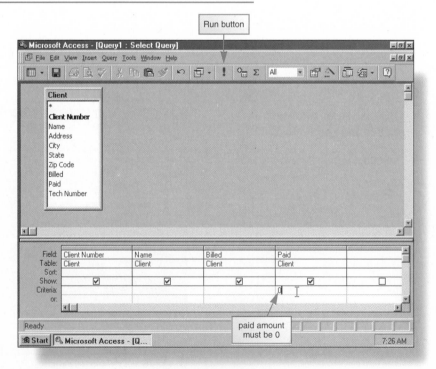

Run button

paid amount must be 0

FIGURE 2-30

3 **Click the Run button on the toolbar.**

The results display (Figure 2-31). Only those clients that have a paid amount of $0.00 are included.

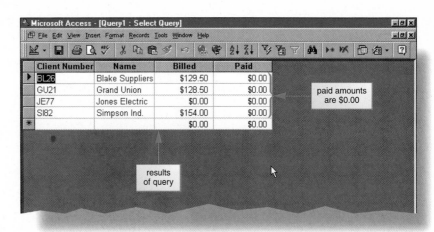

FIGURE 2-31

Using Comparison Operators

Unless you specify otherwise, Access assumes that the criteria you enter involve equality (exact matches). In the last query, for example, you were requesting those clients whose paid amount is equal to 0. If you want something other than an exact match, you must enter the appropriate **comparison operator**. The comparison operators are > (greater than), < (less than), >= (greater than or equal to), <= (less than or equal to), and NOT (not equal to).

Perform the following steps to use the > operator to find all clients whose billed amount is greater than $300.

 Steps **To Use a Comparison Operator in a Criterion**

1 **Click the View button on the toolbar to return to the Query1 : Select Query window. On the Edit menu, click Clear Grid.**

Access clears the design grid so you can enter the next query.

2 **Include the Client Number, Name, Billed, and Paid fields in the query. Type** >300 **as the criterion for the Billed field.**

The fields are selected and the criterion is entered (Figure 2-32).

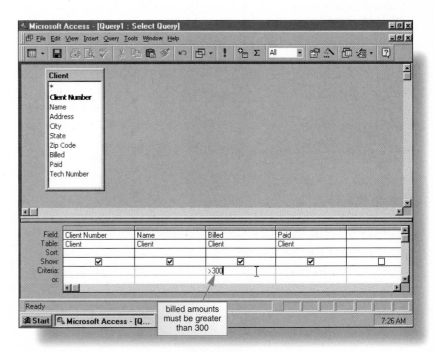

FIGURE 2-32

3 **Click the Run button on the toolbar.**

The results display (Figure 2-33). Only those clients that have a billed amount more than $300 are included.

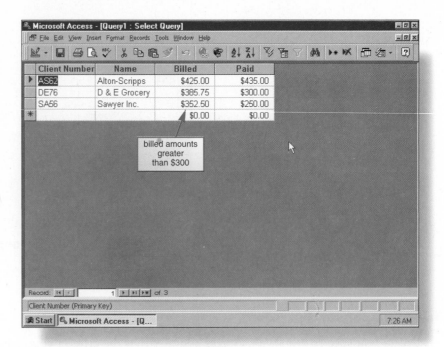

FIGURE 2-33

Using Compound Criteria

Often you will have more than one criterion that the data for which you are searching must satisfy. This type of criterion is called a **compound criterion**. Two types of compound criteria exist.

In **AND criterion**, each individual criterion must be true in order for the compound criterion to be true. For example, an AND criterion would allow you to find those clients that have a billed amount greater than $300 and whose technician is technician 12.

Conversely, **OR criterion** is true provided either individual criterion is true. An OR criterion would allow you to find those clients that have a billed amount greater than $300 or whose technician is technician 12. In this case, any client whose billed amount is greater than $300 would be included in the answer whether or not the client's technician is technician 12. Likewise, any client whose technician is technician 12 would be included whether or not the client had a billed amount greater than $300.

To combine criteria with AND, place the criteria on the same line. Perform the following steps to use an AND criterion to find those clients whose billed amount is greater than $300 and whose technician is technician 12.

Steps **To Use a Compound Criterion Involving AND**

1 **Click the View button on the toolbar to return to the Query1 : Select Query window. On the Edit menu, click Clear Grid.**

Access clears the design grid so you can enter the next query.

2 **Include the Client Number, Name, Billed, Paid, and Tech Number fields in the query.**

3 **Click the Criteria entry for the Billed field, and then type** >300 **as a criterion for the Billed field. Click the Criteria entry for the Tech Number field and then type** 12 **as the criterion for the Tech Number field.**

The fields shift to the left (Figure 2-34). Criteria have been entered for the Billed and Tech Number fields.

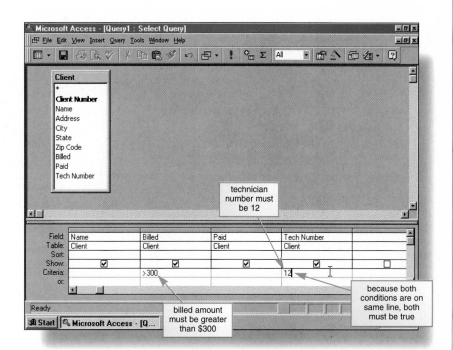

FIGURE 2-34

4 **Click the Run button on the toolbar.**

The results display (Figure 2-35). Only the single client whose billed amount is greater than $300.00 and whose technician number is 12 is included.

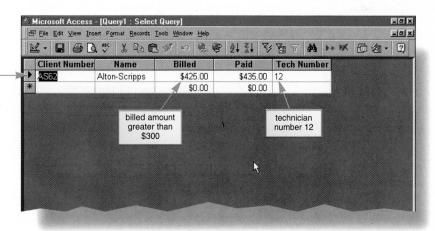

FIGURE 2-35

To combine criteria with OR, the criteria must go on separate lines in the Criteria area of the grid. The steps on the next page use an OR criterion to find those clients whose billed amount is more than $300.00 or whose technician is technician 12 (or both).

Steps To Use a Compound Criterion Involving OR

1 Click the View button on the toolbar to return to the Query1 : Select Query window.

2 Click the Criteria entry for the Tech Number field. Use the BACKSPACE key to delete the entry ("12"). Click the or entry (below Criteria) for the Tech Number field and then type 12 as the entry.

The criteria are entered for the Billed and Tech Number fields on different lines (Figure 2-36).

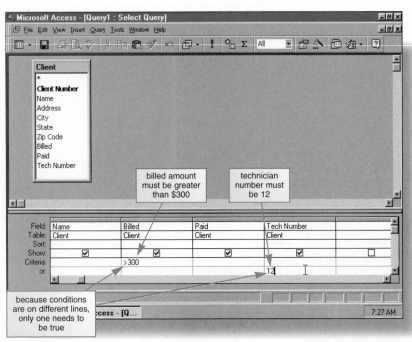

FIGURE 2-36

3 Click the Run button on the toolbar.

The results display (Figure 2-37). Only those clients whose billed amount is more than $300.00 or whose technician number is 12 are included.

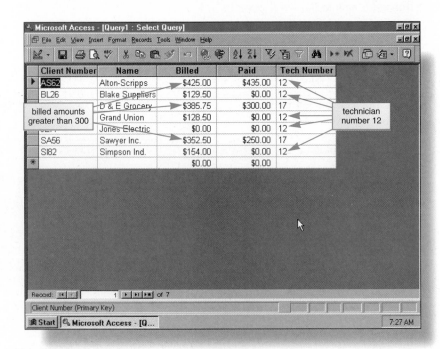

FIGURE 2-37

Sorting Data in a Query

In some queries, the order in which the records are displayed really does not matter. All you need be concerned about are the records that appear in the results. It does not matter which one is first or which one is last.

In other queries, however, the order can be very important. You may want to see the cities in which clients are located and would like them arranged alphabetically. Perhaps you want to see the clients listed by technician number. Further, within all the clients of any given technician, you would like them to be listed by billed amount.

To order the records in the answer to a query in a particular way, you **sort** the records. The field or fields on which the records are sorted is called the **sort key**. If you are sorting on more than one field (such as sorting by billed amount within technician number), the more important field (Tech Number) is called the **major key** (also called the **primary sort key**) and the less important field (Billed) is called the **minor key** (also called the **secondary sort key**).

To sort in Microsoft Access, specify the sort order in the Sort line of the design grid below the field that is the sort key. If you specify more than one sort key, the sort key on the left will be the major sort key and the one on the right will be the minor key.

The following steps sort the cities in the Client table.

Steps To Sort Data in a Query

More *About*
Sorting Data in a Query

When sorting data in a query, the records in the underlying tables (the tables on which the query is based) are not actually rearranged. Instead, the DBMS will determine the most efficient method of simply displaying the records in the requested order. The records in the underlying tables remain in their original order.

1 Click the View button on the toolbar to return to the Query1 : Select Query window. On the Edit menu, click Clear Grid. Click the left scroll arrow so no space exists between the scroll arrow and the scroll box.

2 Include the City field in the design grid. Click the Sort row below the City field, and then click the down arrow that appears.

The City field is included (Figure 2-38). A list of available sort orders displays.

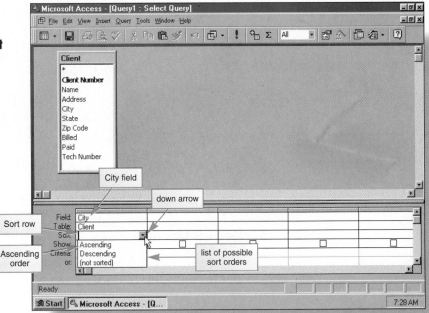

FIGURE 2-38

3   Click Ascending.

Ascending is selected as the order (Figure 2-39).

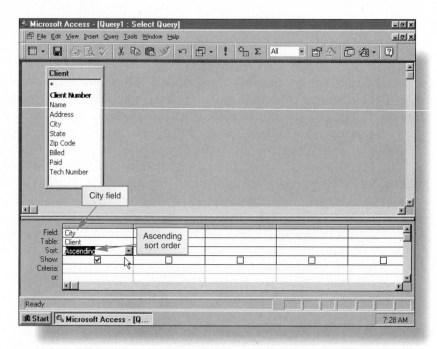

FIGURE 2-39

4   Run the query by clicking the Run button on the toolbar.

The results contain the cities from the Client table (Figure 2-40). The cities display in alphabetical order. Duplicates, that is, identical rows, are included.

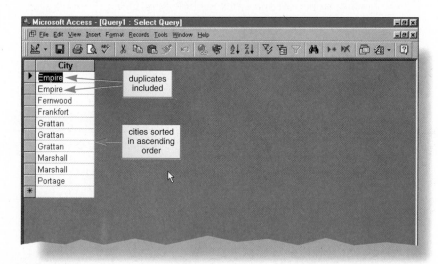

FIGURE 2-40

Sorting on Multiple Keys

The next example lists the number, name, technician number, and billed amount for all clients. The data is to be sorted by descending billed amount (high to low) within technician number, which means that the Tech Number field is the major key and the Billed field is the minor key. It also means that the Billed field should be sorted in descending order.

The following steps accomplish this sorting by specifying the Tech Number and Billed fields as sort keys and by selecting Descending as the sort order for the Billed field.

Steps **To Sort on Multiple Keys**

1 Click the View button on the toolbar to return to the Query1 : Select Query window. On the Edit menu, click Clear Grid.

2 Include the Client Number, Name, Tech Number, and Billed fields in the query in this order. Select Ascending as the sort order for the Tech Number field and Descending as the sort order for the Billed field (Figure 2-41).

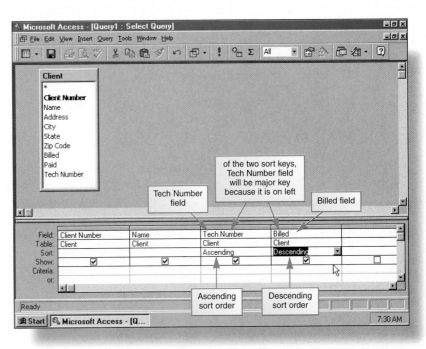

FIGURE 2-41

3 Run the query.

The results display (Figure 2-42). The clients are sorted by technician number. Within the collection of clients having the same technician, the clients are sorted by descending billed amount.

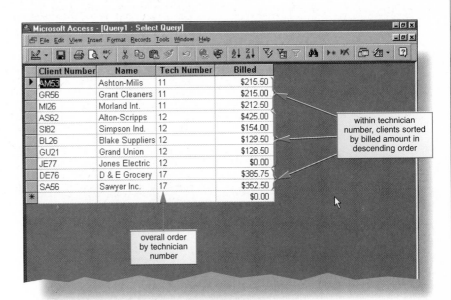

FIGURE 2-42

It is important to remember that the major sort key must appear to the left of the minor sort key in the design grid. If you attempted to sort by billed amount within technician number, but placed the Billed field to the left of the Tech Number field, your results would be incorrect.

Omitting Duplicates

As you saw earlier, when you sort data, duplicates are included. In Figure 2-40 on page A 2.28, for example, Empire appeared twice, Grattan appeared three times, and Marshall appeared twice. If you do not want duplicates included, use the Properties command and specify Unique Values Only. Perform the following steps to produce a sorted list of the cities in the Client table in which each city is listed only once.

Steps To Omit Duplicates

1 **Click the View button on the toolbar to return to the Query1 : Select Query window. On the Edit menu, click Clear Grid.**

2 **Include the City field, click Ascending as the sort order, and right-click the second field in the design grid (the empty field following City).**

The shortcut menu displays (Figure 2-43).

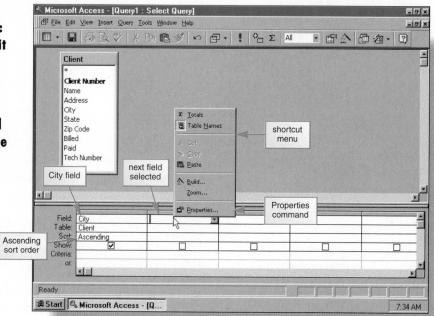

FIGURE 2-43

3 **Click Properties on the shortcut menu.**

The Query Properties sheet displays (Figure 2-44).

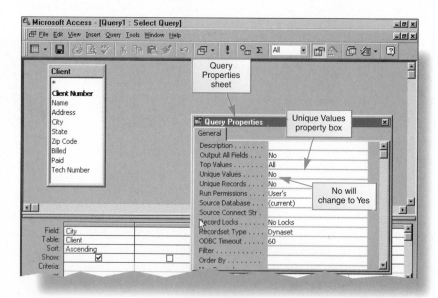

FIGURE 2-44

4 Click the Unique Values property box, and then click the down arrow that displays to produce a list of available choices for Unique Values (Figure 2-45).

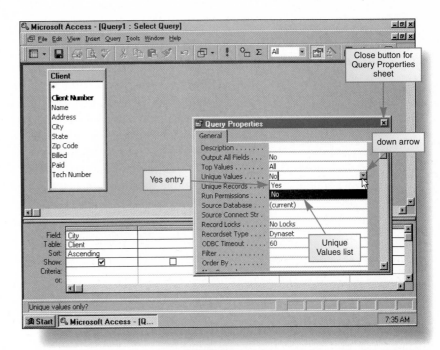

FIGURE 2-45

5 Click Yes, and then close the Query Properties sheet by clicking its Close button. Run the query.

The results display (Figure 2-46). The cities are sorted alphabetically. Each city is included only once.

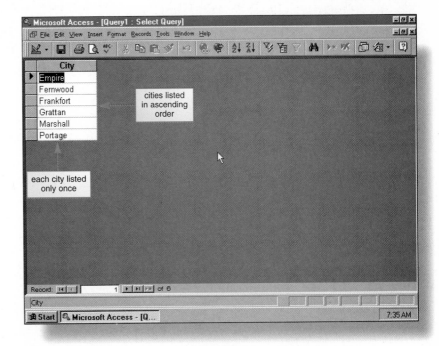

FIGURE 2-46

OtherWays

1. Click Properties button on toolbar
2. On View menu click Properties

Joining Tables

Pilotech Services needs to list the number and name of each client along with the number and name of the client's technician. The client's name is in the Client table, whereas the technician's name is in the Technician table. Thus, this query cannot be satisfied using a single table. You need to **join** the tables; that is, to find records in the two tables that have identical values in matching fields (Figure 2-47). In this example, you need to find records in the Client table and the Technician table that have the same value in the Tech Number fields.

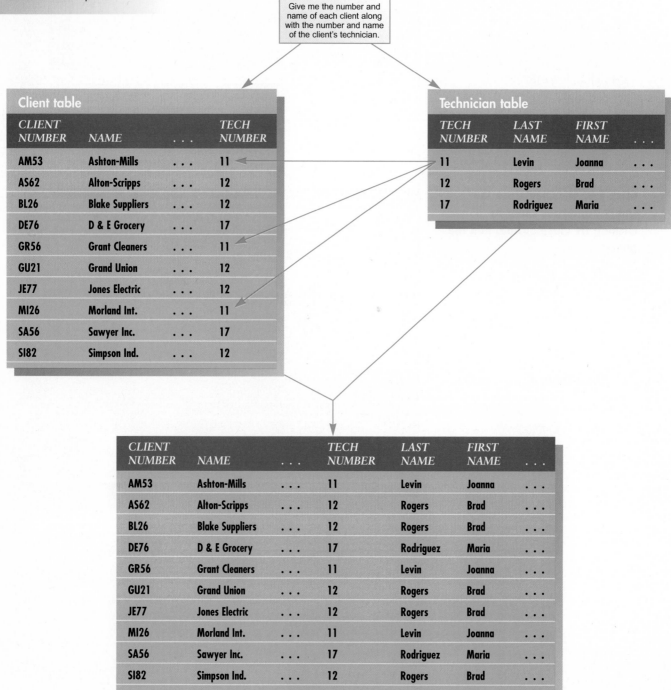

FIGURE 2-47

To join tables in Access, first you bring field lists for both tables to the upper pane of the Select Query window. Access will draw a line, called a **join line**, between matching fields in the two tables indicating that the tables are related. You then can select fields from either table. Access will join the tables automatically.

The first step is to add an additional table to the query as illustrated in the following steps, which add the Technician table.

Steps To Join Tables

1 Click the View button on the toolbar to return to the Query1 : Select Query window. On the Edit menu, click Clear Grid.

2 Right-click any open area in the upper pane of the Query1 : Select Query window.

The shortcut menu displays (Figure 2-48).

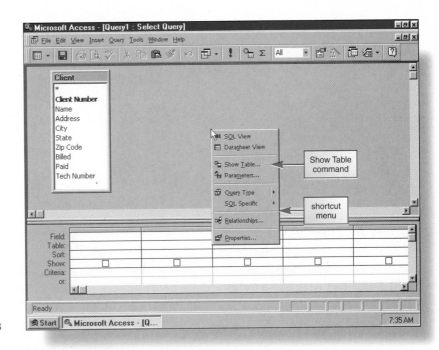

FIGURE 2-48

3 Click Show Table on the shortcut menu.

The Show Table dialog box displays (Figure 2-49).

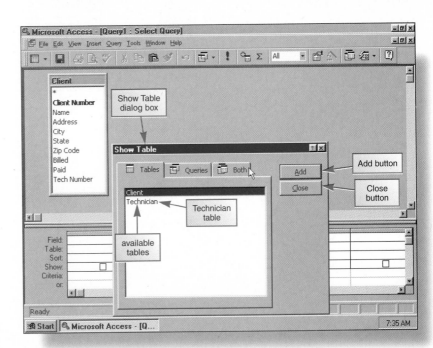

FIGURE 2-49

4 **Click Technician to select the Technician table, and then click the Add button. Close the Show Table dialog box by clicking the Close button. Expand the size of the field list so all the fields in the Technician table display.**

A field list for the Technician table displays (Figure 2-50). It has been enlarged so all the technician fields are visible. A join line appears joining the Tech Number fields in the two field lists. The join line indicates how the tables are related; that is, linked through the matching fields. (If you fail to give the matching fields the same name, Access will not insert the line. You can insert it manually, however, by clicking one of the two matching fields and dragging the mouse pointer to the other matching field.)

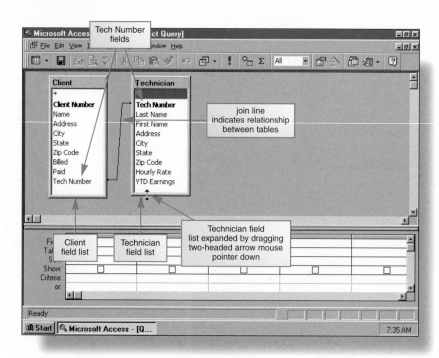

FIGURE 2-50

5 **Include the Client Number, Name, and Tech Number fields from the Client table and the Last Name and First Name fields from the Technician table.**

The fields from both tables are selected (Figure 2-51).

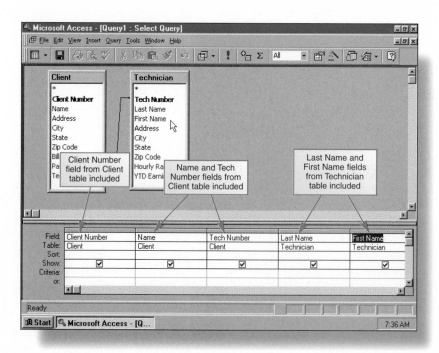

FIGURE 2-51

6 **Run the query.**

The results display (Figure 2-52). They contain data from the Client table as well as data from the Technician table.

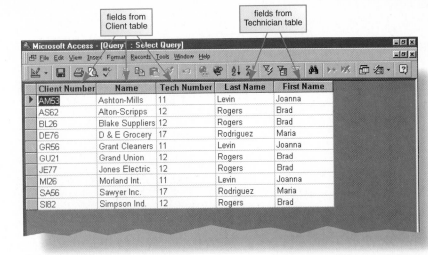

FIGURE 2-52

Other Ways

1. Click Show Table button on toolbar
2. On Query menu click Show Table

Restricting Records in a Join

Sometimes you will want to join tables, but you will not want to include all possible records. In such cases, you will relate the tables and include fields just as you did before. You also will include criteria. For example, to include the same fields as in the previous query, but only those clients whose billed amount is more than $300, you will make the same entries as before and then also type >300 as a criterion for the Billed field.

The following steps modify the query from the previous example to restrict the records that will be included in the join.

Steps **To Restrict the Records in a Join**

1 **Click the View button on the toolbar to return to the Query1 : Select Query window. Add the Billed field to the query. If necessary, scroll the fields to the left so the Billed field displays in the design grid. Type >300 as the criterion for the Billed field and then click the Show check box for the Billed field to remove the check mark.**

The Billed field displays in the design grid (Figure 2-53). A criterion is entered for the Billed field and the Show check box is empty, indicating that the field will not display in the results of the query.

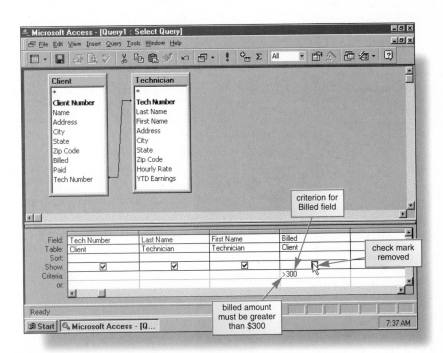

FIGURE 2-53

2 **Run the query.**

The results display (Figure 2-54). Only those clients with a billed amount greater than $300 appear in the result. The Billed field does not display.

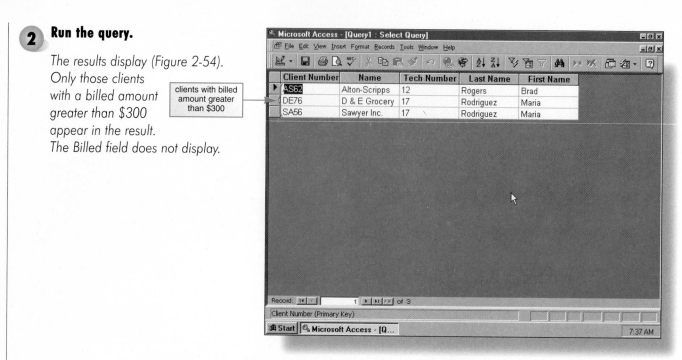

clients with billed amount greater than $300

FIGURE 2-54

Using Computed Fields in a Query

It is important to Pilotech Services to know the outstanding amount for each client; that is, the amount billed to the client minus the amount the client already has paid. This poses a problem because the Client table does not include a field for outstanding amount. You can compute it, however, because the outstanding amount is equal to the billed amount minus the paid amount. Such a field is called a **computed field**.

To include computed fields in queries, you enter a name for the computed field, a colon, and then the expression in one of the columns in the Field row. For the outstanding amount, for example, you will type Outstanding Amount:[Billed]-[Paid]. You can type this directly into the Field row. You will not be able to see the entire entry, however, because the Field row is not large enough. The preferred way is to select the column in the Field row, right-click to display the shortcut menu, and then click Zoom. The Zoom dialog box displays where you can type the expression.

You are not restricted to subtraction in computations. You can use addition (+), multiplication (*), or division (/). In addition, you can include parentheses in your computations to indicate which computations should be done first.

Perform the following steps to use a computed field to display the number, name, and outstanding amount of all clients.

Steps **To Use a Computed Field in a Query**

1 Click the View button on the toolbar to return to the Query1 : Select Query window. Right-click any field in the Technician table field list.

The shortcut menu displays (Figure 2-55).

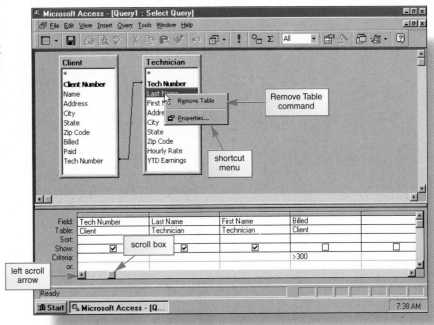

FIGURE 2-55

2 Click Remove Table to remove the Technician table from the Query1 : Select Query window. On the Edit menu, click Clear Grid. Click the left scroll arrow so no space exists between the scroll arrow and the scroll box.

3 Include the Client Number and Name fields. Right-click the Field row in the third column in the design grid and then click Zoom on the shortcut menu. Type `Outstanding Amount:[Billed]-[Paid]` in the Zoom dialog box that displays.

The Zoom dialog box displays (Figure 2-56). The expression you typed displays within the dialog box.

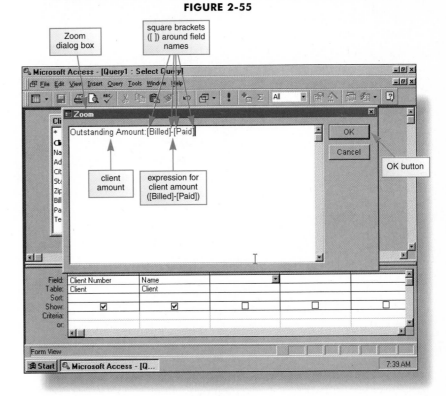

FIGURE 2-56

4 **Click the OK button.**

The Zoom dialog box no longer displays (Figure 2-57). A portion of the expression you entered displays in the third field within the design grid.

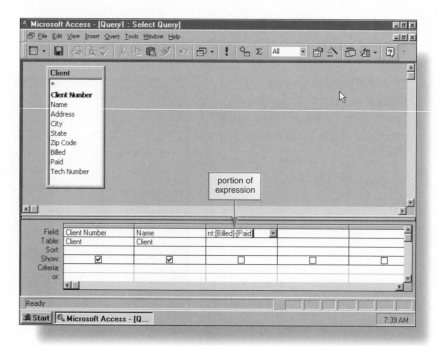

FIGURE 2-57

5 **Run the query.**

The results display (Figure 2-58). Microsoft Access has calculated and displayed the client amounts. The parentheses around $10.00 and $10.75 indicate they are negative numbers; that is, the clients possibly paid more than the amount that was billed.

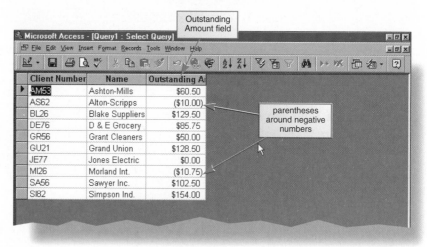

FIGURE 2-58

OtherWays

1. Press SHIFT+F2

Calculating Statistics

Microsoft Access supports the built-in **statistics**: COUNT, SUM, AVG (average), MAX (largest value), MIN (smallest value), STDEV (standard deviation), VAR (variance), FIRST, and LAST. To use any of these in a query, you include it in the Total row in the design grid. The Total row routinely does not appear in the grid. To include it, right-click the grid, and then click Totals on the shortcut menu.

The following example illustrates how you use these functions by calculating the average billed amount for all clients.

Steps To Calculate Statistics

1 Click the View button on the toolbar to return to the Query1 : Select Query window. On the Edit menu, click Clear Grid.

2 Right-click the grid.

The shortcut menu displays (Figure 2-59).

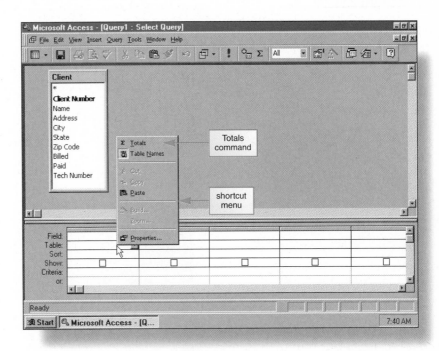

FIGURE 2-59

3 Click Totals on the shortcut menu and then include the Billed field. Point to the Total row in the Billed column.

The Total row now is included in the design grid (Figure 2-60). The Billed field is included, and the entry in the Total row is Group By. The mouse pointer, which has changed shape to an I-beam, is positioned on the Total row under the Billed field.

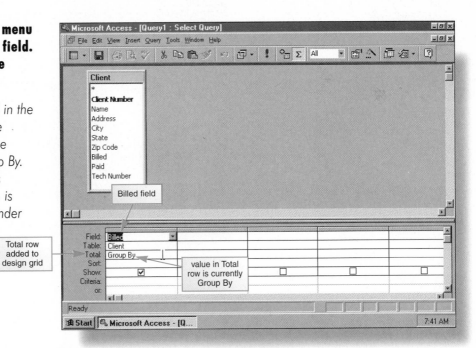

FIGURE 2-60

4 **Click the Total row in the Billed column, and then click the arrow that displays.**

The list of available selections displays (Figure 2-61).

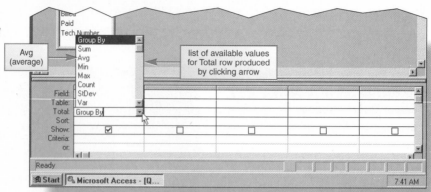

FIGURE 2-61

5 **Click Avg.**

Avg is selected (Figure 2-62).

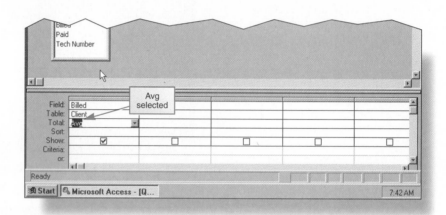

FIGURE 2-62

6 **Run the query.**

The result displays (Figure 2-63), showing the average billed amount for all clients.

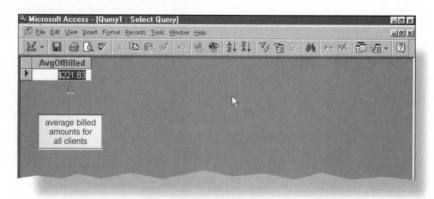

FIGURE 2-63

Other Ways

1. Click Totals button on toolbar
2. On View menu click Totals

Using Criteria in Calculating Statistics

Sometimes calculating statistics for all the records in the table is appropriate. In other cases, however, you will need to calculate the statistics for only those records that satisfy certain criteria. To enter a criterion in a field, first you select Where as the entry in the Total row for the field and then enter the criterion in the Criteria row. The following steps use this technique to calculate the average billed amount for clients of technician 12.

Steps: To Use Criteria in Calculating Statistics

1 Click the View button on the toolbar to return to the Query1 : Select Query window.

2 Include the Tech Number field in the design grid. Next, produce the list of available options for the Total entry just as you did when you selected Avg for the Billed field. Use the vertical scroll bar to move through the options until the word, Where, displays.

The list of available selections displays (Figure 2-64). The Group By entry in the Tech Number field may not be highlighted on your screen depending where you clicked in the Total row.

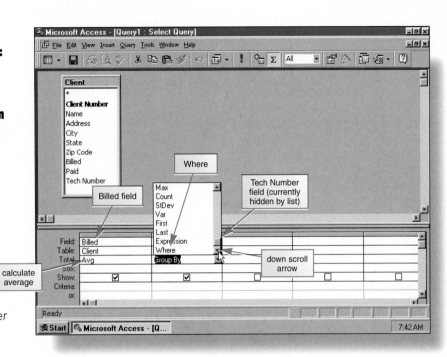

FIGURE 2-64

3 Click Where. Then, type 12 as criterion for the Tech Number field.

Where is selected as the entry in the Total row for the Tech Number field (Figure 2-65) and 12 is entered as the Criteria.

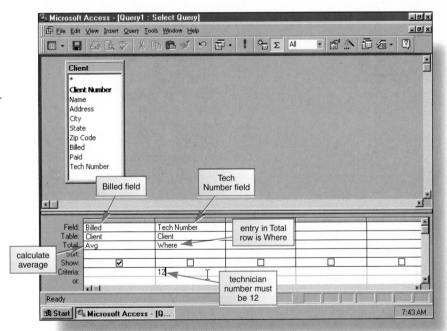

FIGURE 2-65

4 **Run the query.**

The result displays (Figure 2-66), giving the average billed amount for clients of technician 12.

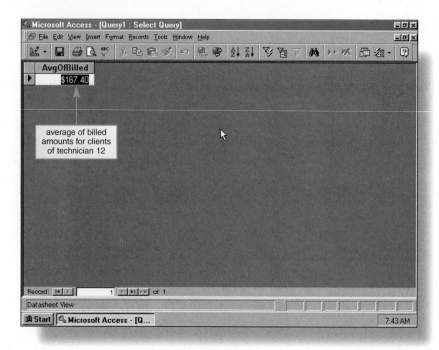

average of billed amounts for clients of technician 12

FIGURE 2-66

Grouping

Another way statistics often are used is in combination with grouping, in which statistics are calculated for groups of records. You may, for example, need to calculate the average billed amount for the clients of each technician. You will want the average for the clients of technician 11, the average for clients of technician 12, and so on.

Grouping means creating groups of records that share some common characteristic. In grouping by Tech Number, for example, the clients of technician 11 would form one group, the clients of technician 12 would be a second, and the clients of technician 17 form a third. The calculations then are made for each group. To indicate grouping in Access, select Group By as the entry in the Total row for the field to be used for grouping.

Perform the following steps to calculate the average billed amount for clients of each technician.

Steps To Use Grouping

1 **Click the View button on the toolbar to return to the Query1 : Select Query window. On the Edit menu, click Clear Grid.**

2 **Include the Tech Number field. Include the Billed field, and then click Avg as the calculation.**

The Tech Number and Billed fields are included (Figure 2-67). The Total entry for the Tech Number field currently is Group By, which is correct; thus, it was not changed.

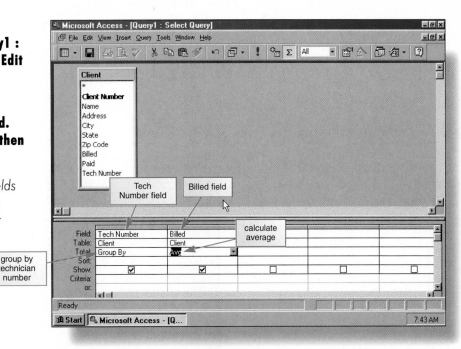

FIGURE 2-67

3 **Run the query.**

The result displays (Figure 2-68), showing each technician's number along with the average billed amount for the clients of that technician.

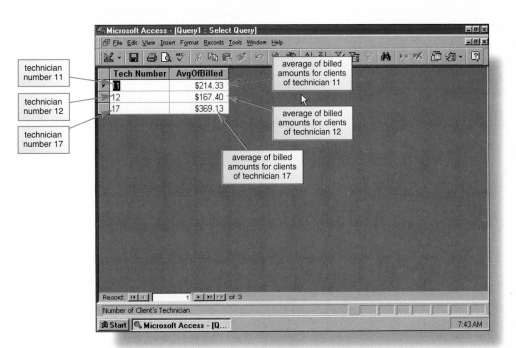

FIGURE 2-68

Saving a Query

In many cases, you will construct a query you will want to use again. By **saving the query**, you will eliminate the need to repeat all your entries. The following steps illustrate the process by saving the query you just have created and assigning it the name Average Billed Amount by Technician.

Steps **To Save a Query**

1 **Return to the Query1 : Select Query window. Point to the Save button (Figure 2-69).**

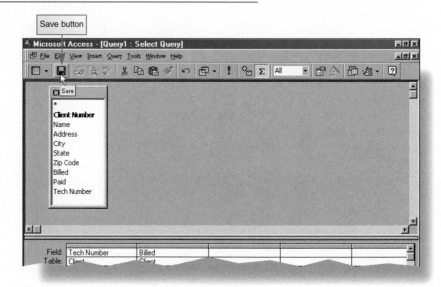

FIGURE 2-69

2 **Click the Save button. Type** Average Billed Amount by Technician **and then point to the OK button.**

The Save As dialog box displays with the query name you typed (Figure 2-70).

3 **Click the OK button to save the query, and then close the query by clicking the Query window's Close button.**

Access saves the query and closes the Query1 : Select Query window.

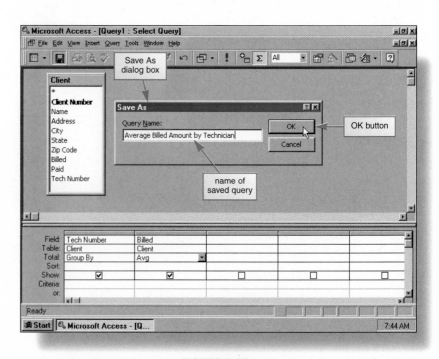

FIGURE 2-70

▶ *Other*Ways

1. On File menu click Save

2. Press CTRL+S

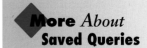

Once you have saved a query, you can use it at any time in the future by opening it. To open a saved query, click the Queries tab in the Database window, right-click the query, and then click Open on the shortcut menu (Figure 2-71).

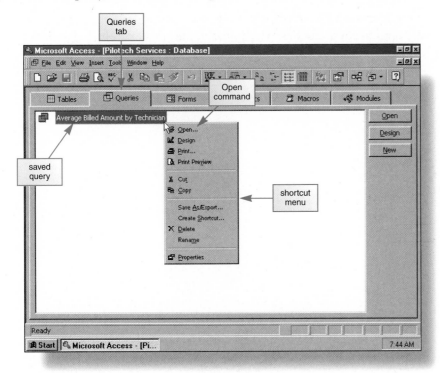

FIGURE 2-71

More *About*
Saved Queries

Forms and reports can be based on either tables or saved queries. To create a report or form based on a query, click the Query tab, select the query, click the New Object button arrow, and then click the appropriate command (Report or Form). From that point on the process is the same as for a table.

The query is run against the current database. Thus, if changes have been made to the data since the last time you ran it, the results of the query may be different.

Closing a Database

The following step closes the database by closing its Database window.

TO CLOSE A DATABASE

Step 1: Click the Close button for the Pilotech Services : Database window.

Project Summary

Project 2 introduced you to querying a database using Access. You created and ran queries for Pilotech Services. You used various types of criteria in these queries. You joined tables in some of the queries. Some Pilotech Services queries used calculated fields and statistics. Finally, you saved one of the queries for future use.

What You Should Know

Having completed this project, you now should be able to perform the following tasks:

- Calculate Statistics *(A 2.39)*
- Clear a Query *(A 2.17)*
- Close a Database *(A 2.45)*
- Close the Query *(A 2.15)*
- Create a Query *(A 2.7)*
- Include All Fields in a Query *(A 2.16)*
- Include Fields in the Design Grid *(A 2.11)*
- Join Tables *(A 2.33)*
- Omit Duplicates *(A 2.30)*
- Open a Database *(A 2.7)*
- Print the Results of a Query *(A 2.13)*
- Restrict the Records in a Join *(A 2.35)*
- Return to the Select Query Window *(A 2.14)*
- Run the Query *(A 2.12)*
- Save a Query *(A 2.44)*
- Sort Data in a Query *(A 2.27)*
- Sort on Multiple Keys *(A 2.29)*
- Use a Comparison Operator in a Criterion *(A 2.23)*
- Use a Compound Criterion Involving AND *(A 2.25)*
- Use a Compound Criterion Involving OR *(A 2.26)*
- Use a Computed Field in a Query *(A 2.37)*
- Use a Number in a Criterion *(A 2.22)*
- Use a Wildcard *(A 2.20)*
- Use Criteria for a Field Not Included in the Results *(A 2.21)*
- Use Criteria in Calculating Statistics *(A 2.41)*
- Use Grouping *(A 2.43)*
- Use Text Data in a Criterion *(A 2.18)*

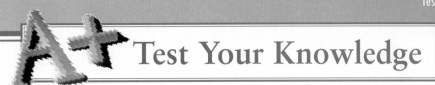 Test Your Knowledge

1 True/False

Instructions: Circle T if the statement is true or F if the statement is false.

T F 1. To include all the fields in a record in a query, click the word ALL that appears at the top of the field list.

T F 2. To create a compound criterion using OR, enter each criterion on a separate line.

T F 3. To create a compound criterion using AND, type the word, INTERSECT, before the second criterion.

T F 4. To create a criterion involving Equals, you do not need to type the equal sign (=).

T F 5. When you enter a criteria for a particular field, that field must appear in the results of the query.

T F 6. To find all clients whose billed amount is $100 or more, type >=100 as the criterion for the Billed field.

T F 7. To clear all the entries in a design grid, on the Query menu, click Clear Grid.

T F 8. When you sort a query on more than one key, the major sort key must appear to the right of the minor sort key.

T F 9. To omit duplicates from a query, use the Properties command and specify Unique Values Only.

T F 10. The wildcard symbols available for use in a query are ? and *.

2 Multiple Choice

Instructions: Circle the correct response.

1. To list only certain records in a table, use a(n) _____.
   a. list
   b. answer
   c. question
   d. query

2. To find all clients whose billed amount is $100 or more, type _____ as the criteria for the Billed field.
   a. >= $100.00
   b. >=100
   c. =>$100.00
   d. =>100

3. To clear all the entries in a design grid, on the _____ menu, click Clear Grid.
   a. Edit
   b. File
   c. Query
   d. View

(continued)

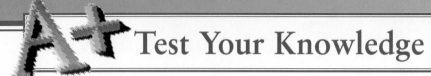

Multiple Choice *(continued)*

4. The wildcard symbols available for use in a query are the _____ and the _____.
   a. double period (..), asterisk (*)
   b. question mark (?), asterisk (*)
   c. double period (..), at symbol (@)
   d. question mark (?), ampersand (&)

5. Equal to (=), less than (<), and greater than (>) are examples of _____.
   a. criteria
   b. values
   c. comparison operators
   d. compound criteria

6. When two or more criteria are connected with AND or OR, the result is called a _____.
   a. simple criterion
   b. pattern criterion
   c. character criterion
   d. compound criterion

7. To add an additional table to a query, click _____ on the shortcut menu for the Select Query window.
   a. Join Table
   b. Show Table
   c. Add Table
   d. Include Table

8. Use a query to _____ tables; that is, find records in two tables that have identical values in matching fields.
   a. merge
   b. match
   c. combine
   d. join

9. To remove a table from a query, right-click any field in the field list for the table and then click _____ on the shortcut menu.
   a. Remove Table
   b. Delete Table
   c. Clear Table
   d. Erase Table

10. To add a Total row to a design grid, click _____ on the shortcut menu for the Select Query window.
    a. Aggregates
    b. Functions
    c. Statistics
    d. Totals

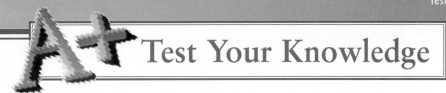

3 Understanding the Select Query Window

Instructions: In Figure 2-72, arrows point to the major components of the Select Query window. Identify the various parts of the Query window in the spaces provided.

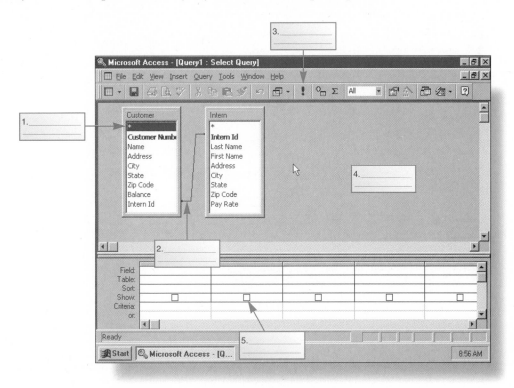

FIGURE 2-72

4 Understanding Statistics

Instructions: Figure 2-73 on the next page shows a created query using statistics for the Customer table and Figure 2-74 on the next page lists the contents of the Customer table. List the answer to this query in the spaces provided.

(continued)

Understanding Statistics *(continued)*

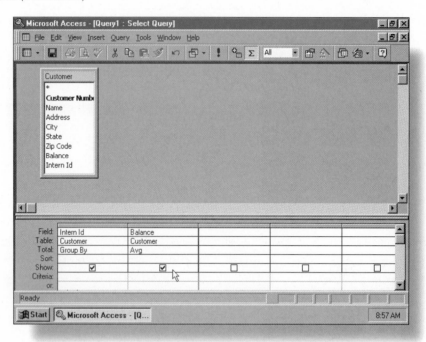

FIGURE 2-73

Data for Customer table							
CUSTOMER NUMBER	NAME	ADDRESS	CITY	STATE	ZIP CODE	BALANCE	INTERN ID
AS36	Asterman Ind.	200 Bard	Howden	MO	59444	$85.00	102
AU54	Author Books	142 Birchwood	Howden	MO	59445	$50.00	109
BI92	Bike Shop	433 Chester	Howden	MO	59441	$40.00	109
CI76	Cinderton Co.	73 Fleming	Dorchester	IL	57342	$0.00	113
CJ16	CJ's Music	277 Fordham	Dorchester	IL	57342	$105.00	102
JO62	Jordan Diner	250 Bard	Howden	MO	59444	$74.00	109
KL55	Klingon Toys	215 Scott	Evansville	MO	59335	$115.00	105
ME71	Meat & Cleaver	543 Fleming	Dorchester	IL	57342	$138.00	102
MO13	Moore Foods	876 Grove	Evansville	MO	59335	$0.00	113
RO32	Royal Mfg Co.	954 Cline	Evansville	MO	59331	$93.00	109

FIGURE 2-74

Use Help

1 Reviewing Project Activities

Instructions: Perform the following tasks using a computer.

1. Start Access.
2. If the Office Assistant is on your screen, then click it to display its balloon. If the Office Assistant is not on your screen, click the Office Assistant button on the toolbar.
3. Type working with queries in the What would you like to do? text box. Click the Search button. Click Queries: What they are and how they work.
4. Read the Help information. Use the page number links in the upper-left corner of the screen to move to the next Help windows. A total of three Help windows will display. When you finish reading the Help information, click the Close button.
5. Click the Office Assistant. Type perform calculations in a query in the What would you like to do? text box. Click the Search button. Click Ways to perform calculations in queries. Read and print the Help information. Hand in the printout to your instructor. Click the Help Topics button.
6. If necessary, click the Index tab. Type wildcard in the top text box labeled 1, and then double-click wildcard characters in the list box labeled 2. Double-click the Search for partial or matching values using wildcard characters topics. When the Help information displays, read it. Next, right-click within the box, and then click Print Topic. Hand in the printout to your instructor. Click the Help Topics button to return to the Help Topics: Microsoft Access 97 dialog box.
7. Click the Find tab. Type sorting in the top text box labeled 1. Double-click The records the query retrieves are in the wrong order in the bottom box labeled 3. When the Help information displays, read it, ready the printer, right-click, and click Print Topic. Hand in the printout to your instructor. Click the Close button.

2 Expanding on the Basics

Instructions: Use Access Help to learn about the topics listed below. If you cannot print the Help information, then answer the question on your own paper.

1. Using the Office Assistant, answer the following questions:
   a. How do you insert a field between other fields in the design grid of a query?
   b. How do you remove a field from the design grid?
   c. How do you change a field name in a query?
   d. When you use the asterisk (*) to select all fields, how do you specify criteria for fields?
   e. How do you insert a Criteria row in the design grid?
2. Using the word, format, and the Find sheet in the Help Topics: Microsoft Access 97 dialog box, display and print information on defining the data display format for a field in query Design view. Then, answer the following questions:
   a. How can you display a field's property sheet using the menu bar?
   b. How do the Regional Settings on the Windows Control Panel affect the formats in a query?
3. Using the word, OR, and the Index sheet in the Help Topics: Microsoft Access 97 dialog box, display and then print information about ways to use multiple criteria in a query. Then answer the following questions:
   a. How do you enter criteria to OR two values in one field?
   b. How do you enter criteria to AND two values in one field?
   c. How do you enter criteria to OR and AND in three fields?
4. Use the Office Assistant to display and print information on searching for a range of values.

Apply Your Knowledge

1 Querying the Green Thumb Database

Instructions: Start Access. Open the Green Thumb database from the Access folder on the Data Disk that accompanies this book. Perform the following tasks.

1. Create a new query for the Customer table.
2. Add the Customer Number, Name, and Balance fields to the design grid as shown in Figure 2-75.
3. Restrict retrieval to only those records where the balance is greater than $100.
4. Run the query and print the results.
5. Return to the Select Query window and clear the grid.
6. Add the Customer Number, Name, City, Balance, and Intern Id fields to the design grid.
7. Restrict retrieval to only those records where the Intern Id is either 109 or 113.
8. Sort the records in order by Balance (descending) within City (ascending).
9. Run the query and print the results.
10. Return to the Select Query window and clear the grid.
11. Join the Customer and Intern tables. Add the Customer Number, Name, and Intern Id fields from the Customer table and the Last Name and First Name fields from the Intern table.
12. Sort the records in ascending order by Intern Id.
13. Run the query and print the results.

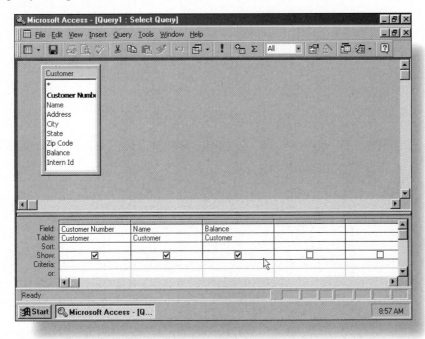

FIGURE 2-75

In the Lab

1 Querying the Museum Mercantile Database

Problem: The volunteers who staff Museum Mercantile have determined a number of questions they want the database management system to answer. You must obtain answers to the questions posed by the volunteers.

Instructions: Use the database created in the In the Lab 1 of Project 1 for this assignment. Perform the following tasks.

1. Open the Museum Mercantile database and create a new query for the Product table.
2. Display and print the Product Id, Description, and Selling Price for all records in the table as shown in Figure 2-76.
3. Display all fields and print all the records in the table.
4. Display and print the Product Id, Description, Cost, and Vendor Code for all products where the Vendor Code is MS.
5. Display and print the Product Id and Description for all products where the Description begins with the letters, Wi.
6. Display and print the Product Id, Description, and Vendor Code for all products that cost more than $20.
7. Display and print the Product Id and Description for all products that have a Selling Price of $5 or less.
8. Display and print all fields for those products that cost more than $10 and where the number of units on hand is less than 10.
9. Display and print all fields for those products that have a Vendor Code of WW or have a Selling Price less than $10.
10. Join the Product table and the Vendor table. Display the Product Id, Description, Cost, Name, and Telephone Number fields. Run the query and print the results.
11. Restrict the records retrieved in task 10 above to only those products where the number of units on hand is less than 10. Display and print the results.
12. Remove the Vendor table and clear the design grid.
13. Include the Product Id and Description in the design grid. Compute the on-hand value (on hand * cost) for all records in the table. Display and print the results.
14. Display and print the average selling price of all products.
15. Display and print the average selling price of products grouped by Vendor Code.
16. Join the Product and Vendor tables. Include the Vendor Code and Name fields from the Vendor table. Include the Product Id, Description, Cost, and On Hand fields from the Product table. Save the query as Vendors and Products. Run the query and print the results.

In the Lab

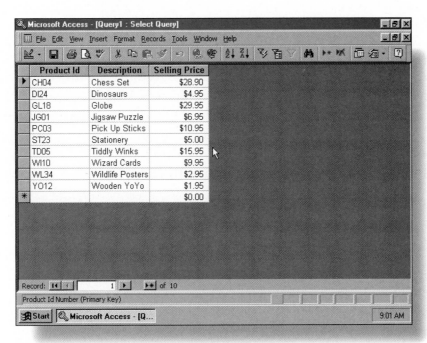

FIGURE 2-76

2 Querying the City Telephone System Database

Problem: The telephone manager has determined a number of questions that she wants the database management system to answer. You must obtain answers to the questions posed by the telephone manager.

Instructions: Use the database created in the In the Lab 2 of Project 1 for this assignment. Perform the following tasks.

1. Open the City Telephone System database and create a new query for the User table.
2. Display and print the User Id, Last Name, First Name, Phone Ext, and Office for all the records in the table as shown in Figure 2-77 on the next page.
3. Display all fields and print all the records in the table.
4. Display and print the User Id, First Name, Last Name, Basic Charge, and Extra Charges for all users in the department with the code of PLN.
5. Display and print the User Id, First Name, Last Name, and Phone Ext for all users whose basic charge is $13 per month.
6. Display and print the User Id, First Name, Last Name, and Extra Charges for all users in the department with a code ITD who have Extra Charges greater than $20. List the records in descending order by Extra Charges.

(continued)

In the Lab

Querying the City Telephone System Database *(continued)*

7. Display and print the User Id, First Name, Last Name, and Extra Charges for all users who have extra charges greater than $25 and are in either the Assessment (APV) or Planning (PLN) department. (*Hint*: Use information from Use Help 2 on page A 2.52 to solve this problem.)
8. Display and print the Basic Charge in ascending order. List each Basic Charge only once.
9. Join the User table and the Department table. Display and print the User Id, Last Name, First Name, Basic Charge, Extra Charges, and Name of the department.
10. Restrict the records retrieved in task 10 above to only those users who have extra charges greater than $20.
11. Remove the Department table and clear the design grid.
12. Include the User Id, First Name, Last Name, Basic Charge, and Extra Charges fields in the design grid. Compute the total bill for each user (Basic Charge + Extra Charges). Display and print the results.
13. Display and print the average extra charges.
14. Display and print the highest extra charge.
15. Display and print the total extra charges for each department.
16. Join the User and Department tables. Include the Department Name, User Id, Last Name, First Name, Phone Ext, Basic Charge, and Extra Charges fields. Save the query as Departments and Users. Run the query and print the results.

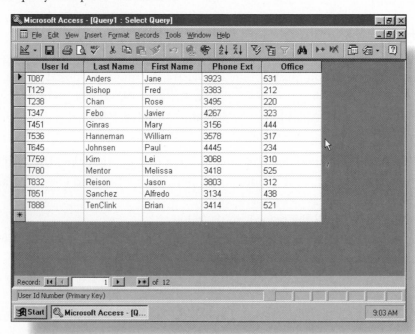

FIGURE 2-77

In the Lab

3 Querying the City Scene Database

Problem: The managing editor of the *City Scene* magazine has determined a number of questions that he wants the database management system to answer. You must obtain answers to the questions posed by the managing editor.

Instructions: Use the database created in the In the Lab 3 of Project 1 for this assignment. Perform the following tasks.

1. Open the City Scene database and create a new query for the Advertiser table.
2. Display and print the Advertiser Number, Name, Balance, and Amount Paid for all the records in the table as shown in Figure 2-78 on the next page.
3. Display and print the Advertiser Number, Name, and Balance for all advertisers where the Ad Rep Number is 19.
4. Display and print the Advertiser Number, Name, and Balance for all advertisers where the Balance is greater than $100.
5. Display and print the Advertiser Number, Name, and Amount Paid for all advertisers where the Ad Rep Number is 16 and the Amount Paid is greater than $250.
6. Display and print the Advertiser Number and Name of all advertisers where the Name begins with C.
7. Display and print the Advertiser Number, Name, and Balance for all advertisers where the Ad Rep Number is 19 or the Balance is less than $100.
8. Include the Advertiser Number, Name, City, and State in the design grid. Sort the records in ascending order by City within State. Display and print the results. The City field should display in the result to the left of the State field. (*Hint*: Use information from Use Help 1 on page A 2.51.)
9. Display and print the cities in ascending order. Each city should display only once.
10. Display and print the Advertiser Number, Name, Balance, and Amount Paid fields from the Advertiser table and the First Name, Last Name, and Comm Rate fields from the Ad Rep table.
11. Restrict the records retrieved in task 10 above to only those advertisers that are in WA. Display and print the results.
12. Clear the design grid and add the Last Name, First Name, and Comm Rate fields from the Ad Rep table to the grid. Add the Amount Paid field from the Advertiser table. Compute the Commission (Amount Paid * Comm Rate) for the Ad Rep table. Sort the records in ascending order by Last Name and format Commission as currency. (*Hint*: Use information from Use Help 2 on page A 2.52 to solve this problem.) Run the query and print the results.
13. Display and print the following statistics: the total balance and amount paid for all advertisers; the total balance for advertisers of ad rep 16; and the total amount paid for each ad rep.
14. Display and print the Ad Rep Number, Last Name, First Name, Advertiser Number, Name, Balance, and Amount Paid. Save the query as Ad Reps and Advertisers.

(continued)

In the Lab

Querying the City Scene Database (continued)

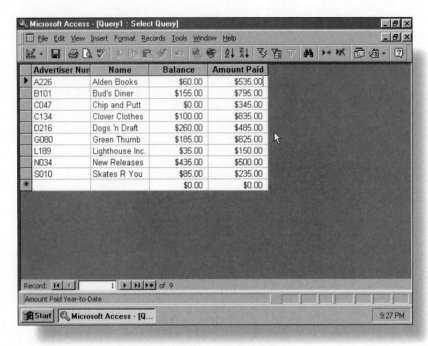

FIGURE 2-78

Cases and Places

The difficulty of these case studies varies: ◗ are the least difficult; ◗◗ are more difficult; and ◗◗◗ are the most difficult.

1 ◗ Use the textbook database created in Case Study 1 of Project 1 for this assignment. Perform the following: (a) The textbook cooperative receives a call asking if anyone is selling a book for Eng 150. Display and print the sellers' names and telephone numbers and their asking prices for books available for that course. (b) Karen Sing asks which books she has submitted. Display and print the titles, authors, and courses of her books. (c) Several nursing students call to ask which textbooks from that department are available. Display and print the titles, authors, and courses of the nursing books. (d) Display and print the titles, authors, and prices of books listed for less than $20. (e) Display and print the titles and course numbers for books in excellent condition.

Cases and Places

2 ▶ Use the restaurant database created in Case Study 2 of Project 1 for this assignment. You decide to survey the campus community to get some marketing ideas for your meal delivery service. You want to know the students' restaurant habits. Perform the following: (a) It is 10:30 p.m. and a student has a craving for pizza. Display and print the names and telephone numbers of all Italian restaurants open that will deliver the order. (b) Students are cramming for an exam at 2:00 a.m. and would settle for any type of food. Display and print the names, telephone numbers, addresses, and closing times of all restaurants that are open. (c) A student's last class on Wednesday ends at 3:50 p.m., and he wants to pick up some food to take home to eat before he leaves for work. Display and print the names, addresses, and opening times of all restaurants that open before 5:00 p.m. (d) Payday for student employees is Friday, and they are short on cash at midweek. Display and print the names, addresses, telephone numbers, and food types of all restaurants that have specials on Wednesday or Thursday. (e) A group of students decides to meet for lunch. Display and print the names, addresses, telephone numbers, and opening times of all restaurants that open before noon.

3 ▶▶ Use the movie collection database created in Case Study 3 of Project 1 for this assignment. Perform the following: (a) Display and print the movie titles in ascending order, along with the two actors and year produced. (b) You have less than two hours to show a movie to the nursing home residents. Display and print the movie titles and running times that would fit this time constraint. (c) Display and print the movie titles starring John Wayne. (d) Display and print the movie titles starring Jean Arthur. (e) The nursing home is having a comedy night. Display and print the movies starring Abbott and Costello. (f) Display and print the movie titles and leading actors of films rated more than two stars. (g) It's Grandparents' Weekend at the nursing home. Display and print the movies produced in the 1930s and 1940s.

4 ▶▶ The American Heart Association recommends a maximum of two, three-ounce cooked servings of lean meat, or six ounces total daily. A three-ounce serving is the size of a woman's palm. Use the nutritional content database created in Case Study 4 of Project 1 for this assignment. Perform the following: (a) Display and print the cuts of beef with less than 70 milligrams of cholesterol in one, three-ounce serving. (b) Display and print the cuts of beef with more than 160 calories in a three-ounce serving. (c) For your research project, you are to consume less than 20 grams of fat daily. During the day, you have eaten food with a total fat gram content of 15. Display and print the cuts of beef that would be within the project's requirements.

Cases and Places

5 ▶▶▶ Use the product comparison database created in Case Study 5 of Project 1 for this assignment. Display and print the following: (a) The six specific items in ascending order, along with sizes and prices for the dairy items at the convenience, grocery, and discount stores. (b) The six specific items in ascending order, along with sizes and prices for the snack items at the convenience, grocery, and discount stores. (c) The six specific items in ascending order, along with sizes and prices for the cosmetics/toiletries items at the convenience, grocery, and discount stores. (d) The six specific items in ascending order, along with sizes and prices for the kitchen supplies items at the convenience, grocery, and discount stores.

6 ▶▶▶ Use the campus directory database created in Case Study 6 of Project 1 for this assignment. Display and print the following: (a) The names of your instructors in ascending order, along with their telephone numbers and room numbers. (b) The names of the administrators in ascending order, along with their telephone numbers and room numbers. (c) The services in ascending order, including telephone numbers and room numbers.

7 ▶▶▶ Use the financial institutions database created in Case Study 7 of Project 1 for this assignment. Display and print the following: (a) The names of the financial institutions and total values of the IRAs at age 65 in descending order. (b) The names and telephone numbers of the financial institutions and total amounts of interest earned at age 65 in descending order. (c) The average value of the IRAs at age 65. (d) The average interest rates for the banks, savings and loans, and credit unions. (e) The name, address, and interest rate of the financial institution with the highest interest rate. (f) The name, telephone number, and interest rate of the financial institution with the lowest interest rate. (g) The names of the financial institutions and penalties for early withdrawal in two years in ascending order. (h) The names of the financial institutions and annual fees in descending order.

Maintaining a Database Using the Design and Update Features of Access

Objectives:

You will have mastered the material in this project when you can:

▶ Add records to a table
▶ Locate records
▶ Change the contents of records in a table
▶ Delete records from a table
▶ Restructure a table
▶ Change field characteristics
▶ Add a field
▶ Save the changes to the structure
▶ Update the contents of a single field
▶ Make changes to groups of records
▶ Delete groups of records
▶ Specify a required field
▶ Specify a range
▶ Specify a default value
▶ Specify legal values
▶ Specify a format
▶ Update a table with validation rules
▶ Specify referential integrity
▶ Order records
▶ Create single-field and multiple-field indexes

Project 3

Enterprise to Earth:
The View Is Superb!

When you hear the name *Enterprise*, what comes to mind? A Federation starship? The aircraft carrier that became the most decorated American ship of World War II? A business venture?

On June 18, 1861, the first electronic message from the skies flashed down from 500 feet above Washington, DC via telegraph wire to President Lincoln, sent by the intrepid Dr. Thaddeus S.C. Lowe from the hot air balloon *Enterprise*. Lowe went on to organize the Federal Balloon Corps, providing the first aerial fire control for Union artillery during the Civil War. The Confederacy soon emulated this feat, but alas! the Federals captured one Confederate balloon — made of silk dresses contributed by dozens of patriotic Southern ladies — before it ever flew.

Since 1783, when Benjamin Franklin watched the Montgolfier brothers of France send their hot air balloon aloft, innovators and daredevils alike have built and flown hundreds of different designs for balloons and dirigibles. Count von Zeppelin of Germany took the science to its highest form with enormous hydrogen-filled dirigibles carrying wealthy passengers on luxury cruises from Germany to America, Rio de Janeiro, Tokyo, Siberia, and other exotic destinations. This form of air service came to an abrupt halt on May 6, 1937, when the 803-foot monster dirigible *Hindenburg* ignited at Lakehurst, New Jersey and seven million cubic feet of gas erupted like Vesuvius. In thirty-two seconds, the mighty lord of the air was gone.

That spectacular disaster, however, did not end the interest in lighter-than-air vessels. From convoy escorts and barrage balloons during World War II, lighter-than-air craft have evolved into commercial and pleasure vehicles. After glimpsing the world through the Goodyear blimp's television camera, one can readily imagine the excitement of scudding through the heavens dangling beneath a hot air balloon, while exchanging wedding vows over California's Napa Valley or watching gazelles and wildebeests bounding across the Serengeti Plain.

A captivating subject, the exploits of pioneers who went aloft in sometimes-crazy contraptions are but a few of the billions of facts that historians, encylopedists, and librarians spend their lifetimes collecting and preserving. In the monumental task of managing ever-accumulating mountains of historical data, computer databases are indispensable.

Maintaining such important archives is an essential, on-going operation. Modern revision tools, such as those provided by Microsoft Access 97, have streamlined the business of updating or restructuring databases significantly. Unlike past programs, which could require hours to add or delete a field, the design and update features found in Access allow you to make global changes to your own databases in just minutes.

Although warp speed is great when doing updates, think how much fun it would have been to accompany Phileas Fogg in his balloon on the leisurely first leg of his trip *Around the World in Eighty Days*. Now, that's flying!

Smart Revision Tools

Microsoft
Access 97

Maintaining a Database Using the Design and Update Features of Access

Case Perspective

Pilotech Services has created a database and loaded it with client and technician data. The management and staff have received many benefits from the database, including the ability to ask a variety of questions concerning the data in the database. They now face the task of keeping the database up to date. They must add new records as they take on new clients and technicians. They must make changes to existing records to reflect additional billings, payments, changes of address, and so on. Pilotech Services also found that it needed to change the structure of the database in two specific ways. The management decided the database needed to categorize the clients by type (regular, non-profit, and educational organization) and so they needed to add a Client Type field to the Client table. They found the Name field was too short to contain the name of one of the clients. They also determined they could improve the efficiency of certain types of database processing and found that to do so, they needed to create indexes, which are similar to indexes found in the back of books.

Introduction

Once a database has been created and loaded with data, it must be maintained. **Maintaining the database** means modifying the data to keep it up to date, such as adding new records, changing the data for existing records, and deleting records. **Updating** can include **mass updates** or **mass deletions**; that is, updates to, or deletions of, many records at the same time.

In addition to adding, changing, and deleting records, maintenance of a database periodically can involve the need to **restructure** the database; that is, to change the database structure. This can include adding new fields to a table, changing the characteristics of existing fields, and removing existing fields. It also can involve the creation of **indexes**, which are similar to indexes found in the back of books and which are used to improve the efficiency of certain operations.

Figure 3-1 summarizes some of the various types of activities involved in maintaining a database.

Project Three — Maintaining the Pilotech Services Database

You are to make the changes to the data in the Pilotech Services database as requested by the management of

Pilotech Services. You also must restructure the database to meet the current needs of Pilotech. This includes adding an additional field as well as increasing the width of one of the existing fields. You also must modify the structure of the database in a way that prevents users from entering invalid data. Finally, management is concerned that some operations, for example, those involving sorting the data, are taking longer than they would like. You are to create indexes to attempt to address this problem.

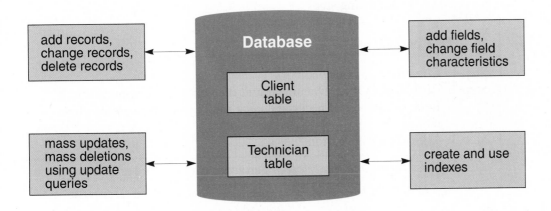

FIGURE 3-1

Overview of Project Steps

These steps give you an overview of how the Pilotech Services database will be maintained. The following tasks will be completed in this project.

1. Start Access and open the Pilotech Services database.
2. Use a form to add a new record to the Client table.
3. Locate the record for client GU21 and then change the name of the client.
4. Delete the record for client BL26.
5. Increase the width of the Name field to accommodate a client name that will not fit in the current structure.
6. Add a field for client category (called Client Type) to the Client table.
7. Change the name of client GU21 (the one that previously would not fit).
8. Resize the columns in Datasheet view.
9. Use an update query to set all the values in the Client Type field initially to REG, which is the most common client category.
10. Use a delete query to delete all clients in zip code 52018.

11. Create a validation rule to make the Name field a required field.
12. Create a validation rule to ensure that only values between $0.00 and $800.00 may be entered in the Billed field.
13. Specify that REG is to be the default value for the Client Type field.
14. Create a validation rule to ensure that only the values of REG, NPR, or EDU may be entered in the Client Type field.
15. Specify that any letters entered in the Client Number field are to be converted automatically to uppercase.
16. Specify referential integrity between the Client and Technician tables.
17. Use the Sort buttons to sort records in the database.
18. Create and use indexes to improve performance.

Opening the Database

Before carrying out the steps in this project, first you must open the database. To do so, perform the following steps.

TO OPEN A DATABASE

Step 1: Click the Start button.
Step 2: Click Open Office Document and then click 3½ Floppy (A:) in the Look in list box. If necessary, click the Pilotech Services database name.
Step 3: Click the Open button.

The database opens and the Pilotech Services : Database window displays.

Adding, Changing, and Deleting

Keeping the data in a database up to date requires three tasks: adding new records, changing the data in existing records, and deleting existing records.

Adding Records

In Project 1, you added records to a database using Datasheet view; that is, as you were adding records, the records were displayed on the screen in the form of a datasheet, or table. When you need to add additional records, you can use the same techniques.

In Project 1, you used a form to view records. This is called **Form view**. You also can use Form view to update the data in a table. To add new records, change existing records, or delete records, you will use the same techniques you used in Datasheet view. To add a record to the Client table with a form, for example, use the following steps. These steps use the Client form you created in Project 1.

Steps To Use a Form to Add Records

1 With the Pilotech Services database open, point to the Forms tab (Figure 3-2).

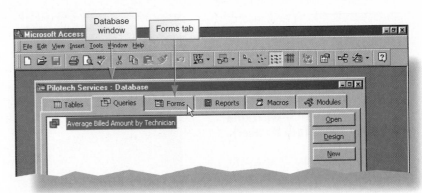

FIGURE 3-2

2 Click the Forms tab. Right-click Client.

The shortcut menu displays (Figure 3-3).

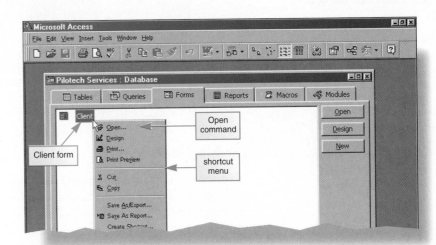

FIGURE 3-3

3 Click Open on the shortcut menu.

The form for the Client table displays (Figure 3-4).

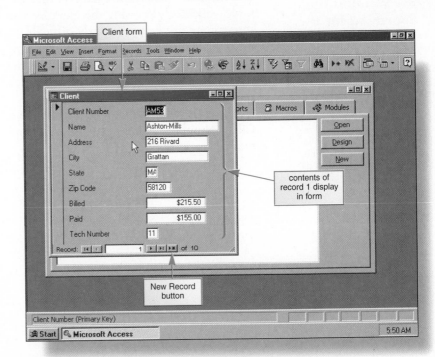

FIGURE 3-4

4 Click the New Record button.

The contents of the form are erased in preparation for a new record.

5 Type the data for the new record as shown in Figure 3-5. Press the TAB key after typing the data in each field, except after typing the final field (Tech Number).

The record appears as shown in Figure 3-5.

6 Press the TAB key.

The record now is added to the Client table and the contents of the form erased.

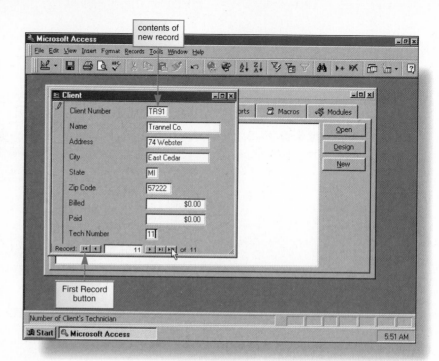

FIGURE 3-5

More *About* **Searching for a Record**

When you are searching for a record, your current position in the database is immaterial if you click the Find First button. The position will change to the first record that satisfies the condition. Your current position is important if you click the Find Next button, because the search then will begin at the current position.

Searching for a Record

In the database environment, **searching** means looking for records that satisfy some criteria. Looking for the client whose number is GU21 is an example of searching. The queries in Project 2 also were examples of searching. Access had to locate those records that satisfied the criteria.

A need for searching also exists when using Form view or Datasheet view. To update client GU21, for example, first you need to find the client. In a small table, repeatedly pressing the Next Record button until client GU21 is on the screen may not be particularly difficult. In a large table with many records, however, this would be extremely cumbersome. You need a way to be able to go directly to a record just by giving the value in some field. This is the function of the **Find button** on the toolbar. Before clicking the Find button, select the field for the search.

Perform the following steps to move to the first record in the file, select the Client Number field, and then use the Find button to search for the client whose number is GU21.

Steps To Search for a Record

1 **Make sure the Client table is open and the form for the Client table is on the screen. Click the First Record button (see Figure 3-5) to display the first record. If the Client Number field is not currently selected, select it by clicking the field name. Point to the Find button on the toolbar.**

The first record displays in the form (Figure 3-6).

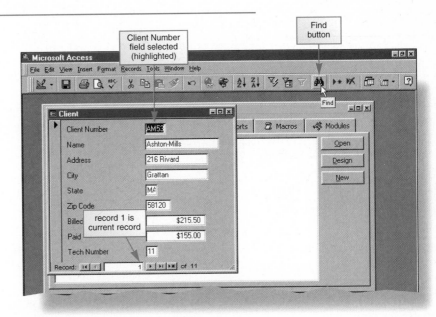

FIGURE 3-6

2 **Click the Find button. Type** GU21 **in the Find What text box.**

The Find in field: 'Client Number' dialog box displays (Figure 3-7). The Find What text box contains the entry, GU21.

3 **Click the Find First button and then click the Close button.**

Access locates the record for client GU21.

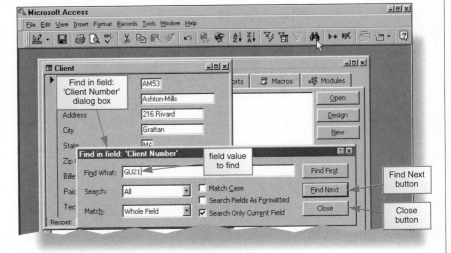

FIGURE 3-7

Other Ways

1. On Edit menu click Find
2. Press CTRL+F

In some cases, after locating a record that satisfies a criterion, you might need to find the next record that satisfies the same criterion. For example, if you have just found the first client whose technician number is 11, you then may want to find the second such client, then the third, and so on. To do so, repeat the same process. You will not need to retype the value, however.

Changing the Contents of a Record

After locating the record to be changed, select the field to be changed by clicking the field. You also can repeatedly press the TAB key. Then make the appropriate changes. Clicking the field name automatically produces an insertion point in the field name text box. If you use the TAB key, you will need to press F2 to produce an insertion point.

More *About*
Changing the Contents of a Record

When you are changing the value in a field, clicking within the field will produce an insertion point. Clicking the name of the field will select the entire field. The new entry typed then will completely replace the previous entry.

Normally, Access is in Insert mode, so the characters typed will be inserted at the appropriate position. To change to Overtype mode, press the INSERT key. The letters, OVR, will display near the bottom right edge of the status bar. To return to Insert mode, press the INSERT key. In **Insert mode**, if the data in the field completely fills the field, no additional characters can be inserted. In this case, increase the size of the field before inserting the characters. You will see how to do this later in the project.

Complete the following steps to use Form view to change the name of client GU21 to Grand Union Supply by inserting the word, Supply, at the end of the name. Sufficient room exists in the field to make this change.

Steps To Update the Contents of a Field

1 **Position the mouse pointer in the Name field text box for client GU21 after the word, Union.**

The mouse pointer shape is an I-beam (Figure 3-8).

2 **Click to produce an insertion point, press the SPACEBAR to insert a space and then type** Supply **to correct the name.**

The name is now Grand Union Supply.

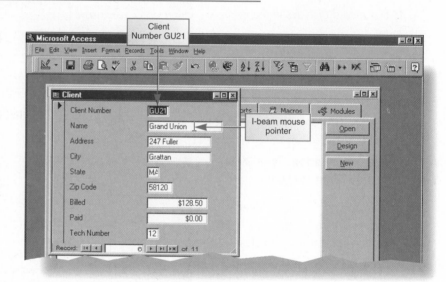

FIGURE 3-8

Switching Between Views

Sometimes, after working in Form view where you can see all fields, but only one record, it would be helpful to see several records at a time. To do so, switch to Datasheet view by clicking the View button arrow and then clicking Datasheet View. Perform the following steps to switch from Form view to Datasheet view.

Steps To Switch from Form View to Datasheet View

1 **Point to the View button arrow on the toolbar (Figure 3-9).**

FIGURE 3-9

2 **Click the View button arrow. Point to Datasheet View.**

The View list displays (Figure 3-10).

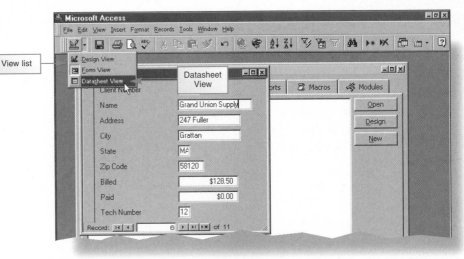

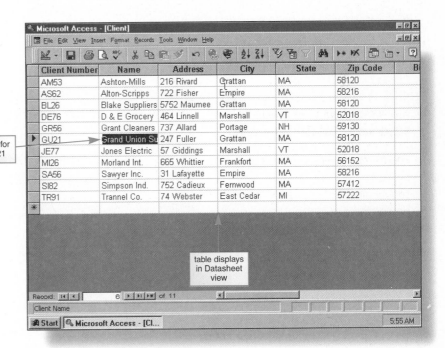

FIGURE 3-10

3 **Click Datasheet View, and then maximize the window containing the datasheet.**

The datasheet displays (Figure 3-11). The position in the table is maintained. The current record selector points to client GU21, the client that displayed on the screen in Form view. The Name field, the field in which the insertion point is displayed, is selected.

FIGURE 3-11

Other Ways

1. On View menu click Datasheet View

If you wanted to return to Form view, you would use the same process. The only difference is that you would click Form View rather than Datasheet View.

Deleting Records

When records are no longer needed, **delete the records** (remove them) from the table. If, for example, client BL26 has moved its offices to a city that is not served by Pilotech and already has settled its final bill, that client's record should be deleted. To delete a record, first locate it and then press the DELETE key. Complete the steps on the next page to delete client BL26.

More *About*
the View Button

You can use the View button to transfer easily between viewing the form, called Form view, and viewing the design of the form, called Design view. To move to Datasheet view, you *must* click the down arrow, and then click Datasheet view in the list that displays.

Steps To Delete a Record

1 **With the datasheet for the Client table on the screen, position the mouse pointer on the record selector of the record in which the client number is BL26 (Figure 3-12).**

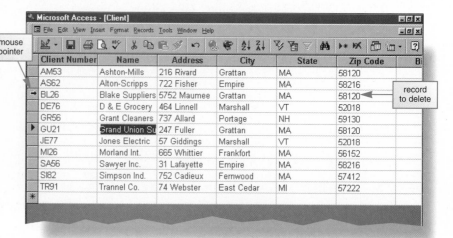

FIGURE 3-12

2 **Click the record selector to select the record, and then press the DELETE key to delete the record.**

The Microsoft Access dialog box displays (Figure 3-13). The message indicates that one record will be deleted.

3 **Click the Yes button to complete the deletion. Close the window containing the table by clicking its Close button.**

The record is deleted and the table disappears from the screen.

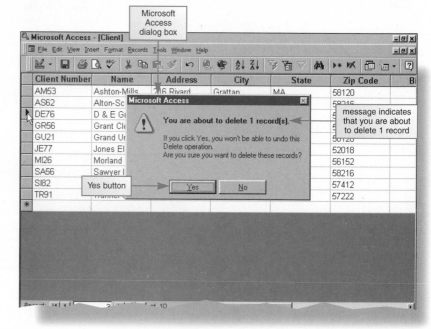

FIGURE 3-13

OtherWays

1. Click record to delete, click Delete Record button on toolbar
2. Click record to delete, on Edit menu click Delete Record

Changing the Structure

When you initially create a database, you define its **structure**; that is, you indicate the names, types, and sizes of all the fields. In many cases, the structure you first defined will not continue to be appropriate as you use the database. A variety of reasons exist why the structure of a table might need to change. Changes in the needs of users of the database may require additional fields to be added. In the Client table, for example, if it is important to store a code indicating the client type of a client, you need to add such a field.

Characteristics of a given field might need to change. For example, the client Grand Union Supply's name is stored incorrectly in the database. It actually should be Grand Union Supply, Inc. The Name field is not large enough, however, to hold the correct name. To accommodate this change, you need to increase the width of the Name field.

It may be that a field currently in the table no longer is necessary. If no one ever uses a particular field, it is not needed in the table. Because it is occupying space and serving no useful purpose, it should be removed from the table. You also would need to delete the field from any forms, reports, or queries that include it.

To make any of these changes, click Design on the shortcut menu.

Changing the Size of a Field

The following steps change the size of the Name field from 20 to 25 to accommodate the change of name from Grand Union Supply to Grand Union Supply, Inc.

More *About* Changing the Structure

A major advantage of using a full-featured database management system is the ease with which you can change the structure of the tables that make up the database. In a nondatabase environment, changes to the structure can be very cumbersome, requiring difficult and time-consuming changes to many programs.

Steps To Change the Size of a Field

1 **With the Database window on the screen, click the Tables tab and then right-click Client.**

The shortcut menu displays (Figure 3-14).

2 **Click Design on the shortcut menu and then point to the row selector for the Name field.**

The Client : Table window displays (Figure 3-15).

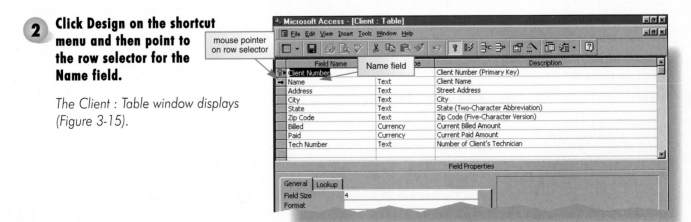

FIGURE 3-14

FIGURE 3-15

3 Click the row selector for the Name field.

The Name field is selected (Figure 3-16).

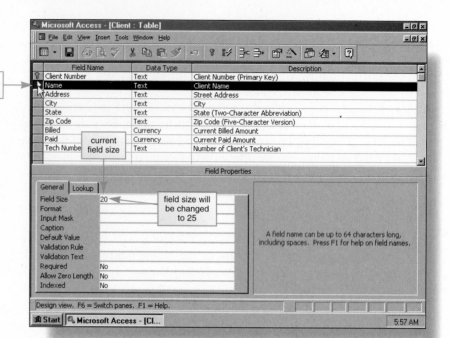

FIGURE 3-16

4 Press F6 to select the field size, type 25 as the new size, and press F6 again.

The size is changed (Figure 3-17).

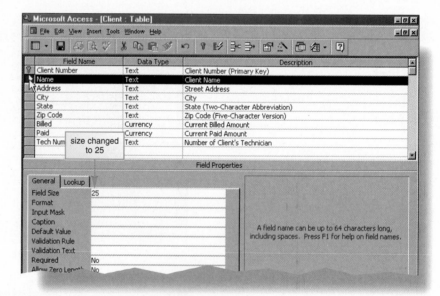

FIGURE 3-17

More *About*
Adding a New Field

Tables frequently need to be expanded to include additional fields for a variety of reasons. Users needs can change. The field may have been omitted by mistake when the table was first created. Government regulations may change in such a way that the organization needs to maintain additional information.

Adding a New Field

The following steps add a new field, called Client Type, to the table. This field is used to indicate the type of client. The possible entries in this field are REG (regular client), NPR (nonprofit organization), and EDU (educational institution). The new field will follow the Zip Code in the list of fields; that is, it will be the seventh field in the restructured table. The current seventh field (Billed) will become the eighth field, Paid will become the ninth field, and so on. Complete the following steps to add the field.

Steps   To Add a Field to a Table

1 Point to the row selector for the Billed field (Figure 3-18).

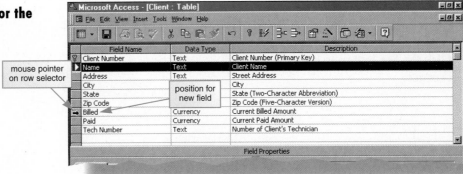

FIGURE 3-18

2 Click the row selector for the Billed field and then press the INSERT key to insert a blank row.

A blank row displays in the position for the new field (Figure 3-19).

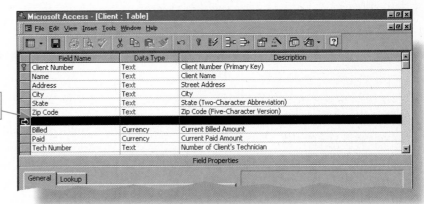

FIGURE 3-19

3 Click the Field Name column for the new field. Type Client Type **(field name) and then press the TAB key. Select the Text data type by pressing the TAB key. Type** Client Type (REG, NPR, or EDU) **as the description. Press F6 to move to the Field Size text box, type** 3 **(the size of the Client Type field), and press F6 again.**

The entries for the new field are complete (Figure 3-20).

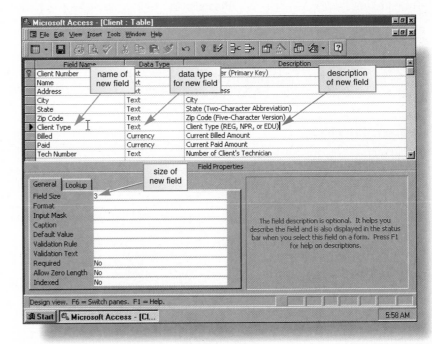

FIGURE 3-20

4 Close the Client : Table window by clicking its Close button.

The Microsoft Access dialog box displays (Figure 3-21).

5 Click the Yes button to save the changes.

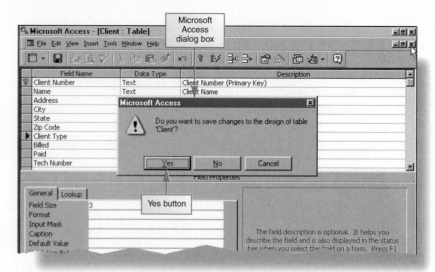

FIGURE 3-21

*Other*Ways

1. Click row selector below where new field is to be added, click Insert Rows button on toolbar
2. Click row selector below where new field is to be added, on Insert menu click Rows

Updating the Restructured Database

Changes to the structure are available immediately. The Name field is longer, although it does not appear that way on the screen, and the new Client Type field is included.

To make a change to a single field, such as changing the name from Grand Union Supply to Grand Union Supply, Inc., click the field to be changed, and then type the new value. If the record to be changed is not on the screen, use the Navigation buttons (Next Record, Previous Record) to move to it. If the field to be corrected simply is not visible on the screen, use the horizontal scroll bar along the bottom of the screen to shift all the fields until the correct one displays. Then make the change.

Perform the following steps to change the name of Grand Union Supply to Grand Union Supply, Inc.

Steps **To Update the Contents of a Field**

1 Right-click Client.

The shortcut menu displays (Figure 3-22).

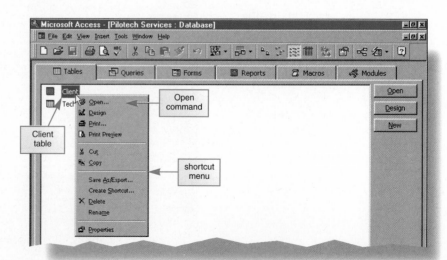

FIGURE 3-22

2 Click Open on the shortcut menu. Position the I-beam mouse pointer to the right of the u of Grand Union Supply (client GU21).

The datasheet displays (Figure 3-23).

3 Click in the field, use the RIGHT ARROW key to move to the end of the name, and then type , Inc. as the addition to the name.

The name is changed from Grand Union Supply to Grand Union Supply, Inc.

FIGURE 3-23

Resizing Columns

The default column sizes provided by Access do not always allow all the data in the field to display. You can correct this problem by **resizing the column** (changing its size) in the datasheet. In some instances, you actually may want to reduce the size of a column. The City field, for example, is short enough that it does not require all the space on the screen that is allotted to it.

Both types of changes are made the same way. Position the mouse pointer on the right boundary of the column's **field selector** (the line in the column heading immediately to the right of the name of the column to be resized). The mouse pointer will change to a two-headed arrow with a vertical bar. You then can drag the line to resize the column. In addition, you can double-click in the line, in which case Access will determine the best size for the column.

The following steps illustrate the process for resizing the Name column to the size that best fits the data.

▶ **M**ore *About*
Updating a Restructured Database

After changing the structure in a nondatabase environment, it can take several hours before the new structure is available for use. Computer jobs to change the structure often would run overnight or even over a weekend. Having the changes available immediately is a major benefit to using a system like Access.

 Steps To Resize a Column

1 Point to the right boundary of the field selector for the Name field (Figure 3-24).

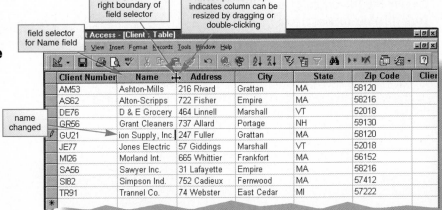

FIGURE 3-24

2 Double-click the right boundary of the field selector for the Name field.

The Name column has been resized (Figure 3-25).

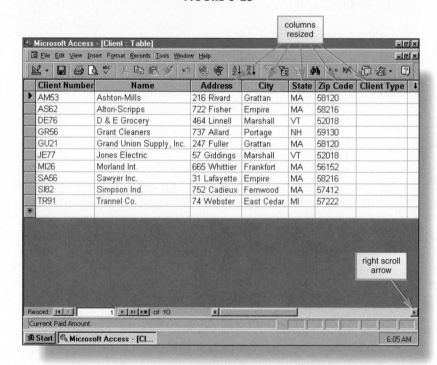

FIGURE 3-25

3 Use the same technique to resize the Address, City, State, Zip Code, and Client Type columns to best fit the data.

The columns have been resized (Figure 3-26).

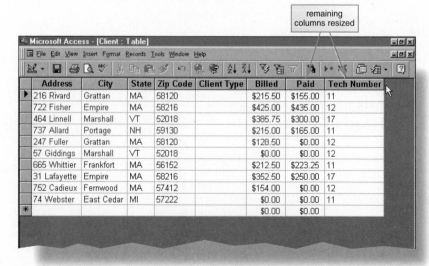

FIGURE 3-26

4 Click the right scroll arrow to display the Billed, Paid, and Tech Number columns, and then resize the columns to best fit the data.

All the columns have been resized (Figure 3-27).

Address	City	State	Zip Code	Client Type	Billed	Paid	Tech Number
216 Rivard	Grattan	MA	58120		$215.50	$155.00	11
722 Fisher	Empire	MA	58216		$425.00	$435.00	12
464 Linnell	Marshall	VT	52018		$385.75	$300.00	17
737 Allard	Portage	NH	59130		$215.00	$165.00	11
247 Fuller	Grattan	MA	58120		$128.50	$0.00	12
57 Giddings	Marshall	VT	52018		$0.00	$0.00	12
665 Whittier	Frankfort	MA	56152		$212.50	$223.25	11
31 Lafayette	Empire	MA	58216		$352.50	$250.00	17
752 Cadieux	Fernwood	MA	57412		$154.00	$0.00	12
74 Webster	East Cedar	MI	57222		$0.00	$0.00	11
					$0.00	$0.00	

FIGURE 3-27

5 **Close the Client : Table window by clicking its Close button.**

The Microsoft Access dialog box displays (Figure 3-28).

6 **Click the Yes button.**

The change is saved. The next time the datasheet displays, the columns will have the new widths.

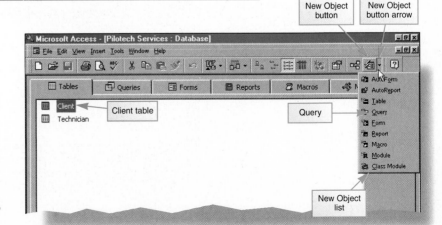

Address	City	State	Zip Code	Client Type	Billed	Paid	Tech Number
216 Rivard	Grattan	MA	58120		$215.50	$155.00	11
722 Fisher	Empire						12
464 Linnell	Marshall						17
737 Allard	Portage						11
247 Fuller	Grattan						12
57 Giddings	Marshall						12
665 Whittier	Frankfort						11
31 Lafayette	Empire						17
752 Cadieux	Fernwood	MA	5 412		$154.00	$0.00	12
74 Webster	East Cedar	MI	57222		$0.00	$0.00	11
*					$0.00	$0.00	

Microsoft Access — Do you want to save changes to the layout of table 'Client'? Yes / No / Cancel

FIGURE 3-28

Other Ways

1. On Format menu click Column Width, click Best Fit

Using an Update Query

The Client Type field is blank on every record. One approach to entering the information for the field would be to step through the entire table, assigning each record its appropriate value. If most of the clients have the same type, a simpler approach is available.

Suppose, for example, that more clients are type REG. Initially, you can set all the values to REG. To accomplish this quickly and easily, you use a special type of query called an **update query**. Later, you can change the type for the nonprofit and educational clients.

The process for creating an update query begins the same as the process for creating the queries in Project 2. After selecting the table for the query, right-click any open area of the upper pane, click Query Type on the shortcut menu, and then click Update Query on the menu of available query types. An extra row, Update To:, displays in the design grid. Use this additional row to indicate the way the data will be updated. If a criterion is entered, then only those records that satisfy the criterion will be updated.

Perform the following steps to change the value in the Client Type field to REG for all the records. Because all records are to be updated, no criteria will be entered.

More About Resizing Columns

After you have changed the size of a field, the forms you have created will not reflect your changes. If you used the Auto-Form command, you can change the field sizes by simply recreating the form. To do so, right-click the form, click Delete, and create the form as you did in Project 1.

 Steps To Use an Update Query to Update All Records

1 **With the Client table selected, click the New Object: AutoForm button arrow on the toolbar.**

The New Object list displays (Figure 3-29).

Microsoft Access - [Pilotech Services : Database] — Tables / Queries / Forms / Reports / Macros — Client, Technician. New Object list: AutoForm, AutoReport, Table, Query, Form, Report, Macro, Module, Class Module

FIGURE 3-29

2 **Click Query.**

The New Query dialog box displays (Figure 3-30). Design View is selected.

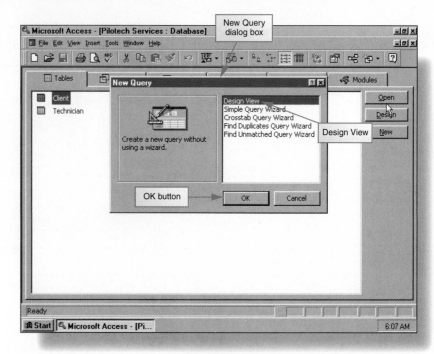

FIGURE 3-30

3 **Click the OK button, and be sure the Query1 : Select Query window is maximized. Resize the upper and lower panes of the window as well as the Client field list so all fields in the Client table field list display (see page A 2.9 in Project 2). Right-click the upper pane and point to Query Type on the shortcut menu.**

The shortcut menu displays (Figure 3-31). The Query Type submenu displays the available query types.

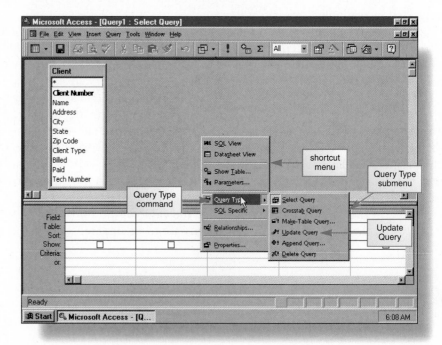

4 **Click Update Query on the submenu, double-click the Client Type field to select the field, click the Update To text box in the first column of the design grid, and type REG as the new value.**

The Client Type field is selected (Figure 3-32). In an Update Query, the Update To row displays in the design grid. The value to which the field is to be changed is entered as REG. Because no criteria are entered, the Client Type value on every row will be changed to REG.

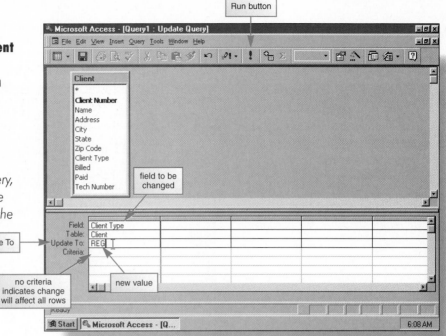

FIGURE 3-32

5 **Click the Run button on the toolbar.**

The Microsoft Access dialog box displays (Figure 3-33). The message indicates that 10 rows will be updated by the query.

6 **Click the Yes button.**

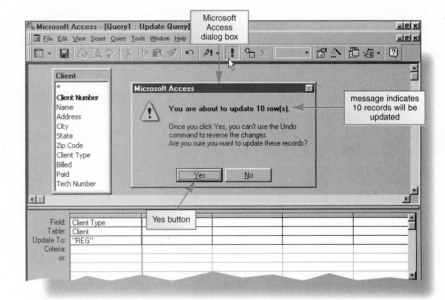

FIGURE 3-33

Using a Delete Query to Delete a Group of Records

In some cases, you may need to delete several records at a time. If, for example, all clients in a particular zip code are to be serviced by another firm, the clients with this zip code can be deleted from the Pilotech Services database. Rather than deleting these clients individually, which could be very cumbersome, you can delete them in one operation by using a **delete query**, which is a query that will delete all the records satisfying the criteria entered in the query.

Perform the steps on the next page to use a delete query to delete all clients whose zip code is 52018.

Other Ways

1. Click Query Type button arrow on toolbar, click Update Query

2. On Query menu click Update Query

Steps **To Use a Delete Query to Delete a Group of Records**

1 Clear the grid by clicking Edit on the menu bar and then clicking Clear Grid. Right-click the upper pane and then point to Query Type on the shortcut menu.

The shortcut menu displays (Figure 3-34). The Query Type submenu displays the available query types.

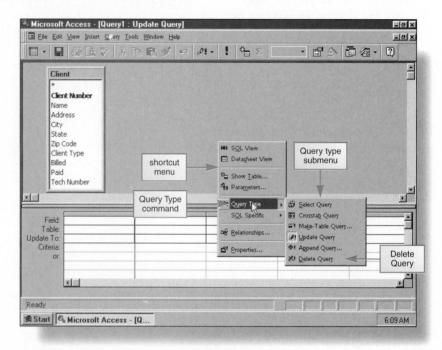

FIGURE 3-34

2 Click Delete Query on the submenu, double-click the Zip Code field to select the field, and click the Criteria box. Type 52018 as the criterion.

The criterion is entered in the Zip Code column (Figure 3-35). In a Delete Query, the Delete row displays in the design grid.

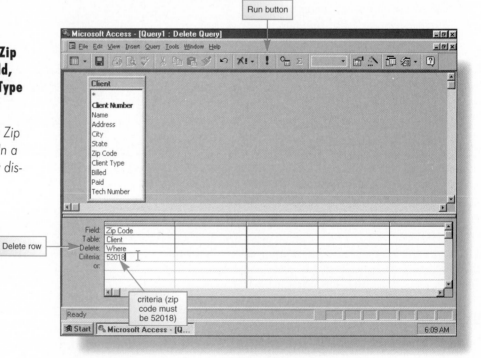

FIGURE 3-35

③ Run the query.

The Microsoft Access dialog box displays (Figure 3-36). The message indicates the query will delete 2 rows (records).

④ Click the Yes button. Close the Query window. Do not save the query.

The two clients with zip code 52018 have been removed from the table.

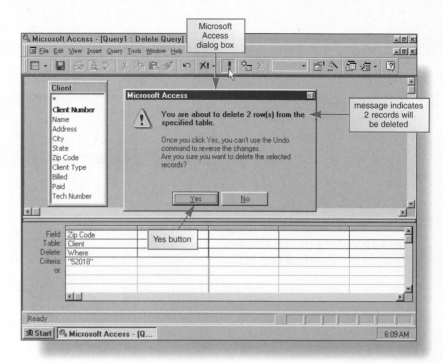

FIGURE 3-36

Creating Validation Rules

Up to this point in this book, you have created, loaded, queried, and updated a database. Nothing done so far, however, ensures that users enter only valid data. This section explains how to create **validation rules**; that is, rules that the data entered by a user must follow. As you will see, Access will prevent users from entering data that does not follow the rules. The steps also specify **validation text**, which is the message that will be displayed if a user violates the validation rule.

Validation rules can indicate a **required field**, a field in which the user actually must enter data. For example, by making the Name field a required field, a user actually must enter a name (that is, the field cannot be blank). Validation rules can make sure a user's entry lies within a certain **range of values**; for example, that the values in the Billed field are between $0.00 and $800.00. They can specify a **default value**; that is, a value that Access will display on the screen in a particular field before the user begins adding a record. To make data entry of client numbers more convenient, you also can have lowercase letters converted automatically to uppercase letters. Finally, validation rules can specify a collection of acceptable values; for example, that the only legitimate entries for the Client Type field are REG, NPR, and EDU.

Specifying a Required Field

To specify that a field is to be required, change the value in the Required text box from No to Yes. The steps on the next page specify that the Name field is to be a required field.

OtherWays

1. Click Query Type button arrow on toolbar, click Delete Query
2. On Query menu click Delete Query

More *About* **Update Queries**

Any full-featured database management system will offer some mechanism for updating multiple records at a time, that is, for making the same change to all the records that satisfy some criterion. Some systems, including Access, accomplish this through the query tool by providing a special type of query for this purpose.

More *About* **Delete Queries**

Any full-featured database management system will offer some mechanism for deleting multiple records at a time, that is, for deleting all the records that satisfy some criterion. Some systems, including Access, accomplish this through the query tool by providing a special type of query for this purpose.

Steps   To Specify a Required Field

1 **With the Database window on the screen and the Tables tab selected, right-click Client.**

The shortcut menu displays.

2 **Click Design on the shortcut menu, and then select the Name field by clicking its row selector. Point to the Required text box.**

The Client : Table window displays (Figure 3-37). The Name field is selected.

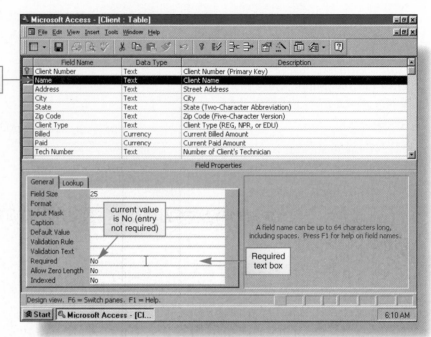

FIGURE 3-37

3 **Click the Required text box in the Field Properties area, and then click the down arrow that displays. Click Yes in the list.**

The value in the Required text box changes to Yes (Figure 3-38). It now is required that the user enter data into the Name field when adding a record.

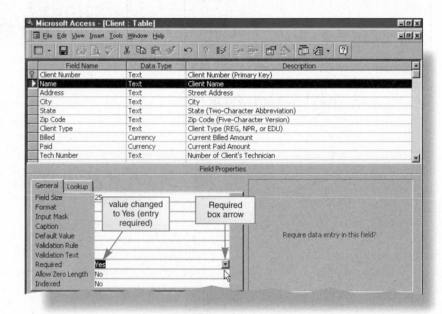

FIGURE 3-38

Specifying a Range

The following step specifies that entries in the Billed field must be between $0.00 and $800.00. To indicate this range, you will enter a condition that specifies that the billed amount must be both $>= 0$ (greater than or equal to zero) and $<= 800$ (less than or equal to 800).

Steps To Specify a Range

① Select the Billed field by clicking its row selector. Click the Validation Rule text box to produce an insertion point, and then type >=0 and <=800 as the rule. Click the Validation Text text box to produce an insertion point, and then type Must be between $0.00 and $800.00 as the text. You must type all the text, including the dollar signs in this text box.

The validation rule and text are entered (Figure 3-39).

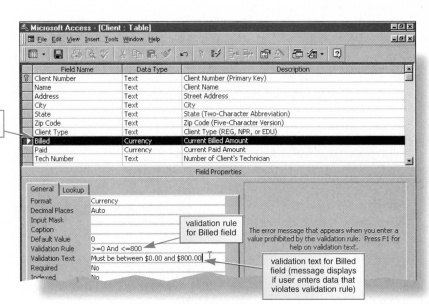

FIGURE 3-39

Users now will be prohibited from entering a billed amount that is either less than $0.00 or greater than $800.00 when they add records or change the value in the Billed field.

Specifying a Default Value

To specify a default value, enter the value in the Default Value text box. The following step specifies REG as the default value for the Client Type field. This simply means that if users do not enter a client type, the type will be REG.

Steps To Specify a Default Value

① Select the Client Type field. Click the Default Value text box and then type =REG as the value.

The Client Type field is selected. The default value is entered in the Default Value text box (Figure 3-40).

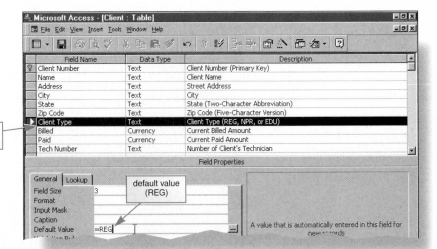

FIGURE 3-40

From this point on, if users do not make an entry in the Client Type field when adding records, Access will set the value to REG.

Specifying a Collection of Legal Values

The only **legal values** for the Client Type field are REG, NPR, and EDU. An appropriate validation rule for this field can direct Access to reject any entry other than these three possibilities. Perform the following step to specify the legal values for the Client Type field.

Steps To Specify a Collection of Legal Values

1 **Make sure the Client Type field is selected. Click the Validation Rule text box and then type** =REG or =NPR or =EDU **as the validation rule. Click the Validation Text text box and then type** Must be REG, NPR, or EDU **as the validation text.**

The Client Type field is selected. The validation rule and text have been entered (Figure 3-41). In the Validation Rule text box, Access automatically inserted quotation marks around the REG, NPR, and EDU values and changed the lowercase letter, o, to uppercase in the word, or.

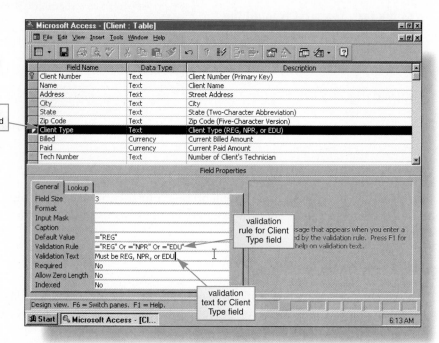

FIGURE 3-41

Users now will be allowed to enter only REG, NPR, or EDU in the Client Type field when they add records or make changes to this field.

Using a Format

To affect the way data is entered in a field, you can use a **format**. To use a format, you enter a special symbol, called a **format symbol**, in the field's Format text box. The following step specifies a format for the Client Number field in the Client table. The format symbol used in the example is >, which causes Access to convert lowercase letters automatically to uppercase. The format symbol < would cause Access to convert uppercase letters automatically to lowercase.

Steps To Specify a Format

1 **Select the Client Number field. Click the Format text box and then type > (Figure 3-42).**

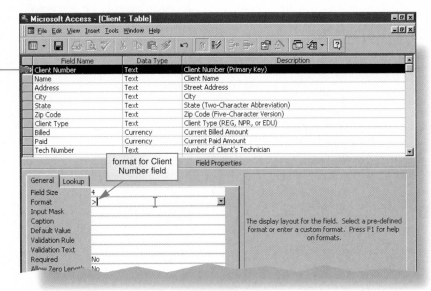

FIGURE 3-42

From this point on, any lowercase letters will be converted to uppercase automatically when users add records or change the value in the Client Number field.

Saving Rules, Values, and Formats

To save the validation rules, default values, and formats, perform the following steps.

Steps To Save the Validation Rules, Default Values, and Formats

1 **Click the Close button for the Client : Table window to close the window.**

The Microsoft Access dialog box displays, asking if you want to save your changes (Figure 3-43).

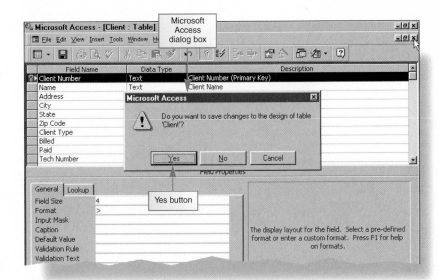

FIGURE 3-43

2 Click the Yes button to save the changes.

The Microsoft Access dialog box displays (Figure 3-44). This message asks if you want the new rules applied to current records. If this were a database used to run a business or to solve some other critical need, you would click Yes. You would want to be sure that the data already in the database does not violate the rules.

3 Click the No button.

The rules are not violated by the data in the Client table. The changes are made.

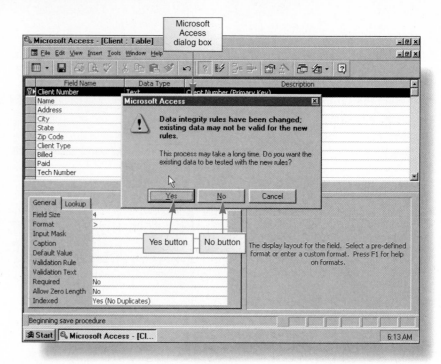

FIGURE 3-44

Updating a Table that Contains Validation Rules

When updating a table that contains validation rules, Access provides assistance in making sure the data entered is valid. It helps in making sure that data is formatted correctly. Access also will not accept invalid data. Entering a number that is out of the required range, for example, or entering a value that is not one of the possible choices, will produce an error message in the form of a dialog box. The database will not be updated until the error is corrected.

If the Client number entered contains lowercase letters, such as da24 (Figure 3-45), Access will convert the data automatically to DA24 (Figure 3-46).

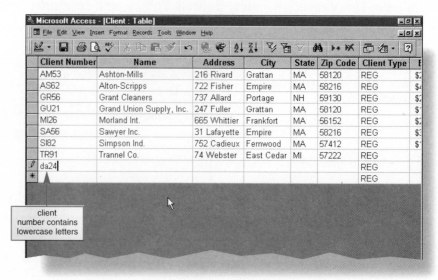

FIGURE 3-45

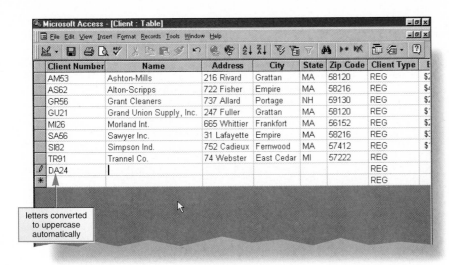

FIGURE 3-46

Instead of the Client Type field initially being blank, it now contains the value REG, because REG is the default value. Thus, for any client whose type is REG, it is not necessary to enter the value. By pressing the TAB key, the value REG is accepted.

If the client type is not valid, such as abc, Access will display the text message you specified (Figure 3-47) and not allow the data to enter the database.

If the Billed value is not valid, such as 900, Access also displays the appropriate message (Figure 3-48) and refuses to accept the data.

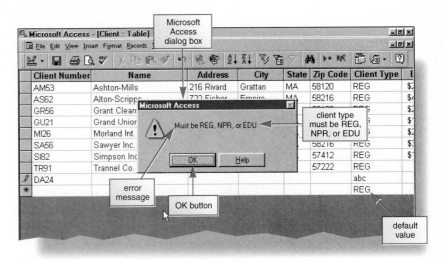

FIGURE 3-47

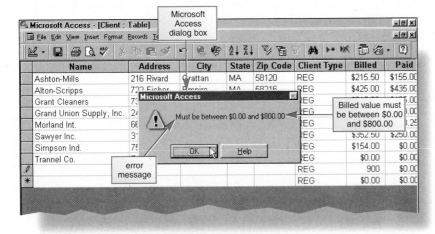

FIGURE 3-48

If a required field contains no data, Access indicates this by displaying an error message as soon as you attempt to leave the record (Figure 3-49 on the next page). The field must contain a valid entry before Access will move to a different record.

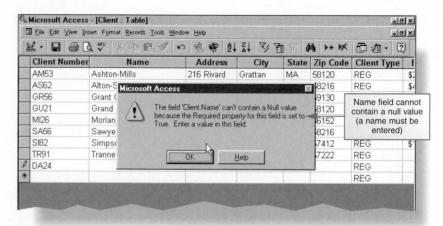

FIGURE 3-49

Take care when creating validation rules as you may come to an impasse where you can neither leave the field nor close the table because you have entered data into a field that violates the validation rule. It may be that you cannot remember the validation rule you created or it was created incorrectly.

First, try to type an acceptable entry. If this does not work, repeatedly press the BACKSPACE key to erase the contents of the field and then try to leave the field. If you are unsuccessful using this procedure, press the ESC key until the record is removed from the screen. The record will not be added to the database.

Should the need arise to take this drastic action, you probably have a faulty validation rule. Use the techniques of the previous sections to correct the existing validation rules for the field.

Making Individual Changes to a Field

Earlier, you changed all the entries in the Client Type field to REG. You now have created a rule that will ensure that only legitimate values (REG, NPR, or EDU) can be entered in the field. To make a change, click the field to be changed to produce an insertion point, use the BACKSPACE or DELETE key to delete the current entry, and then type the new entry.

Complete the following steps to change the Client Type value on the second record to NPR and on the fifth record to EDU.

 Steps **To Make Individual Changes**

1 **Make sure the Client table displays in Datasheet view (Figure 3-50).**

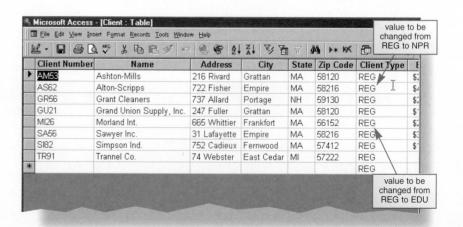

FIGURE 3-50

2 Click to the right of the REG entry in the Client Type field on the second record to produce an insertion point. Press the **BACKSPACE** key three times to delete REG and then type NPR **as the new value. In a similar fashion, change the REG on the fifth record to EDU (Figure 3-51).**

3 Close the Client : Table window by clicking its Close button.

The Client Type field changes now are complete.

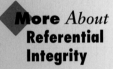

Client Number	Name	Address	City	State	Zip Code	Client Type	
AM53	Ashton-Mills	216 Rivard	Grattan	MA	58120	REG	$
AS62	Alton-Scripps	722 Fisher	Empire	MA	58216	NPR	$
GR56	Grant Cleaners	737 Allard	Portage	NH	59130	REG	$
GU21	Grand Union Supply, Inc.	247 Fuller	Grattan	MA	58120	REG	$
MI26	Morland Int.	665 Whittier	Frankfort	MA	56152	EDU	$
SA56	Sawyer Inc.	31 Lafayette	Empire	MA	58216	REG	$
SI82	Simpson Ind.	752 Cadieux	Fernwood	MA	57412	REG	$
TR91	Trannel Co.	74 Webster	East Cedar	MI	57222	REG	
*						REG	

Record: 5 of 8

Client Type (REG, NPR, or EDU)

FIGURE 3-51

Specifying Referential Integrity

The property that ensures that the value in a foreign key must match that of another table's primary key is called **referential integrity**. A **foreign key** is a field in one table whose values are required to match the *primary key* of another table. In the Client table, the Tech Number field is a foreign key that must match the primary key of the Technician table; that is, the technician number for any client must be a technician currently in the Technician table. A client whose technician number is 02, for example, should not be stored if technician 02 does not exist.

In Access, to specify referential integrity, you must define a relationship between the tables by using the Relationships command. Access then prohibits any updates to the database that would violate the referential integrity. Access will not allow you to store a client with a technician number that does not match a technician currently in the Technician table. Access also will prevent you from deleting a technician who currently has clients. Technician 12, for example, currently has several clients in the Client table. If you deleted technician 12, these clients' technician numbers would no longer match anyone in the Technician table.

The type of relationship between two tables specified by the Relationships command is referred to as a **one-to-many relationship**. This means that one record in the first table is related to (matches) many records in the second table, but each record in the second table is related to only one record in the first. In the sample database, for example, a one-to-many relationship exists between the Technician table and the Client table. *One* technician is associated with *many* clients, but each client is associated with only a single technician. In general, the table containing the foreign key will be the *many* part of the relationship.

> **More About Referential Integrity**
>
> Referential integrity is an essential property for databases, but providing support for it proved to be one of the more difficult tasks facing the developers of relational database management systems. Although the problem was worked on throughout the 1970s, it was not until the late 1980s that relational systems were able to satisfactorily enforce referential integrity.

The following steps use the Relationships command to specify referential integrity by specifying a relationship between the Technician and Client tables.

Steps **To Specify Referential Integrity**

1 Close any open datasheet on the screen by clicking its Close button. Then, point to the Relationships button on the toolbar (Figure 3-52).

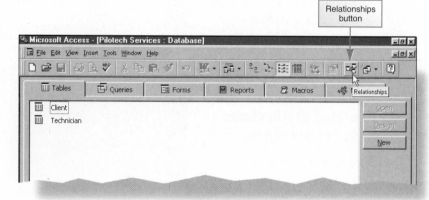

FIGURE 3-52

2 Click the Relationships button.

The Show Table dialog box displays (Figure 3-53).

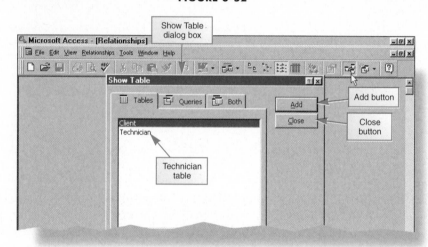

FIGURE 3-53

3 Click the Technician table, click the Add button, click the Client table, click the Add button again, and then click the Close button. Resize the field list boxes that display so all fields are visible. Point to the Tech Number field in the field list for the Technician table.

Field list boxes for the Technician and Client tables display (Figure 3-54). The boxes have been resized so all fields are visible.

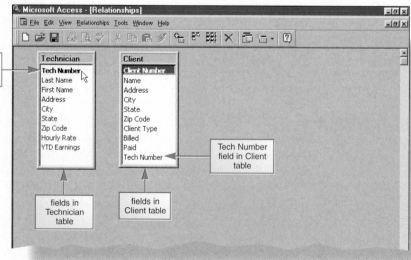

FIGURE 3-54

4 Drag the Tech Number field in the Technician table field list box to the Tech Number field in the Client table field list box.

The Relationships dialog box displays (Figure 3-55). The correct fields (the Tech Number fields) have been identified as the matching fields.

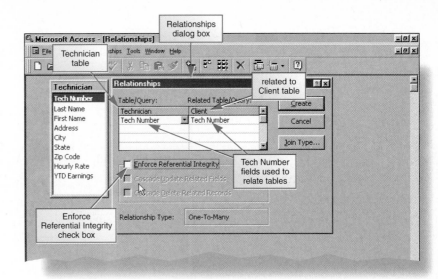

FIGURE 3-55

5 Click Enforce Referential Integrity.

Enforce Referential Integrity is selected (Figure 3-56). With Enforce Referential Integrity selected, Access will reject any update that would violate referential integrity.

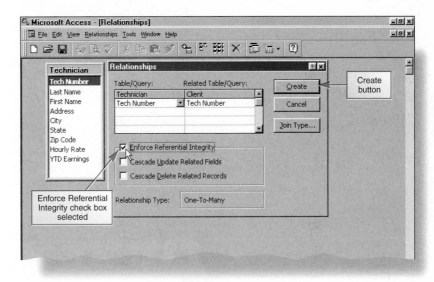

FIGURE 3-56

6 Click the Create button.

*Access creates the relationship and displays it visually with the **relationship line** joining the two Tech Number fields (Figure 3-57). The number 1 at the top of the relationship line close to the Tech Number field in the Technician table indicates that the Technician table is the one part of the relationship. The ∞ symbol at the other end of the relationship line indicates that the Client table is the many part of the relationship.*

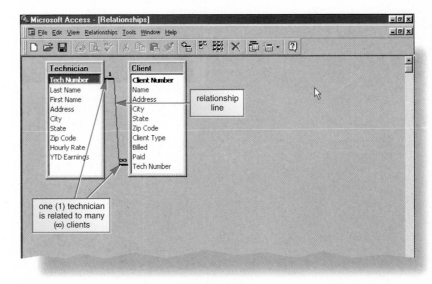

FIGURE 3-57

7 Close the Relationships window by clicking its Close button.

The Microsoft Access dialog box displays (Figure 3-58).

8 Click the Yes button to save your work.

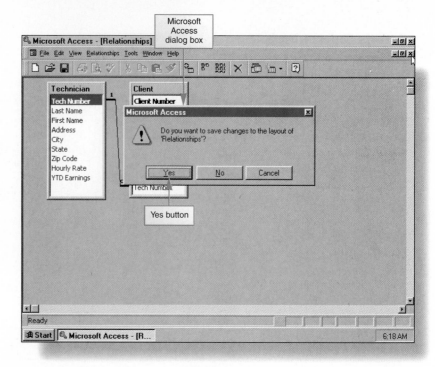

FIGURE 3-58

Access now will reject any number in the Tech Number field in the Client table that does not match a technician number in the Technician table. Trying to add a client whose Tech Number field does not match would result in the error message shown in Figure 3-59.

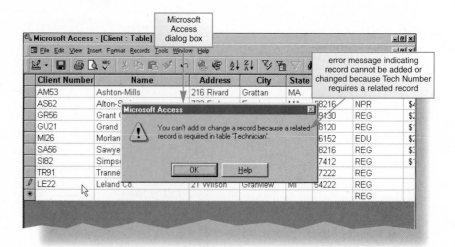

FIGURE 3-59

A deletion of a technician for whom related clients exist also would be rejected. Attempting to delete technician 11 from the Technician table, for example, would result in the message shown in Figure 3-60.

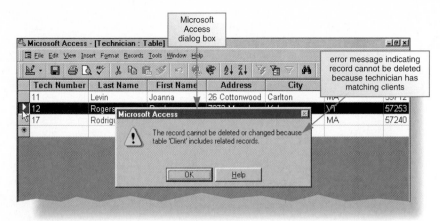

FIGURE 3-60

Ordering Records

Recall from previous discussions that Access sequences the records by client number whenever listing them because the Client Number field is the primary key. To change the order in which records appear, use the Sort Ascending or Sort Descending buttons on the toolbar. Either button reorders the records based on the field in which the insertion point is located.

Perform the following steps to order the records by client name using the Sort Ascending button.

Steps **To Use the Sort Ascending Button to Order Records**

1 **Open the Client table in Datasheet view, and then click the Name field on the first record (any other record would do as well). Point to the Sort Ascending button on the toolbar (Figure 3-61).**

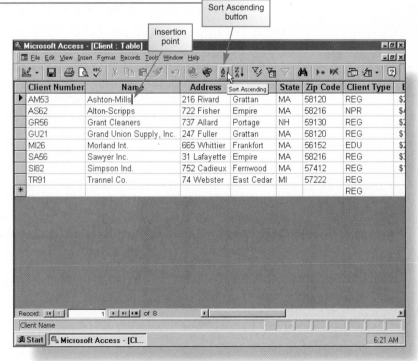

FIGURE 3-61

2 **Click the Sort Ascending button.**

The rows now are ordered by name (Figure 3-62).

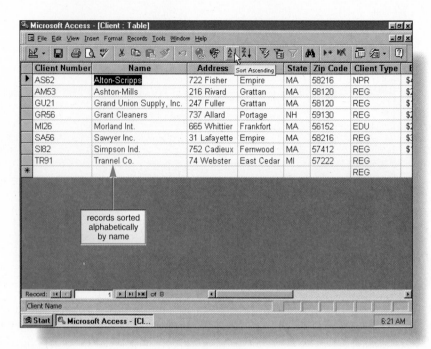

FIGURE 3-62

If you wanted to sort the data in reverse order, you would click the Sort Descending button instead of the Sort Ascending button.

Ordering Records on Multiple Fields

Just as you are able to sort the answer to a query on multiple fields, you also can sort the data that displays in a datasheet on multiple fields. To do so, the major key and minor key must be next to each other in the datasheet with the major key on the left. (If this is not the case, you can drag the columns into the correct position. Instead of dragging, however, usually it will be easier to use a query that has the data sorted in the desired order.)

Given that the major and minor keys are in the correct position, select both fields and then click the Sort Ascending button on the toolbar. To select the fields, click the **field selector** for the first field (the major key). Next, hold down the SHIFT key and then click the field selector for the second field (the minor key). A **field selector** is the small bar at the top of the column that you click to select an entire field in a datasheet.

Order records on the combination of the Client Type and Billed fields using the Sort Ascending button by completing the following steps.

Steps To Use the Sort Ascending Button to Order Records on Multiple Fields

1 **Scroll the table to bring both the Client Type and Billed fields into view. Click the field selector at the top of the Client Type column to select the entire column. Hold down the SHIFT key and then click the field selector for the Billed column.**

The Client Type and Billed fields are selected (Figure 3-63).

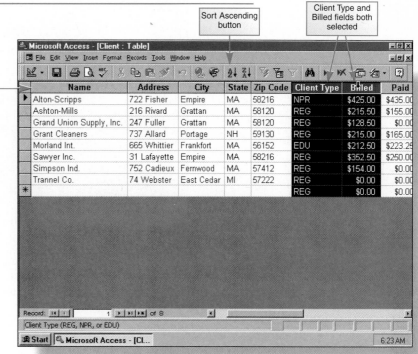

FIGURE 3-63

2 **Click the Sort Ascending button on the toolbar.**

The rows are ordered by client type (Figure 3-64). Within each group of clients of the same type, the rows are ordered by billed.

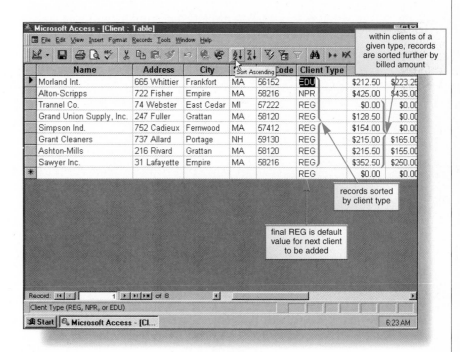

FIGURE 3-64

3 **Close the Client : Table window by clicking its Close button.**

The Microsoft Access dialog box displays (Figure 3-65). The message asks if you want to save the changes to the design; that is, do you want to save the order in which the records currently display?

4 **Click the No button to abandon changes.**

The next time the table is open, the records will display in their original order.

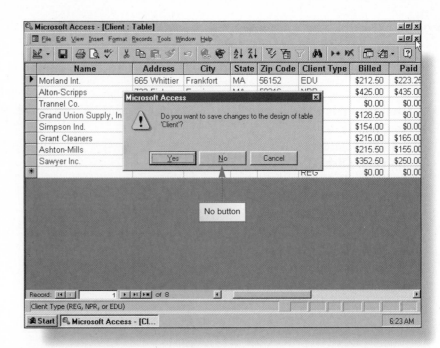

FIGURE 3-65

Creating and Using Indexes

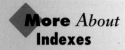

More *About*
Indexes

The most common structure for high-performance indexes is called a B-tree. It is a highly efficient structure that supports very rapid access to records in the database as well as a rapid alternative to sorting records. Virtually all systems use some version of the B-tree structure.

You already are familiar with the concept of an index. The index in the back of a book contains important words or phrases together with a list of pages on which the given words or phrases can be found. An **index** for a table is similar. Figure 3-66, for example, shows the Client table along with an index built on names. In this case, the items of interest are names rather than keywords or phrases as is the case in the back of this book. The field or fields on which the index is built is called the **index key**. Thus, in Figure 3-66, the Name field is the index key.

Index on Name		Client table							
NAME	RECORD NUMBER	RECORD NUMBER	CLIENT NUMBER	NAME	ADDRESS	CITY	STATE	ZIP CODE	...
Alton-Scripps	2	1	AM53	Ashton-Mills	216 Rivard	Grattan	MA	58120	...
Ashton-Mills	1	2	AS62	Alton-Scripps	722 Fisher	Empire	MA	58216	...
Grand Union Supply, Inc.	4	3	GR56	Grant Cleaners	737 Allard	Portage	NH	59130	...
		4	GU21	Grand Union Supply, Inc.	247 Fuller	Grattan	MA	58120	...
Grant Cleaners	3								
Morland Int.	5	5	MI26	Morland Int.	665 Whittier	Frankfort	MA	56152	...
Sawyer Inc.	6	6	SA56	Sawyer Inc.	31 Lafayette	Empire	MA	58216	...
Simpson Ind.	7	7	SI82	Simpson Ind.	752 Cadieux	Fernwood	MA	57412	...
Trannel Co.	8	8	TR91	Trannel Co.	74 Webster	East Cedar	MI	57222	...

FIGURE 3-66

Each name occurs in the index along with the number of the record on which the corresponding client is located. Further, the names appear in the index in alphabetical order. If Access were to use this index to find the record on which the name is Grant Cleaners, for example, it could scan rapidly the names in the index to find Grant Cleaners. Once it did, it would determine the corresponding record number (3) and then go immediately to record 3 in the Client table, thus finding this client more quickly than if it had to look through the entire Client table one record at a time. Indexes make the process of retrieving records very fast and efficient.

Because no two clients happen to have the same name, the Record Number column contains only single values. This may not always be the case. Consider the index on the Zip Code field shown in Figure 3-67 on the next page. In this index, the Record Number column contains several values, namely all the records on which the corresponding zip code appears. The first row, for example, indicates that zip code 56152 is found only on record 5; whereas, the fourth row indicates that zip code 58120 is found on records 1 and 4. If Access were to use this index to find all clients in zip code 58120, it could scan rapidly the zip codes in the index to find 58120. Once it did, it would determine the corresponding record numbers (1 and 4) and then go immediately to these records. It would not have to examine any other records in the Client table.

FIGURE 3-67

Another benefit of indexes is that they provide an efficient way to order records. That is, if the records are to appear in a certain order, Access can use an index instead of physically having to rearrange the records in the database file. Physically rearranging the records in a different order, which is called **sorting**, can be a very time-consuming process.

To see how indexes can be used for alphabetizing records, look at the record numbers in the index (Figure 3-66 on the previous page) and suppose you used these to list all clients. That is, simply follow down the Record Number column, listing the corresponding clients. In this example, first you would list the client on record 2 (Alton-Scripps), then the client on record 1 (Ashton-Mills), then the client on record 4 (Grand Union Supply, Inc.), and so on. The clients would be listed alphabetically by name without actually sorting the table.

To gain the benefits from an index, you first must create one. Access automatically creates an index on the primary key as well as some other special fields. If, as is the case with both the Client and Technician tables, a table contains a field called Zip Code, for example, Access will create an index for it automatically. You must create any other indexes you feel you need, indicating the field or fields on which the index is to be built.

Although the index key usually will be a single field, it can be a combination of fields. For example, you might want to sort records by Billed within Tech Number. In other words, the records are ordered by a combination of fields: Tech Number and Billed. An index can be used for this purpose by using a combination of fields for the index key. In this case, you must assign a name to the index. It is a good idea to assign a name that represents the combination of fields. For example, an index whose key is the combination of Tech Number and Billed, might be called Techbill.

How Does Access Use an Index?

Access creates an index whenever you request that it do so. It takes care of all the work in setting up and maintaining the index. In addition, it will use the index automatically.

If you request that data be sorted in a particular order and Access determines that an index is available that it can use to make the process efficient, it will do so. If no index is available, it still will sort the data in the order you requested; it will just take longer.

Similarly, if you request that Access locate a particular record that has a certain value in a particular field, Access will use an index if an appropriate one exists. If not, it will have to examine each record until it finds the one you want.

In both cases, the added efficiency provided by an index will not be readily apparent in tables that have only a few records. As you add more records to your tables, however, the difference can be dramatic. Even with only fifty to one hundred records, you will notice a difference. You can imagine how dramatic the difference would be in a table with fifty thousand records.

When Should You Create an Index?

An index improves efficiency for sorting and finding records. On the other hand, indexes occupy space on your disk. They also require Access to do extra work. Access must maintain all the indexes that have been created up to date. Thus, both advantages and disadvantages exist to using indexes. Consequently, the decision as to which indexes to create is an important one. The following guidelines should help you in this process.

Create an index on a field (or combination of fields) if one or more of the following conditions are present:

1. The field is the primary key of the table (Access will create this index automatically)
2. The field is the foreign key in a relationship you have created (Access also will create this index automatically when you specify the relationship)
3. You frequently will need your data to be sorted on the field
4. You frequently will need to locate a record based on a value in this field

Because Access handles 1 and 2 automatically, you need only to concern yourself about 3 and 4. If you think you will need to see client data arranged in order of billed amounts, for example, you should create an index on the Billed field. If you think you will need to see the data arranged by billed within technician number, you should create an index on the combination of the Tech Number field and the Billed field. Similarly, if you think you will need to find a client given the client's name, you should create an index on the Name field.

Creating Single-Field Indexes

A **single-field index** is an index whose key is a single field. In this case, the index key is to be the Name field. In creating an index, you need to indicate whether to allow duplicates in the index key; that is, two records that have the same value. For example, in the index for the Name field, if duplicates are not allowed, Access would not allow the addition of a client whose name is the same as the name of a client already in the database. In the index for the Name field, duplicates will be allowed. Perform the following steps to create a single-field index.

 Steps To Create a Single-Field Index

1 **Right-click Client.**

The shortcut menu displays.

2 **Click Design on the shortcut menu, and then, if necessary, maximize the Client : Table window. Click the row selector to select the Name field. Point to the Indexed text box.**

A maximized Client : Table window displays (Figure 3-68). The Name field is selected.

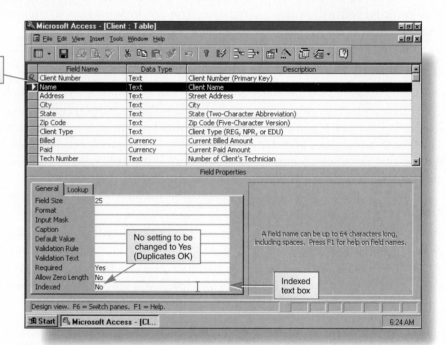

FIGURE 3-68

3 Click the Indexed text box in the Field Properties pane. Click the down arrow that displays.

The Indexed list displays (Figure 3-69). The settings are No (no index), Yes (Duplicates OK) (create an index and allow duplicates), and Yes (No Duplicates) (create an index but reject (do not allow) duplicates).

4 Click Yes (Duplicates OK).

The index on the Name field now will be created and is ready for use as soon as you save your work.

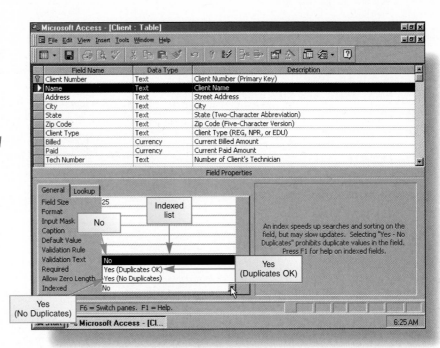

FIGURE 3-69

Creating Multiple-Field Indexes

Creating **multiple-field indexes**, that is, indexes whose key is a combination of fields, involves a different process from creating single-field indexes. To create multiple-field indexes, you will use the **Indexes button** on the toolbar, enter a name for the index, and then enter the combination of fields that make up the index key. The following steps create a multiple-field index with the name Techbill. The key will be the combination of the Tech Number field and the Billed field.

Steps **To Create a Multiple-Field Index**

1 Point to the Indexes button on the toolbar (Figure 3-70).

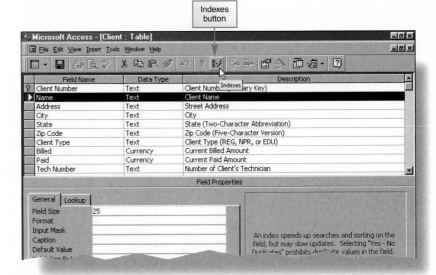

FIGURE 3-70

2 **Click the Indexes button.
Click the blank row (the row
following Name) in the Index
Name column. Type** Techbill **as
the index name, and then press
the TAB key. Point to the down
arrow.**

*The Indexes: Client dialog box dis-
plays. It shows the indexes that
already have been created and
allows you to create additional
indexes (Figure 3-71). The index
name has been entered as Techbill.
An insertion point displays in the
Field Name column. The index on
Client Number is the primary index
and was created automatically by
Access. The index on Name is the
one just created. Access created
other indexes (Paid and Zip Code)
automatically. In this dialog box,
you can create additional indexes.*

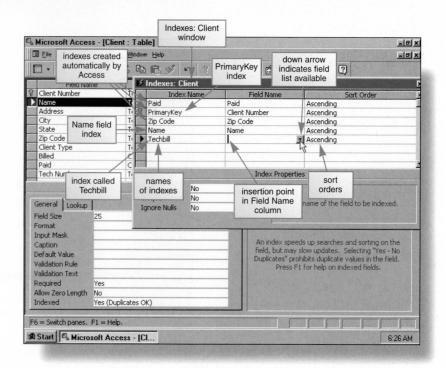

FIGURE 3-71

3 **Click the down arrow in the Field
Name column to produce a list
box of fields in the Client table,
scroll down the list, and select
Tech Number. Press the TAB key
three times to move to the Field
Name column on the following
row. Select the Billed field in the
same manner as the Tech
Number field.**

*Tech Number and Billed are
selected as the two fields for the
Techbill index (Figure 3-72). The
absence of an index name on the
row containing the Billed field indicates that it is part of the previous
index, Techbill.*

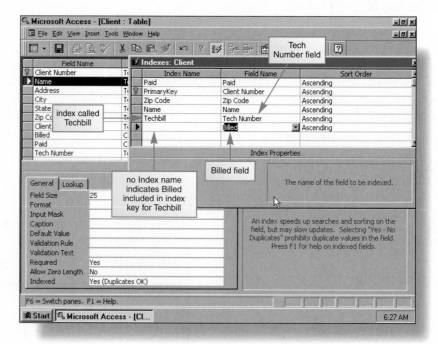

FIGURE 3-72

4 **Close the Indexes: Client dialog
box by clicking its Close button,
and then close the Client : Table
window by clicking its Close button.
When the Microsoft Access dialog
box displays, click the Yes button to save your changes.**

The indexes are created and the Database window displays.

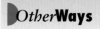

Other Ways

1. On View menu click Indexes

Closing the Database

The following step closes the database by closing its Database window.

TO CLOSE A DATABASE

Step 1: Click the Close button for the Pilotech Services : Database window.

The database closes.

The indexes now have been created. Access will use them automatically whenever possible to improve efficiency of ordering or finding records. Access also will maintain them automatically. That is, whenever the data in the Client table is changed, Access will make appropriate changes in the indexes automatically.

Project Summary

Project 3 covered the issues involved in maintaining a database. You used Form view to add a record to the Pilotech Services database and searched for a record satisfying a criterion. You changed and deleted records. You changed the structure of the Client table in the Pilotech Services database, created validation rules, and specified referential integrity between the Client and the Technician tables by creating relationships. You made mass changes to the Client table. Finally, you created indexes to improve performance.

What You Should Know

Having completed this project, you now should be able to perform the following tasks:

- Add a Field to a Table *(A 3.15)*
- Change the Size of a Field *(A 3.13)*
- Close a Database *(A 3.45)*
- Create a Multiple-Field Index *(A 3.43)*
- Create a Single-Field Index *(A 3.42)*
- Delete a Record *(A 3.12)*
- Make Individual Changes *(A 3.30)*
- Open a Database *(A 3.6)*
- Resize a Column *(A 3.17)*
- Save the Validation Rules, Default Values, and Formats *(A 3.27)*
- Search for a Record *(A 3.9)*
- Specify a Collection of Legal Values *(A 3.26)*
- Specify a Default Value *(A 3.25)*
- Specify a Format *(A 3.27)*
- Specify a Range *(A 3.25)*
- Specify a Required Field *(A 3.24)*
- Specify Referential Integrity *(A 3.32)*
- Switch from Form View to Datasheet View *(A 3.10)*
- Update the Contents of a Field *(A 3.10, A 3.16)*
- Use a Delete Query to Delete a Group of Records *(A 3.22)*
- Use a Form to Add Records *(A 3.7)*
- Use an Update Query to Update All Records *(A 3.19)*
- Use the Sort Ascending Button to Order Records *(A 3.35)*
- Use the Sort Ascending Button to Order Records on Multiple Fields *(A 3.37)*

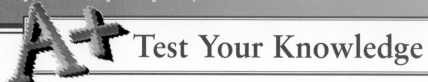

Test Your Knowledge

1 True/False

Instructions: Circle T if the statement is true or F if the statement is false.

T F 1. Access sorts records automatically by the primary index.

T F 2. Indexes provide an efficient alternative to sorting.

T F 3. To force all letters in a field to display as uppercase, use the ! symbol in the Format text box.

T F 4. You can add and change records using Datasheet view, but you can only delete records using Form view.

T F 5. To change the order in which records appear in a table, click the Order Records Ascending or Order Records Descending button on the toolbar.

T F 6. To delete a record from a table, click the record selector for the record, and then press the DELETE key.

T F 7. To delete a group of records that satisfy a criteria, use a query.

T F 8. A secondary key is a field in one table whose values are required to match a primary key of another table.

T F 9. The property that the value in a foreign key must match that of another table's primary key is called referential integrity.

T F 10. To specify referential integrity, click the Relationships button on the toolbar.

2 Multiple Choice

Instructions: Circle the correct response.

1. Indexes _____.
    a. allow rapid retrieval of tables
    b. allow rapid retrieval of records
    c. provide an efficient alternative to sorting
    d. both b and c

2. To create a multiple-field index, click the _____ button on the toolbar in the Table Design window.
    a. Secondary Index
    b. Create Secondary Indexes
    c. Indexes
    d. Create Indexes

3. _____ rules are rules that the data entered by a user must follow.
    a. Data
    b. Validation
    c. Integrity
    d. Edit

 Test Your Knowledge

4. To search for a specific record in a table, select the field to search and then click the _____ button on the toolbar.
   a. Search
   b. Locate
   c. Find
   d. Query

5. To force all letters in a field to display as uppercase, use the _____ symbol in the Format text box.
   a. ?
   b. >
   c. !
   d. &

6. A(n) _____ key is a field in one table whose values are required to match a primary key of another table.
   a. secondary
   b. auxiliary
   c. foreign
   d. matching

7. The property that the value in a foreign key must match that of another table's primary key is called _____ integrity.
   a. entity
   b. interrelation
   c. relationship
   d. referential

8. To delete a record from a table, click the record selector for the record, and then press the _____ key(s).
   a. CTRL+DELETE
   b. DELETE
   c. CTRL+D
   d. CTRL+U

9. To specify referential integrity, click the _____ button on the toolbar.
   a. Referential Integrity
   b. Relationships
   c. Integrity
   d. Primary Key

10. To add a field to a table structure, select the field below where you would like the new field inserted and then press the _____ key(s).
    a. CTRL+N
    b. CTRL+I
    c. ALT+INSERT
    d. INSERT

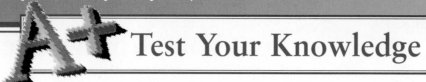

3 Adding, Changing, and Deleting Records

Instructions: Figure 3-73 shows the first record in the Customer table in Form view. Use this figure to help explain how to perform the following tasks in Form view. Write your answers on your own paper.

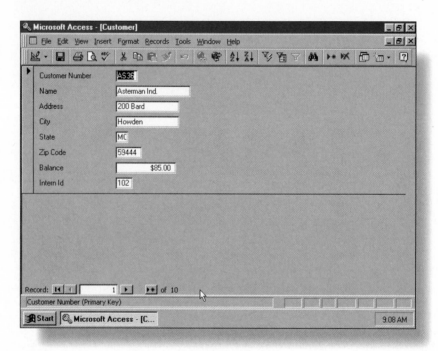

FIGURE 3-73

1. Change the Address from 200 Bard to 200 Bardsen.
2. Add a new record to the Customer table.
3. Locate the record that contains the value ME71 in the Customer Number field.
4. Switch to Datasheet view.
5. In Datasheet view, delete the record where the Customer Number is ME71.

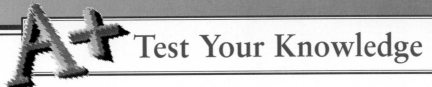

4 Understanding Validation Rules and Indexes

Instructions: Figure 3-74 shows the Intern table in Design view. Use this figure to help explain how to create the following validation rules and indexes. For each question, assume that the proper field already has been selected. Write your answers on your own paper.

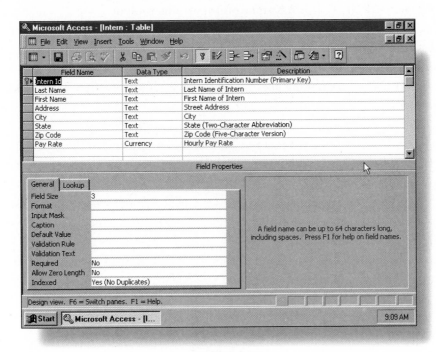

FIGURE 3-74

1. Make the Last Name field a required field.
2. Specify a default value of $7.25 for the Pay Rate field.
3. Specify that any value entered in the Pay Rate field must be greater than or equal to $7.25 and less than or equal to $10.00.
4. Create an index on the Last Name field that allows duplicates.

Use Help

1 Reviewing Project Activities

Instructions: Perform the following tasks using a computer.

1. Start Access.

2. If the Office Assistant is on your screen, then click it to display its balloon. If the Office Assistant is not on your screen, click the Office Assistant button on the toolbar.

3. Type find records in the What would you like to do? text box. Click the Search button. Click Find data. Read the Help information and then click The Find dialog box link under Which method do you want to use to find data?

4. Read the Help information on finding specific occurrences of a value in a field. Next, right-click within the box, and then click Print Topic. Hand in the printout to your instructor. Click the Help Topics button to return to the Help Topics: Microsoft Access 97 dialog box.

5. Click the Index tab. Type sort in the top text box labeled 1 and then double-click tables under sorting data in the list box labeled 2. Double-click Ways to work with data in a table's datasheet in the Topics Found dialog box. Click each of the links and read the Help information. When you are finished, click the Help Topics button to return to the Help Topics: Microsoft Access 97 dialog box.

6. Click the Find tab. Type validation in the top text box labeled 1. Click Validation in the list box labeled 2. Double-click Define validation rules to control what values can be entered into a field in the bottom box labeled 3. When the Help information displays, read it, ready the printer, right-click, and click Print Topic. Hand in the printout to your instructor. Click the Close button in the Microsoft Access 97 Help window.

7. Click the Office Assistant to display its balloon. Type indexes in the What would you like to do? text box. Click the Search button. Click Create an index to find and sort records faster. Read and print the Help information. Hand in the printout to your instructor.

Use Help

2 Expanding the Basics

Instructions: Use Access Help to learn about the topics listed below. If you are unable to print the Help information, then answer the question on your own paper.

1. Using the Creating, Importing, and Linking Tables book on the Contents sheet in the Help Topics: Microsoft Access 97 dialog box, answer the following questions:
   a. How do you delete an index?
   b. You cannot create indexes on fields of certain data types. What are these data types?
   c. What is the maximum number of fields in a multiple-field index?
   d. How can you create a primary key that includes more than one field?
2. Using the word, update, and the Index sheet in the Help Topics: Microsoft Access 97 dialog box, display and print information on update queries. Then, answer the following questions:
   a. How can you see a list of records that will be updated?
   b. How can you stop a query after you start it?
3. Use the Find sheet in the Help Topics: Microsoft Access 97 dialog box to display and then print information about replacing specific occurrences of a value in a field. Then answer the following questions:
   a. What are the advantages of using the Replace command instead of an update query?
   b. What is a null value?
4. Use the Office Assistant to display and print information on defining a custom data display format for a field.

Apply Your Knowledge

1 Maintaining the Green Thumb Database

Instructions: Start Access. Open the Green Thumb database from the Access folder on the Data Disk that accompanies this book. Perform the following tasks.

1. Open the Customer table in Design view as shown in Figure 3-75.

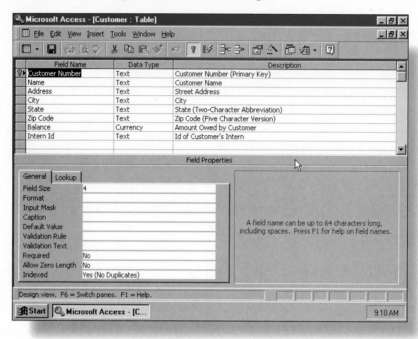

FIGURE 3-75

Apply Your Knowledge

2. Increase the size of the Name field to 25.
3. Format the Customer Number field so any lowercase letters display in uppercase.
4. Make the Name field a required field.
5. Specify that Balance amounts must be greater than or equal to $0.00 and less than or equal to $150.00. Include validation text.
6. Create an index that allows duplicates for the Name field.
7. Save the changes to the structure.
8. Open the Customer table in Datasheet view.
9. Change the name of Customer Number CJ16 to CJ's Music and Videos.
10. Resize the Name column so the complete name for customer CJ16 displays. Resize the City, State, Zip Code, Balance, and Intern Id columns to the best size.
11. Close the table and click Yes to save the changes to the layout of the table.
12. Print the table.
13. Open the Customer table and delete the record of Customer Number ME71.
14. Print the table.
15. Sort the data in ascending order by Zip Code within State.
16. Print the table. Close the table. If you are asked to save changes to the design of the table, click the No button.
17. Establish referential integrity between the Intern table (the one table) and the Customer table (the many table).

In the Lab

1 Maintaining the Museum Mercantile Database

Problem: The Museum Mercantile volunteers would like to make some changes to the database structure. They need to increase the size of the Description field and add an additional index. Because several different individuals update the data, the volunteers also would like to add some validation rules to the database. Finally, some new products must be added to the database.

Instructions: Use the database created in the In the Lab 1 of Project 1 for this assignment. Perform the following tasks.

1. Open the Museum Mercantile database and open the Product table in Design view as shown in Figure 3-76.
2. Create an index for the Description field. Be sure to allow duplicates.
3. Create and save the following validation rules for the Product table. List the steps involved on your own paper.
   a. Make the Description field a required field.
   b. Ensure that any lowercase letters entered in the Product Id field are converted to uppercase.
   c. Specify that the on hand units must be between 0 and 100. Include validation text.

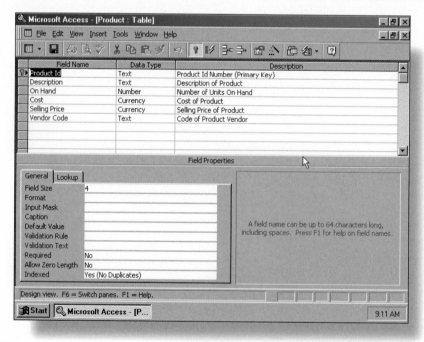

FIGURE 3-76

In the Lab

4. Save the changes.

5. Open the Product form you created in Project 1, and then add the following record to the Product table:

MN04	Mancala	4	$17.50	$21.95	WW

6. Switch to Datasheet view and sort the records in ascending order by Description.

7. Print the table. Close the table. If you are asked to save changes to the design of the table, click the No button.

8. Create a new query for the Product table.

9. Using a query, delete all records in the Product table where the Description starts with the letter T. (*Hint*: Use information from Use Help Exercise 2 to solve this problem.) Close the query without saving it.

10. Print the Product table.

11. Open the Vendor table in Design view, change the field width of the Name field to 22, and save the change.

12. Open the Vendor table in Datasheet view, and then change the name on the third record to Woodcrafters Guild. Resize the column so the complete name displays.

13. Print the table. Save the change to the layout of the table.

14. Specify referential integrity between the Vendor table (the one table) and the Product table (the many table). List the steps involved on your own paper.

In the Lab

2 Maintaining the City Telephone System Database

Problem: The manager of the City Telephone System would like to make some changes to the database structure. Another field must be added to the database, and the size of the First Name field must be increased. Because several different individuals update the data, the manager also would like to add some validation rules to the database. Finally, some additions and deletions are to be made to the database.

Instructions: Use the database created in the In the Lab 2 of Project 1 for this assignment. Perform the following tasks.

1. Open the City Telephone System database and open the User table in Design view as shown in Figure 3-77.

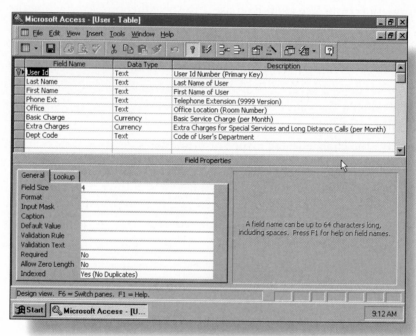

FIGURE 3-77

In the Lab

2. Create an index for the Last Name field. Be sure to allow duplicates.

3. Create an index on the combination of the Dept Code and Last Name fields. Name the index Deptname.

4. Change the field width of the First Name field to 15.

5. Save these changes and display the User table in Datasheet view.

6. Change the first name for User Id T451 to Mary Catherine.

7. Print the table.

8. Sort the records in ascending order by Dept Code.

9. Print the table. Close the table. If you are asked to save changes to the design of the table, click the No button.

10. Open the User table in Design view, and then add a Phone Code field to the User table. Define the field as Text with a width of 3. Insert the Phone Code field after the Extra Charges field. This field will contain data on whether the type of telephone is a regular single-line telephone (REG), multi-line telephone (MLT), or portable telephone (POR). Save the changes to the User table.

11. Create a new query for the User table.

12. Using this query, change all the entries in the Phone Code column to REG. This will be the status of most telephones. Do not save the query.

13. Print the table.

14. Open the User table in Design view and create the following validation rules for the User table. List the steps involved on your own paper.

    a. Make First Name and Last Name required fields.

    b. Specify the legal values, REG, MLT, and POR for the Phone Code field. Include validation text.

    c. Ensure that any letters entered in the User Id field are converted to uppercase.

    d. Specify a default value of $10.00 for the Basic Charge field.

15. Save the changes.

16. You can use either Form view or Datasheet view to add records to a table. To use Form view, you must replace the form you created in Project 1 with a form that includes the new field, Phone Code. With the User table selected, click the New Object: AutoForm button arrow on the toolbar. Click AutoForm. Use this form that contains the phone code to add the following record:

T890	Tartar	Joan	4655	240	$10.00	$0.00	REG	HRS

(continued)

In the Lab

Maintaining the City Telephone System Database *(continued)*

17. Close the form. Click the Yes button when asked if you want to save the form. Save the form as User. Click the Yes button when asked if you want to replace the User form you created in Project 1.

18. Open the User form and then locate the users with User Ids T645 and T759. Change the Phone Code for each record to MLT. Locate the user with User Id T888 and change the Phone Code to POR.

19. Switch to Datasheet view and print the table in order by last name. Close the table. If you are asked to save changes to the design of the table, click the No button.

20. Create a new query for the User table.

21. Using a query, delete all records in the User table where the Dept Code is ENG.

22. Close the query without saving it.

23. Print the User table.

24. Specify referential integrity between the Department table (the one table) and the User table (the many table). List the steps involved on your own paper.

3 Maintaining the City Scene Database

Problem: The managing editor has determined that some changes must be made to the database structure. Another field must be added and the size of the Name field must be increased. Because several different individuals update the data, the editor also would like to add some validation rules to the database. Finally, some additions and deletions are required to the database.

Instructions: Use the database created in the In the Lab 3 of Project 1 for this assignment. Perform the following tasks.

1. Open the City Scene database and open the Advertiser table in Design view as shown in Figure 3-78.

2. Create an index for the Name field. Be sure to allow duplicates. Create an index on the combination of the State and Zip Code fields. Name the index Statezip. Save these changes.

In the Lab

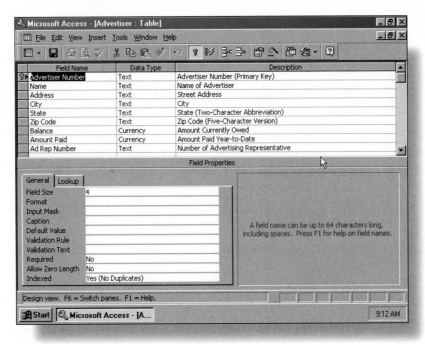

FIGURE 3-78

3. Display the Advertiser table in Datasheet view and order the records by Zip Code within State.

4. Print the table. Close the table. If you are asked to save changes to the design of the table, click the No button.

5. Change the field width of the Name field to 25.

6. Add the field, Ad Type, to the Advertiser table. Define the field as Text with a width of 3. Insert the Ad Type field after the Zip Code field. This field will contain data on the type of advertising account. Advertisers are classified as retail (RET), service (SER), and dining (DIN).

7. Save these changes and display the Advertiser table in Datasheet view.

8. Change the name of account C134 to Baker & Clover Clothes.

9. Resize the Name column to fit the changed entry. Decrease the width of the remaining columns.

10. Print the table. If necessary, change the margins so the table prints on one page in landscape orientation. Close the table. Save the layout changes to the table.

11. Using a query, change all the entries in the Ad Type column to RET. This will be the type of most accounts. Do not save the query.

12. Open the Advertiser table and order the records by name. Print the table. Close the table. If you are asked to save changes to the design of the table, click the No button.

(continued)

In the Lab

Maintaining the City Scene Database (continued)

13. Create the following validation rules for the Advertiser table and save the changes to the table. List the steps involved on your own paper.
    a. Make Name a required field.
    b. Specify the legal values RET, SER, and DIN for the Ad Type field. Include validation text.
    c. Ensure that any letters entered in the Advertiser Number and State fields are converted to uppercase.
    d. Specify that Balance must be between $0.00 and $450.00. Include validation text.
14. You can use either Form view or Datasheet view to add records to a table. To use Form view, you must replace the form you created in Project 1 with a form that includes the new field, Ad Type. With the Advertiser table selected, click the New Object: AutoForm button arrow on the toolbar. Click AutoForm. Use this form that contains Ad Type to add the following record:

| M121 | Shoe Salon | 113 Main | Fernwood | WA | 91191 | RET | $50.00 | $0.00 | 22 |

15. Close the form. Click the Yes button when asked if you want to save the form. Save the form as Advertiser. Click the Yes button when asked if you want to replace the Advertiser form you created in Project 1.
16. Open the Advertiser form and locate the advertisers with Advertiser Numbers B101, and D216 and then change the Ad Type for each record to DIN. Change the Ad Type for advertisers C047 and G080 to SER.
17. Change to Datasheet view and print the table.
18. Using a query, delete all records in the table where the account has the Ad Type of SER and is located in the state of OR. Do not save the query.
19. Print the Advertiser table. Specify referential integrity between the Ad Rep table (the one table) and the Advertiser table (the many table). List the steps involved on your own paper.

Cases and Places

The difficulty of these case studies varies: ❱ are the least difficult; ❱❱ are more difficult; and ❱❱❱ are the most difficult.

1 ❱ Use the textbook database created in Case Study 1 of Project 1 for this assignment. Execute each of these tasks and then print the results: (a) Mary Healy has dropped the price of her textbook from $36 to $30. (b) John Mott has sold his book, so you can delete his record from your database. (c) Sandi Radle informs you she gave you the wrong course number for her textbook. It is used in Phi 210 instead of Phi 310. (d) You decide to sell the computer book you are using in this class for $35. It is in good condition. (e) The Psychology department has changed textbooks in the introductory course for the upcoming semester. Delete the books listed for Psy 101. (f) Dave Corsi's book is in good condition. (g) Peter Rudd has changed his telephone number to 555-1782.

2 ❱ Use the restaurant database created in Case Study 2 of Project 1 for this assignment. Execute each of these tasks and then print the results: (a) Ye Old Cafe now occupies the location formerly occupied by Curry and More, which has gone out of business. Ye Old Cafe serves Continental cuisine, is open from 6:00 a.m. to 9:00 p.m., and has carryout but no delivery service. Its telephone number is (714) 555-3628. You like the all-you-can-eat special on Wednesday. (b) Ole Taco now offers delivery service. (c) New Crete now opens at 11:00 a.m. and closes at 11:00 p.m. (d) Little Venice has moved to 532 S. Madison. (e) Texas Diner has changed its special from Thursday to Friday. (f) Red Rose now offers carryout service.

3 ❱❱ Use the movie collection database created in Case Study 3 of Project 1 for this assignment. Add five of your favorite movie titles to the table. Print the entire table sorted by movie title in ascending order.

4 ❱❱ Use the nutritional content database created in Case Study 4 of Project 1 for this assignment. Execute each of these tasks and then print the results: (a) Other meat also can be considered lean. For example, pork tenderloin has the same calories and fat as eye of round and has 65 mg of cholesterol. Top pork loin chop and center chop both have 170 calories, 7 grams of fat, and 70 mg of cholesterol. Boneless ham is one of the most nutritional meats, with 125 calories, 4 grams of fat, and 45 mg of cholesterol. Lamb loin chop has 180 calories, 8 grams of fat, and 80 mg of cholesterol, and whole leg of lamb has 160 calories, 7 grams of fat, and 75 mg of cholesterol. Add these cuts of meat to the database. (b) Display and print the cuts of meat with less than 70 milligrams of cholesterol in a three-ounce serving. (c) Display and print the cuts of meat with more than 160 calories in a three-ounce serving. (d) Your nutrition instructor wants you to experiment by consuming less than 20 grams of fat daily. During the day, you have eaten food with a total fat gram content of 15. Display and print the cuts of meat that would be within the experiment guidelines.

Cases and Places

5 ▶▶▶ Use the product comparison database you created in Case Study 5 of Project 1 for this assignment. Often generic items are available for products on your shopping list. During your next shopping trip, locate any generic items that you could substitute for the 24 items in the table. Create a new field in the table and add the generic prices. Then, print the six items in each of the four categories in ascending order, along with the sizes and prices.

6 ▶▶▶ You have found the campus directory database you created in Case Study 6 of Project 1 to be invaluable. You have been handwriting additional names and telephone numbers and making changes to the printout, and now you want to update the table. Add a new category called departmental coordinators, and add the names, telephone numbers, and room numbers of departmental coordinators you call. In the faculty category, list your favorite instructors from previous semesters. Add your current instructors' office hours to the table. In the administration category, add data for the president and vice president of the school. In the services category, add the library circulation desk, athletic office, and theatre box office data. Print the entire table. Then print the instructors' names in ascending order, along with their telephone numbers, office hours, and office room numbers. Create a similar printout for the administrators and for the departmental coordinators. Finally, print the services in ascending order, including telephone numbers and room numbers.

7 ▶▶▶ Many national brokers offer IRAs. Call three of these brokerage companies and obtain the same information for investing $1,000 that you needed to complete Case Study 7 of Project 1 in the financial institutions database. Add these records to the table. Then, display and print the following: (a) The names of all the financial institutions in the table and total values of the IRAs at age 65 in descending order. (b) The names and telephone numbers of the financial institutions and total amounts of interest earned at age 65 in descending order. (c) The average value of the IRAs at age 65. (d) The average interest rates for the banks, savings and loans, credit unions, and brokerage companies. (e) The name, address, and interest rate of the financial institution with the highest interest rate. (f) The name, telephone number, and interest rate of the financial institution with the lowest interest rate. (g) The names of the financial institutions and penalties for early withdrawal in two years in ascending order. (h) The names of the financial institutions and annual fees in ascending order.

Integrating Excel Worksheet Data into an Access Database

INTEGRATION FEATURE

Case Perspective

Tamalex Industries has used Excel to automate a variety of tasks for several years. Employees at Tamalex have created several useful worksheets that have simplified their work. Along with the worksheets, they have created attractive charts for visual representation of the data.

When Tamalex decided it needed to maintain employee data, the familiarity with Excel led to the decision to maintain the data as an Excel worksheet. This worked well for a while. Then, they began to question whether Excel was the best choice. Their counterparts at other companies indicated that they were using Access to maintain employee data. Access had worked well for them. As the structure of their data became more complex, Access easily adapted to the increased complexity. They appreciated the power of the query and reporting features in Access. Finally, officials at Tamalex decided that they should follow the lead of the other companies. The company decided to convert its data from Excel to Access.

Introduction

It is not uncommon for people to use an application for some specific purpose, only to find later that another application may be better suited. For example, a company such as Tamalex Industries initially might keep data in an Excel worksheet, only to discover later that the data would be better maintained in an Access database. Some common reasons for using a database instead of a worksheet are:

1. The worksheet contains a great deal of redundant data. As discussed in Project 1 on pages A 1.54 through A 1.56, databases can be designed to eliminate redundant data.
2. The worksheet would need to be larger than Excel can handle. Excel has a limit of 16,384 rows. In Access, no such limit exists.
3. The data to be maintained consists of multiple interrelated items. For example, Pilotech Services needed to maintain data on two items, clients and technicians, and these items are interrelated. A client has a single technician and each technician services several clients. The Pilotech Services database is a very simple one. Databases easily can contain 30 or more interrelated items.
4. You want to use the extremely powerful query and report capabilities of Microsoft Access.

More *About*
Converting Data:
Worksheets

It is possible to convert a single worksheet within a Microsoft Excel multiple-worksheet workbook to an Access table. With other spreadsheet packages, however, you first must save the worksheet as an individual file and then convert the individual file.

Regardless of the reasons for making the change from a worksheet to a database, it is important to be able to make the change easily. In the not-too-distant past, converting data from one tool to another often could be a very difficult, time-consuming task. Fortunately, an easy way of converting data from Excel to Access is available.

Figures 1 and 2 illustrate the conversion process. The type of worksheet that can be converted is one in which the data is stored as a **list**, that is, a labeled series of rows in which each row contains the same type of data. For example, in the worksheet in Figure 1, the first row contains the labels, which are entries indicating the type of data found in the column. The entry in the first column, for example, is SS Number, indicating that all the other values in the column are Social Security numbers. The entry in the second column is Last Name, indicating that all the other values in the column are last names. Other than the first row, which contains the labels, all the rows contain precisely the same type of data: a Social Security number in the first column, a last name in the second column, a first name in the third column, and so on.

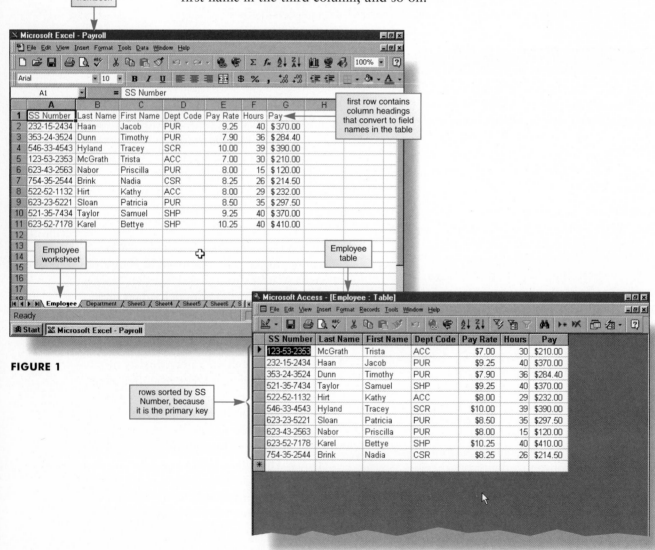

FIGURE 1

FIGURE 2

As the figures illustrate, the worksheet, shown in Figure 1, is converted to a database table, shown in Figure 2. The columns in the worksheet become the fields. The column headings in the first row of the worksheet become the field names. The rows of the worksheet, other than the first row, which contains the labels, become the records in the table. In the process, each field will be assigned the data type that seems the most reasonable, given the data currently in the worksheet.

The conversion process uses the **Import Spreadsheet Wizard**. The wizard takes you through some basic steps, asking a few simple questions. Once you have answered the questions, the wizard will perform the conversion.

Creating an Access Database

Before converting the data, you need to create the database that will contain the data. Perform the following steps to create the Tamalex Industries database.

TO CREATE A NEW DATABASE

Step 1: Click the Start button and then click New Office Document on the Start menu.

Step 2: Click the General tab, make sure the Blank Database icon is selected, and then click the OK button.

Step 3: Click the Save in box arrow and then click 3½ Floppy (A:).

Step 4: Type Tamalex Industries as the file name and then click the Create button.

Converting an Excel Worksheet to an Access Database

To convert the data, you will use the Import Spreadsheet Wizard. In the process, you will indicate that the first row contains the column headings. These column headings then will become the field names in the Access table. In addition, you will indicate the primary key for the table. As part of the process, you can choose not to include all the fields from the worksheet in the resulting table. You should be aware that some of the steps on the next page might take a significant amount of time for Access to execute.

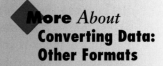

More *About* **Converting Data: Databases**

It is possible to convert data from objects other than spreadsheets to a database. You can also convert data from one database management system to another. Access, for example, provides tools for easily converting data from such database systems as dBASE III, dBASE IV, and Paradox.

More *About* **Converting Data: Other Formats**

It is possible to convert data to a database from a variety of special file formats, including delimited and fixed-width text files. If you cannot convert directly from another spreadsheet or database directly to Access, you often can convert to one of these special formats and then convert the resulting file to Access.

Steps **To Convert an Excel Worksheet to an Access Database**

1 **With the Tamalex Industries database open, click File on the menu bar and then click Get External Data. Point to Import.**

The submenu of commands for getting external data displays (Figure 3).

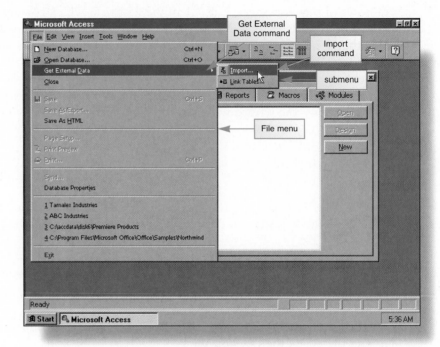

FIGURE 3

2 **Click Import. Click the Files of type box arrow in the Import dialog box and then click Microsoft Excel. Click 3½ Floppy (A:) in the Look in list box, and then select the Access folder. Make sure the Payroll workbook is selected and then click the Import button.**

The Import Spreadsheet Wizard dialog box displays (Figure 4). It displays the list of worksheets in the Payroll workbook.

FIGURE 4

3 Be sure the Employee worksheet is selected and then click the Next button.

The Import Spreadsheet Wizard dialog box displays (Figure 5). It displays a portion of the worksheet that is being converted. In this dialog box, you indicate that the first row of the worksheet contains the column headings. The wizard uses these values as the field names in the Access table.

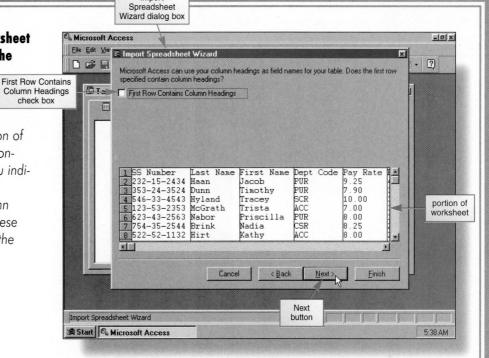

FIGURE 5

4 Click First Row Contains Column Headings and then click the Next button.

The Import Spreadsheet Wizard dialog box displays asking whether the data is to be placed in a new table or in an existing table (Figure 6).

FIGURE 6

5 **Be sure that In a New Table is selected and then click the Next button.**

The Import Spreadsheet Wizard dialog box displays giving you the opportunity to specify field options (Figure 7). You can specify that indexes are to be created for certain fields. You also can specify that certain fields should not be included in the Access table.

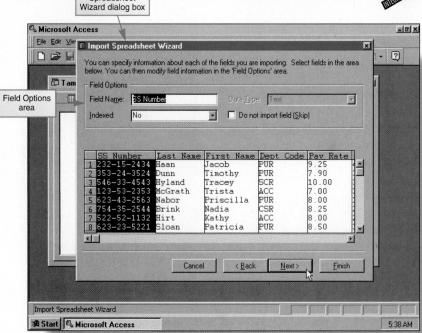

FIGURE 7

6 **Click the Next button.**

The Import Spreadsheet Wizard dialog box displays (Figure 8). In this dialog box, you indicate the primary key of the Access table. You can allow Access to add a special field to serve as the primary key as illustrated in the figure. You can choose an existing field to serve as the primary key. You also can indicate no primary key. Most of the time, one of the existing fields will serve as the primary key. In this worksheet, for example, the SS Number serves as the primary key.

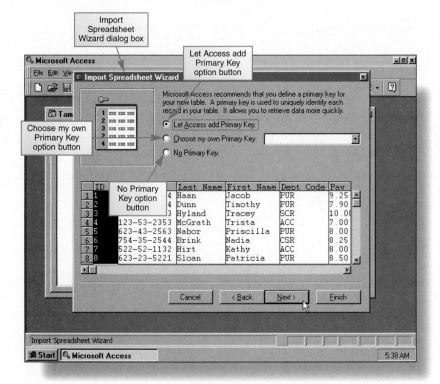

FIGURE 8

7 Click **Choose my own Primary Key.**

The SS Number field, which is the correct field, will be the primary key. If some other field were to be the primary key, you could click the down arrow and select the other field from the list of available fields.

8 Click the **Next button. Be sure Employee displays in the Import to Table text box.**

The Import Spreadsheet Wizard dialog box displays (Figure 9). The name of the table will be Employee.

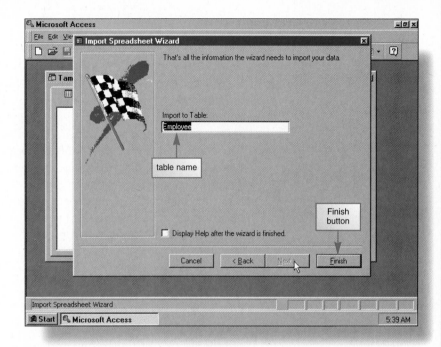

FIGURE 9

9 Click the **Finish button.**

The worksheet will be converted into an Access table. When the process is completed, the Import Spreadsheet Wizard dialog box will display (Figure 10).

10 Click the **OK button.**

The table now has been created (see Figure 2 on page AI 1.2).

11 Close **Access.**

The Employee table has been created in the Tamalex Industries database.

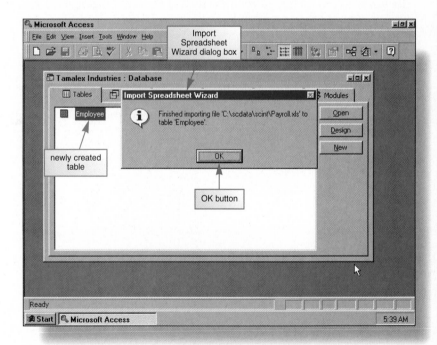

FIGURE 10

Using the Access Table

Once the Access version of the table has been created, you can treat it as you would any other table. After first opening the database containing the table, you can open the table in Datasheet view (Figure 2 on page AI 1.2). You can make changes to the data. You can create queries that use the data in the table.

By clicking Design on the table's shortcut menu, you can view the table's structure and make any necessary changes to the structure. The changes may include changing field sizes and types, creating indexes, or adding additional fields. To accomplish any of these tasks, use the same steps you used in Project 3. In the Employee table shown in Figure 2, for example, the data type for the Pay Rate field has been changed to Currency and the columns have all been resized to best fit the data.

Summary

The Integration Feature covered the process of integrating an Excel worksheet into an Access database. To convert a worksheet to an Access table, you learned to use the Import Spreadsheet Wizard. Working with the wizard, you identified the first row of the worksheet as the row containing the column headings and you indicated the primary key. The wizard then created the table for you and placed it in a new database.

What You Should Know

Having completed this Integration Feature, you now should be able to perform the following tasks:

▶ Convert an Excel Worksheet to an Access Database *(AI 1.4)*

▶ Create a New Database *(AI 1.3)*

1 Use Help

Instructions: Perform the following tasks using a computer.

1. Start Access.
2. If the Office Assistant is on your screen, then click it to display its balloon. If the Office Assistant is not on your screen, click the Office Assistant button on the toolbar.
3. Type spreadsheets in the What would you like to do? text box. Click the Search button. Click Import or link data from a spreadsheet. When the Help information displays, read it. Next, right-click within the box, and then click Print Topic. Hand in the printout to your instructor. Click the Help Topics button to return to the Help Topics: Microsoft Access 97 dialog box.
4. Click the Index tab. Type troubleshooting in the top text box labeled 1 and then double-click troubleshooting imported and linked data in the list box labeled 2. Double-click Troubleshoot text or spreadsheet import errors in the Topics Found dialog box. When the Help information displays, click the first link and read the information. Next, right-click within the box and click Print Topic. Click the Back button and then click the second link. Read and print the information. Hand in the printouts to your instructor.

2 Converting the Inventory Worksheet

Problem: The Tennis Is Everything Catalog Company has been using Excel to keep track of its inventory. Employees at Tennis Is Everything use several worksheets to reorder products, keep track of carrying costs, and graph trends in buying. The company is expanding rapidly and branching out into other sports-related products. They now need to maintain additional data and would like to produce reports and queries that are more sophisticated. The company management has asked you to convert its inventory data to an Access database.

Instructions: Perform the following tasks.

1. Create a new database in which to store all the objects related to the inventory data. Call the database Tennis Is Everything.
2. Open the Inventory workbook in the Access folder on the Data Disk that accompanies this book. Import the Product worksheet into Access.
3. Use Product as the name of the Access table and Product Number as the primary key.
4. Open and print the Product table shown in Figure 11 on the next page.

(continued)

In the Lab

Converting the Inventory Worksheet *(continued)*

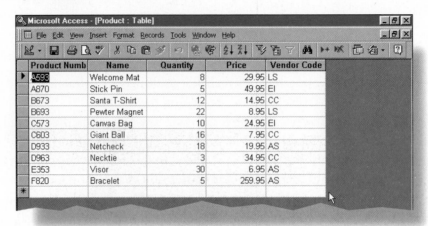

Product Numb	Name	Quantity	Price	Vendor Code
A593	Welcome Mat	8	29.95	LS
A870	Stick Pin	5	49.95	EI
B673	Santa T-Shirt	12	14.95	CC
B693	Pewter Magnet	22	8.95	LS
C573	Canvas Bag	10	24.95	EI
C603	Giant Ball	16	7.95	CC
D933	Netcheck	18	19.95	AS
D963	Necktie	3	34.95	CC
E353	Visor	30	6.95	AS
F820	Bracelet	5	259.95	AS

FIGURE 11

3 Converting the Customer Worksheet

Problem: Midwest Computer Supply has been using Excel to keep track of its customer data. Employees at Midwest Computer Supply use several worksheets to maintain information on inventory as well as customers. The company realizes that customer data would be better handled in Access. A Midwest employee created a database to store the data but has not yet imported the data. The company management has asked you to complete the conversion of its customer data to an Access database.

Instructions: Perform the following tasks.

1. Open the Midwest Computer Supply database in the Access folder on the Data Disk that accompanies this book.

2. Open the Sales workbook in the Access folder on the Data Disk that accompanies this book. Import the Customer worksheet into Access.

3. Append the worksheet data to the Customer table that already exists in the Midwest Computer Supply database. *(Hint:* Use Help on the previous page can help you solve this problem.)

4. Open the Customer table, resize the columns, and print the table shown in Figure 12.

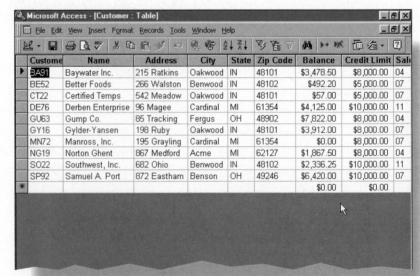

Custome	Name	Address	City	State	Zip Code	Balance	Credit Limit	Sal
BA91	Baywater Inc.	215 Ratkins	Oakwood	IN	48101	$3,478.50	$8,000.00	04
BE52	Better Foods	266 Walston	Benwood	IN	48102	$492.20	$5,000.00	07
CT22	Certified Temps	542 Meadow	Oakwood	IN	48101	$57.00	$5,000.00	07
DE76	Derben Enterprise	96 Magee	Cardinal	MI	61354	$4,125.00	$10,000.00	11
GU63	Gump Co.	85 Tracking	Fergus	OH	48902	$7,822.00	$8,000.00	04
GY16	Gylder-Yansen	198 Ruby	Oakwood	IN	48101	$3,912.00	$8,000.00	07
MN72	Manross, Inc.	195 Grayling	Cardinal	MI	61354	$0.00	$8,000.00	07
NG19	Norton Ghent	867 Medford	Acme	MI	62127	$1,867.50	$8,000.00	04
SO22	Southwest, Inc.	682 Ohio	Benwood	IN	48102	$2,336.25	$10,000.00	11
SP92	Samuel A. Port	872 Eastham	Benson	OH	49246	$6,420.00	$10,000.00	07
*						$0.00	$0.00	

FIGURE 12

Microsoft Access 97

Microsoft Access 97

Reports, Forms, and Publishing Reports to the Web

Objectives:

You will have mastered the material in this project when you can:

▶ Create a query for a report

▶ Use the Report Wizard to create a report

▶ Use the Report window to modify a report design

▶ Move between Design view and Print Preview

▶ Recognize sections in a report

▶ Save a report

▶ Close a report

▶ Print a report

▶ Create a report with grouping and subtotals

▶ Change headings in a report

▶ Move and resize controls on a report

▶ Use the Form Wizard to create an initial form

▶ Use the Form window to modify a form design

▶ Move fields on a form

▶ Place a calculated field on a form

▶ Change the format of a field on a form

▶ Place a combo box on a form

▶ Place a title on a form

▶ Change colors on a form

▶ View data using a form

▶ Publish database data to the Web

Outrageous Oddities

and Meaningful Data

Pelicans on the moon? In 1834, the *New York Sun* had its readers believing exactly that. Later, Edgar Allen Poe displayed a similar zest for practical jokes when he published a "news" dispatch detailing a bogus trans-Atlantic hot air balloon crossing. These were blatant hoaxes, but people loved them. Into this climate of practical jokes and humbug strode a man who was arguably the all-time giant of American entertainment. For sixty years, Phineas Taylor Barnum reigned as "The Showman to the World."

Best remembered today for his monumental circuses, he promoted some of the more outrageous oddities America and the world have ever seen, most of them legitimate, others born of Barnum's fertile imagination and love for a prank.

After it became known that the Feejee Mermaid was the head and torso of an orangutan sewn onto the body of a fish, crowds still flocked to see it. The public not only expected the outrageous from Barnum, but required it.

Far outweighing his hoaxes was the unending stream of genuine rarities he produced: Jenny Lind, the Swedish Nightingale; General Tom Thumb, measuring 25 inches tall and weighing 15 pounds, who became the toast of Europe and Commodore Nutt, who was even tinier; Anna Swan, the Nova Scotia giantess; Chang and Eng, Siamese Twins who fathered 22 children between them; Mrs. Myers, the bearded lady; *industrious* fleas trained to pull tiny wagons; a knitting machine operated by a dog; the armless man who loaded and fired a pistol and played musical instruments — with his feet; and Jumbo the Elephant, the mainstay of Barnum circuses.

What made Barnum's name a household word around the world? A consummate master of the art of presentation, he preceded each new attraction with a concentrated public relations campaign. Editors then were just as desperate as now for news and advertising and Barnum fed them a steady diet of both, always well-written and humorous. Above all, he loved people.

Although you may never have the opportunity to manage an event of such magnitude as a grand-scale Barnum circus, you are likely to require in your profession the Microsoft Access tools illustrated in this project to present data. If relational database power had existed in the days of P.T. Barnum, he might have used an Access Event Management database. Access eases the tasks of report and form creation with improved Report and Form Wizards that create tables and reports from database information with little user intervention.

Today, almost 100 years since Barnum first introduced "The Greatest Show on Earth," you can access information about it on the World Wide Web. The new Access Internet tool, Publish to the Web Wizard, shown in this project, automates the publishing of your database information dynamically. Now, you can share timely data on the World Wide Web.

With Microsoft Access 97, you get organized, get connected, and get results, quickly.

Project 4

Microsoft
Access 97

Case Perspective

Pilotech Services has realized several benefits from its database of clients and technicians. The management and staff of Pilotech Services greatly appreciate, for example, the ease with which they can query the database. They hope to realize additional benefits using two custom reports that meet their exact needs. The first report includes the number, name, address, city, state, zip code, and outstanding amount (billed amount minus paid amount) of all clients. The second report groups the records by technician number. Subtotals of the billed and paid amounts appear after each group, and grand totals appear at the end of the report. They also want to improve the data entry process by using a custom form. In addition to a title, the form will contain the fields arranged in two columns and display the outstanding amount, which will be calculated automatically by subtracting the paid amount from the billed amount. To assist users in entering the correct technician number, users should be able to select from a list of existing technician numbers. Finally, Pilotech would like to make copies of the reports available on the Web.

Reports, Forms, and Publishing Reports to the Web

Introduction

This project creates two reports and a form. The two reports will be printed and made available on the Web. The first report is shown in Figure 4-1. This report includes the number, name, address, city, state, zip code, and outstanding amount (Billed minus Paid) of all clients. It is similar to the one produced by clicking the Print button on the toolbar. It has two significant differences, however.

First, not all fields are included. The Client table includes a Client Type field (added in Project 3), a Billed field, a Paid field, and a Tech Number field, none of which appears on this report. Second, this report contains an Outstanding Amount field, which does not appear in the Client table.

The second report is shown in Figure 4-2 on page A 4.8. It is similar to the report in Figure 4-1, but contains an additional feature, grouping. **Grouping** means creating separate collections of records sharing some common characteristic. In the report in Figure 4-2, for example, the records have been grouped by Technician Number. Three separate groups exist: one for Technician 11, one for Technician 12, and one for Technician 17. The appropriate Technician Number appears before each group, and the total of the billed and paid amounts for the clients in the group (called a **subtotal**) appears after the group. At the end of the report is a grand total of the billed and paid amounts.

Client Amount Report

Client Number	Name	Address	City	State	Zip Code	Outstanding Amount
AM53	Ashton-Mills	216 Rivard	Grattan	MA	58120	$60.50
AS62	Alton-Scripps	722 Fisher	Empire	MA	58216	($10.00)
GR56	Grant Cleaners	737 Allard	Portage	NH	59130	$50.00
GU21	Grand Union Supply, Inc.	247 Fuller	Grattan	MA	58120	$128.50
MI26	Morland Int.	665 Whittier	Frankfort	MA	56152	($10.75)
SA56	Sawyer Inc.	31 Lafayette	Empire	MA	58216	$102.50
SI82	Simpson Ind.	752 Cadieux	Fernwood	MA	57412	$154.00
TR91	Trannel Co.	74 Webster	East Cedar	MI	57222	$0.00

FIGURE 4-1

Clients by Technician

Technician Number	First Name	Last Name	Client Number	Name	Billed	Paid
11	Joanna	Levin				
			AM53	Ashton-Mills	$215.50	$155.00
			GR56	Grant Cleaners	$215.00	$165.00
			MI26	Morland Int.	$212.50	$223.25
			TR91	Trannel Co.	$0.00	$0.00
					$643.00	$543.25
12	Brad	Rogers				
			AS62	Alton-Scripps	$425.00	$435.00
			GU21	Grand Union Supply, Inc.	$128.50	$0.00
			SI82	Simpson Ind.	$154.00	$0.00
					$707.50	$435.00
17	Maria	Rodriguez				
			SA56	Sawyer Inc.	$352.50	$250.00
					$352.50	$250.00
					$1,703.00	1,228.25

FIGURE 4-2

The **custom form** to be created is shown in Figure 4-3. Although similar to the form created in Project 1, it offers some distinct advantages. Some of the differences are merely aesthetic. The form has a title and the fields have been rearranged in two columns. In addition, two other major differences are present. This form displays the outstanding amount and will calculate it automatically by subtracting the amount paid from the amount billed. Second, to assist users in entering the correct technician, the form contains a **combo box**, which is a box that allows you to select entries from a list. An arrow displays in the Technician Number field. Clicking the arrow causes a list of the technicians in the Technician table to display as shown in the figure. You then can type either the desired technician number or simply click the desired technician.

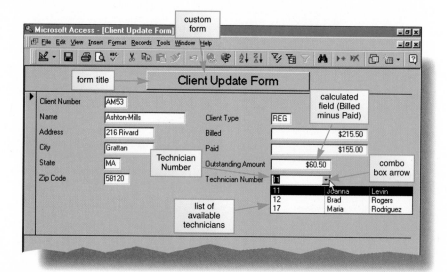

FIGURE 4-3

Note: The Data Disk that accompanies this book contains an Access folder containing compressed versions of five databases: Pilotech Services, Green Thumb, Museum Mercantile, City Telephone System, and City Scene. Pilotech Services is required if you plan to step through the project on a PC. The other files are required for the exercises at the end of the project. It is recommended that you create a copy of the Data Disk for each database you will be using.

To create a copy for an individual database, do the following: [1] Insert the Data Disk in drive A; [2] start Explorer; [3] right-click the 3½ Floppy (A:) folder in the All Folders side of the window; [4] click Copy Disk; [5] click Start and OK as required; [6] insert the blank floppy disk when requested; [7] delete any folder other then the Access folder from the newly-created floppy disk; [8] double-click the Access folder in the All Folders side of the window and then double-click the name of the database on the Contents of 'Access' side of the window; and [9] clearly label this floppy disk with the name of the database. The database will be contained in the Access folder.

If possible, you should place your data on your hard disk or on a network drive, because the databases can become rather large, especially after adding the pictures in Project 5. If this is not possible, you should not insert the pictures in Project 5. (There is a note in Project 5, showing you precisely which steps you should skip.)

Project Four – Creating Custom Reports and a Form for Pilotech Services

You are to create the reports requested by the management of Pilotech Services. You also must create the form that the management deems to be important to the data-entry process.

Overview of Project Steps

The database preparation steps give you an overview of how the reports and form shown in Figures 4-1 through 4-3 will be created in this project.

1. Start Access and open the Pilotech Services database.
2. Create a query for the first report.
3. Use the Report Wizard to create an initial version of the first report.
4. Use the Report window to complete the creation of the first report by changing one of the properties.
5. Create a query for the second report.
6. Use the Report Wizard to create an initial version of the second report.
7. Use the Report window to complete the creation of the second report.
8. Remove unwanted controls from the second report.
9. Enlarge the Page Header section on the second report.
10. Change the column headings on the second report.
11. Use the Form Wizard to create an initial version of the form.
12. Use the Form window to complete the creation of the form.
13. Move fields on the form.
14. Add a new field to the form.
15. Change the format of a field on the form.
16. Add a combo box to the form.
17. Add a title to the form.
18. Enhance the title on the form by changing some of its properties.
19. Publish the reports created in this project to the Web.

The following pages contain a detailed explanation of these steps.

Opening the Database

Before creating reports or forms, first you must open the database. Perform the following steps to complete this task.

TO OPEN A DATABASE

Step 1: Click the Start button.
Step 2: Click Open Office Document on the Start menu and then click 3½ Floppy (A:) in the Look in list box. If necessary, double-click the Access folder. Make sure the database called Pilotech Services is selected.
Step 3: Click the Open button.

The database is open and the Pilotech Services : Database window displays.

More *About*
Creating a Report

There are two alternatives to using the Report Wizard to create reports. You can use AutoReport to create a very simple report that includes all fields and records in the table or query. Using Design View allows you to create a report from scratch.

More *About*
Using Queries for Reports

The records in the report will appear in the specified order if you have sorted the data in the query. You also can enter criteria in the query, in which case only records that satisfy the criteria will be included in the report.

Report Creation

The simplest way to create a report design is to use the **Report Wizard**. For some reports, the Report Wizard can produce exactly the desired report. For others, however, first use the Report Wizard to produce a report that is as close as possible to the desired report. Then use the **Report window** to modify the report, transforming it into exactly the correct report. In either case, once the report is created and saved, you can print it at any time. Access will use the current data in the database for the report, formatting and arranging it in exactly the way you specified when the report was created.

If a report uses only the fields in a single table, use the table as a basis for the report. If the report uses extra fields (such as Outstanding Amount) or uses multiple tables, however, the simplest way to create the report is first to create a query using the steps you learned in Project 2. The query should contain exactly the fields and tables required for the report. This query forms the basis for the report.

Creating a Query

The process of creating a query for a report is identical to the process of creating queries for any other purpose. Perform the following steps to create the query for the first report.

Steps To Create a Query

1 **In the Database window, click the Tables tab, if necessary, and then click the Client table. Click the New Object: AutoForm button arrow on the toolbar. Click Query. Be sure Design View is selected, and then click the OK button. Maximize the Select Query window. Resize the upper and lower panes and the Client field list so all the fields in the Client table display.**

2 **Double-click Client Number. Select Ascending as the sort order for the field. Include the Name, Address, City, State, and Zip Code fields in the design grid. Click the right scroll arrow to shift the fields to the left so the space for an extra field is visible. Right-click in the Field row of the space for the extra field. Point to Zoom on the shortcut menu.**

The shortcut menu for the extra field displays (Figure 4-4).

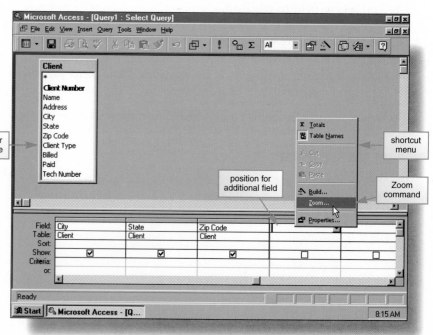

FIGURE 4-4

3 Click Zoom on the shortcut menu. Type Outstanding Amount:[Billed]-[Paid] in the Zoom dialog box and point to the OK button (Figure 4-5).

4 Click the OK button. Click the Close button for the Select Query window and then click the Yes button.

5 Type Client Amount Query as the name of the query and then click the OK button.

The query is saved.

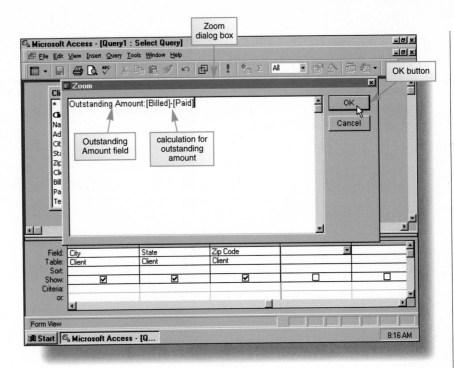

FIGURE 4-5

Creating a Report

Next, you will create a report using the Report Wizard. Access leads you through a series of choices and questions, and then creates the report automatically. Perform the following steps to create the report shown in Figure 4-1 on page A 4.7.

Steps To Create a Report

1 Click the Reports tab in the Database window and then point to the New button (Figure 4-6).

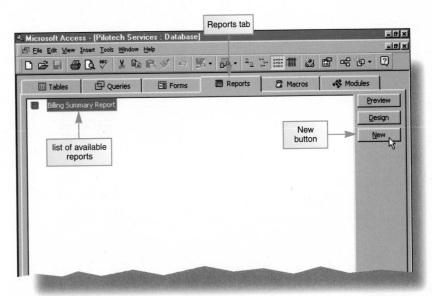

FIGURE 4-6

2 **Click the New button. Click Report Wizard, click the list box arrow to display a list of available tables and queries, click Client Amount Query, and then point to the OK button.**

The New Report dialog box displays and the Client Amount Query is selected (Figure 4-7).

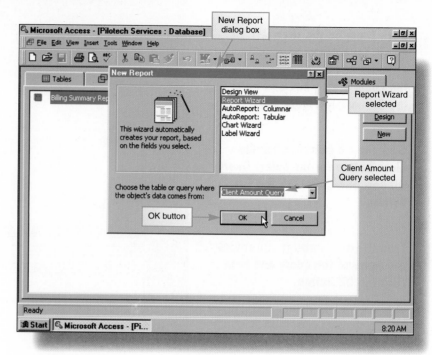

FIGURE 4-7

3 **Click the OK button and then point to the Add All Fields button.**

The Report Wizard dialog box displays, requesting the fields for the report (Figure 4-8). To add the selected field to the list of fields on the report, use the Add Field button. To add all fields, use the Add All Fields button.

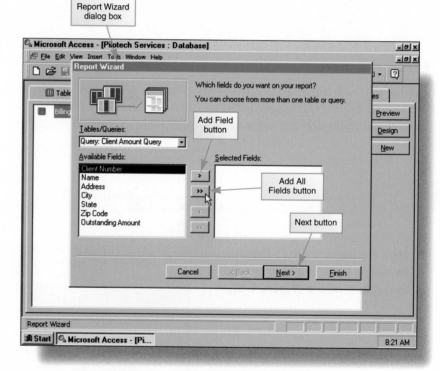

FIGURE 4-8

4 Click the Add All Fields button to add all the fields, and then click the Next button.

The next Report Wizard dialog box displays, requesting the field or fields for grouping levels (Figure 4-9). No grouping takes place in this report being created.

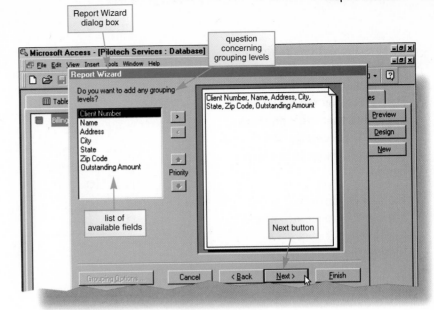

FIGURE 4-9

5 Click the Next button. No grouping levels are required.

The next Report Wizard dialog box displays, requesting the sort order for the report (Figure 4-10).

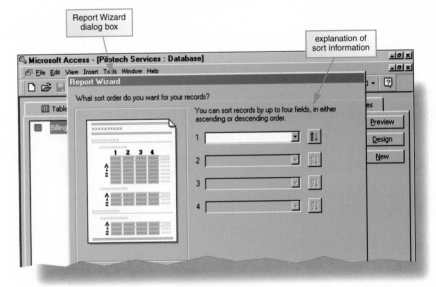

FIGURE 4-10

6 Click the Next button. The query already is sorted in the appropriate order, so you need not specify a sort order.

The next Report Wizard dialog box displays, requesting your report layout preference (Figure 4-11).

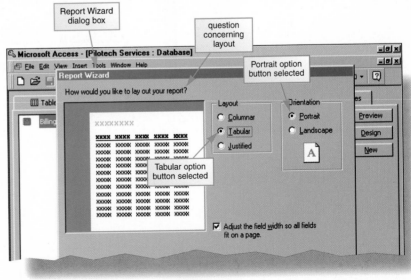

FIGURE 4-11

7 Be sure the options selected in the Report Wizard dialog box on your screen match those in Figure 4-11 on the previous page, and then click the Next button. If necessary, click Formal to select it. Point to the Next button.

The next Report Wizard dialog box displays, requesting a style for the report (Figure 4-12). The Formal style is selected.

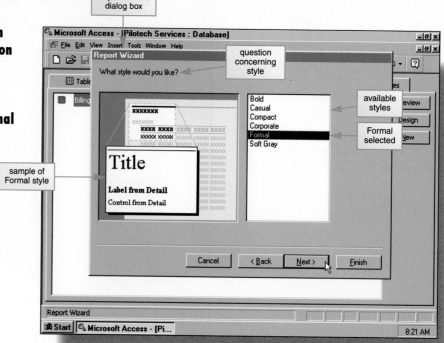

FIGURE 4-12

8 Click the Next button and then type Client Amount Report as the report title. Point to the Finish button.

The next Report Wizard dialog box displays, requesting a title for the report (Figure 4-13). Client Amount Report is entered as the title.

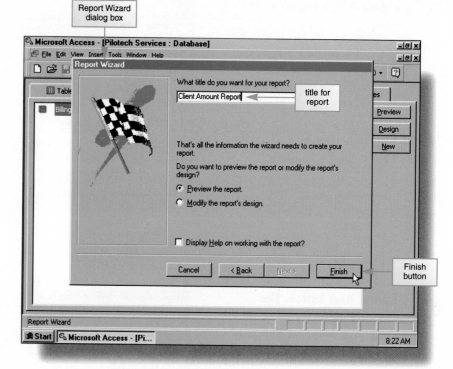

FIGURE 4-13

9 Click the Finish button.

The report design is complete and displays in Print Preview (Figure 4-14). (If your computer displays an entire page of the report, click the portion of the report where the mouse pointer displays in the figure.)

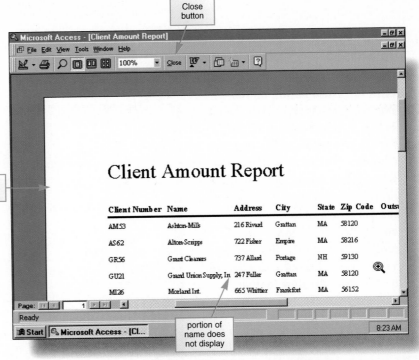

FIGURE 4-14

Because of insufficient space allowed in the report shown in Figure 4-14, some of the data does not display completely. The final portion of the name of Grand Union Supply, Inc. does not display, for example. You will need to correct this problem.

Using Design View

Within the Report window, the different possible views are Design view and Print Preview. Use **Design view** to modify the design (layout) of the report. Use **Print Preview** to see the report with sample data. To move from Design view to Print Preview, click the Print Preview button on the toolbar. To move from Print Preview to Design view, click the button labeled Close on the toolbar.

Within Print Preview, you can switch between viewing an entire page or a portion of a page. To do so, click somewhere within the report (the mouse pointer will change shape to a magnifying glass).

In Design view, you can modify the design of the report. A **toolbox** is available in Design view that allows you to create special objects for the report. The toolbox obscures a portion of the report, so it is common practice to remove the toolbox when you are not using it by clicking the Toolbox button on the toolbar. You can return the toolbox to the screen whenever you need it by clicking the Toolbox button again.

Perform the steps on the next page to move from Print Preview to Design view and remove the toolbox from the screen.

Other Ways

1. With table selected, click New Object button arrow on toolbar, click Report, click Report Wizard to create report
2. On Insert menu click Report, click Report Wizard to create report

More About Previewing a Report

You can view two pages at the same time when previewing a report by clicking the Two Page button on the toolbar. You can view multiple pages by clicking View on the menu bar, clicking Pages, and then clicking the number of pages to view.

Steps To Move to Design View and Remove the Toolbox

1 Click the Close button on the Print Preview toolbar (see Figure 4-14). If Access returns to the Database window, right-click the report, and then click Design on the shortcut menu. If the toolbox displays, point to the Toolbox button on the Report Design toolbar. In the list, click Design View. Then click the Close button on the Print Preview toolbar.

Print Preview is replaced by Design view (Figure 4-15). In the figure, the toolbox displays, obscuring some of the left edge of the report design.

2 If the toolbox displays, click the Toolbox button on the toolbar.

The toolbox no longer displays.

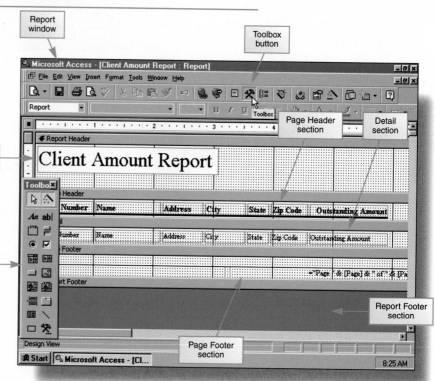

FIGURE 4-15

OtherWays

1. Click View button arrow on toolbar, click Design View
2. On View menu click Design View

More *About*
Report Sections

Another common term for the sections in a report is "band." The term "band-oriented" applied to a report tool means that the tool is very similar to the report tool in Access; that is, you design a report by simply modifying the contents of the various sections (bands).

Report Sections

Each of the different portions of the report is described in what is termed a **section**. The sections are labeled on the screen (see Figure 4-15). Notice the following sections: the Report Header section, Page Header section, Detail section, Page Footer section, and Report Footer section.

The contents of the **Report Header section** print once at the beginning of the report. The contents of the **Report Footer section** print once at the end of the report. The contents of the **Page Header section** print once at the top of each page, and the contents of the **Page Footer section** print once at the bottom of each page. The contents of the **Detail section** print once for each record in the table.

The various rectangles appearing in Figure 4-15 (Client Amount Report, Client Number, Name, and so on) are called **controls**. The control containing Client Amount Report displays the report title; that is, it displays the words, Client Amount Report. The control in the Page Header section containing Name displays the word, Name.

The controls in the Detail section display the contents of the corresponding fields. The control containing Name, for example, will display the client's name. The controls in the Page Header section serve as **captions** for the data. The Client Number control in this section, for example, will display the words, Client Number, immediately above the column of client numbers, thus making it clear to anyone reading the report that the items in the column are, in fact, client numbers.

To move, resize, delete, or modify a control, click it. Small squares called **sizing handles** appear around the border of the control. Drag the control to move it, drag one of the sizing handles to resize it, or press the DELETE key to delete it. Clicking a second time produces an insertion point in the control in order to modify its contents.

Changing Properties

Some of the changes you may make will involve using the property sheet for the control to be changed. The **property sheet** is a list of properties for the control that can be modified. By using the property sheet, you can change one or more of the control's properties. To produce the property sheet, right-click the desired control and then click Properties on the shortcut menu.

The problem of missing data in the report in Figure 4-14 on page A 4.15 can be corrected in several ways.

1. Move the controls to allow more space in between them. Then, drag the appropriate handles on the controls that need to be expanded to enlarge them.
2. Use the Font Size property to select a smaller font size. This would enable more data to print in the same space.
3. Use the Can Grow property. By changing the value of this property from No to Yes, the data can be spread over two lines, thus enabling all the data to print. The name of customer GU21, for example, will have Grand Union Supply, on one line and Inc. on the next. Access will split data at natural break points, such as commas, spaces, and hyphens.

The first approach will work, but it can be cumbersome. The second approach would work, but makes the report difficult to read. The third approach, changing the Can Grow property, is the simplest and produces a very readable report. Perform the following steps to change the Can Grow property for the Detail section.

> ### More *About* Changing Properties
>
> There are a large number of properties that can be changed using the property sheet. The properties determine the structure and appearance of a control. They also determine the characteristics of the data the control contains. For details on a particular property, click the Help button, then click the property.

 To Change the Can Grow Property

1 **Point below the section selector for the Detail section (Figure 4-16).**

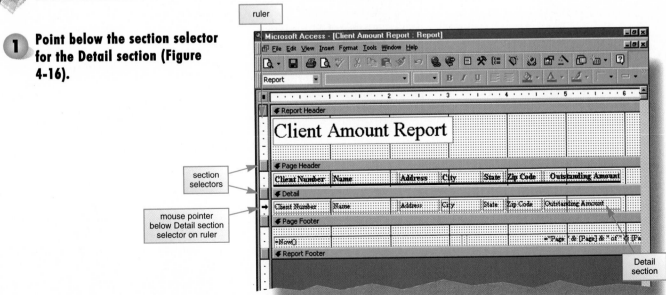

FIGURE 4-16

2 **Right-click and then point to Properties on the shortcut menu.**

The shortcut menu displays (Figure 4-17).

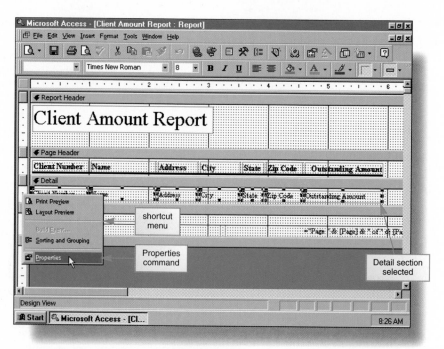

FIGURE 4-17

3 **Click Properties and then click the All tab, if necessary, to ensure that all available properties display. Click the Can Grow property, click the Can Grow box arrow, and then click Yes in the list that displays.**

The Multiple selection property sheet displays (Figure 4-18). All the properties display on the All sheet. The value for the Can Grow property has been changed to Yes.

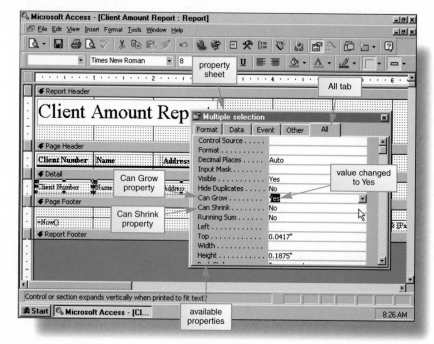

FIGURE 4-18

4 Close the property sheet by clicking its Close button, and then point to the Print Preview button on the toolbar (Figure 4-19).

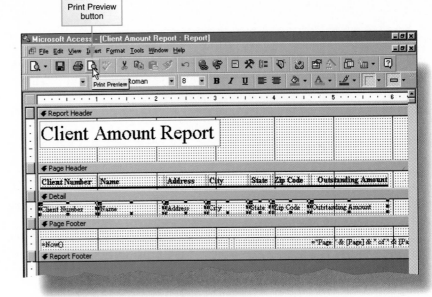

Print Preview button

FIGURE 4-19

5 Click the Print Preview button.

A portion of the report displays (Figure 4-20). The names now display completely by extending to a second line. (If your computer displays an entire page, click the portion of the report where the mouse pointer displays in the figure.)

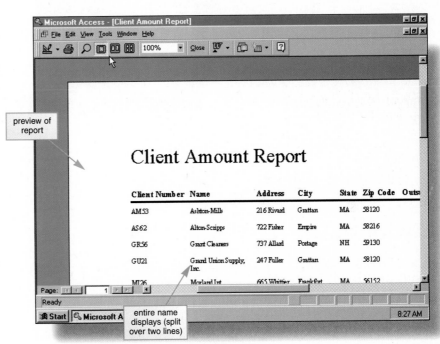

preview of report

entire name displays (split over two lines)

FIGURE 4-20

Closing and Saving a Report

To close a report, close the window using the window's Close button in the upper-right corner of the window. Then indicate whether or not you want to save your changes. Perform the following step to close the report.

TO CLOSE AND SAVE A REPORT

Step 1: Close the Report window and then click the Yes button to save the report.

*Other*Ways

1. On File menu click Close

Printing a Report

To print a report, right-click the report in the Database window, and then click Print on the shortcut menu. Perform the following steps to print the Client Amount Report.

Steps To Print a Report

1 **In the Database window, if necessary, click the Reports tab. Right-click the Client Amount Report. Point to Print on the shortcut menu.**

The shortcut menu for the Client Amount Report displays (Figure 4-21).

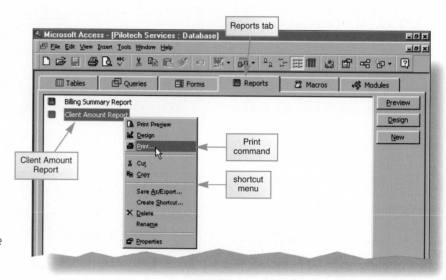

FIGURE 4-21

2 **Click Print.**

The report prints. It should look like the report shown in Figure 4-1 on page A 4.7.

Other Ways

1. Click Reports tab, select report, click Print button on toolbar
2. Click Reports tab, select report, on File menu click Print
3. Click Reports tab, select report, press CTRL+P

Grouping in a Report

Grouping arranges the records in your report. When records are grouped in a report, separate collections of records are created that share some common characteristic. In the report in Figure 4-2 on page A 4.8, for example, the records are grouped by Technician Number. Three separate groups exist, one for each technician.

In grouping, reports typically include two other types of sections: a group header and a group footer. A **group header** is printed before the records in a particular group and a **group footer** is printed after the group. In Figure 4-2, the group header indicates the technician number and name. The group footer includes the total of the billed and paid amounts for the clients of that technician. Such a total is called a **subtotal**, because it is just a subset of the overall total.

Again, you should create an appropriate query before creating the report. Perform the following steps to create the query for the report shown in Figure 4-2.

Creating a Query

Because the report involves data from two tables, the query needs to draw data from two tables. To create such a query, you will need to create a multi-table query. Perform the following steps to create a query for the report.

More *About*
Grouping in a Report

To force each group to begin on a new page of the report, change the value of the ForceNewPage property for the group header section from None to Before Section. You can change the ForceNewPage property for any section except the page header and page footer.

TO CREATE A QUERY

Step 1: In the Database window, click the Tables tab and then, if necessary, click the Client table. Click the New Object: AutoForm button arrow on the toolbar. Click Query. Be sure Design View is selected, and then click the OK button.

Step 2: If necessary, maximize the Select Query window. Resize the upper and lower panes and the Client field list so that all fields in the Client table display. Add the Technician table by right-clicking any open area in the upper pane of the Select Query window, clicking Show Table on the shortcut menu, clicking the Technician table, clicking the Add button, and clicking the Close button. Expand the size of the field list so all the fields display.

Step 3: Include the Tech Number field from the Technician table and then select Ascending as the sort order. Include the First Name and Last Name fields from the Technician table. Include the Client Number, Name, Billed, and Paid fields from the Client table.

All the necessary fields are included (Figure 4-22), although currently some are off the right edge of the design grid.

Step 4: Click the Close button for the Select Query window, click the Yes button, type Clients by Technician as the name, and click the OK button.

The query is created and saved.

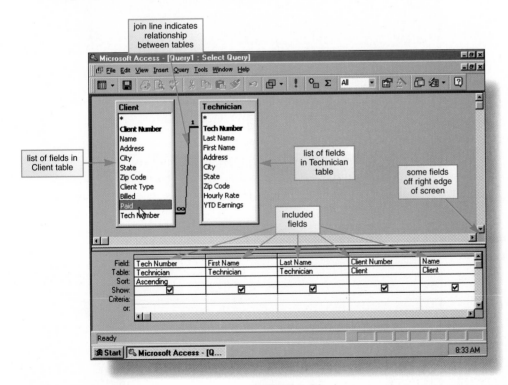

FIGURE 4-22

Creating a Second Report

As you did when creating the first report, you will use the Report Wizard to create the second report. Perform the steps on the next page to create the report shown in Figure 4-2 on page A 4.8.

Steps To Create a Second Report

1 In the Database window, click the Reports tab and then click the New button. Click Report Wizard, select the Clients by Technician query, and then point to the OK button.

The New Report dialog box displays and the Clients by Technician query is selected (Figure 4-23).

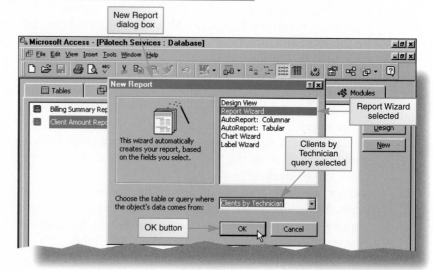

FIGURE 4-23

2 Click the OK button and then point to the Add All Fields button.

The Report Wizard dialog box displays, requesting the fields for the report (Figure 4-24).

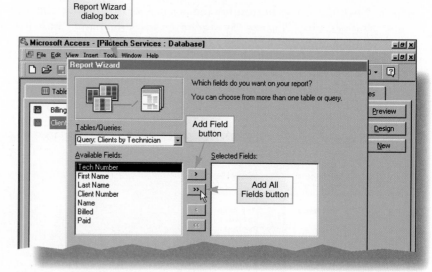

FIGURE 4-24

3 Click the Add All Fields button to add all the fields, and then click the Next button.

The next Report Wizard dialog box displays (Figure 4-25). Because two tables are in the query, the wizard is asking you to indicate how the data is to be viewed; that is, the way the report is to be organized. The report may be organized by Technician or by Client.

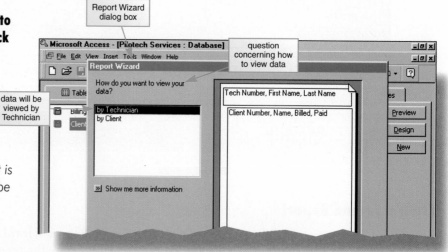

FIGURE 4-25

4 Because the report is to be viewed by technician and by Technician already is selected, click the Next button.

Access groups the report automatically by Tech Number, which is the key to the Technician table. The next Report Wizard dialog box displays, asking for additional grouping levels other than the Tech Number.

5 Because no additional grouping levels are required, click the Next button. Click the box 1 arrow and then click the Client Number field. Point to the Summary Options button.

The next Report Wizard dialog box displays, requesting the sort order for detail records in the report; that is, the way in which records will be sorted within each of the groups (Figure 4-26). The Client Number field is selected for the sort order, indicating that within the group of clients of any technician, the clients will be sorted by client number.

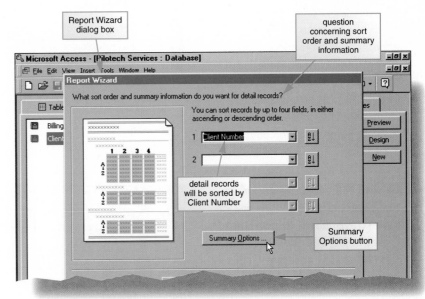

FIGURE 4-26

6 Click the Summary Options button. Point to the Sum check box in the row labeled Billed.

The Summary Options dialog box displays (Figure 4-27). This dialog box allows you to indicate any statistics you want calculated in the report by clicking the appropriate check box.

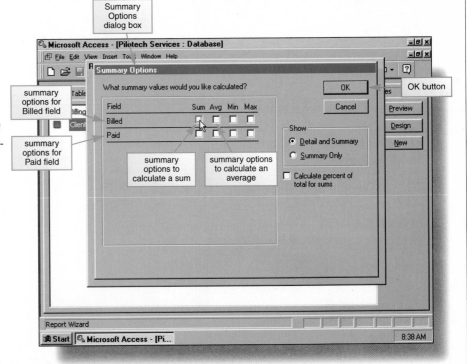

FIGURE 4-27

7 Click the Sum check box in the Billed row and the Sum check box in the Paid row. Click the OK button in the Summary Options dialog box, and then click the Next button.

The next Report Wizard dialog box displays, requesting your report layout preference (Figure 4-28). The Stepped layout, which is the correct one, already is selected. To see the effect of any of the others, click the appropriate option button. The sample layout displayed on the left side of this screen will change to represent the layout you select. The Stepped option button should be selected before you proceed.

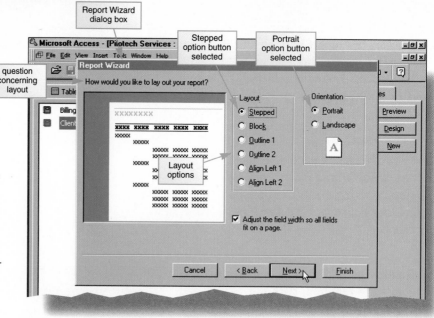

FIGURE 4-28

8 Be sure the options selected in the Report Wizard dialog box on your screen match those shown in Figure 4-28, and then click the Next button. If necessary, click Formal to select it.

The next Report Wizard dialog box displays, requesting a style for the report. The Formal style is selected (Figure 4-29).

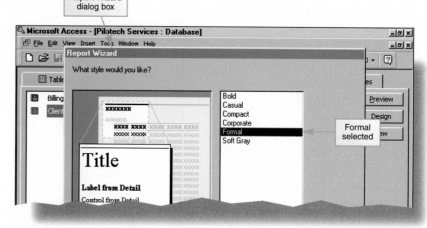

FIGURE 4-29

9 Click the Next button and then type Clients by Technician as the report title. Point to the Finish button.

The next Report Wizard dialog box displays, requesting a title for the report (Figure 4-30). Clients by Technician is typed as the title.

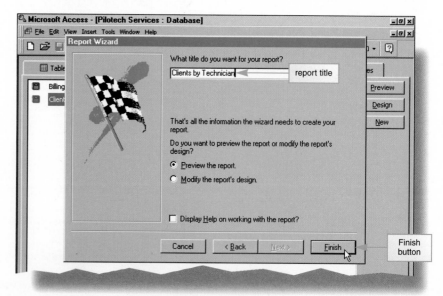

FIGURE 4-30

10 Click the Finish button.

The report design is complete and displays in the Print Preview window (Figure 4-31).

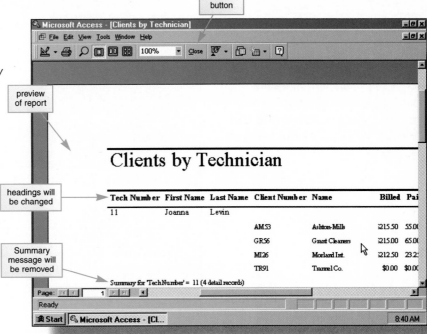

FIGURE 4-31

Reviewing the Report Design

Three major differences exist between the report in Figure 4-31 and the one in Figure 4-2 on page A 4.8. The first is that all the column headings in Figure 4-31 are on a single line, whereas they extend over two lines in the report in Figure 4-2. The first column heading in Figure 4-2 is Technician Number, rather than Tech Number. The second difference is that the report in Figure 4-2 does not contain the message that begins, Summary for Tech Number. Other messages are on the report in Figure 4-31 that are not on the report in Figure 4-2, but they are included on a portion of the report that currently does not display. The final difference is that the Billed and Paid fields do not display completely.

To complete the report design, you must change the column headings and remove these extra messages. In addition, you will move and resize the Billed and Paid fields so the values display completely. (Changing the Can Grow property would not work here because it places part of the number on one line and the rest on the next line. While this is appropriate for names, it is not appropriate for numbers.)

Removing Unwanted Controls

To remove the extra messages, or any other control, first click the control to select it. Then press the DELETE key to remove the unwanted control. Perform the steps on the next page to remove the unwanted controls from the report.

Steps To Remove Unwanted Controls

1 **Click the Close button on the toolbar to return to the Report window. Point to the control that begins, ="Summary for " (Figure 4-32).**

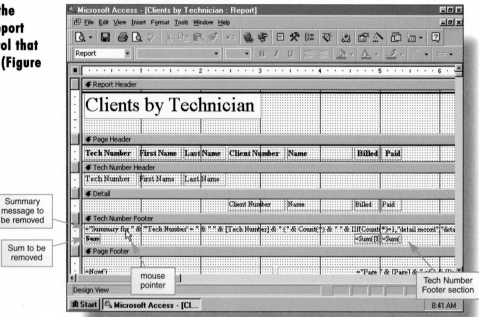

FIGURE 4-32

2 **Click the control to select it, and then press the DELETE key to delete it. In a similar fashion, delete the control below that reads, Sum. Click the down scroll arrow so the Report Footer displays and then delete the control that begins, Grand.**

The controls have been removed (Figure 4-33).

FIGURE 4-33

Enlarging the Page Header Section

The current Page Header section is not large enough to encompass the desired column headings because several of them extend over two lines. Thus, before changing the column headings, you must **enlarge** the Page Header. To do so, drag the bottom border of the Page Header section down. A bold line in the Page Header section immediately below the column headings also must be dragged down.

Perform the following steps to enlarge the Page Header section and move the bold line.

 Steps To Enlarge the Page Header Section

1 Click the up scroll arrow to move to the top of the report. Point to the bottom border of the Page Header section (Figure 4-34). The mouse pointer shape changes to a two-headed vertical arrow.

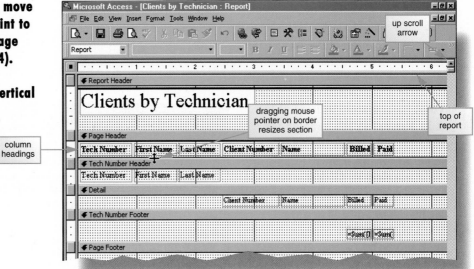

FIGURE 4-34

2 Drag the mouse pointer down to enlarge the size of the Page Header section to that shown in Figure 4-35 and then drag the bold line in the Page Header section down to the position shown in the figure. The mouse pointer will display as a hand as you drag the line.

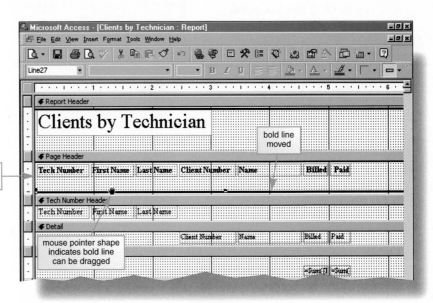

FIGURE 4-35

Changing Column Headings

To change a column heading, point to the position at which you would like to produce an insertion point. Click once to select the heading. Handles will appear around the border of the heading after clicking. Then, click a second time to produce the insertion point. Once you have produced the insertion point, you can make the desired changes. To delete a character, press the DELETE key to delete the character following the insertion point, or the BACKSPACE key to delete the character preceding the insertion point. To insert a new character, simply type the character. To move the portion following the insertion point to a second line, press the SHIFT+ENTER keys.

If you click the second time too rapidly, Access will assume that you have double-clicked the heading. Double-clicking a control is another way to produce the control's property sheet. If this happens, simply close the property sheet and begin the process again.

Perform the following steps to change the column headings.

Steps To Change the Column Headings

1 Point immediately in front of the N in Number in the heading for the first field. Click the column heading for the first field to select it. Click it a second time to produce an insertion point in front of the N, and then press the SHIFT+ENTER keys. Click immediately after the h in Tech and then type nician to complete the word, Technician, on the first line.

The heading is split over two lines (Figure 4-36). The heading has been changed to Technician Number.

FIGURE 4-36

2 Use the same technique to split the headings for the First Name, Last Name, and Client Number fields over two lines.

The changes to the header now are complete.

Moving and Resizing Controls

To move, resize, delete, or modify a single control, click it. **Sizing handles** display around the border of the control. To move the control, point to the boundary of the control, but away from any sizing handle. The mouse pointer changes shape to a hand. You then can drag the control to move it. To resize the control, drag one of the sizing handles.

You can move or resize several controls at the same time by selecting them all before dragging. This is especially useful when controls must line up in a column. For example, the Paid control in the Page Header should line up above the Paid control in the Detail section. These controls also should line up with the controls in the Tech Number Footer and Report Footer sections that will display the sum of the paid amounts.

To select multiple controls, click the first control you wish to select. Then hold down the SHIFT key while you click each of the others. The following steps first will select the controls in the Page Header, Detail, Tech Number Footer, and Report Footer sections that relate to the Paid amount. You then will move and resize all these controls at once. Next, you will use the same technique to move and resize the controls that relate to the Billed amount. Finally, to ensure enough room for complete names, you will enlarge the Name controls in the Page Header and Detail sections.

 Steps **To Move and Resize Controls**

1 **Click the down scroll arrow so the Report Footer displays. Click the Paid control in the Page Header section to select it. Hold down the SHIFT key and click the Paid control in the Detail section, the control for the sum of the Paid amounts in the Tech Number Footer section, and the control for the sum of the Paid amounts in the Report Footer section. Release the SHIFT key. Point to the border of the Paid control in the Page Header section but away from any handle.**

Multiple controls are selected (Figure 4-37).

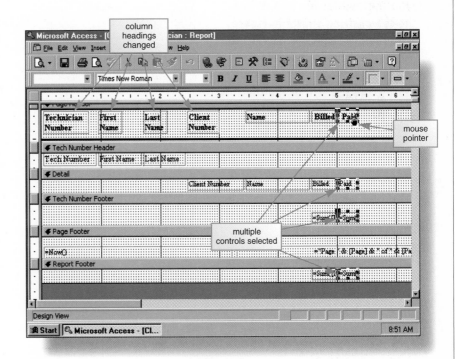

FIGURE 4-37

2 Drag the Paid control in the Page Header section to the position shown in Figure 4-38. Drag the right sizing handle of the Paid control in the Page Header section to change the size of the control to the one shown in the figure. (You need not be exact.)

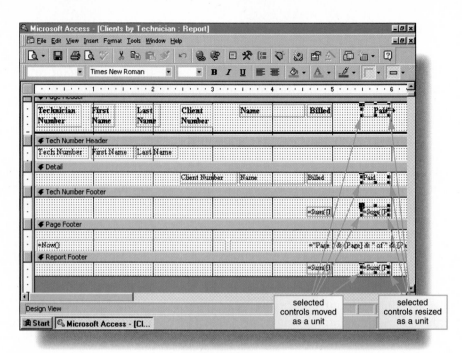

FIGURE 4-38

3 Use the same technique to move the controls for the Billed field to the position shown in Figure 4-39 and change the size of the controls to those shown in the figure. Use the same technique to change the size of the controls for the Name field to those shown in the figure. (Again, you need not be exact.)

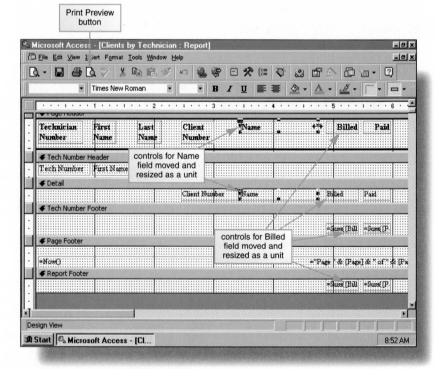

FIGURE 4-39

Previewing a Report

To see what the report looks like with sample data, preview the report by clicking the Print Preview button on the toolbar as illustrated in the following step.

TO PREVIEW A REPORT

Step 1: Click the Print Preview button on the toolbar. If the entire width of the report does not display, click anywhere within the report.

A preview of the report displays (Figure 4-40). The extra messages have been removed. The column headings have been changed and now extend over two lines.

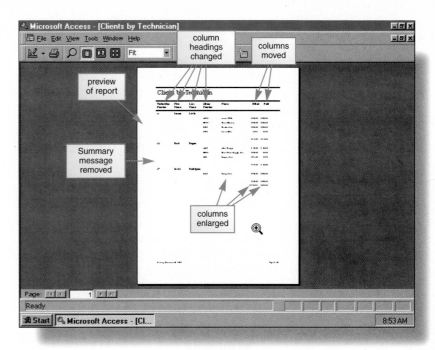

FIGURE 4-40

Closing and Saving a Report

To close a report, close the window using the window's Close button. Then, indicate whether you want to save your changes. Perform the following step to close and save the report.

TO CLOSE AND SAVE A REPORT

Step 1: Click the window's Close button to close the window. Click the Yes button to save the design of the report.

Printing a Report

To print the report, right-click the report name in the Database window, and then click Print on the shortcut menu as shown in the following step.

TO PRINT A REPORT

Step 1: Make sure that the reports display in the Database window. Right-click the Clients by Technician report and then click Print on the shortcut menu.

The report prints. It should look like the report shown in Figure 4-2 on page A 4.8.

▶**Other**Ways

1. Click View button on toolbar, click Print Preview
2. On View menu click Print Preview

Report Design Considerations

When designing and creating reports, keep in mind the following guidelines.

1. The purpose of any report is to provide specific information. Ask yourself if the report conveys this information effectively. Are the meanings of the rows and columns in the report clear? Are the column captions easily understood? Are any abbreviations contained on the report that may not be clear to those looking at the report?
2. Be sure to allow sufficient white space between groups. If you feel the amount is insufficient, add more by enlarging the group footer.

3. You can use different fonts and sizes, but do not overuse them. Using more than two or three different fonts and/or sizes often gives a cluttered and amateurish look to the report.
4. Be consistent when creating reports. Once you have decided on a general style, stick with it.

Creating and Using Custom Forms

Thus far, you have used a form to add new records to a table and change existing records. When you did, you created a basic form using the New Object: AutoForm button. Although the form did provide some assistance in the task, the form was not particularly pleasing. The standard form stacked fields on top of each other at the left side of the screen. This section covers custom forms that you can use in place of the basic form created by the Report Wizard. To create such a form, first use the Form Wizard to create a basic form. Then, you can modify the design of this form, transforming it into the one you want.

More *About*
Creating Forms

There are two alternatives to using the Form Wizard to create forms. You can use AutoForm to create a very simple form that includes all fields in the table or query. You also can use Design View to create a form totally from scratch.

Beginning the Form Creation

To create a form, first click the Forms tab and then click the New button. Next, use the Form Wizard to create the form. The Form Wizard leads you through a series of choices and questions. Access then will create the form automatically.

Perform the following steps to create an initial form. This form later will be modified to produce the form shown in Figure 4-3 on page A 4.8.

Steps **To Begin Creating a Form**

1 **Click the Forms tab, click the New button, click Form Wizard, click the list box arrow, and then click the Client table.**

The New Form dialog box displays. Form Wizard and the Client table are both selected.

2 **Click the OK button and then point to the Add Field button.**

The Form Wizard dialog box displays (Figure 4-41). The Client Number field is selected.

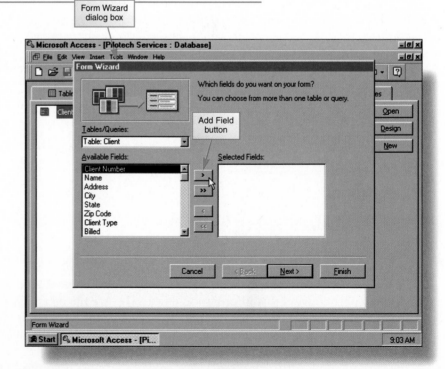

FIGURE 4-41

3 Use the Add Field button to add all the fields except the Tech Number field, and then click the Next button. When asked for a layout, be sure Columnar is selected, and then click the Next button again.

The Form Wizard dialog box displays, requesting a form style (Figure 4-42).

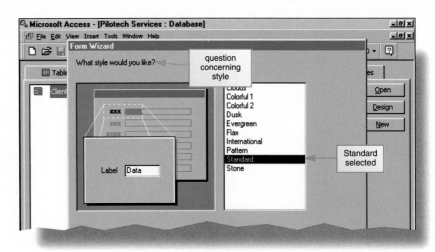

FIGURE 4-42

4 Be sure Standard is selected, click the Next button, type Client Update Form **as the title for the form. Click the Finish button to complete and display the form.**

The form displays (Figure 4-43).

5 Click the Close button for the Client Update Form window to close the form.

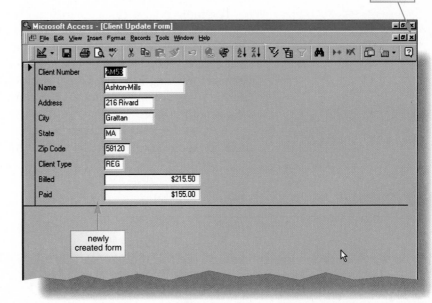

FIGURE 4-43

Modifying the Form Design

To modify the design of an existing form, right-click the form in the Database window, and then click Design on the shortcut menu. Then, modify the design. The modifications can include moving fields, adding new fields, and changing field characteristics. In addition, they can include adding special features, such as combo boxes and titles. The modifications also can involve changes to colors.

Just as with reports, the various items on a form are called **controls**. The three types are **bound controls**, which are used to display data that comes from the database, such as the client number and name. Bound controls have attached labels that typically display the name of the field that furnishes the data for the control. The **attached label** for the Client Number field, for example, is the portion of the screen immediately to the left of the field. It contains the words, Client Number.

Other Ways

1. With table selected, click New Object button arrow on toolbar, click Form, click Form Wizard to create form

2. On Insert menu click Form, click Form Wizard to create form

More *About*
Attached Labels

You can remove an attached label by clicking the label and then pressing the DELETE key. The label will be removed, but the control will remain. To attach a label to a control, create the label, click the Cut button, click the Control, and then click the Paste button.

Unbound controls are not associated with data from the database and are used to display such things as the form's title. Finally, **calculated controls** are used to display data that is calculated from data in the database, such as the outstanding amount, which is calculated by subtracting the paid amount from the billed amount.

To move, resize, delete, or modify a control, click it. Handles display around the border of the control and, if appropriate, around the attached label. If you point to the border of the control, but away from any handle, the pointer shape will change to a hand. You then can drag the control to move it. If an attached label is present, it will move along with the control. If you wish to move the control or the attached label separately, drag the large handle in the upper-left corner of the control or label. You also can drag one of the sizing handles to resize the control, or press the DELETE key to delete it. Clicking a second time produces an insertion point in the control in order to modify its contents.

Just as with reports, some of the changes involve using the property sheet for the control to be changed. You will use the property sheet of the Outstanding Amount control, for example, to change the format that Access uses to display the contents of the control.

The toolbox also can obscure a portion of the form as it obscured a portion of a report. You can use the Toolbox button to remove it and return it to the screen when needed. Because you use the toolbox frequently when modifying form designs, it is desirable to be able to leave it on the screen, however. You can do this by moving it to a different position on the screen, which is a process referred to as **docking**. To do so, you simply drag the title bar of the toolbox to the desired position.

Perform the following steps to modify the design of the Client Update Form and dock the toolbox at the bottom of the screen.

Steps To Modify the Form Design

1 In the Pilotech Services database window, click the Forms tab. Right-click the Client Update Form to display its shortcut menu.

The shortcut menu for the Client Update Form displays.

2 Click Design on the shortcut menu. Maximize the window, if necessary. Be sure the toolbox displays. (If it does not, click the Toolbox button on the toolbar). Point to the title bar of the toolbox (Figure 4-44).

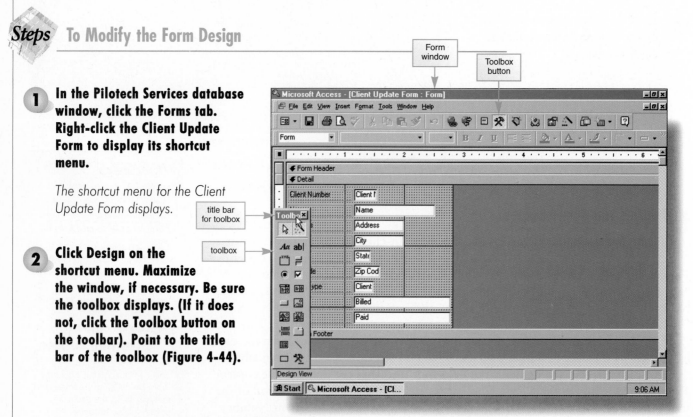

FIGURE 4-44

3 If the toolbox is not already docked at the bottom of the screen, drag the title bar of the toolbox below the scroll bar at the bottom of the screen and release the left mouse button.

The toolbox is docked at the bottom of the screen (Figure 4-45).

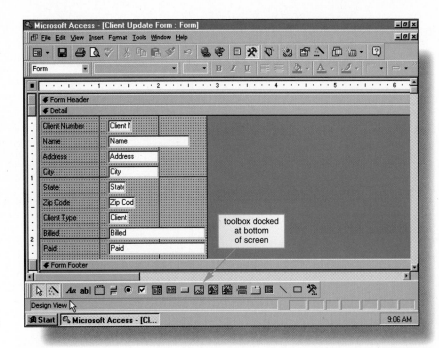

FIGURE 4-45

4 Click the control for the Client Type field, and then move the mouse pointer until the shape changes to a hand. (You will need to point to the border of the control but away from any handle.)

Move handles display, indicating the field is selected (Figure 4-46). The shape of the mouse pointer has changed to a hand.

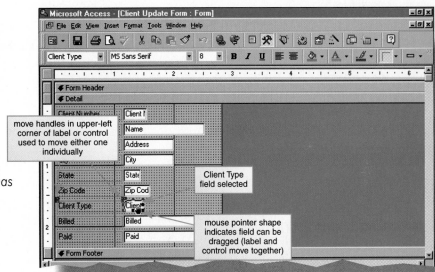

FIGURE 4-46

5 Drag the Client Type field to the approximate position shown in Figure 4-47. The form will expand automatically in size to accommodate the new position for the field.

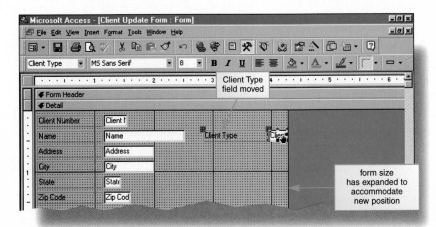

FIGURE 4-47

6 Use the same steps to move the Billed and Paid fields to the positions shown in Figure 4-48.

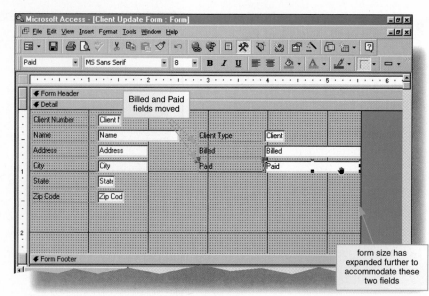

FIGURE 4-48

More *About*
Adding a Field

You can receive assistance in entering the expression for a field you are adding by using the Expression Builder. To do so, click the Control Source property on the control's property sheet and then click the Build button. The Expression Builder dialog box then will display.

Adding a New Field

To add a new field, use the **Text Box button** in the toolbox to add a field. After clicking the Text Box button, click the position for the field on the form, and then indicate the contents of the field. Perform the following steps to add the Outstanding Amount field to the form.

Steps To Add a New Field

1 Point to the Text Box button in the toolbox (Figure 4-49).

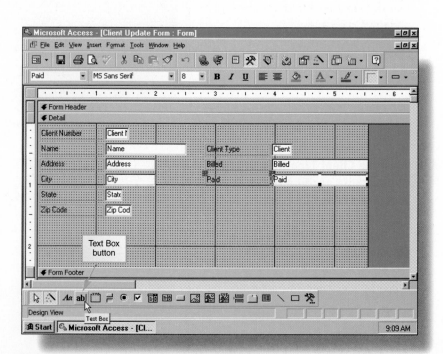

FIGURE 4-49

2 Click the Text Box button in the toolbox, and then move the mouse pointer, which has changed shape to a small plus sign accompanied by a text box, to the position shown in Figure 4-50.

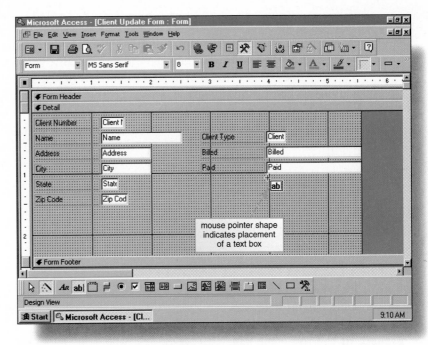

FIGURE 4-50

3 Click the position shown in Figure 4-50 to place a text box. Type =[Billed]-[Paid] as the expression in the text box. Click the field label (the box that contains the word Text) twice, once to select it and a second time to produce an insertion point. Use the DELETE key or the BACKSPACE key to delete the current entry. Type Outstanding Amount as the new entry.

The expression for the field has been entered and the label has been changed to Outstanding Amount (Figure 4-51).

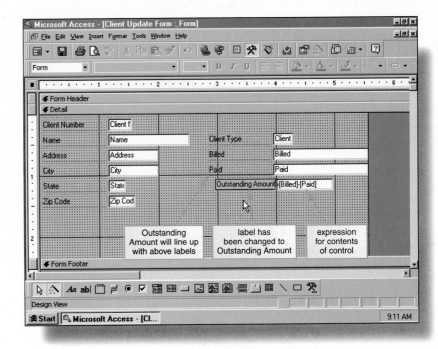

FIGURE 4-51

4 Click outside the Outstanding Amount control to deselect it. Then, click the control to select it once more. Handles will display around the control. Move the label portion so its left edge lines up with the labels for the Client Type, Billed, and Paid fields by dragging the move handle in its upper-left corner.

More *About*
Changing a Format

Access assigns formats to database fields, but these formats can be changed by changing the Format property. The specific formats that are available depend on the data type of the field. The Format list also contains samples of the way the data would display with the various formats.

Changing the Format of a Field

Access automatically formats fields from the database appropriately, because it knows their data types. Usually, you will find the formats assigned by Access to be acceptable. For calculated fields, such as Outstanding Amount, however, Access just assigns a general format. The value will not display automatically with two decimal places and a dollar sign.

A special format, such as Currency, which displays the number with a dollar sign and two decimal places, requires using the field's property sheet to change the Format property. Perform the following steps to change the format for the Outstanding Amount field to Currency.

Steps **To Change the Format of a Field**

1 Right-click the control for the Outstanding Amount field (the box containing the expression) to produce its shortcut menu and then click Properties on the shortcut menu. Click the All tab, if necessary, so all the properties display, and then click the Format property. Point to the Format box arrow.

The property sheet for the field displays in the Text Box window (Figure 4-52).

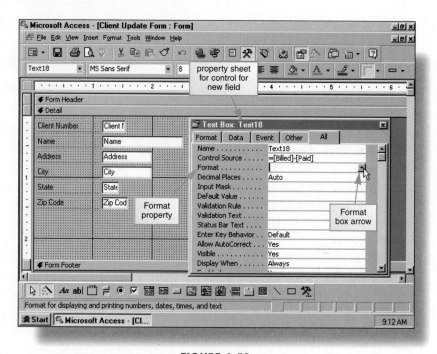

FIGURE 4-52

2 Click the Format box arrow to produce a list of available formats. Scroll down so Currency displays and then click Currency. Close the property sheet by clicking its Close button.

The values in the Outstanding Amount field now display in Currency format, which includes a dollar sign and two decimal places.

Placing a Combo Box

To place a combo box, use the Combo Box button in the toolbox. If the **Control Wizards button** in the toolbox is recessed, you can use a wizard to guide you through the process of creating the combo box. Perform the following steps to place a combo box for the Tech Number on the form.

Steps To Place a Combo Box

1 Make sure the Control Wizards button in the toolbox is recessed. Point to the Combo Box button in the toolbox (Figure 4-53).

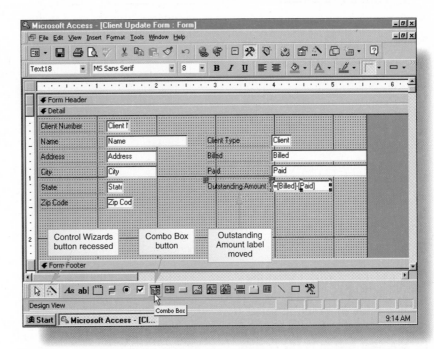

FIGURE 4-53

2 Click the Combo Box button in the toolbox, and then move the mouse pointer, whose shape has changed to a small plus sign accompanied by a combo box, to the position shown in Figure 4-54.

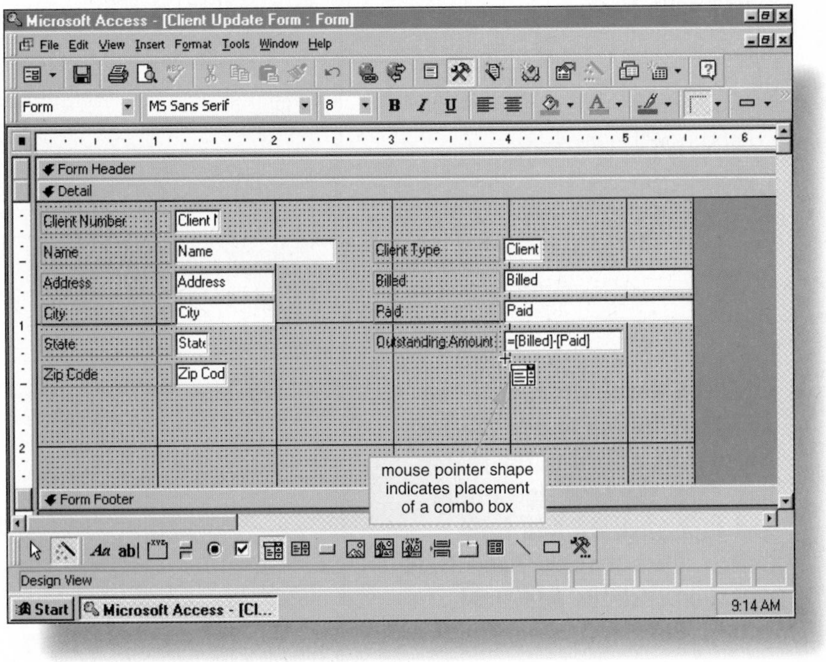

FIGURE 4-54

3 Click the position shown in Figure 4-54 on the previous page to place a combo box.

The Combo Box Wizard dialog box displays, requesting that you indicate how the combo box is to receive values for the list (Figure 4-55).

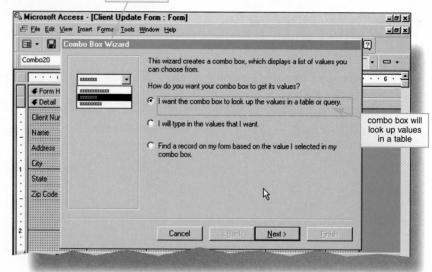

FIGURE 4-55

4 If necessary, click I want the combo box to look up the values in a table or query. to select it as shown in Figure 4-55. Click the Next button in the Combo Box Wizard dialog box, click the Technician table, and then point to the Next button.

The Technician table is selected as the table to provide values for the combo box (Figure 4-56).

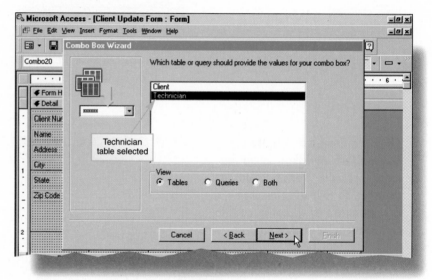

FIGURE 4-56

5 Click the Next button. Click the Add Field button to add the Tech Number as a field in the combo box. Click the First Name field and then click the Add Field button. Click the Last Name field and then click the Add Field button. Point to the Next button.

The Tech Number, First Name, and Last Name fields are selected for the combo box (Figure 4-57).

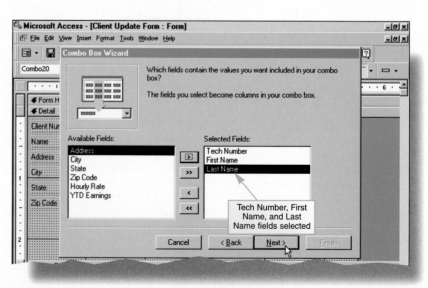

FIGURE 4-57

6 Click the Next button. Point to the Hide key column (recommended) check box.

The next Combo Box Wizard dialog box displays (Figure 4-58). You can use this dialog box to change the sizes of the fields. You also can use it to indicate whether the key field, in this case the Tech Number field, should be hidden.

7 Click Hide key column (recommended) to remove the check mark to ensure the Tech Number field displays along with the First Name and Last Name fields. Resize each column to best fit the data by double-clicking the right-hand border of the column heading. Click the Next button.

The Combo Box Wizard dialog box displays, asking you to choose a field that uniquely identifies a row in the combo box. The Tech Number field, which is the correct field, already is selected.

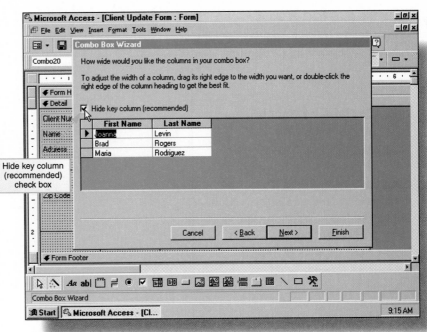

FIGURE 4-58

8 Click the Next button. Click Store that value in this field. Click the Store that value in this field box arrow, scroll down and then click Tech Number.

The Store that value in this field option button is selected and the Tech Number field is selected (Figure 4-59).

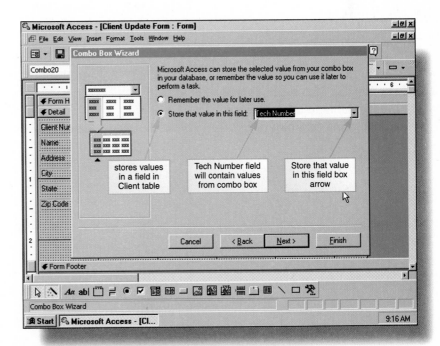

FIGURE 4-59

9 Click the Next button. Type Technician Number as the label for the combo box (Figure 4-60).

10 Click the Finish button. Click the label for the combo box, and then move the label so its left edge aligns with the left edge of the Client Type, Billed, Paid, and Outstanding Amount fields. Select the label and then expand it by double-clicking the handle on its right edge so the entire Technician Number label displays.

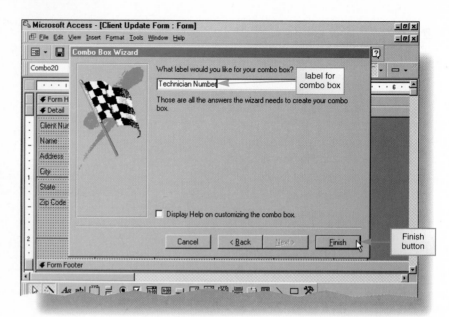

FIGURE 4-60

Adding a Title

The form in Figure 4-3 on page A 4.8 contains a title, Client Update Form that displays in a large, light blue label at the top of the form. To add a title, first expand the Form Header to allow room for the title. Next, use the Label button in the toolbox to place the label in the Form Header. Finally, type the title in the label. Perform the following steps to add a title to the form.

Steps To Add a Title

1 Point to the bottom border of the Form Header. The mouse pointer changes shape to a two-headed vertical arrow as shown in Figure 4-61.

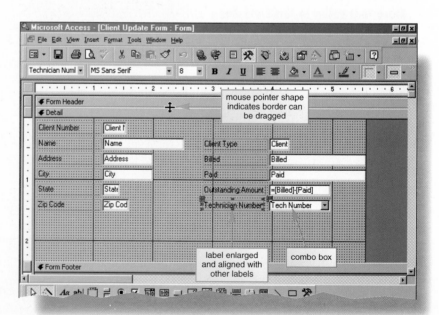

FIGURE 4-61

2 Drag the bottom border of the Form Header to the approximate position shown in Figure 4-62, and then point to the Label button in the toolbox.

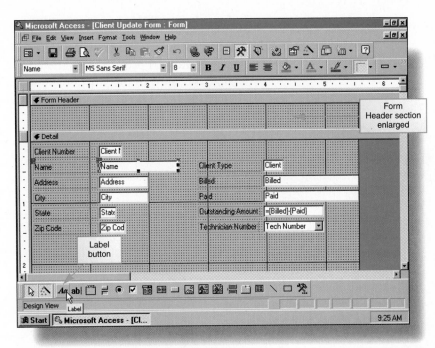

FIGURE 4-62

3 Click the Label button in the toolbox and move the mouse pointer, whose shape has changed to a small plus sign accompanied by a label, into the position shown in Figure 4-63.

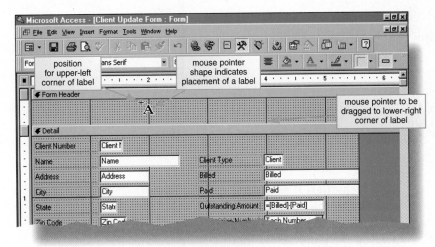

FIGURE 4-63

4 Press the left mouse button and drag the pointer to the opposite corner of the Form Header to form the label shown in Figure 4-64.

5 Type Client Update Form as the form title.

The title is entered.

FIGURE 4-64

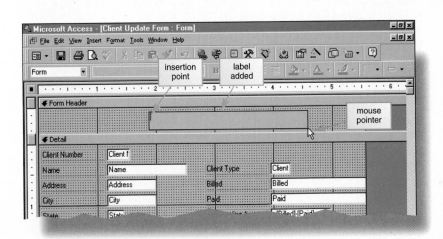

Enhancing a Title

The form now contains a title. You can enhance the appearance of the title by changing various properties of the label containing the title. The following steps change the color of the label, make the label appear to be raised from the screen, change the font size of the title, and change the alignment of the title within the label.

Steps **To Enhance a Title**

1 **Click somewhere outside the label containing the title to deselect the label. Deselecting is required or right-clicking the label will have no effect. Next, right-click the label containing the title. Point to Properties on the shortcut menu.**

The shortcut menu for the label displays (Figure 4-65).

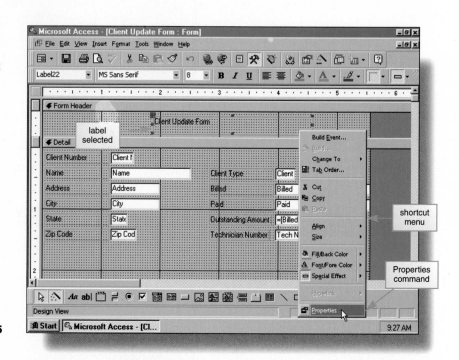

FIGURE 4-65

2 **Click Properties. If necessary, click the All tab on the property sheet. Click Back Color and then point to the Build button (the button with the three dots).**

The property sheet for the label displays. The insertion point displays in the Back Color property (Figure 4-66).

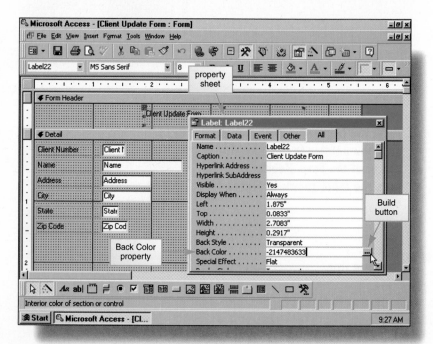

FIGURE 4-66

3 Click the Build button and then point to the color light blue in the Color dialog box that displays (Figure 4-67).

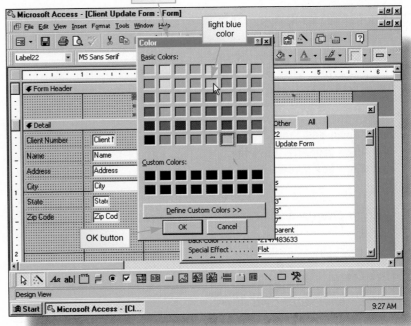

FIGURE 4-67

4 Click the color light blue, and then click the OK button. Click the Special Effect property, and then click the Special Effect box arrow.

The list of available values for the Special Effect property displays (Figure 4-68).

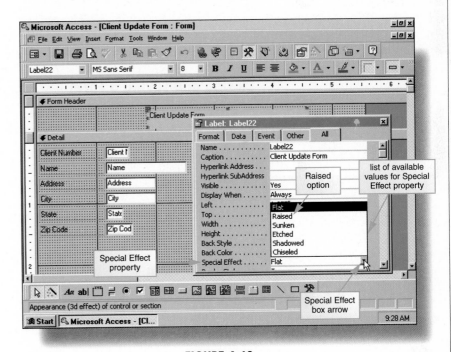

FIGURE 4-68

5 Click Raised. Scroll down the property sheet and then click the Font Size property. Click the Font Size box arrow. Click 14 in the list of font sizes that displays.

6 Scroll down and then click the Text Align property. Click the Text Align box arrow.

The list of available values for the Text Align property displays (Figure 4-69).

7 Click Center. Close the property sheet by clicking its Close button.

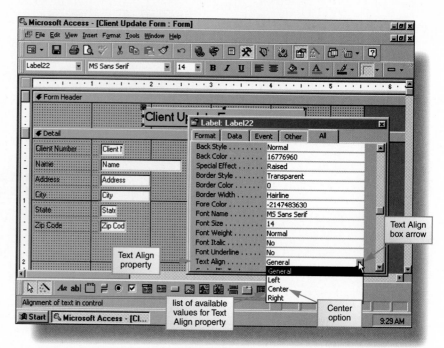

FIGURE 4-69

The enhancements to the title now are complete.

Closing and Saving a Form

To close a form, close the window using the window's Close button. Then indicate whether you want to save your changes. Perform the following step to close and save the form.

OtherWays

1. On File menu click Close

TO CLOSE AND SAVE A FORM

Step 1: Click the window's Close button to close the window, and then click the Yes button to save the design of the form.

Opening a Form

To open a form, right-click a form in the Database window, and then click Open on the shortcut menu. The form will display and can be used to examine and update data. Perform the following steps to open the Client Update Form.

Steps To Open a Form

1 **Right-click the Client Update Form to display the shortcut menu. Point to Open on the shortcut menu.**

The shortcut menu for the Client Update Form displays (Figure 4-70).

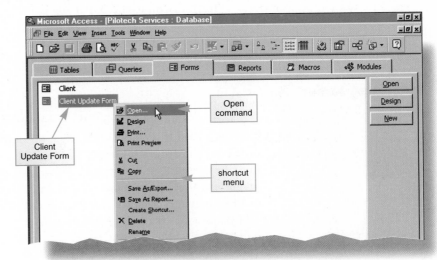

FIGURE 4-70

2 **Click Open on the shortcut menu.**

The form displays. It should look like the form shown in Figure 4-3 on page A 4.8.

Using a Form

You use this form as you used the form in Project 3, with two differences. Access will not allow changes to the outstanding amount, because Access calculates this amount automatically by subtracting the paid amount from the billed amount. The other difference is that this form contains a combo box, which you can use to select a Technician Number (Figure 4-3 on page A 4.8).

To use the combo box, click the arrow. The numbers and names of available technicians display as shown in Figure 4-3. Either you can type the appropriate technician number from the list you see on the screen or you can click the appropriate technician. In either case, the combo box helps you make sure you enter the correct number.

Closing a Form

To close a form, simply close the window containing the form. Perform the following step to close the form.

TO CLOSE A FORM

Step 1: Click the Close button for the Form window.

Form Design Considerations

As you design and create custom forms, keep in mind the following guidelines.

1. Remember that someone using your form may be looking at the form for several hours at a time. Forms that are cluttered excessively or that contain too many different effects (colors, fonts, frame styles, and so on) can become very hard on the eyes.

2. Place the fields in logical groupings. Fields that relate to each other should be close to each other on the form.

3. If the data that a user will enter comes from a paper form, make the screen form resemble the paper form as closely as possible.

Publishing to the Web

More *About*
Publishing to the Web

Access creates one Web page for each report page, datasheet, and form that you publish to the Web. You can use the Publish to the Web wizard to publish custom forms that allow you to view data as well as add, change, and delete records in the database.

Access provides the capability of creating a version of a datasheet, form, or report in a format that can be viewed on the **Internet**, specifically on a portion of the Internet called the **World Wide Web**, or simply the **Web**. (It also could be viewed on an organization's **intranet**.) To do so, the version of the object to be viewed must be stored as a **Web page**. Web pages are stored in a language called **HTML** (**hypertext markup language**). Fortunately, you do not need to know the details of this language, because Access will create this version for you automatically. The process of creating such a version is referred to as **publishing to the Web**. The tool in Access that assists you in the process is the Publish to the Web Wizard.

Publishing an Object to the Web

To publish an object to the Web, you first must save the object as HTML. The Publish to the Web Wizard then will lead you through the necessary steps to create the HTML version of the object. Perform the following steps to publish the Client Amount Report to the Web.

Steps To Publish a Report to the Web

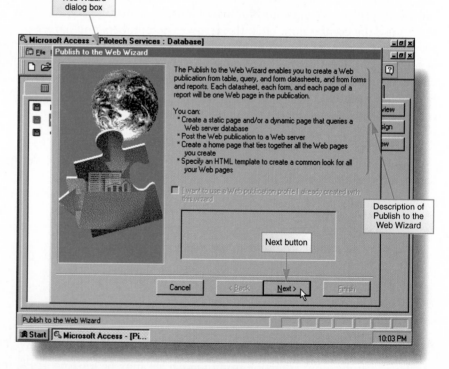

1 **With the Database window on the screen, click File on the menu bar and then click Save as HTML. Point to the Next button.**

The Publish to the Web Wizard dialog box displays (Figure 4-71).

More *About*
Static and Dynamic HTML Format

When you publish a report to the Web, the report is stored in static HTML format. The resulting Web page is a snapshot of the data at the time you published your report. If your data changes, you must publish your report again. When you publish a custom form to the Web, you should use dynamic format to store and retrieve live data from your database.

FIGURE 4-71

2 Click the Next button. Click the Reports tab in the next Publish to the Web Wizard dialog box that displays, and then click the check box for the Client Amount Report.

The Publish to the Web Wizard dialog box displays, requesting you to select the objects you wish to publish (Figure 4-72). The Client Amount Report is selected.

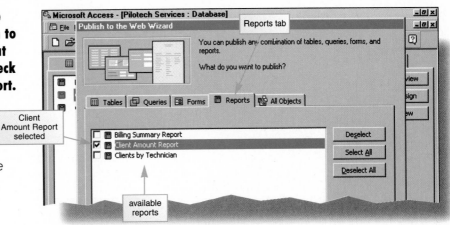

FIGURE 4-72

3 Click the Next button. No HTML document is to be used as a template in this project. Click the Next button. Be sure Static HTML is selected as the default format type, and then click the Next button. Point to the Browse button.

The Publish to the Web Wizard dialog box displays, asking where you want to place the Web publication (Figure 4-73).

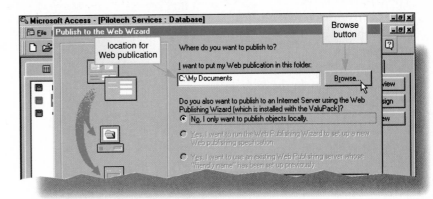

FIGURE 4-73

4 Click the Browse button. Click the Look in box arrow, click 3½ Floppy (A:), click the Access folder, and then click the Select button. Click the Next button.

The Publish to the Web Wizard dialog box displays, asking if you want to create a home page (Figure 4-74). If you were publishing several objects at once, a home page would be a convenient way to tie them together.

5 Be sure the Yes, I want to create a home page. check box is not checked and then click the Next button. Click the Finish button to complete the process.

The Publish to the Web Wizard creates a Web page for the Client Amount Report.

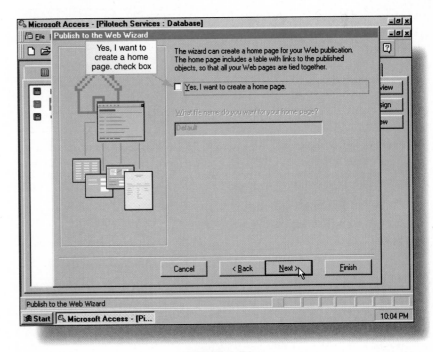

FIGURE 4-74

Viewing a Web Page

Once the Client Amount Report is saved as a Web page, you can use your browser or the **Web toolbar** in Access to display it. The following steps show how to launch your browser using the Access Web toolbar and Address text box on the Web toolbar.

 Steps To View a Web Page

1 **Insert the floppy disk with the HTML file into drive A. Right-click the toolbar and then click Web on the shortcut menu. When the Web toolbar displays, type the file path** a:\access\Client Amount Report_1.html **in the Address text box.**

The Web toolbar displays (Figure 4-75). The file path displays in the Address text box.

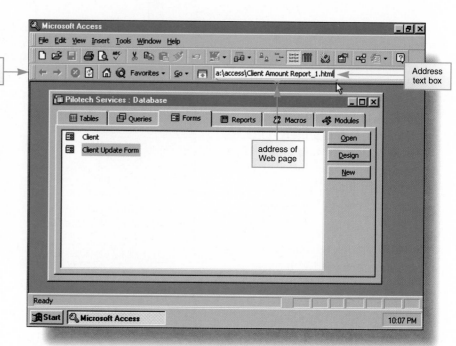

FIGURE 4-75

2 **Press the ENTER key.**

Your browser starts and displays the Client Amount Report Web page (Figure 4-76).

3 **Close the Microsoft Internet Explorer by clicking its Close button.**

4 **Right-Click the toolbar and then click Web on the shortcut menu.**

The Web toolbar no longer displays.

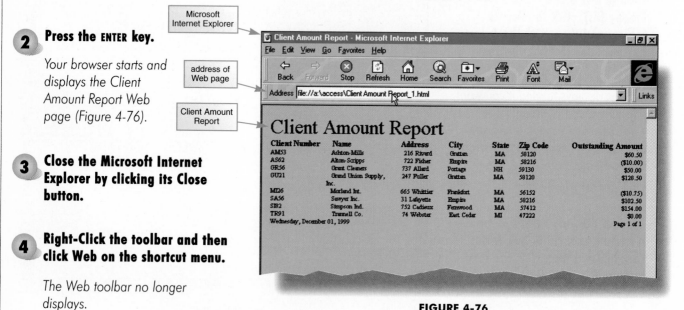

FIGURE 4-76

Closing a Database

The following step closes the database by closing its Database window.

TO CLOSE A DATABASE

Step 1: Click the Close button for the Pilotech Services : Database window.

Project Summary

Project 4 covered the creation of reports and forms. To create the reports for Pilotech Services, you learned the purpose of the various sections and how to modify their contents. You used grouping in a report. You created and used a custom form. Steps and techniques were presented showing you how to move controls, create new controls, add combo boxes, and add a title. You changed the characteristics of various objects in a form. General principles to help you design effective reports and forms were explained. Finally, you learned how to publish an object to the Web (or an intranet connection) using the Publish to the Web Wizard.

What You Should Know

Having completed this project, you now should be able to perform the following tasks:

▶ Add a New Field *(A 4.36)*
▶ Add a Title *(A 4.42)*
▶ Begin Creating a Form *(A 4.32)*
▶ Change the Can Grow Property *(A 4.17)*
▶ Change the Column Headings *(A 4.28)*
▶ Change the Format of a Field *(A 4.38)*
▶ Close a Database *(A 4.51)*
▶ Close a Form *(A 4.47)*
▶ Close and Save a Form *(A 4.46)*
▶ Close and Save a Report *(A 4.19, A 4.31)*
▶ Create a Report *(A 4.11)*
▶ Create a Second Report *(A 4.22)*
▶ Create a Query *(A 4.10, A 4.21)*
▶ Enhance a Title *(A 4.44)*

▶ Enlarge the Page Header Section *(A 4.27)*
▶ Modify the Form Design *(A 4.34)*
▶ Move and Resize Controls *(A 4.29)*
▶ Move to Design View and Remove the Toolbox *(A 4.16)*
▶ Open a Database *(A 4.9)*
▶ Open a Form *(A 4.47)*
▶ Place a Combo Box *(A 4.39)*
▶ Preview a Report *(A 4.31)*
▶ Print a Report *(A 4.20, A 4.31)*
▶ Publish a Report to the Web *(A 4.48)*
▶ Remove Unwanted Controls *(A 4.26)*
▶ View a Web Page *(A 4.50)*

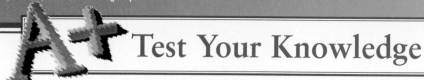

Test Your Knowledge

1 True/False

Instructions: Circle T if the statement is true or F if the statement is false.

T F 1. Only a report that does not need to be modified in any way can be created with the Report Wizard.

T F 2. The contents of the Page Footer section will display only once on a report.

T F 3. The Report window uses small squares called sizing handles to indicate which portion of a report currently is selected.

T F 4. The various entries appearing in a report, such as the report title and a column heading, are called containers.

T F 5. To remove a control from a report, select the control and press the CTRL+D keys.

T F 6. To split a column heading over two lines, place the insertion point at the position where you would like to split the heading, and then press the TAB+ENTER keys.

T F 7. The three types of controls on a form are bound controls, unbound controls, and calculated controls.

T F 8. On a form, unbound controls are used to display the title.

T F 9. To add a new field to a form, use the Label button in the toolbox.

T F 10. A combo box is a box that allows you to select entries from a list.

2 Multiple Choice

Instructions: Circle the correct response.

1. The process of creating separate collections of records sharing some common characteristic is known as _____.
   a. collecting
   b. matching
   c. categorizing
   d. grouping

2. By changing the value of the _____ property, data can be split over two lines on a report.
   a. Enlarge
   b. Can Grow
   c. Magnify
   d. Expand

3. To remove a control from a report, select the control and then _____.
   a. press the DELETE key
   b. press the CTRL+DELETE keys
   c. press the CTRL+D keys
   d. right-click

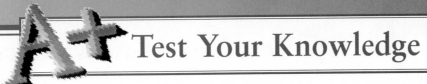

Test Your Knowledge

4. Portions of the Report window such as Report Header or Page Header are called _____.
   a. segments
   b. sections
   c. areas
   d. bands

5. The Report window uses small squares called _____ to indicate which portion of the report currently is selected.
   a. handholds
   b. braces
   c. handles
   d. grippers

6. To split a column heading over two lines, place the insertion point at the position where you would like to split the heading, and then press the _____ keys.
   a. SHIFT+ENTER
   b. ENTER
   c. ALT+ENTER
   d. TAB+ENTER

7. On a custom form, controls that are used to display data in a database are called _____ controls.
   a. bound
   b. field
   c. unbound
   d. data

8. On a form, _____ controls are used to display data that is calculated from data in the database.
   a. tabulated
   b. calculated
   c. defined
   d. extended

9. Controls that are not associated with data in a database are called _____ controls.
   a. text
   b. bound
   c. unbound
   d. outside

10. To add a new field to a form, use the _____ button in the toolbox.
   a. Object Box
   b. Control Box
   c. Field Box
   d. Text Box

Test Your Knowledge

3 Understanding the Report Window

Instructions: In Figure 4-77, arrows point to the major components of the Report window. Identify the various parts of the Report window in the spaces provided. Answer the following questions about the window on your own paper.

1. How many times will the control with the label =Sum([Balance]) print?

2. How can you delete the control that begins ="Summary for"?

3. What values will print once at the top of every page?

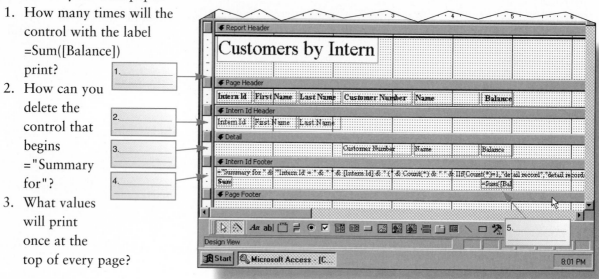

FIGURE 4-77

4 Understanding the Form Design Window

Instructions: In Figure 4-78, arrows point to various items in the Form Design window. Identify these items in the spaces provided. Answer the following questions about the window on your own paper.

1. Which control currently is selected?

2. Identify the unbound control(s) on the form.

3. Identify the bound control(s) on the form.

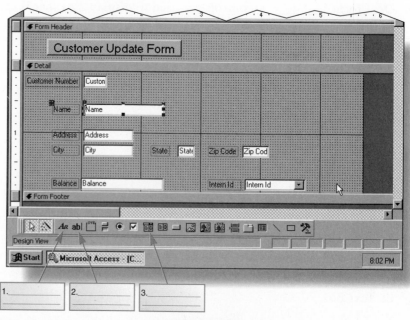

FIGURE 4-78

Use Help

1 Reviewing Project Activities

Instructions: Perform the following tasks using a computer.

1. Start Access.
2. If the Office Assistant is on your screen, then click it to display its balloon. If the Office Assistant is not on your screen, click the Office Assistant button on the toolbar.
3. Type property sheet in the What would you like to do? text box. Click the Search button. Click What is a property sheet?.
4. Read the Help information in the Microsoft Access 97 Help window. Next, right-click within the box, and then click Print Topic. Hand the printout in to your instructor. Click the Help Topics button to the return to the Help Topics: Microsoft Access 97 dialog box.
5. Click the Index tab. Type grouping in the top text box labeled 1, and then double-click grouping records in reports in the middle list box labeled 2. Double-click Example of grouped records in a report in the Topics Found dialog box. Read the Help information. Use the page number buttons in the upper-left corner of the screen to move to the next Help windows. Three Help windows will display. When you are finished, click the Close button.
6. Click the Office Assistant. Type controls in the What would you like to do? text box. Click the Search button. Click Move a control and its label. Read and print the Help information. Hand the printout in to your instructor.

2 Expanding the Basics

Instructions: Use Access Help to better understand the topics listed below. If you cannot print the Help information, then answer the question on your own paper.

1. Using the Office Assistant, answer the following questions:
   a. How can you change the page orientation for a report?
   b. Do you need to reset special page setup options each time you print a report?
   c. How can you preview just the layout of a report?
2. Use the Index tab in the Help Topics: Microsoft Access 97 dialog box to answer the following questions about fonts on forms and reports:
   a. How do you italicize text using the property sheet?
   b. What is the Formatting toolbar?
   c. Where is the Formatting toolbar located?
   d. How else can you italicize text?
3. Use the Find tab in the Help Topics: Microsoft Access 97 dialog box to display and print information on adding the current date and time to a form.
4. Use the Office Assistant to display and print information on exporting a table, query, form, or report to HTML format. Then, answer the following questions:
   a. What is an HTML template file?
   b. When do you use dynamic HTML format?

 Apply Your Knowledge

1 Presenting Data in the Green Thumb Database

Instructions: Start Access and open the Green Thumb database from the Access folder on the Data Disk that accompanies this book. Perform the following tasks.

1. Create a query that includes both the Customer and Intern tables. Include the Intern Id, First Name, and Last Name from the Intern table. Include the Customer Number, Name, and Balance from the Customer table.

2. Using the query, create the report shown in Figure 4-79.

Customers by Intern

Intern Id	First Name	Last Name	Customer Number	Name	Balance
102	Chou	Dang			
			AS36	Asterman Ind.	$85.00
			CJ16	CJ's Music and Videos	$105.00
					$190.00
105	Lois	Eckels			
			KL55	Klingon Toys	$115.00
					$115.00
109	Michelle	Hyde			
			AU54	Author Books	$50.00
			BI92	Bike Shop	$40.00
			JO62	Jordan Diner	$74.00
			RO32	Royal Mfg Co.	$93.00
					$257.00
113	Javier	Lopez			
			CI76	Cinderton Co.	$0.00
			MO13	Moore Foods	$0.00
					$0.00
					$562.00

Wednesday, December 30, 1998

Page 1 of 1

FIGURE 4-79

Apply Your Knowledge

3. Print the report.
4. Using the Form Wizard, create a form for the Customer table. Include all fields except Intern Id on the form. Use Customer Update Form as the title for the form.
5. Modify the form in the Design window to create the form shown in Figure 4-80. The form includes a combo box for the Intern Id field.

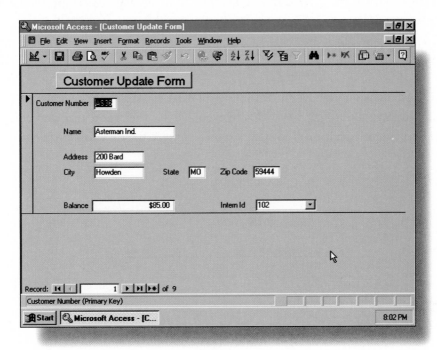

FIGURE 4-80

6. Print the form. To print the form, open the form, click File on the menu bar and then click Print. Click Selected Record(s) as the Print Range. Click the OK button.

In the Lab

1 Presenting Data in the Museum Mercantile Database

Problem: Museum Mercantile already has realized the benefits from the database of products and vendors that you created. The Museum director must now prepare reports for auditors as well as the executive board of the Museum. The director and volunteer staff greatly appreciate the validation rules that were added to ensure that data is entered correctly. They now feel they can improve the data entry process even further by creating custom forms.

Instructions: Open the Museum Mercantile database in the Access folder (see the note on page A 4.8). Perform the following tasks.

1. Create the On Hand Value Report shown in Figure 4-81 for the Product table. On Hand Value is the result of multiplying On Hand by Cost. In Figure 4-81, the report title and column headings are italicized. (*Hint*: Use information from Use Help Exercise 2 to solve this problem.)

On Hand Value Report

Product Id	Description	On Hand	Cost	On Hand Value
CH04	Chess Set	11	$26.75	$294.25
DI24	Dinosaurs	14	$3.75	$52.50
GL18	Globe	2	$27.50	$55.00
JG01	Jigsaw Puzzle	3	$5.40	$16.20
MN04	Mancala	4	$17.50	$70.00
PC03	Pick Up Sticks	5	$8.50	$42.50
ST23	Stationery	8	$3.95	$31.60
WI10	Wizard Cards	10	$7.50	$75.00
WL34	Wildlife Posters	15	$2.50	$37.50
YO12	Wooden YoYo	9	$1.60	$14.40

FIGURE 4-81

2. Print the report.
3. Create the Products by Vendor report shown in Figure 4-82. Profit is the difference between Selling Price and Cost.

In the Lab

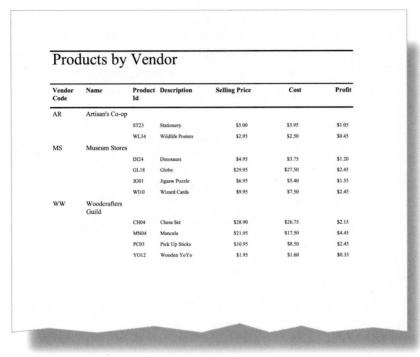

Products by Vendor

Vendor Code	Name	Product Id	Description	Selling Price	Cost	Profit
AR	Artisan's Co-op					
		ST23	Stationery	$5.00	$3.95	$1.05
		WL34	Wildlife Posters	$2.95	$2.50	$0.45
MS	Museum Stores					
		DI24	Dinosaurs	$4.95	$3.75	$1.20
		GL18	Globe	$29.95	$27.50	$2.45
		JG01	Jigsaw Puzzle	$6.95	$5.40	$1.55
		WI10	Wizard Cards	$9.95	$7.50	$2.45
WW	Woodcrafters Guild					
		CH04	Chess Set	$28.90	$26.75	$2.15
		MN04	Mancala	$21.95	$17.50	$4.45
		PC03	Pick Up Sticks	$10.95	$8.50	$2.45
		YO12	Wooden YoYo	$1.95	$1.60	$0.35

FIGURE 4-82

4. Print the report.
5. Create the form shown in Figure 4-83. On Hand Value is a calculated control and is the result of multiplying On Hand by Cost. Include a combo box for Vendor Code.
6. Print the form. To print the form, open the form, click File on the menu bar and then click Print. Click Selected Record(s) as the Print Range. Click the OK button.

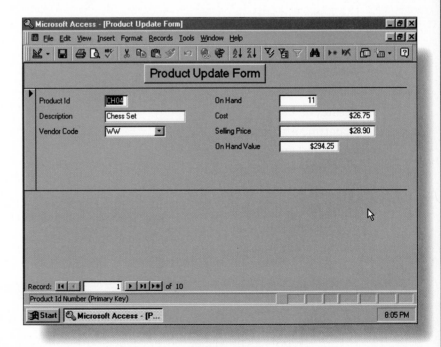

FIGURE 4-83

In the Lab

2 Presenting Data in the City Telephone System Database

Problem: The Telephone manager already has realized several benefits from the database of users and departments that you created. The manager now would like to prepare reports from the database that can be used for hourly rate purposes. She greatly appreciates the validation rules that were added to ensure that data is entered correctly. She now feels that the data entry process can be improved even further by creating custom forms.

Instructions: Open the City Telephone System database in the Access folder (see the note on page A 4.8). Perform the following tasks.

1. Create the Total Charges Report shown in Figure 4-84. Total Charges is the sum of Basic Charge and Extra Charges. The report is sorted by last name. (*Hint*: Sort the query by last name rather than using the Report Wizard to sort the records.)

2. Print the report.

3. Create the Users by Department report shown in Figure 4-85. Notice that the date appears at the top of the report. (*Hint*: Use information from Use Help Exercise 1 to solve this problem.)

Total Charges Report

User Id	Last Name	First Name	Phone Ext	Office	Total Charges
T087	Anders	Jane	3923	531	$10.00
T129	Bishop	Fred	3383	212	$32.00
T238	Chan	Rose	3495	220	$42.95
T347	Febo	Javier	4267	323	$17.75
T451	Ginras	Mary Catherin	3156	444	$69.85
T536	Hanneman	William	3578	317	$31.75
T645	Johnsen	Paul	4445	234	$28.75
T780	Mentor	Melissa	3418	525	$90.95
T851	Sanchez	Alfredo	3134	438	$17.25
T890	Tartar	Joan	4655	240	$10.00
T888	TenClink	Brian	3414	521	$47.45

Wednesday, December 30, 1998   Page 1 of 1

FIGURE 4-84

In the Lab

Users by Department

Wednesday, December 30, 1998

Dept Code	Dept Name	User Id	Last Name	First Name	Basic Charge	Extra Charges	Total Charges
APV	Assessment						
		T451	Ginras	Mary Catherin	$17.00	$52.85	$69.85
		T851	Sanchez	Alfredo	$11.00	$6.25	$17.25
					$28.00	$59.10	$87.10
HRS	Housing						
		T347	Febo	Javier	$10.00	$7.75	$17.75
		T536	Hanneman	William	$13.00	$18.75	$31.75
		T890	Tartar	Joan	$10.00	$0.00	$10.00
					$33.00	$26.50	$59.50
ITD	Income Tax						
		T129	Bishop	Fred	$10.00	$22.00	$32.00
		T238	Chan	Rose	$13.00	$29.95	$42.95
		T645	Johnsen	Paul	$21.00	$7.75	$28.75
					$44.00	$59.70	$103.70
PLN	Planning						
		T087	Anders	Jane	$10.00	$0.00	$10.00
		T780	Mentor	Melissa	$17.00	$73.95	$90.95
		T888	TenClink	Brian	$10.00	$37.45	$47.45
					$37.00	$111.40	$148.40
					$142.00	$256.70	$398.70

Page 1 of 1

FIGURE 4-85

4. Print the report.
5. Create the form shown in Figure 4-86 on the next page. Total Charges is a calculated control and is the sum of Basic Charge and Extra Charges. Dept Code is a combo box.
6. Print the form. To print the form, open the form, click File on the menu bar and then click Print. Click Selected Record(s) as the Print Range. Click the OK button.
7. Publish the Total Charges Report to the Web.

(continued)

In the Lab

Presenting Data in the City Telephone System Database *(continued)*

FIGURE 4-86

3 **Presenting Data in the City Scene Database**

Problem: *City Scene* magazine already has realized several benefits from the database of accounts and account reps that you created. The managing editor now would like to prepare reports from the database that can be used for financial analysis and future planning. He greatly appreciates the validation rules that were added to ensure that data is entered correctly. He now feels that the data entry process can be improved even further by creating custom forms.

Instructions: Open the City Scene database in the Access folder (see the note on page A 4.8). Perform the following tasks.

1. Create the Advertising Income Report shown in Figure 4-87. Advertising Income is the sum of Balance and Amount Paid.

In the Lab

Advertising Income Report

Advertiser Number	Name	City	Balance	Amount Paid	Advertising Income
A226	Alden Books	Fernwood	$60.00	$535.00	$595.00
B101	Bud's Diner	Crestview	$155.00	$795.00	$950.00
C134	Baker & Clover Clothes	New Castle	$100.00	$835.00	$935.00
D216	Dogs 'n Draft	Crestview	$260.00	$485.00	$745.00
G080	Green Thumb	New Castle	$185.00	$825.00	$1,010.00
L189	Lighthouse Inc.	Crestview	$35.00	$150.00	$185.00
M121	Shoe Salon	Fernwood	$50.00	$0.00	$50.00
N034	New Releases	Fernwood	$435.00	$500.00	$935.00
S010	Skates R You	New Castle	$85.00	$235.00	$320.00

Wednesday, December 30, 1998   Page 1 of 1

FIGURE 4-87

2. Print the report.
3. Create the Advertisers by Ad Rep report shown in Figure 4-88 on the next page.

(continued)

In the Lab

Presenting Data in the City Scene Database *(continued)*

Advertisers by Ad Rep

Ad Rep Number	First Name	Last Name	Advertiser Number	Name	Ad Type	Balance	Amount Paid
16	Anne	Hammond					
			A226	Alden Books	RET	$60.00	$535.00
			D216	Dogs 'n Draft	DIN	$260.00	$485.00
			L189	Lighthouse Inc.	RET	$35.00	$150.00
			S010	Skates R You	RET	$85.00	$235.00
						$440.00	$1,405.00
19	Louis	Morales					
			B101	Bud's Diner	DIN	$155.00	$795.00
			G080	Green Thumb	SER	$185.00	$825.00
						$340.00	$1,620.00
22	Elaine	Rodgers					
			C134	Baker & Clover Clothes	RET	$100.00	$835.00
			M121	Shoe Salon	RET	$50.00	$0.00
			N034	New Releases	RET	$435.00	$500.00
						$585.00	$1,335.00
						$1,365.00	$4,360.00

Wednesday, December 30, 1998   Page 1 of 1

FIGURE 4-88

4. Print the report.
5. Create the form shown in Figure 4-89. Advertising Income is a calculated control and is the sum of Balance and Amount Paid. Ad Rep Number is a combo box.

In the Lab

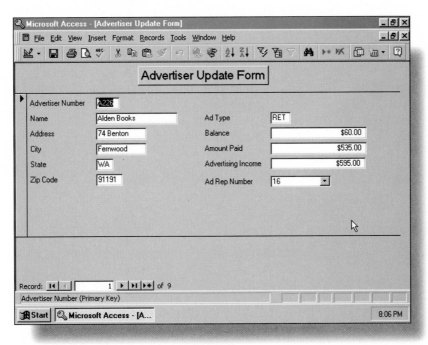

FIGURE 4-89

6. Add the current date to the form. (*Hint*: Use information from Use Help Exercise 2 to solve this problem.)

7. Print the form. To print the form, open the form, click File on the menu bar and then click Print. Click Selected Record(s) as the Print Range. Click the OK button.

8. Publish the Advertisers by Ad Rep report to the Web.

Cases and Places

The difficulty of these case studies varies: ❱ are the least difficult, ❱❱ are more difficult; and ❱❱❱ are the most difficult.

1 ❱ The Athletic department has decided to offer golf clinics emphasizing particular skills. Create a Lesson Revenue Report similar in format to Figure 4-81 on page A 4.58 that shows the maximum revenue that can be generated in each class. Use the data in Figure 4-90. Use the heading, Maximum Revenue, for the last column, and calculate the maximum revenue by multiplying Maximum Students by Fee. Print the report.

Lesson Revenue Table

CLASS ID	DESCRIPTION	MAXIMUM STUDENTS	FEE	PRO'S SALARY	PRO'S INITIALS
101	Grip	25	$15	$135	GC
102	Setup	15	$22	$168	CW
103	Alignment	20	$18	$180	VM
104	Posture	25	$20	$180	VM
105	Pitching	20	$25	$168	VM
106	Bunker Play	10	$30	$210	CW
107	Chipping	15	$28	$388	GC
108	Putting	10	$30	$388	SP
109	Finishing and Balance	15	$24	$158	GC
110	Distance	10	$20	$175	SP

FIGURE 4-90

2 ❱ Using the database from Case Study 1 above, create a Classes By Pro report similar in format to Figure 4-82 on page A 4.59 that shows each pro's name, classes taught, maximum revenue in the classes, pro's salary, and profit. Profit is calculated by subtracting the pro's salary from the maximum revenue. Use the data in Figure 4-91. Print the report.

Pro Table

PRO'S INITIALS	PRO'S NAME
GC	Greg Cotter
CW	Christy Walton
VM	Vishnu Mahraj
SP	Sue Pendleton

FIGURE 4-91

Cases and Places

3 ▶▶ Using the database from Case Studies 1 and 2, create a Class Update Form similar to the one in Figure 4-83 on page A 4.59. Use a calculated control called Revenue that is the result of multiplying Maximum Students by Fee. Include a combo box for Pro's Initials. Print the form.

4 ▶▶ The textbook exchange system you created in Case Study 1 of the Cases and Places section of Project 1 has become extremely successful. Student government has had a tremendous response and has decided to charge a 10 percent commission on each book exchanged. The money collected will be used to fund various student activities. Create and print a Textbook Exchange Report that shows book title, author, seller's name, seller's telephone number, price, and commission. Commission is calculated by multiplying the price by 10 percent (0.10). In addition, create and print a form that helps you input and delete books in the textbook database.

5 ▶▶▶ Finding restaurants that match an individual's food preferences and schedule often is a time-consuming process. Restaurants seem to open and close overnight, or the hours and cuisine of the established restaurants change frequently depending on seasons and trends. You have found the database you created in Case Study 2 of the Cases and Places section of Project 1 to be valuable, so you need a form to help you make frequent updates easily. Create and print this form. In addition, create and print a report organized by food type.

6 ▶▶▶ You have a part-time job on campus working at the Information Desk. Visitors often approach you to ask the room number of particular instructors and offices, and callers ask for telephone extensions and office hours. Currently, you must consult several directories and guides to answer their questions, so you decide to create a database resembling the one in Case Study 6 of the Cases and Places section of Project 1. Create and print a report showing pertinent campus information in the categories of faculty, administration, and services. In addition, create and print a form to help you update the database easily.

Cases and Places

7   ▶▶▶ Few people have addressed adequately the goal of financial security in retirement. The rule of thumb is a retiree needs 80 percent of annual, after-tax pre-retirement income to live comfortably. To estimate how much you will need to have saved on your last day on the job, compute 80 percent of your current annual, after-tax income and divide that number by four percent, which is the annual rate of return you can expect from investments adjusted for inflation. With that investing goal in mind, your accounting instructor wants you to add $20,000 you have inherited from your favorite aunt to the $1,000 he had you invest in an Individual Retirement Account in Case Study 7 of the Cases and Places section of Project 1. Create and print an IRA Future Value Report that shows the names, addresses, and telephone numbers of financial institutions, current interest rates, and total values of the IRAs by age 65. Include a column comparing these IRA values to how much you will need to have invested when you retire.

Microsoft Access *97*

Enhancing Forms with OLE Fields, Hyperlinks, and Subforms

Objectives:

You will have mastered the material in this project when you can:

▶ Use date, memo, and OLE fields
▶ Enter data in date fields
▶ Enter data in memo fields
▶ Enter pictures into OLE fields
▶ Change row and column spacing in tables
▶ Save table properties
▶ Create a form with a subform
▶ Move and resize fields on a form
▶ Use a form that contains a subform
▶ Change styles and colors of labels
▶ Use date and memo fields in a query

Project 5

Illuminate Your Work

I n futuristic 32 A.D., carefully avoiding the Valley of the Misborn, feckless Brother Francis rode a scrawny burro along a narrow trail, carrying a most sacred manuscript concealed beneath his robe. For fifteen years he had toiled, first copying the wondrous drawing created by the *Beatus*, Irving E. Leibowitz, onto bleached sheepskin, then illuminating the copy with brilliantly hued letters, embellished with leaves and vines, and inlaid with scrollwork of gold and silver. Now, he was en route to New Rome, where he would deliver the holy document to Pope Leo XXII, who soon would canonize Leibowitz as a saint. Just when Brother Francis thought he had passed out of harm's way, however, three humanoid creatures — one of them sporting two heads — sprang from hiding. Not satisfied with seizing his poor burro as the main course for their dinner, they plucked the precious manuscript — a copy of a blueprint entitled *Transistorized Control System for Unit Six-B*.

In *A Canticle for Leibowitz*, written during the height of 50s concern over the danger of nuclear war, *Canticle* was the most literarily successful science fiction novel written on the subject. Walter Michael Miller, Jr. paints a world where knowledge has been lost after the great Flame Deluge of the twentieth century. The setting is post-holocaust America where scraps of pre-war knowledge are gathered and preserved by monks who no longer understand that knowledge. After the fall of the Roman Empire, knowledge was preserved in Western Europe almost exclusively in small, isolated communities of priests and monks during a centuries-long dark age, recopied by men who often understood little of the ancient manuscripts of which they were the custodians.

An unexpected by-product of that activity was the enhanced works of art that these copies became; priceless pieces often bound in covers of gold or carved ivory. More importantly, they preserved knowledge that might otherwise have been lost and passed it on.

In today's world, knowledge flourishes. It is preserved, recalled, manipulated, enhanced, and stored. The process of enhancing documents is simplified by the capabilities of integration such as object linking an embedding (OLE). In Microsoft Access, along with other Microsoft products offering the OLE feature, it now is a simple matter to enhance a form in a database by inserting objects such as scanned-in photographs, clip art from the Microsoft Clip Gallery, and text from other applications.

In the topics presented in this project, you will experience the ease with which you can enter data and pictures into OLE fields, change styles and colors, and move and redesign objects on your forms. Data is everywhere on your PC, on local networks, and on the Internet. With such power at your fingertips, perhaps a form you create will become a model for the future.

Microsoft

Access 97

Enhancing Forms with OLE Fields, Hyperlinks, and Subforms

Case Perspective

The management of Pilotech Services has found it needs to maintain additional data on its technicians. Managers need to keep the start date of each technician in the database. They also would like the database to contain a description of the specialties of each technician as well as the technician's picture. In addition, each technician now has a page on the Web and the managers want to access this page easily from the database.

Once these fields have been added to the database, they would like to have a form created that incorporates the four new fields along with several existing fields. In addition, they would like the form to contain the client number, name, billed, and paid amounts for the clients of the technician. They would like to have two or three clients display on the screen at the same time, and the ability to scroll through all the clients of the technician. Finally, they would like to be able to access the technician's Web page directly from the form.

Introduction

This project creates the form shown in Figure 5-1. The form incorporates the following features not covered in previous projects:

- Four new fields are added to the Technician table. The Start Date field gives the date the technician began working for Pilotech Services. A Specialties field allows the organization to store a paragraph describing the specialties of the technician. The Specialties entry can be as long or short as the organization desires. The Picture field holds a picture of the technician. Finally, the Web Page field gives the ability to access the Technician's Web page directly from the database.
- The form not only shows data concerning the technician, but also the technician's clients. The clients are displayed as a table on the form. The form also contains the Web Page field. Clicking this field will access the technician's Web page automatically.

Project Five – Enhancing the Pilotech Services Forms

Before creating the form required by the management of Pilotech Services, first you must change the structure of the Technician table to incorporate the four new fields:

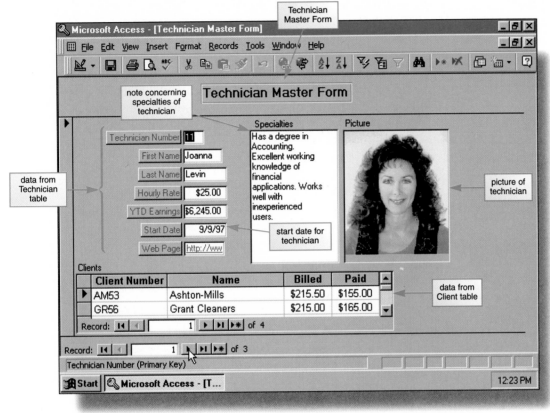

FIGURE 5-1

Start Date, Specialties, Picture, and Web Page. Each of the new fields uses a field type you have not encountered before. Then, you must fill in these new fields with appropriate data. The way this is achieved depends on the field type. After filling in the fields, you are to create the form including the table of client data. Finally, you will create queries to obtain the answer to two important questions that reference the new fields.

Overview of Project Steps

The database preparation steps give you an overview of how the new fields will be added and the form shown in Figure 5-1 will be created. The following tasks will be completed in this project.

1. Start Access.
2. Open the Pilotech Services database.
3. Add the Start Date, Specialties, Picture, and Web Page fields to the Technician table.
4. Update the Start Date, Specialties, Picture, and Web Page fields for the three technicians currently in the table.
5. Create a form that includes both technician and client data.

6. Move and resize objects on the form.
7. Change the size mode of the picture on the form so the entire picture displays.
8. Change special effects and colors of objects on the form.
9. Add a title to the form.
10. Use the form to view data.
11. Use the form to access the technicians' Web pages.
12. Create a query that uses the Start Date and Specialties fields.

The following pages contain a detailed explanation of these steps.

Opening the Database

Before modifying the Technician table and creating the form, first you must open the database. Perform the following steps to complete this task.

TO OPEN A DATABASE

Step 1: Click the Start button.
Step 2: Click Open Office Document, and then click 3½ Floppy (A:) in the Look in list box. If necessary, double-click the Access folder. Make sure the database called Pilotech Services is selected.
Step 3: Click the Open button.

The database is open and the Pilotech Services : Database window displays.

Date, Memo, OLE, and Hyperlink Fields

The data shown in the form in Figure 5-1 on the previous page incorporates the following field types:

1. **Date** (**D**) — The field can contain only valid dates.
2. **Memo** (**M**) — The field can contain text that is variable in length. The length of the text stored in memo fields virtually is unlimited.
3. **OLE** (**O**) — The field can contain objects created by other applications that support **OLE** (**Object Linking and Embedding**) as a server. Object Linking and Embedding is a special feature of Microsoft Windows that creates a special relationship between Microsoft Access and the application that created the object. When you edit the object, Microsoft Access returns automatically to the application that created the object.
4. **Hyperlink** (**H**) — This field can contain links to other office documents or to Web pages. If the link is to a Web page, the field will contain the **URL** (**Uniform Resource Locator**) of the Web page.

Adding Fields to a Table

You add the new fields to the Technician table by modifying the design of the table and inserting the fields at the appropriate position in the table structure. Perform the following steps to add the Start Date, Specialties, Picture, and Web Page fields to the Technician table.

Steps   To Add Fields to a Table

1 **If necessary, click the Tables tab. Right-click the Technician table, and then point to Design on the shortcut menu.**

The shortcut menu for the Technician table displays (Figure 5-2).

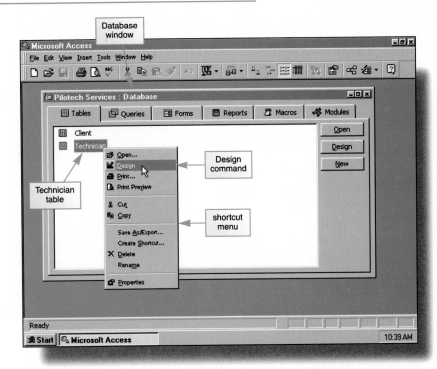

FIGURE 5-2

2 **Click Design on the shortcut menu and then maximize the Technician : Table window. Point to the position for the new field (the Field Name column in the row following the YTD Earnings field).**

The Technician : Table window displays (Figure 5-3).

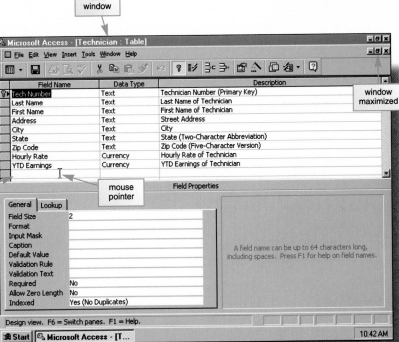

FIGURE 5-3

3 Click the position for the new field. Type Start Date as the field name, press the TAB key, select Date/Time as the data type, press the TAB key, type Start Date as the description, and then press the TAB key to move to the next field.

4 Type Specialties as the field name, press the TAB key, select Memo as the data type, press the TAB key, type Note Containing Details of Technician's Specialties as the description, and then press the TAB key to move to the next field. Type Picture as the field name, press the TAB key, select OLE Object as the data type, press the TAB key, type Picture of Technician as the description, and then press the TAB key to move to the next field. Type Web Page as the field name, press the TAB key, select Hyperlink as the data type, press the TAB key, and type Address of Technician's Web Page as the description. Point to the Close button.

The new fields are entered (Figure 5-4).

5 Close the window by clicking its Close button. Click the Yes button in the Microsoft Access dialog box to save the changes.

The new fields have been added to the structure.

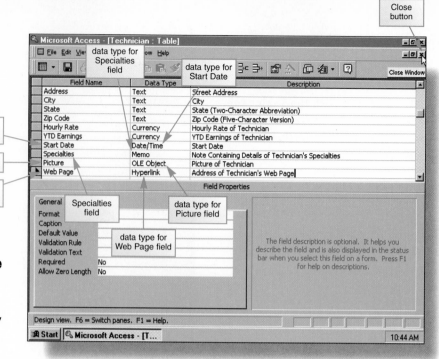

FIGURE 5-4

Updating the New Fields

After adding the new fields to the table, the next task is to enter data into the fields. The manner in which this is accomplished depends on the field type. The following sections cover the methods for updating date fields, memo fields, OLE fields, and Hyperlink fields.

Updating Date Fields

To enter **date fields**, simply type the dates including slashes (/). Perform the following steps to add the Start Dates for all three technicians using Datasheet view.

 Steps To Enter Data in Date Fields

1 **With the Database window on the screen, right-click the Technician table. Point to Open on the shortcut menu.**

The shortcut menu displays (Figure 5-5).

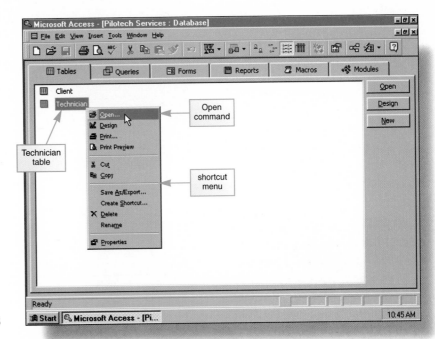

FIGURE 5-5

2 **Click Open on the shortcut menu and then, if necessary, maximize the window. Point to the right scroll arrow.**

The Technician table displays in Datasheet view in a maximized window (Figure 5-6).

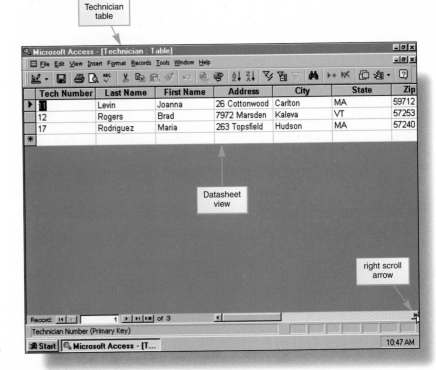

FIGURE 5-6

3 Repeatedly click the right scroll arrow until the new fields display (Figure 5-7). Point to the Start Date field on the first record.

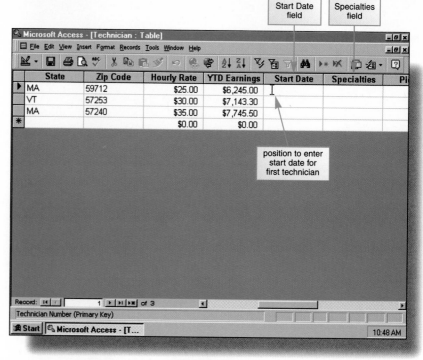

FIGURE 5-7

4 Click the Start Date field on the first record and then type 9/9/97 as the date. Press the DOWN ARROW key. Type 10/6/98 as the Start Date on the second record and then press the DOWN ARROW key. Type 11/12/98 as the date on the third record.

The dates are entered (Figure 5-8).

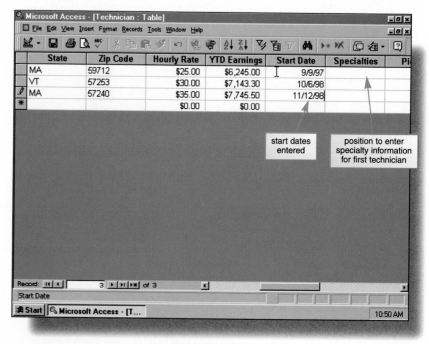

FIGURE 5-8

Updating Memo Fields

To **update a memo field,** simply type the data in the field. With the current spacing on the screen, only a small portion of the memo will display. To correct this problem, you later will change the spacing to allow more room for the memo. Perform the following steps to enter each technician's specialties.

To Enter Data in Memo Fields

1 **If necessary, click the right scroll arrow so that the Specialties field displays. Click the Specialties field on the first record. Type** Has a degree in Accounting. Excellent working knowledge of financial applications. Works well with inexperienced users. **as the entry.**

The last portion of the memo displays (Figure 5-9).

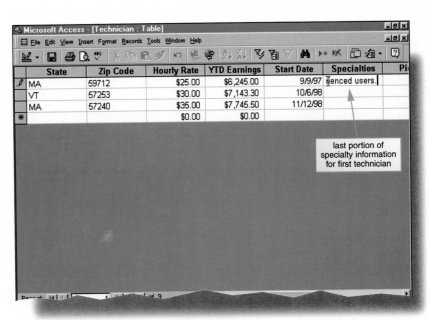

FIGURE 5-9

2 **Click the Specialties field on the second record. Type** Specializes in network design and maintenance. Is a certified network administrator. Teaches networking courses at local community college. **as the entry.**

3 **Click the Specialties field on the third record. Type** Excellent diagnostic skills. Enjoys challenging hardware problems. Works well with inexperienced users. **as the entry.**

The Specialties are all entered (Figure 5-10). The first portion of the specialty information for the first two Technicians displays. Because the insertion point is still in the field for the third Technician, only the last portion displays.

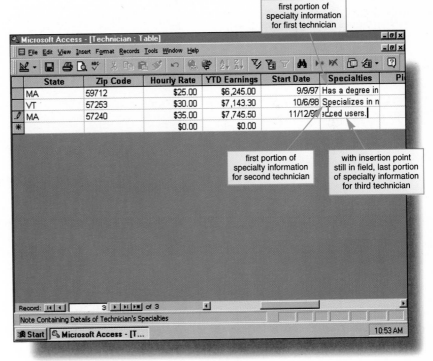

FIGURE 5-10

Changing the Row and Column Size

Only a small portion of the specialties display in the datasheet. To allow more of the specialties to display, you can expand the size of the rows and the columns. You can change the size of a column using the field selector. The **field selector** is the bar containing the field name. To select an entire column, you click the field selector. You then drag to change the size of the column. To change the size of a row, you use a record's **row selector**, which is the small box at the beginning of each record. You then click to select the record and drag to resize the row.

The following steps resize the column containing the Specialties field and resize the rows of the table so a larger portion of the Specialties field text will display.

Steps To Change the Row and Column Size

1 Click the right scroll arrow so the Web Page field displays. Point between the two column headings for the Specialties and Picture columns.

The mouse pointer shape changes to a two-headed vertical arrow, indicating you can drag the line to resize the column (Figure 5-11).

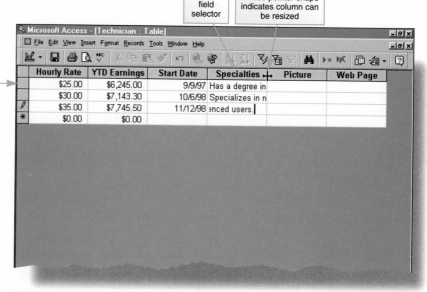

FIGURE 5-11

2 Drag to the right to resize the Specialties column to the approximate size shown in Figure 5-12 and then point between the first and second row selectors as shown in the figure.

The mouse pointer shape changes to a double-headed arrow with a horizontal bar, indicating you can drag the line to resize the row.

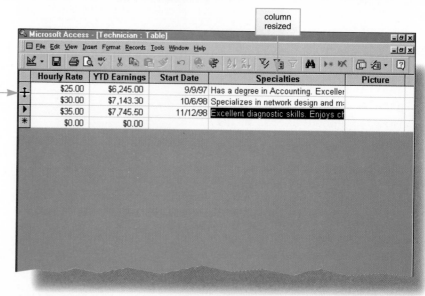

FIGURE 5-12

3 Drag the edge of the row to approximately the position shown in Figure 5-13.

All the rows are resized at the same time (Figure 5-13). The specialties now display in their entirety. The last row has a different appearance from the other two because it still is selected.

Microsoft Access - [Technician : Table]

File Edit View Insert Format Records Tools Window Help

Hourly Rate	YTD Earnings	Start Date	Specialties	Picture
$25.00	$6,245.00	9/9/97	Has a degree in Accounting. Excellent working knowledge of financial applications. Works well with inexperienced users.	
$30.00	$7,143.30	10/6/98	Specializes in network design and maintenance. Is a certified network administrator. Teaches networking courses at local community college.	
$35.00	$7,745.50	11/12/98	Excellent diagnostic skills. Enjoys	

row resized

FIGURE 5-13

Other Ways

1. On Format menu click Row Height to change row spacing

2. On Format menu click Column Width to change column size

Updating OLE Fields

To insert data into an OLE field, you will use the **Insert Object command** on the OLE field's shortcut menu. The Insert Object command presents a list of the various types of objects that can be inserted. Access then opens the corresponding application that is used to create the object, for example, Microsoft Drawing. If the object already is created and stored in a file, as is the case in this project, you simply can insert it directly from the file.

Perform the following steps to insert pictures into the Picture field. The pictures are located in the Access folder on the Data Disk that accompanies this book. If you are not using this floppy disk for your database, you will need to copy the files pict1.pcx, pict2.pcx, and pict3.pcx from the Data Disk to your floppy disk.

The quality of the pictures you see on your screen depends on the particular video driver your system is using. If your pictures do not appear to be as sharp as the ones shown in the text, it simply means your system is using a different video driver.

Note: If you are working on a floppy disk, skip these steps so that your database will not become too large for your disk.

Steps To Enter Data in OLE Fields and Convert the Data to Pictures

1 Click the right scroll arrow so the Picture field displays. Right-click the Picture field on the first record. Point to Insert Object on the shortcut menu.

The shortcut menu for the Picture field displays (Figure 5-14).

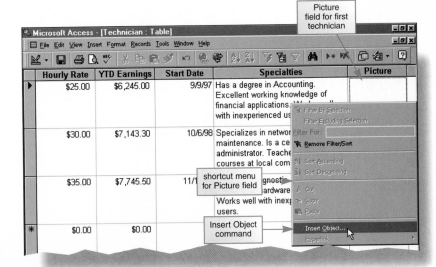

Microsoft Access - [Technician : Table]

File Edit View Insert Format Records Tools Window Help

Hourly Rate	YTD Earnings	Start Date	Specialties	Picture
$25.00	$6,245.00	9/9/97	Has a degree in Accounting. Excellent working knowledge of financial applications. Works well with inexperienced us	
$30.00	$7,143.30	10/6/98	Specializes in networ maintenance. Is a ce administrator. Teache courses at local com	
$35.00	$7,745.50	11/1	gnost ardware Works well with inexp users.	
$0.00	$0.00			

Picture field for first technician

Filter By Selection
Filter Excluding Selection
Filter For:
Remove Filter/Sort
Sort Ascending
Sort Descending
Cut
Copy
Paste
Insert Object...
Hyperlink

shortcut menu for Picture field

Insert Object command

FIGURE 5-14

2

Click the Insert Object command on the shortcut menu. Point to Create from File in the Insert Object dialog box.

The Insert Object dialog box displays (Figure 5-15).

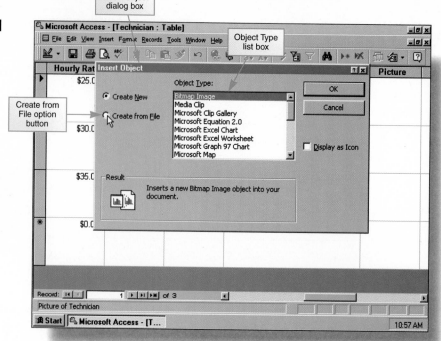

FIGURE 5-15

3

Click Create from File. If necessary, type a : \ **in the File text box and then point to the Browse button.**

The Create from File option button is selected (Figure 5-16).

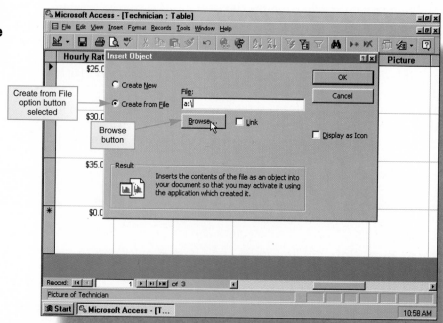

FIGURE 5-16

4 Click the Browse button. If necessary, select a:\, double-click the Access folder in the Directories list to select it, and then point to pict1.pcx.

The Browse dialog box displays (Figure 5-17). If you do not have the pcx files, you will need to locate the folder in which yours are stored.

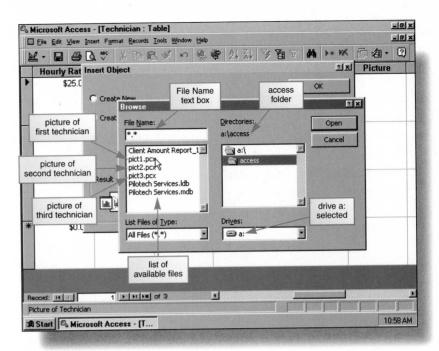

FIGURE 5-17

5 Double-click pict1.pcx and then point to the OK button.

The Browse dialog box closes and the Insert Object dialog box displays (Figure 5-18). The name of the selected picture displays in the File text box.

6 Click the OK button.

7 Insert the pictures in the second and third records using the techniques illustrated in Steps 1 through 6. For the second record, select the picture named pict2.pcx. For the third record, select the picture named pict3.pcx.

The pictures are inserted.

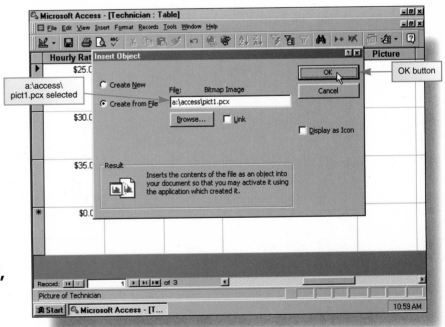

FIGURE 5-18

Other Ways

1. On Insert menu click Object

Updating Hyperlink Fields

To insert data into a Hyperlink field, you will use the **Hyperlink command** on the Hyperlink field's shortcut menu. You then edit the hyperlink. You either can enter the URL for the appropriate Web page or specify a file that contains the document to which you wish to link.

Perform the following steps to insert data into the Web Page field.

Steps ☞ To Enter Data in Hyperlink Fields

1 **Click the right scroll arrow so the Web Page field displays. Right-click the Web Page field on the first record, click Hyperlink on the shortcut menu, and point to Edit Hyperlink.**

The shortcut menu for the Web Page field displays (Figure 5-19).

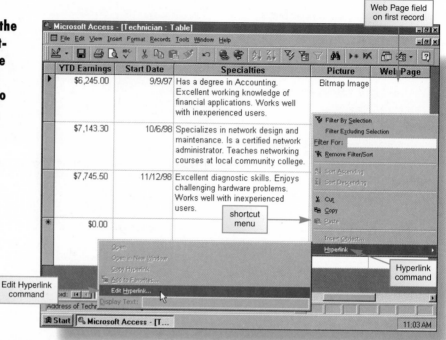

FIGURE 5-19

2 **Click Edit Hyperlink. Type www.scsite.com/ac97/ tech1.htm in the Link to file or URL text box. Point to the OK button. (If you do not have access to the Internet, type a:\access\tech1.html in the Link to file or URL text box instead of www.scsite.com/ac97/ tech1.htm as the URL.)**

The Insert Hyperlink dialog box displays (Figure 5-20).

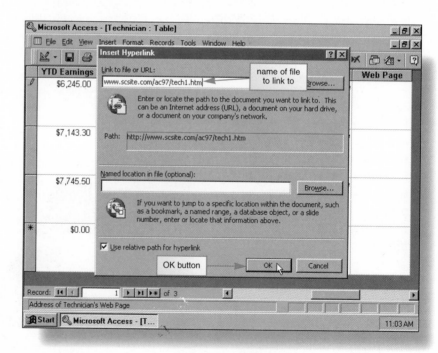

FIGURE 5-20

3 Click the OK button. Use the techniques in Steps 1 and 2 to enter Web page data for the second and third technicians. For the second technician, type `www.scsite.com/ac97/ tech2.htm` **as the URL and for the third, type** `www.scsite.com/ac97/ tech3.htm` **as the URL. (If you do not have access to the Internet, type** `a:\access\tech2.html` **for the second technician, and** `a:\access\tech3.html` **for the third technician.)**

The Web page data is entered (Figure 5-21).

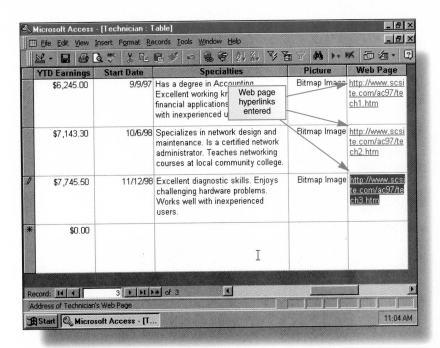

FIGURE 5-21

Other Ways

1. On Insert menu click Hyperlink

Saving the Table Properties

The row and column spacing are **table properties**. When changing any table properties, the changes apply only as long as the table is active *unless they are saved*. If saved, they will apply every time the table is open. To save them, simply close the table. If any properties have changed, a Microsoft Access dialog box will ask if you want to save the changes. By answering Yes, the changes will be saved.

Perform the following steps to close the table and save the properties that have been changed.

 Steps To Close the Table and Save the Properties

1 Close the table by clicking its Close button. Point to the Yes button.

The Microsoft Access dialog box displays (Figure 5-22).

2 Click the Yes button to save the table properties.

The properties now are saved.

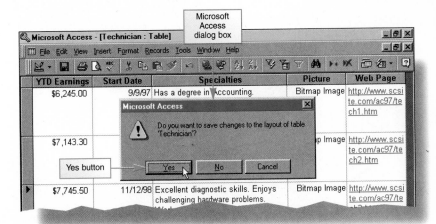

FIGURE 5-22

Although the pictures do not display on the screen, you can view them at any time. To view the picture of a particular *Technician*, point to the Picture field for the *Technician*, and then right-click to produce the shortcut menu. Click Bitmap Image Object on the shortcut menu, and then click Open. The picture then will display. Once you have finished viewing the picture, close the window containing the picture by clicking its Close button. You also can view the Web page for a technician, by clicking the technician's Web Page field.

Advanced Form Techniques

The form in this project includes data from both the Technician and Client tables. The form will display data concerning one technician. It also will display data concerning the technician's many clients. Formally, the relationship between technicians and clients is called a **one-to-many relationship** (*one* technician has *many* clients).

To include the data for the many clients of a technician on the form, the client data must appear in a **subform**, which is a form that is contained in another form. The form in which the subform is contained is called the main form. Thus, the **main form** will contain technician data and the subform will contain client data.

Creating a Form with a Subform

No special action is required to create a form with a subform if you use the Form Wizard. The **Form Wizard** will create both the form and subform automatically once you have selected the tables and indicated the general organization of your data. Perform the following steps to create the form and subform.

Steps **To Create a Form with a Subform Using the Form Wizard**

1 With the Database window on the screen, click the Forms tab and then point to the New button.

The Database window and the Forms sheet display (Figure 5-23).

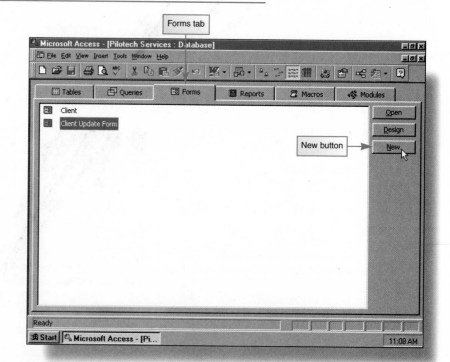

FIGURE 5-23

2 Click the New button, click Form Wizard, click the list box arrow, and then click Technician. Point to the OK button.

The New Form dialog box displays (Figure 5-24). Form Wizard and the Technician table both are selected.

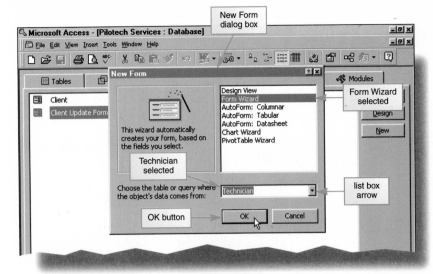

FIGURE 5-24

3 Click the OK button. With the Tech Number field selected in the Available Fields list box, click the Add Field button. Select the First Name, Last Name, Hourly Rate, YTD Earnings, Start Date, Specialties, Picture, and Web Page fields by clicking the field and then clicking the Add Field button. Point to the Table/Queries box arrow.

The fields from the Technician table are selected for the form (Figure 5-25).

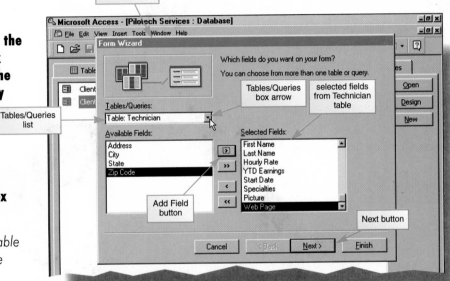

FIGURE 5-25

4 Click the Tables/Queries box arrow. Point to Table: Client in the list that displays (Figure 5-26).

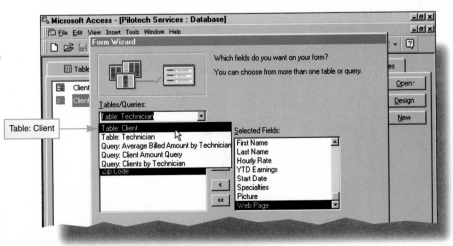

FIGURE 5-26

5 **Click Table: Client. Select the Client Number, Name, Billed, and Paid fields. Point to the Next button.**

All the fields are selected (Figure 5-27).

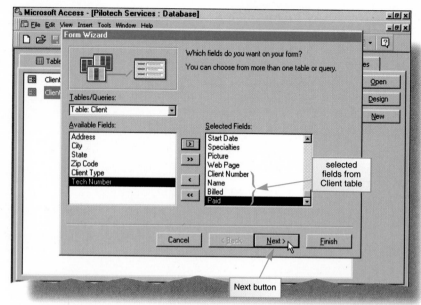

FIGURE 5-27

6 **Click the Next button.**

The Form Wizard dialog box displays, requesting how you want to view the data: by Technician or by Client (Figure 5-28). The highlighted selection, by Technician, is correct. The box on the right indicates visually that the main organization is by Technician, with the Technician fields listed at the top. Contained within the form is a subform that contains Client data.

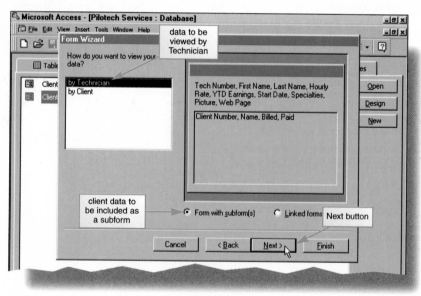

FIGURE 5-28

7 **Click the Next button.**

The Form Wizard dialog box displays, requesting the layout for the subform (Figure 5-29). This subform is to display in Datasheet view.

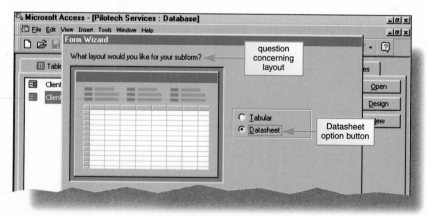

FIGURE 5-29

8 If necessary, click Datasheet and then click the Next button. Make sure the Standard style is selected.

The Form Wizard dialog box displays, requesting a style for the report (Figure 5-30).

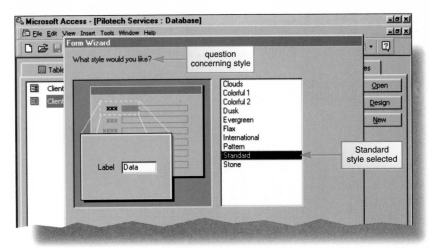

FIGURE 5-30

9 Click the Next button.

The Form Wizard dialog box displays (Figure 5-31). You use this dialog box to change the titles of the form and subform.

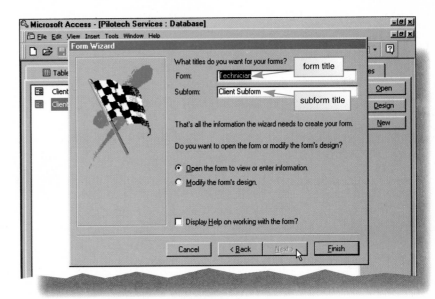

FIGURE 5-31

10 Type Technician Master Form as the title of the form. Click the Subform text box, use the DELETE or BACKSPACE key to erase the current entry, and then type Clients as the name of the subform. Point to the Finish button.

The titles are changed (Figure 5-32).

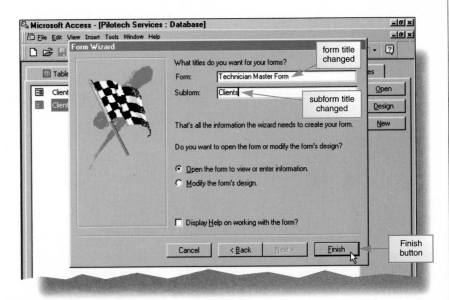

FIGURE 5-32

11 **Click the Finish button.**

The form displays (Figure 5-33).

12 **Close the form by clicking its Close button.**

FIGURE 5-33

The form and subform now have been saved as part of the database and are available for future use.

Modifying the Subform Design

The next task is to modify the spacing of the columns in the subform. The Client Number column is so narrow that only the letters, Clien, display. Conversely, the Billed column is much wider than is needed. You can correct these problems, by right-clicking the subform in the Database window and then clicking Design. When the design of the subform displays, you then can convert it to Datasheet view. At this point, you resize each column by double-clicking the border to the right of the column name.

Perform the following steps to modify the subform design to improve the column spacing.

Steps **To Modify the Subform Design**

1 **On the Forms sheet, right-click Clients. Point to Design on the shortcut menu.**

The shortcut menu for the subform displays (Figure 5-34).

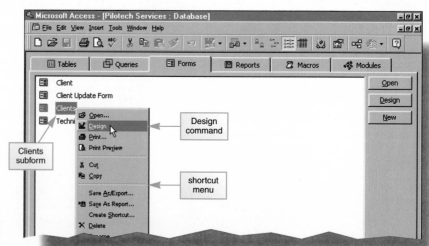

FIGURE 5-34

2 Click Design on the shortcut menu. If necessary, maximize the window. Point to the View button on the toolbar.

The form design displays in a maximized window (Figure 5-35).

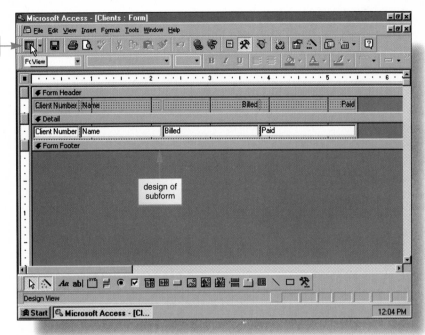

FIGURE 5-35

3 Click the View button to display the subform in Datasheet view. Resize each of the columns by pointing to the right edge of the field selector (the right of the column name) and double-clicking. Point to the Close button.

The subform displays in Datasheet view (Figure 5-36). The columns have been resized. You also can resize each column by dragging the right edge of the field selector.

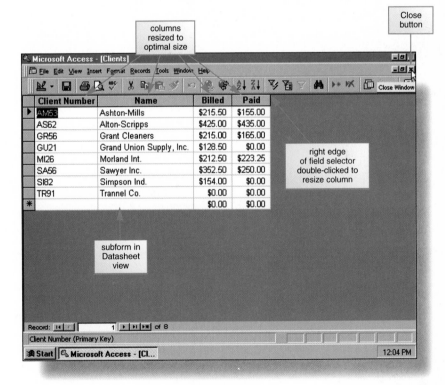

FIGURE 5-36

4 Close the subform by clicking its Close button.

The changes are made and saved.

Modifying the Form Design

The next step is to make several changes to the form. Various objects, including the subform, need to be moved and/or resized. The properties of the picture need to be adjusted so the entire picture displays. The appearance of the labels needs to be changed, and a title needs to be added to the form.

You can make these or other changes to the design of the form by right-clicking the form in the Database window and then clicking Design. If the toolbox is on the screen, make sure it is docked at the bottom of the screen. Perform the following steps to begin the modification of the form design.

Steps To Modify the Form Design

1 **Right-click Technician Master Form. Point to Design on the shortcut menu.**

The shortcut menu for the form displays (Figure 5-37).

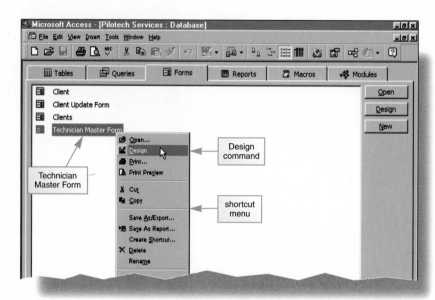

FIGURE 5-37

2 **Click Design on the shortcut menu. If the toolbox does not display, click the Toolbox button on the toolbar. Make sure it is docked at the bottom of the screen (Figure 5-38). If it is not, drag it to the bottom of the screen to dock it there.**

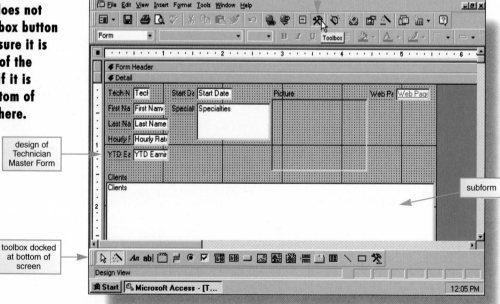

FIGURE 5-38

Resizing and Moving the Subform

To resize or move the subform, click it. **Sizing handles** display around the border of the subform. Drag the control to move it or drag one of the sizing handles to resize it. Perform the following steps first, to reduce the size of the subform, and then to move it to the bottom of the form.

Steps To Resize and Move the Subform

1 **Click the down scroll arrow so the bottom portion of the form design displays (Figure 5-39).**

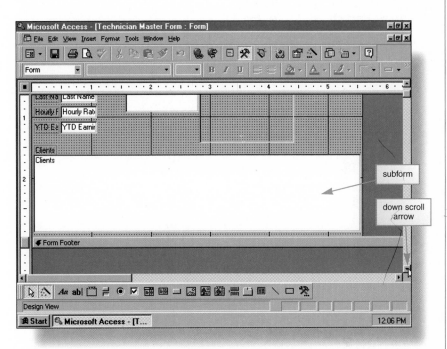

FIGURE 5-39

2 **Click the subform. Point to the sizing handle in the middle of the lower border of the subform.**

The subform is selected (Figure 5-40). Sizing handles display on the border of the subform. The shape of the mouse pointer has changed, indicating that you can drag the sizing handle to resize the subform.

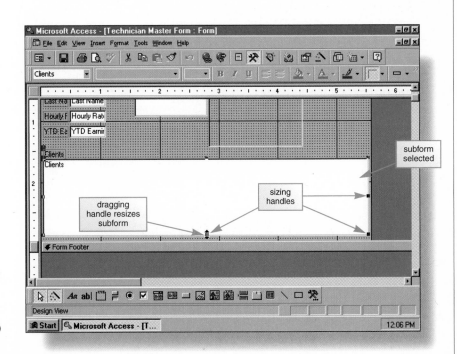

FIGURE 5-40

3 Drag the handle to approximately the position shown in Figure 5-41.

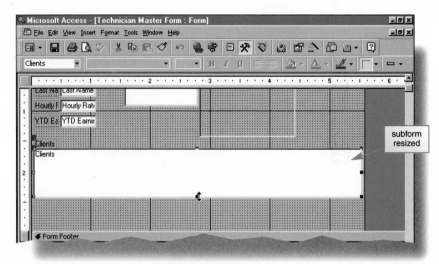

FIGURE 5-41

4 Point to the lower border of the subform, but not to a sizing handle. The shape of the mouse pointer will change to a hand (Figure 5-42).

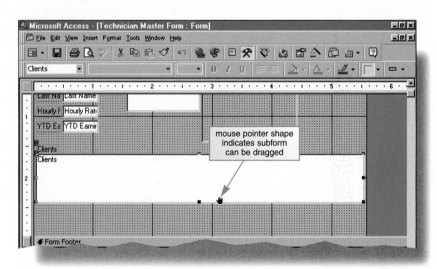

FIGURE 5-42

5 Move the subform by dragging the lower border to approximately the position shown in Figure 5-43.

The subform now has been resized and moved.

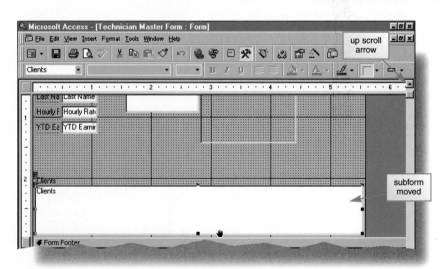

FIGURE 5-43

Moving and Resizing Fields

Fields on this form can be moved or resized just as they were in the form created in the previous project. First, click the field. To move it, move the mouse pointer to the boundary of the field so it becomes a hand, and then drag the field. To resize a field, drag the appropriate sizing handle. The following steps move certain fields on the form. They also resize the fields appropriately.

 Steps **To Move and Resize Fields**

1 **Click the up scroll arrow to scroll up to the top of the form. Click the Start Date control, and then move the mouse pointer until the shape changes to a hand.**

Sizing handles display, indicating the control is selected (Figure 5-44).

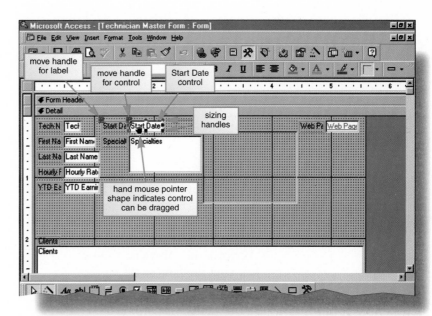

FIGURE 5-44

2 **Drag the Start Date control to the position shown in Figure 5-45.**

The control now has been moved.

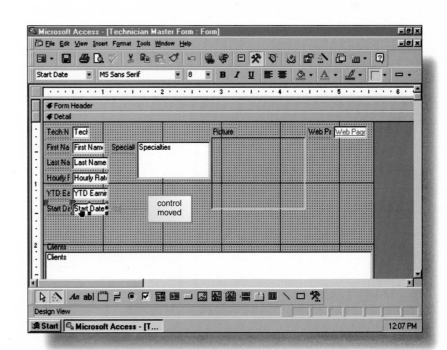

FIGURE 5-45

3 Move the Web Page control to the position shown in Figure 5-46. Move and resize the Picture control to the approximate position and size shown in the figure, and then move and resize the Specialties control to the approximate position and size shown in the figure.

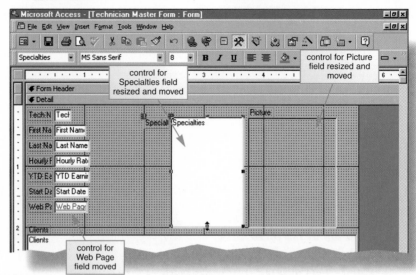

FIGURE 5-46

Moving Labels

To move a label independently from the field with which the label is associated, point to the large, **move handle** in the upper-left corner of the label. The shape of the mouse pointer changes to a hand with a pointing finger. By dragging this move handle, you will move the label without moving the associated field. Perform the following steps to move the label of the Specialties field without moving the field itself.

Steps **To Move Labels**

1 Click the label for the Specialties field and then drag the handle in the upper-left corner to the position shown in Figure 5-47.

The shape of the mouse pointer changes to a hand with a pointing finger.

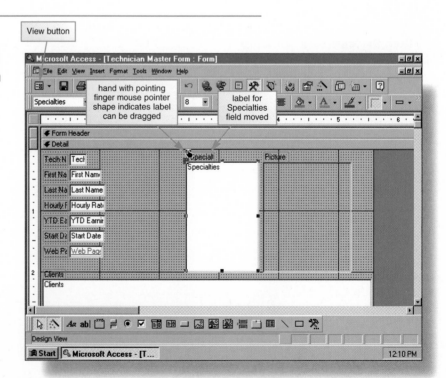

FIGURE 5-47

2 **Click the View button to view the form with the changes.**

The form displays (Figure 5-48).

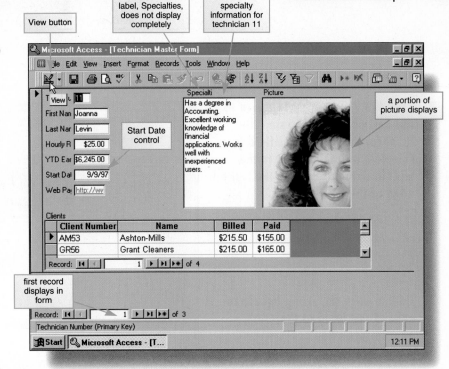

FIGURE 5-48

Changes to the Form

Several changes need to be made to this form to produce the form shown in Figure 5-1 on page A 5.5. The Tech Number, First Name, Last Name, Hourly Rate, YTD Earnings, Start Date, and Web Page fields are not in the correct positions. In addition, the labels for these fields need to be changed in a variety of ways. The label for the Specialties field has the last few letters cut off and only a portion of the picture displays.

Resizing a Label

To resize a label, select the label by clicking it, and then drag an appropriate sizing handle. To resize a label to optimum size, select the label and then double-click an appropriate sizing handle. Perform the steps on the next page to resize the label for the Specialties field by double-clicking the sizing handle on the right.

Steps To Resize a Label

1 Click the View button to return to the design grid. Make sure the label for the Specialties field is selected, and then point to the middle sizing handle on the right edge of the label.

The shape of the mouse pointer changes to a two-headed arrow (Figure 5-49).

2 Double-click the sizing handle to expand the label to the appropriate size.

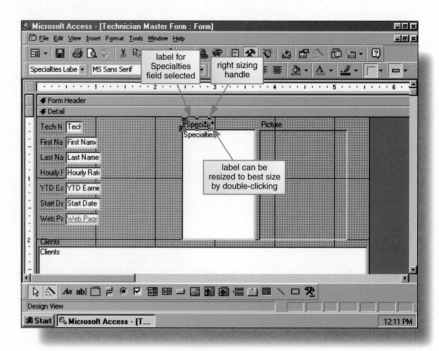

FIGURE 5-49

Changing the Size Mode of a Picture

The portion of a picture that displays as well as the way it displays is determined by the **size mode**. The possible size modes are as follows:

1. **Clip** — Displays only the portion of the picture that will fit in the space allocated to it.
2. **Stretch** — Expands or contracts the picture to fit the precise space allocated on the screen. For photographs, usually this is not a good choice, because fitting a photograph to the allocated space can distort the image, giving it a stretched appearance.
3. **Zoom** — Do the best job of fitting the picture to the allocated space without changing the look of the picture. The entire picture will display and will be proportioned correctly. Some white space may be visible either above or to the right of the picture, however.

Currently, the size mode is Clip and that is why only a portion of the picture displayed. To see the whole picture, use the shortcut menu for the picture to change the size mode to Zoom as in the following steps.

 **More** *About* **Size Mode**

The Clip size mode is the most rapid to display, but may only show a portion of a picture. If your pictures have been created with a size such that the entire picture will display on the form with Clip as the size mode, Clip is the best choice.

Steps To Change the Size Mode of a Picture

1 **Right-click the Picture control to produce its shortcut menu, and then point to Properties.**

The shortcut menu displays (Figure 5-50).

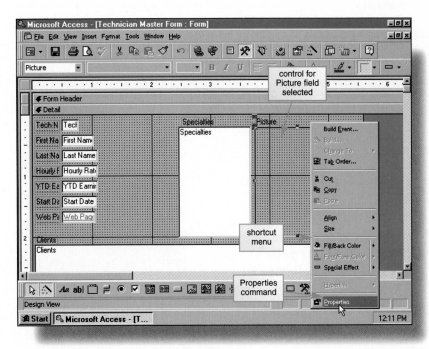

FIGURE 5-50

2 **Click Properties on the shortcut menu. Click the Size Mode property and then click the Size Mode box arrow. Point to Zoom.**

The Bound Object Frame: Picture property sheet displays (Figure 5-51). The list of Size Mode options displays.

3 **Click Zoom and then close the property sheet by clicking its Close button.**

The Size Mode is changed. The entire picture now will display.

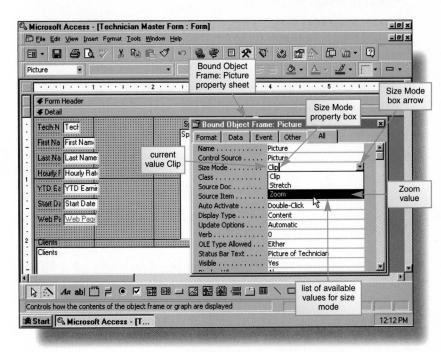

FIGURE 5-51

Other Ways

1. Click Properties button on toolbar
2. On View menu click Properties

More *About*
Selecting Multiple Controls

To select all the controls in a given column or row, you can use the rulers. To select all the controls in a column, click the horizontal ruler above the column. To select all the controls in a row, click the vertical ruler to the left of the row.

Moving a Group of Fields

Fields may be moved individually just as you have done previously. If you need to move a group of fields as a single block, however, a shortcut is available. You can move the group of fields in a single operation by selecting all the fields at once. To do so, click the first field to select it. To select more than one object at a time, press and hold down the SHIFT key as you click the additional objects. Once all the fields have been selected, drag any field to its new position. All the other selected fields will move along with it.

Perform the following step to move the Tech Number, First Name, Last Name, Hourly Rate, YTD Earnings, Start Date, and Web Page fields.

Steps **To Move a Group of Fields**

1 Click the control of the Tech Number field (the white portion, not the label). Select the First Name, Last Name, Hourly Rate, YTD Earnings, Start Date, and Web Page controls by clicking them while holding down the SHIFT key. Release the SHIFT key. Move the mouse pointer until its shape changes to a hand. Drag the Web Page control to approximately the position shown in Figure 5-52. The other controls will move as a block along with the Web Page field.

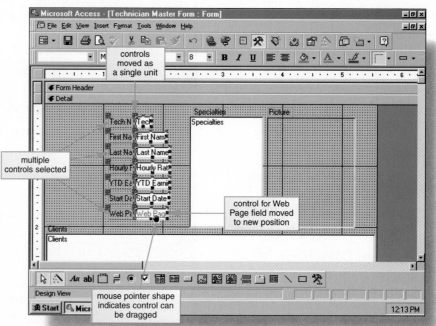

FIGURE 5-52

Changing the Contents of a Label

To change the contents of a label, right-click the label, and then click Properties on the shortcut menu. Select the Caption property and type the new **caption**; that is, the new entry that will display within the label. Perform the following steps to change the contents of the label for the Tech Number field from Tech Number to Technician Number.

 **To Change the Contents of a Label**

1 **Right-click the label for the Tech Number field. Click Properties on the shortcut menu. Click the Caption property, and then change the caption from Tech Number to Technician Number.**

The Label: Tech Number Label property sheet displays (Figure 5-53). The caption has been changed to Technician Number.

2 **Close the Label: Tech Number Label property sheet by clicking its Close button.**

The label is changed.

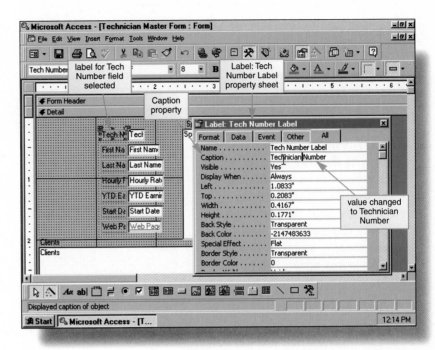

FIGURE 5-53

Changing Label Alignment

The labels for the Technician Number, First Name, Last Name, Hourly Rate, YTD Earnings, Start Date, and Web Page fields in Figure 5-1 on page A 5.5 are **right-aligned**, that is, aligned with the right margin. Because the labels currently are left-aligned, the alignment needs to be changed. To change the **alignment**, you must click the label, right-click to produce the shortcut menu, click Properties, and then click the Text Align property. In the property sheet, you then can select the appropriate alignment.

In some cases, you will want to make the same change to several objects, perhaps to several labels at once. Rather than making the changes individually, you can select all the objects at once, and then make a single change. Perform the steps on the next page to change the alignment of the labels.

Steps To Change Label Alignment

1 If necessary, click the label for the Technician Number field to select it. Select the labels for the First Name, Last Name, Hourly Rate, YTD Earnings, Start Date, and Web Page fields by clicking them while holding down the SHIFT key. Release the SHIFT key. Right-click the Web Page field. Click Properties on the shortcut menu and then click the down scroll arrow until the Text Align property displays. Click the Text Align property, and then click the Text Align box arrow. Point to Right.

The labels are selected (Figure 5-54). The Multiple selection property sheet displays. The Text Align property is selected and the list of available values for the Text Align property displays.

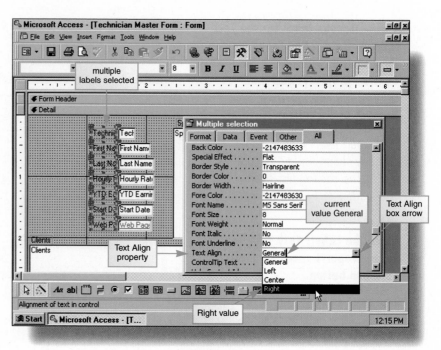

FIGURE 5-54

2 Click Right to select right alignment for the labels. Close the Multiple selection property sheet by clicking its Close button.

The alignment is changed.

Resizing the Labels

To resize a label to optimum size, select the label by clicking it, and then double-click an appropriate sizing handle. Perform the following steps to resize the label for the Technician Number, First Name, Last Name, Hourly Rate, YTD Earnings, Start Date, and Web Page fields just as you resized the label for the Specialties field earlier. The only difference is that you will double-click the sizing handles at the left edge of the labels instead of the right edge. You could resize them individually. It is easier, however, to make sure they are all selected and then resize one of the labels. Access will resize all the others automatically as demonstrated in the following step.

Steps To Resize a Label

1 With all the labels selected, double-click the middle sizing handle on the left edge of the Technician Number label to resize all the labels to the optimal size.

The labels are resized (Figure 5-55).

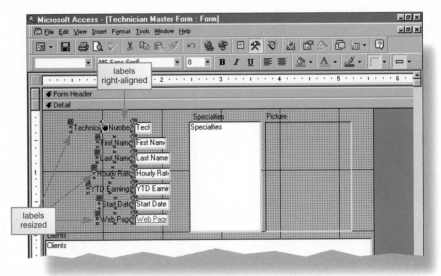

FIGURE 5-55

Changing Special Effects and Colors of Labels

Access allows you to change a variety of **characteristics of the labels** in the form. You can change the border style and color, the background color, the font, and the font size. You also can give the label **special effects**, such as raised or sunken. To change characteristics of a label, such as special effects and colors, perform the following steps.

More About Colors of Labels

There are two different colors you can change for many objects, including labels. Changing Fore Color (foreground) changes the color of the letters that appear in the label. Changing Back Color (background) changes the color of the label itself.

Steps To Change Special Effects and Colors of Labels

1 Be sure the labels for the Technician Number, First Name, Last Name, Hourly Rate, YTD Earnings, Start Date, and Web Page fields are selected. Right-click one of the selected labels, and then click Properties on the shortcut menu that displays. Click the Special Effect property and then click the Special Effect box arrow. Point to Raised.

The Multiple selection property sheet displays (Figure 5-56). The Special Effect property is selected and the list of values for the Special Effect property displays.

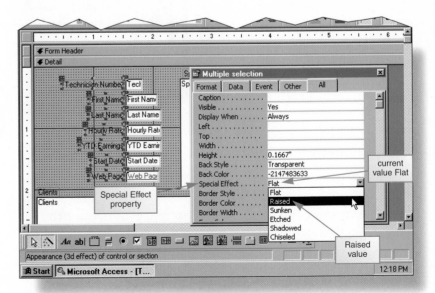

FIGURE 5-56

2 Click Raised. If necessary, click the down scroll arrow until the Fore Color property displays, and then click the Fore Color property. Point to the Build button (the button containing the three dots).

The Fore Color property is selected (Figure 5-57).

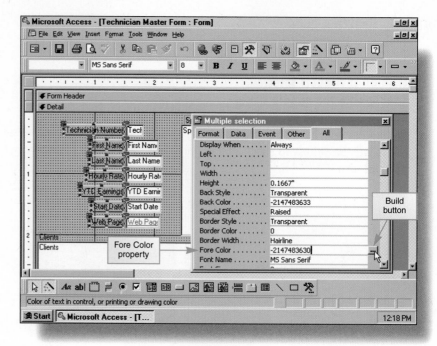

FIGURE 5-57

3 Click the Build button to produce the Color dialog box, and then point to the color blue in row 4, column 5, as shown in Figure 5-58.

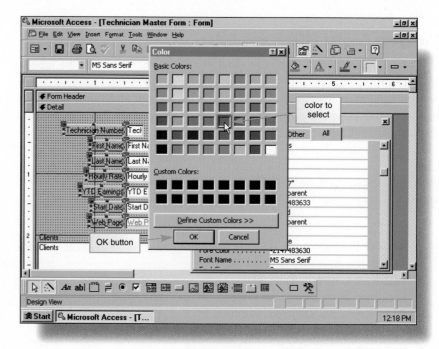

FIGURE 5-58

4 Click the color blue, and then click the OK button. Close the Multiple selection property sheet by clicking its Close button.

The changes to the labels are complete.

5 Click the View button to view the form.

The form displays (Figure 5-59). The fields have been moved and the appearance of the labels has been changed.

6 Click the View button a second time to return to the design grid.

The form design displays.

FIGURE 5-59

Adding a Form Title

Notice in Figure 5-1 on page A 5.5 that the form includes a title. To add a title to a form, add the title as a label in the Form Header section. To accomplish this task, first you will need to expand the size of the Form Header to accommodate the title by dragging the bottom border of the Form Header. Then, you can use the **Label button** in the toolbox to place the label. After placing the label, you can type the title in the label. Using the Properties command on the label's shortcut menu you can change various properties to improve the title's appearance, as well.

Perform the following steps to place a title on the form.

More *About*
Form Headers

You might wish to add more than just a title to a form header. For example, you may wish to add a picture such as a company logo. To do so, click the Image button in the toolbox, click the position where you want to place the picture, and then select the picture to insert.

 Steps **To Add a Form Title**

1 Point to the line separating the Form Header section from the Detail section.

The shape of the mouse pointer changes to a two-headed horizontal arrow, indicating you can drag the line to resize the Form Header section (Figure 5-60).

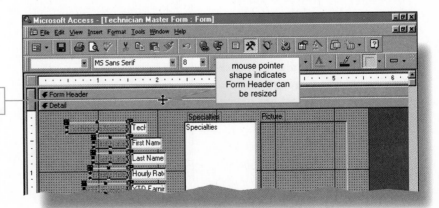

FIGURE 5-60

2 Drag the line to expand the size of the Form Header section to approximately the size shown in Figure 5-61. Point to the Label button in the toolbox as shown in the figure.

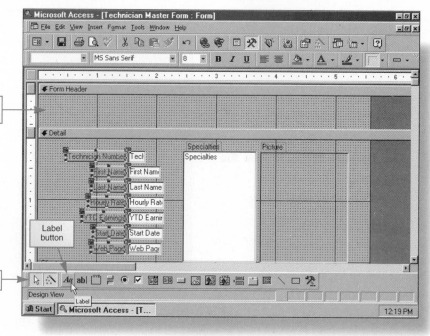

FIGURE 5-61

3 Click the Label button and then position the mouse pointer as shown in Figure 5-62. The shape of the mouse pointer has changed, indicating you are placing a label.

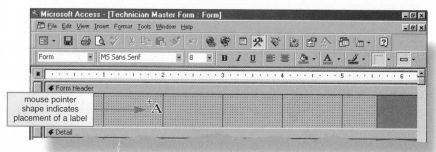

FIGURE 5-62

4 Click the position shown in the figure to place the label on the form. Type Technician Master Form as the title. Click somewhere outside the rectangle containing the title to deselect the rectangle, and then right-click the rectangle containing the title. Click Properties on the shortcut menu that displays, click the Special Effect property, and click the Special Effect box arrow. Point to Etched.

The Label: Label21 property sheet displays (Figure 5-63). The Special Effect property is selected. (Your Label property sheet may contain a different number.)

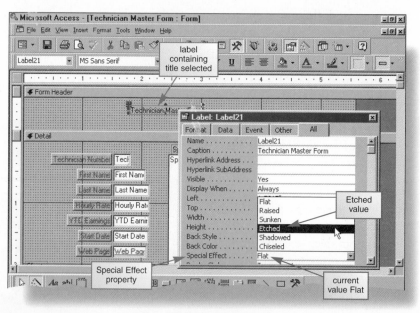

FIGURE 5-63

5 Click Etched. Click the down scroll arrow so the Font Size property displays. Click the Font Size property, click the Font Size box arrow, and then click 12. If necessary, click the down scroll arrow to display the Font Weight property. Click the Font Weight property, click the Font Weight box arrow, and then click Bold. Close the property sheet by clicking its Close button. Resize the label to display the title completely in the larger font size.

The Form Header is complete (Figure 5-64).

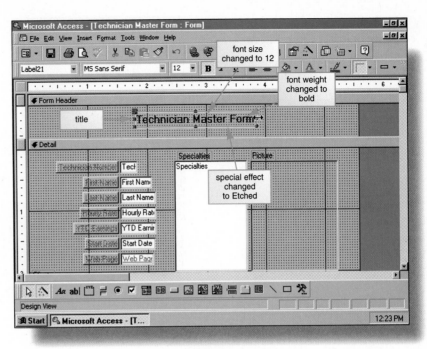

FIGURE 5-64

Adjusting the Subform

After viewing the form in Figure 5-59 on page A 5.37, you can see a problem with the subform. It is wider than it needs to be. The following steps change the size of the subform to remove the extra space.

Steps To Adjust the Subform

1 Scroll down to the bottom of the form. Click the subform and then point to the right middle sizing handle (Figure 5-65).

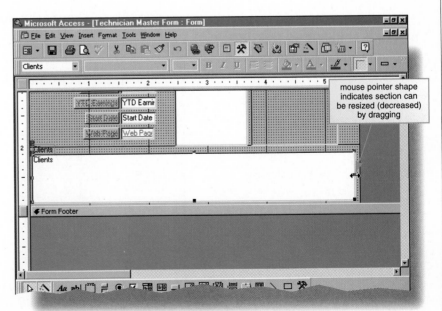

FIGURE 5-65

2 Drag the right edge to approximately the position shown in Figure 5-66.

3 Close the window containing the form. When asked if you want to save the changes to the design of the form, click Yes.

The form is complete.

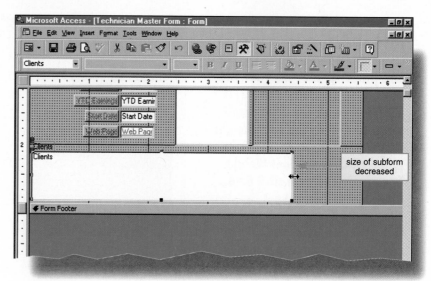

FIGURE 5-66

Viewing Data and Web Pages Using the Form

To use a form to view data, right-click the form in the Database window, and then click Open on the shortcut menu that displays. You then can use the navigation buttons to move among technicians or to move among the clients of the technician who currently is displayed on the screen. By clicking the technician's Web Page field, you can display the technician's Web page. As soon as you close the window containing the Web page, Access returns to the form.

Perform the following steps to display data using the form.

Steps To Use the Form to View Data and Web Pages

1 If necessary, click the Forms tab and then right-click Technician Master Form. Point to Open on the shortcut menu.

The shortcut menu displays (Figure 5-67).

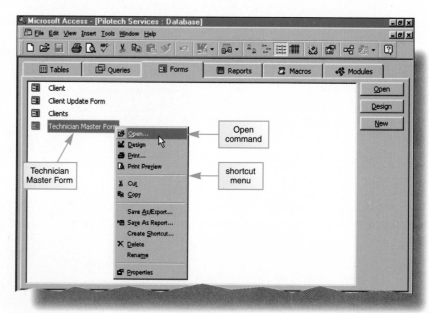

FIGURE 5-67

2 Click Open on the shortcut menu. Be sure the window containing the form is maximized. Point to the Next Record button for the Technician table.

The data from the first record displays in the form (Figure 5-68).

FIGURE 5-68

3 Click the Next Record button to move to the second technician. Point to the Next Record button for the Clients subform (the Next Record button in the set of navigation buttons immediately below the subform).

*The data from the second record displays (Figure 5-69). (The records in your form may display in a different order.) Because more clients are included than will fit in the subform at a single time, Access automatically adds a **vertical scroll bar**. You can use the scroll bar or the navigation buttons to move among clients.*

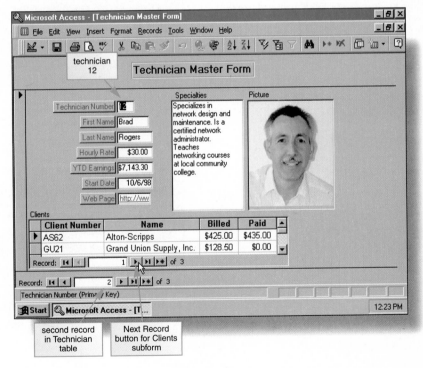

FIGURE 5-69

4 **Click the subform's Next Record button twice.**

The data from the third client of technician 12 displays in the subform (Figure 5-70).

FIGURE 5-70

5 **Point to the control for the technician's Web page (Figure 5-71).**

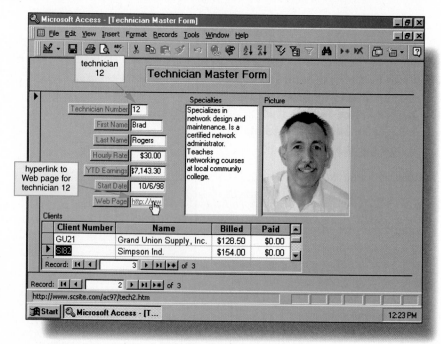

FIGURE 5-71

6 Click the control for the technician's Web page. If a dialog box displays in either this step or the next, follow the directions given in the dialog box.

The technician's Web page displays (Figure 5-72).

7 When you have finished viewing the technician's Web page, click the Close button to return to the form. Close the form by clicking its Close button.

The form no longer displays.

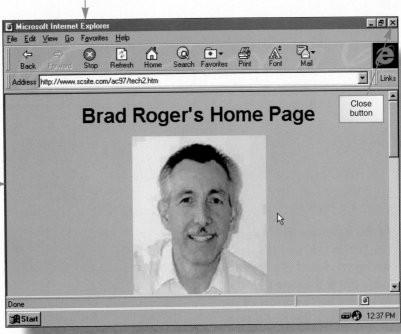

FIGURE 5-72

The previous steps have illustrated the way you work with a main form and subform, as well as how to use a hyperlink (the Web Page control in this form). Clicking the navigation buttons for the main form moves to a different technician. Clicking the navigation buttons for the subform moves to a different client of the technician who displays in the main form. Clicking a hyperlink moves to the corresponding document or Web page. The following are other actions you can take within the form:

1. To move from the last field in the main form to the first field in the subform, press the TAB key. To move back to the last field in the main form, press the CTRL+SHIFT+TAB keys.
2. To move from the last field in the subform to the first field in the main form, press the CTRL+TAB keys. In the process, you also will move to the next record.
3. To switch from the main form to the subform using the mouse, click anywhere in the subform. To switch back to the main form, click any control in the main form. Clicking the background of the main form is not sufficient.

Using Date and Memo Fields in a Query

To use date fields in queries, you simply type the dates including the slashes. To search for records with a specific date, you must type the date. You also can use **comparison operators**. To find all the technicians whose start date is prior to January 1, 1998, for example, you would type the criterion <1/1/98.

More *About* **Date Fields in Queries: Using Date( )**

In a query, to test for the current date, type Date( ) in the criteria row of the appropriate column. Placing <Date( ) in the criteria row for Renewal Date, for example, would find those therapists whose renewal date occurs anytime before the date on which you run the query.

More *About* **Date Fields in Queries: Using Expressions**

Expressions have a special meaning in date fields in queries. Numbers that appear in expressions represent numbers of days. The expression <Date( )+30 for Renewal Date would find therapists whose renewal date occurs anytime prior to 30 days after the day on which you run the query.

You also can use memo fields in queries. Typically, you will want to find all the records on which the memo field contains a specific word or phrase. To do so, you use wildcards. For example, to find all the technicians who have the word, inexperienced, in the Specialties field, you would type the criterion like *inexperienced*.

Perform the following steps to create and run queries that use date and memo fields.

Steps To Use Date and Memo Fields in a Query

1 In the Database window, click the Tables tab, and then, if necessary, select the Technician table. Click the New Object: AutoForm button arrow on the toolbar. Click Query. Be sure Design View is highlighted, and then click the OK button.

2 Maximize the Select Query window that displays. Resize the upper and lower panes and the Technician field list to the sizes shown in Figure 5-73. Double-click the Tech Number, First Name, Last Name, Start Date, and Specialties fields to include them in the query (you may need to scroll down the field list before double-clicking the Specialties field). Click the Criteria row under the Specialties field and then type like *inexperienced* **(Figure 5-73)**. Point to the Run button on the toolbar.

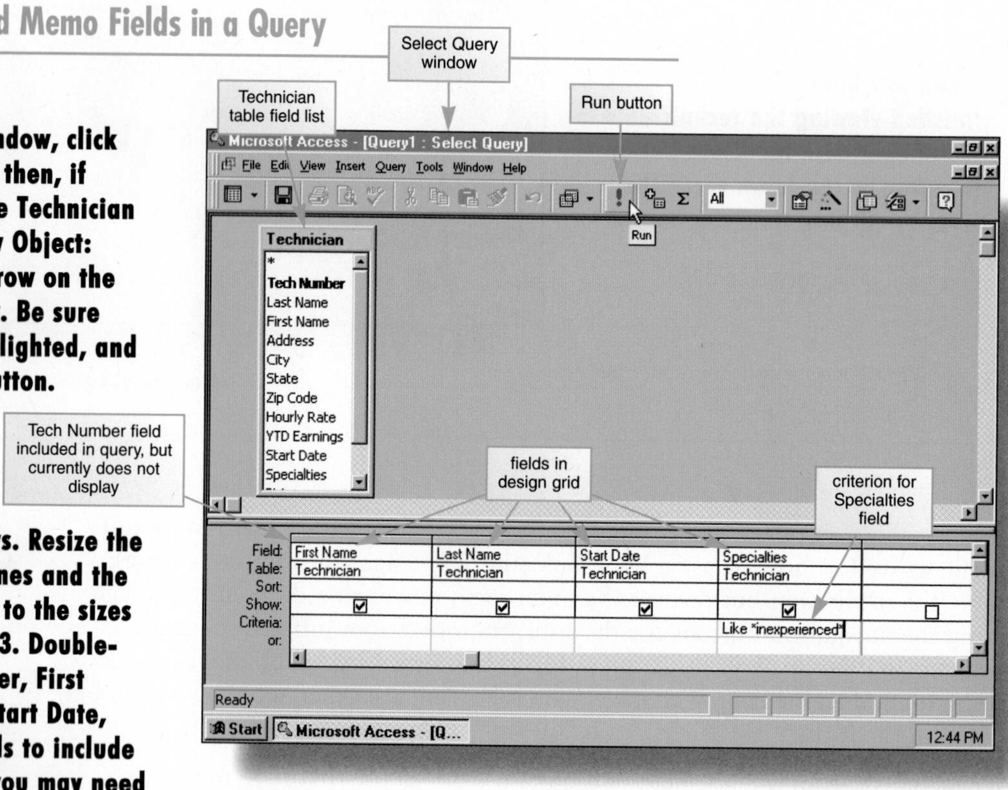

FIGURE 5-73

3 **Click the Run button on the toolbar to run the query.**

The results display in Datasheet view (Figure 5-74). Two records are included.

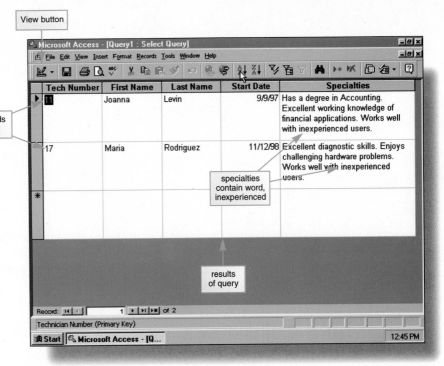

View button

two records included

specialties contain word, inexperienced

results of query

FIGURE 5-74

4 **Click the View button to return to the Select Query window. Click the Criteria row under the Start Date field, and then type** <1/1/98 **(Figure 5-75).**

5 **Click the Run button on the toolbar to run the query.**

The result contains only a single row, because only one technician was hired before January 1, 1998 and has a specialty entry that contains the word, inexperienced.

6 **Close the Select Query window by clicking its Close button. When asked if you want to save the query, click the No button.**

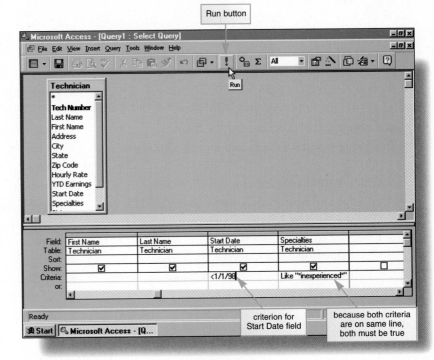

Run button

Run

criterion for Start Date field

because both criteria are on same line, both must be true

FIGURE 5-75

The results of the query are removed from the screen and the Database window again displays.

Closing the Database

The following step closes the database by closing its Database window.

TO CLOSE A DATABASE

Step 1: Click the Close button for the Pilotech Services : Database window.

Project Summary

Project 5 introduced you to some additional field types. To maintain the additional data required at Pilotech Services, you needed to learn how to create and work with date, memo, OLE, and Hyperlink fields. You also learned how to use such fields in a form. You then learned how to build a form on a one-to-many relationship in which you had several records from one of the tables displaying on the screen at the same time in order to create the form required for Pilotech Services. You learned how to use the form to view technician and client data as well as to view the technician's Web page. Finally, you learned how to use date and memo fields in queries to answer two important questions for the organization.

What You Should Know

Having completed this project, you now should be able to perform the following tasks:

▌ Add a Form Title *(A 5.37)*
▌ Add Fields to a Table *(A 5.7)*
▌ Adjust the Subform *(A 5.39)*
▌ Change Label Alignment *(A 5.34)*
▌ Change Special Effects and Colors of Labels *(A 5.35)*
▌ Change the Contents of a Label *(A 5.33)*
▌ Change the Row and Column Size *(A 5.12)*
▌ Change the Size Mode of a Picture *(A 5.31)*
▌ Close a Database *(A 5.46)*
▌ Close the Table and Save the Properties *(A 5.17)*
▌ Create a Form with a Subform Using the Form Wizard *(A 5.18)*
▌ Enter Data in Date Fields *(A 5.9)*
▌ Enter Data in Hyperlink Fields *(A 5.16)*
▌ Enter Data in Memo Fields *(A 5.11)*
▌ Enter Data in OLE Fields and Convert the Data to Pictures *(A 5.13)*
▌ Modify the Form Design *(A 5.24)*
▌ Modify the Subform Design *(A 5.22)*
▌ Move a Group of Fields *(A 5.32)*
▌ Move and Resize Fields *(A 5.27)*
▌ Move Labels *(A 5.28)*
▌ Open a Database *(A 5.6)*
▌ Resize a Label *(A 5.30, A 5.35)*
▌ Resize and Move the Subform *(A 5.25)*
▌ Use Date and Memo Fields in a Query *(A 5.44)*
▌ Use the Form to View Data and Web Pages *(A 5.40)*

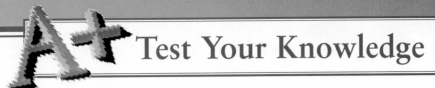 Test Your Knowledge

1 True/False

Instructions: Circle T if the statement is true or F if the statement is false.

T F 1. The term OLE means Object Linking and Embedding.

T F 2. To change the size of a row, position the mouse pointer on the lower border of any record's row selector and drag.

T F 3. To insert data into an OLE field, right-click the field to produce the shortcut menu, and then click Add Picture on the shortcut menu.

T F 4. You can import pictures from files on disk and place them in an OLE field.

T F 5. You cannot resize OLE fields on a form.

T F 6. To change the color of a field label, right-click the object, and then click Color on the shortcut menu.

T F 7. To select more than one object at a time, press and hold down the CTRL key as you select additional objects.

T F 8. You cannot use comparison operators with date fields.

T F 9. To find all records where the text, Java, is included in a memo field, enter Java in the criteria row of the design grid.

T F 10. When you enter date fields in a record, it is not necessary to enter the slashes.

2 Multiple Choice

Instructions: Circle the correct response.

1. The term OLE means _____.
   a. Object Linking and Encoding
   b. Object Locking and Encoding
   c. Object Linking and Embedding
   d. Object Locking and Embedding

2. To enter data in a Hyperlink field, right-click the field, and then click _____ on the shortcut menu.
   a. Hyperlink
   b. WWW
   c. URL
   d. Link

3. In a table, the row containing the list of field names is called the _____.
   a. column selector panel
   b. field label
   c. field selector
   d. column label panel

(continued)

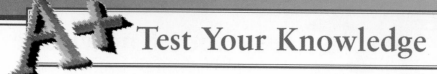

Multiple Choice (continued)

4. The box at the beginning of a record that you can click to select a record is called the _____.
   a. row selector
   b. row identifier
   c. record highlighter
   d. record identifier

5. To insert data in an OLE field, right-click the field, and then click _____ on the shortcut menu.
   a. Insert OLE
   b. Insert Object
   c. Object
   d. OLE

6. A technician may represent many clients but a client can be represented by only one technician. This is a _____ relationship.
   a. one-to-none
   b. one-to-many
   c. one-to-one
   d. many-to-many

7. To select all field objects on a form, click the first object and then press and hold down the _____ key as you click each of the others.
   a. left CTRL
   b. SHIFT
   c. right CTRL
   d. ALT

8. To change the color of a field label, right-click the field, click _____ on the shortcut menu, and then click the Fore Color property.
   a. Color
   b. Label
   c. Properties
   d. Image

9. The Technician table contains a Start Date field. To find all technicians who started after January 1, 1998, enter the criterion _____ in the Criteria row of the Start Date field in the design grid.
   a. >'1/1/98'
   b. >1/1/98
   c. >=1/1/98
   d. >='1/1/98'

10. The Technician table includes a Specialties field that contains notes describing important characteristics of the technicians. To find all technicians with the word, network, in the Specialties field, enter the criterion _____ in the Criteria row of the Specialties field in the design grid.
    a. like ?network
    b. like ?network?
    c. like *network
    d. like *network*

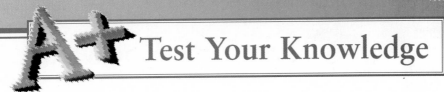

Test Your Knowledge

3 Understanding Forms

Instructions: Figure 5-76 shows a partially completed form for the Intern table. Answer the following questions about the form on your own paper.

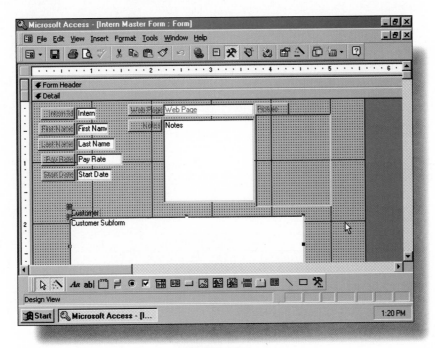

FIGURE 5-76

1. How can you select more than one field object at a time?
2. How would you change the color of the field labels on the form?
3. The form includes a Customer subform. What is a subform?
4. How would you add a title to the form?

4 Understanding the Green Thumb Database

Instructions: In Figure 5-77 on the next page, arrows point to various fields in the Intern table in the Green Thumb database. Identify the data types for these fields in the spaces provided. Answer the following questions about the Green Thumb database on your own paper.

(continued)

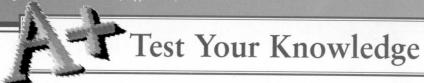

Test Your Knowledge

Understanding the Green Thumb Database *(continued)*

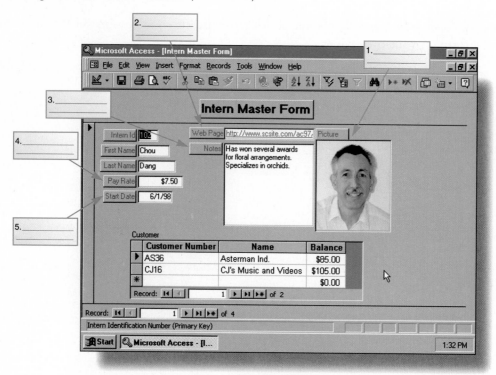

FIGURE 5-77

1. The Intern Master Form depicts a one-to-many relationship between the Intern table and the Customer table. What is a one-to-many relationship?
2. Using the keyboard, how can you move from the last field in the main form to the first field in the subform?
3. Using the mouse, how can you move from the subform to the main form?

Use Help

1 Reviewing Project Activities

Instructions: Perform the following tasks using a computer.

1. Start Access.
2. Click the Contents and Index command on the Help menu to display the Help Topics: Microsoft Access 97 dialog box.

Use Help

3. Click the Contents tab. Double-click the Working with Forms book. Double-click the Creating Multiple-Table or Linked Forms (Subforms) book and then double-click How Microsoft Access links main forms and subforms.

4. Read the Help information when it displays. Next, ready the printer, right-click within the Help window, and then click Print Topic. Hand the printout in to your instructor. Click the Help Topics button to return to the Help Topics: Microsoft Access 97 dialog box.

5. Click the Index tab. Type relationships in the top text box labeled 1 and then double-click forms and subforms under relationships in the middle list box labeled 2. Double-click Subforms - What they are and how they work in the Topics Found dialog box. When the Help information displays, read it, ready the printer, right-click, and click Print Topic. Hand the printout in to your instructor. Click the Help Topics button to return to the Help Topics: Microsoft Access 97 dialog box.

6. Click the Find tab. Type hyperlink in the top text box labeled 1. Double-click About hyperlink addresses in hyperlink fields and controls in the lower list box labeled 3. When the Help information displays, read it, ready the printer, right-click, and click Print Topic. Hand the printout in to your instructor. Click the Close button.

7. If the Office Assistant is on your screen, click it to display its balloon. If the Office Assistant is not on your screen, click the Office Assistant button on the toolbar.

8. Type special effects in the What would you like to do? text box. Click the Search button. Click Make a control appear raised, sunken, shadowed, chiseled, or etched. When the Help information displays, read it, ready the printer, right-click, and click Print Topic. Hand the printout in to your instructor. Click the Close button.

2 Expanding the Basics

Instructions: Use Access Help to better understand the topics listed below. If you cannot print the Help information, then answer the questions on your own paper.

1. Using the Office Assistant, answer the following questions:
   a. What is the maximum size of a text field?
   b. What is the maximum size of a memo field?
   c. Can you create an index for a memo field?
   d. What is the default size for a text field?
2. Using the keyword, sizemode, and the Index sheet in the Help Topics: Microsoft Access 97 dialog box, display and print information on adjusting the size and proportions of a picture. Then, answer the following question. Which setting may distort the image?
3. Use the Find sheet in the Help Topics: Microsoft Access 97 dialog box to display and then print information about changing the layout of a subform displayed in Datasheet view. Then, answer the following questions:
   a. How can you hide a column?
   b. How can you freeze a column?
4. Use the Office Assistant to display and print information on creating hyperlink data types.

Apply Your Knowledge

1 Enhancing the Green Thumb Database

Instructions: Start Access. Open the Green Thumb database from the Access folder on the Data Disk that accompanies this book. Perform the following tasks.

1. Add the fields, Start Date, Notes, Picture, and Web Page to the Intern table structure as shown in Figure 5-78.

2. Save the changes to the structure.

3. Add the data shown in Figure 5-79 to the Intern table. Add pictures and hyperlinks for all interns. Use the same pictures and hyperlinks that you used for the Technician table in this project. You can use the same file for more than one record. Pict1.pcx, and pict3.pcx are pictures of females; pict2.pcx is a male. Adjust the row and column spacing for the table, if necessary.

4. Print and then close the table.

5. Query the Intern table to find all interns who do floral arrangements. Include the Intern's first name, last name, and pay rate in the query. Print the query results. Do not save the query.

6. Use the Form Wizard to create a form/subform for the Intern table. Include the Intern Id, Last Name, First Name, Pay Rate, Start Date, Notes, Picture, and Web Page from the Intern table. Include the Customer Number, Name, and Balance fields from the Customer table.

7. Modify the form design to create the form shown in Figure 5-77 on page A 5.50.

8. Print the form. To print the form, open the form, click File on the menu bar, click Print, and click Selected Record(s) as the Print Range. Click the OK button.

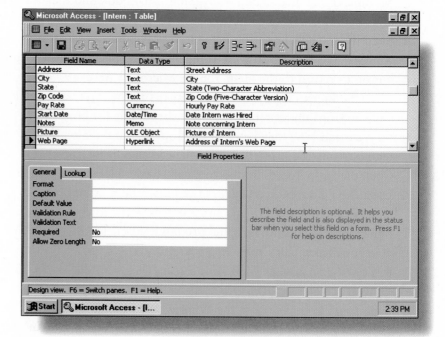

FIGURE 5-78

INTERN ID	START DATE	NOTES
102	6/1/98	Has won several awards for floral arrangements. Specializes in orchids.
105	8/1/98	Has an environmental engineering background. Very knowledgeable on plant toxins and allergies.
109	1/9/99	Has a reputation for innovative floral arrangements. Bonsai enthusiast.
113	3/1/99	Prefers outdoor gardening chores. Has some experience with irrigation systems.

FIGURE 5-79

In the Lab

1 Enhancing the Museum Mercantile Database

Problem: The Museum director has found that Museum Mercantile needs to maintain additional data on vendors. They need to know the last date that they placed an order with a vendor. They also would like to store some notes about each vendor's return policy as well as the URL of each vendor's Web page. The committee requires a form that displays information about the vendor as well as the products that the vendor sells.

Instructions: Open the Museum Mercantile database from the Access folder on the Data Disk that accompanies this book. Perform the following tasks.

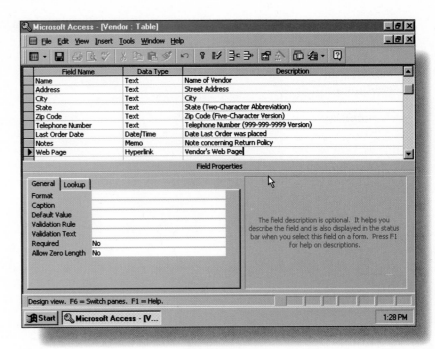

FIGURE 5-80

1. Add the fields Last Order Date, Notes, and Web Page to the Vendor table structure as shown in Figure 5-80 and then save the changes to the structure.

2. Add the data shown in Figure 5-81 to the Vendor table. Adjust the row and column spacing for the table, if necessary.

VENDOR CODE	LAST ORDER DATE	NOTES
AR	1/5/99	Can return all unsold merchandise. No extra charges.
MS	1/17/99	Can return all unsold merchandise. Charges a fee.
WW	2/14/99	Can return only those items ordered for the first time. Charges a fee.

FIGURE 5-81

3. Print the table.
4. Create the form shown in Figure 5-82 on the next page for the Vendor table. Use Vendor Master Form as the name of the form and Products of Vendor (Subform) as the name of the subform.

(continued)

In the Lab

Enhancing the Museum Mercantile Database *(continued)*

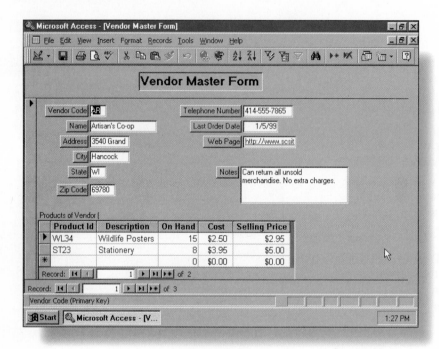

FIGURE 5-82

5. Print the form. To print the form, open the form, click File on the menu bar, click Print, and click Selected Record(s) as the Print Range. Click the OK button.

6. Query the Vendor table to find all vendors that allow all unsold merchandise to be returned. Include the Vendor Code and Name in the query. Print the results. Do not save the query.

2 Enhancing the City Telephone System Database

Problem: The Telephone manager has found that she needs to maintain additional data on the departments. For auditing purposes, she needs to know the start date for each manager. She also needs to store some notes on the billing rate procedures for each department. The manager would like you to create a form that displays information about the department as well as the users in the department.

Instructions: Open the City Telephone System database from the Access folder on the Data Disk that accompanies this book. Perform the following tasks.

1. Add the fields Start Date and Notes to the Department table structure as shown in Figure 5-83. Save the changes to the structure.

In the Lab

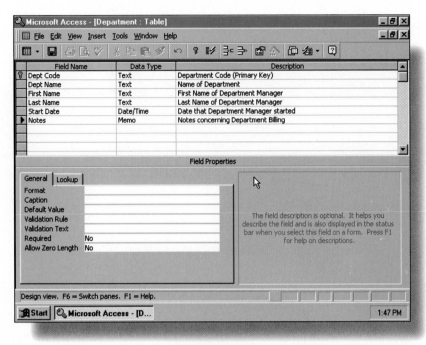

FIGURE 5-83

2. Add the data shown in Figure 5-84 to the Department table. Adjust the row and column spacing for the table, if necessary.

DEPT CODE	START DATE	NOTES
APV	9/1/97	Send all invoices to manager.
ENG	2/1/99	Send invoices to users with summary to manager.
HRS	7/1/98	Send all invoices to manager. Requires two copies.
ITD	3/1/98	Send invoices to users with summary to manager.
PLN	4/1/99	Send all invoices to manager. Also send invoices to users.

FIGURE 5-84

3. Print the table.
4. Create the form shown in Figure 5-85 on the next page. Use Department Master Form as the name of the form and Users as the name of the subform.

(continued)

In the Lab

Enhancing the City Telephone System Database *(continued)*

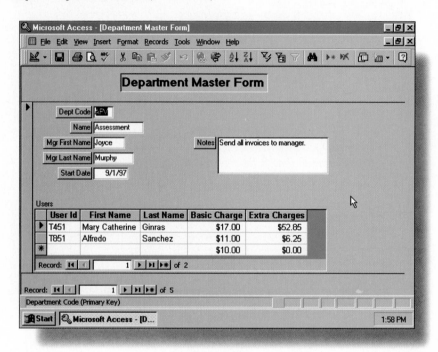

FIGURE 5-85

5. Print the form. To print the form, open the form, click File on the menu bar, click Print, and click Selected Record(s) as the Print Range. Click the OK button.

6. Query the Department table to find all departments whose manager started prior to July 1, 1998. Include the Dept Code, Name, First Name, and Last Name in the query. Print the results. Do not save the query.

3 Enhancing the City Scene Database

Problem: The managing editor has found that he needs to maintain additional data on the advertising representatives. He needs to maintain the date an ad rep started as well as some notes concerning a representative's abilities. He also would like to store a picture of the representative as well as a link to each representative's Web page. The manager wants you to create a form that displays advertising representative information and the advertisers for which they are responsible.

Instructions: Open the City Scene database from the Access folder on the Data Disk that accompanies this book. Perform the following tasks.

1. Add the Start Date, Notes, Picture, and Web Page fields to the Ad Rep table as shown in Figure 5-86. Save the changes to the structure.

In the Lab

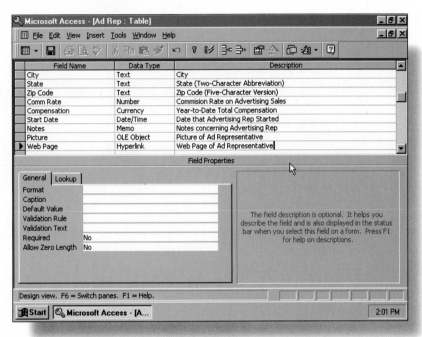

FIGURE 5-86

2. Add the data shown in Figure 5-87 to the Ad Rep table. Add pictures and hyperlinks for each representative. Use the same picture and hyperlink files that you used for the Technician table in this project. Pict1.pcx and pict3.pcx are pictures of females; pict2.pcx is a male.

AD REP NUMBER	START DATE	NOTES
16	4/1/98	Also works as freelance journalist.
19	9/7/98	Records radio advertisements for magazine.
22	3/4/99	Excellent proofreader.

FIGURE 5-87

3. Print the table.
4. Create the form shown in Figure 5-88 on the next page. Use Advertising Rep Master Form as the name of the form and Accounts as the name of the subform.

(continued)

In the Lab

Enhancing the City Scene Database *(continued)*

FIGURE 5-88

5. Add the current date to the form. (*Hint*: Use information from Use Help Exercise 2 of the previous project to solve this problem.)

6. Print the form. To print the form, open the form, click File on the menu bar, click Print, and click Selected Record(s) as the Print Range. Click the OK button.

7. Query the Ad Rep table to find all ad reps who also will work as freelance journalists. Include the Ad Rep Number, Last Name, and First Name in the query. Print the query results. Do not save the query.

8. Query the Ad Rep table to find all ad reps who started before 1999. Include the Ad Rep Number, Last Name, First Name, Compensation, and Comm Rate in the query. Print the query results. Do not save the query.

Cases and Places

The difficulty of these case studies varies: ◗ are the least difficult; ◗◗ are more difficult; and ◗◗◗ are the most difficult.

1 ◗ Use the database created in Case Study 1 of the Cases and Places section of Project 4 for this assignment. Athletic department personnel need additional data on the golf pros. Add the fields and data in Figure 5-89 to the Pro table. Print the Pro table. Create and print a Pro Master Form for the Pro table, which is similar in format to Figure 5-82 on page A 5.54. Query the Pro table to find the instructors who prefer teaching in the afternoons.

INSTRUCTOR	PREFERRED TIMES	PREFERRED STUDENTS
GC	Mornings	Children
CW	Weekends	Beginners
VM	Afternoons	Advanced
SP	Afternoons	Beginners

FIGURE 5-89

2 ◗ Enhance the database created in Case Study 1 above by adding pictures of the four golf pros. Use the same picture files used for the Technician table in Project 5. (Use the picture file of the male for both male golf pros.) In addition, change the special effects and colors of the labels.

3 ◗◗ Use the database created in Case Study 3 of the Cases and Places section of Project 1 for this assignment. Add a memo field to describe the plot of each movie and a date field to indicate when nursing home residents last watched the movie. Use the following data: *The Little Princess*, a sweet child is mistreated at a strict boarding school, 10/15/96; *North by Northwest*, mistaken identity entangles a New York man in murder and espionage, 2/19/98; *Of Mice and Men*, migrant life during the Depression on a California ranch, 4/2/97; *The Quiet Man*, an American ex-boxer returns to Ireland and falls in love, 5/4/98; *On the Waterfront*, corruption in New York tests morality 3/6/98; *Pardon My Sarong*, two Chicago bus drivers experience a Pacific island, 8/25/97; *Ride 'em Cowboy*, two New York peanut vendors experience a dude ranch 12/16/96; *You Can't Take It with You*, an unconventional grandfather and the parents of his granddaughter's fiancé meet, 4/29/98; *The Undefeated*, a Yankee colonel and a Confederate colonel join forces to sell wild horses to the French, 7/31/96; and *Operation Pacific*, a submarine commander tackles the Japanese, 2/7/98. Query the table to find all movies with a New York setting and all movies that have not been watched in the past two years.

Cases and Places

4 ▶▶ You have been using the restaurant form created in Case Study 5 of the Cases and Places section of Project 4 in your meal delivery service. Now, you want to add a memo field to record notes regarding these eating establishments. Add the following facts to the records in the table: Ole Tacos has outstanding taco salads; Little Venice, Red Rose, and House of China accept reservations; Noto's has extremely slow service; Pan Pacific and New Crete have entertainment on weekends; Napoli's Pizza has a romantic decor; Ye Old Cafe and Texas Diner have outdoor seating. Query the table to find all restaurants open past 10:00 p.m. that have outdoor seating and all restaurants open for lunch that accept reservations.

5 ▶▶▶ Although the textbook exchange system you enhanced in Case Study 4 of the Cases and Places section of Project 4 is quite profitable, you believe the system would be more successful by using additional marketing data in the advertisements you have been running on the student government's Web page. Add fields to the table for the current selling price in the bookstore, copyright date, and edition. Use the following data: *Sociology Today*, $35, 1998, 3rd ed.; *Creative Writing*, $27, 1997, 2nd ed.; *Reach for the Stars*, $42, 1996, 4th ed.; *Ethics for Today's Society*, $35, 1998, 3rd ed.; *Electronic Circuitry*, $52, 1997, 3rd ed.; *Nutrition for Our Souls*, $26, 1998, 2nd ed.; *Geriatric Nursing*, $54, 1997, 3rd ed. Query the table for books published after 1996 and for books selling for less than $30.

6 ▶▶▶ The campus directory database you created in Case Study 6 of the Cases and Places section of Project 4 has been very useful. Add fields and data for: (a) athletic coaches and dates of athletic events and (b) computer lab room numbers, open lab times, and telephone extensions. Query the table to find all computer labs that are open on the weekends, all faculty members with office hours on Fridays, and the coaches in charge of the next three athletic events.

7 ▶▶▶ Financial planners suggest saving 10 percent of income as a good start toward preparing for retirement. Your accounting instructor wants you to diversify your investments by putting 10 percent of last year's after-tax income in certificates of deposit. Visit five local banks, credit unions, or savings and loan associations to determine current rates, maturity dates, and the total values of the CDs by age 65. Add fields and this data to the table you created in Case Study 7 of the Cases and Places Section of Project 4, and then print a revised report with the new title of Investment Future Value Report. Query the table to find all the financial institutions with interest rates above 6 percent and all CDs maturing before January 2001.

Microsoft Access 97

Creating an Application System Using Macros, VBA, and the Switchboard Manager

Objectives:

You will have mastered the material in this project when you can:

▶ Create a macro
▶ Add actions and comments to a macro
▶ Modify arguments in a macro
▶ Run a macro
▶ Add command buttons to forms
▶ Modify VBA code associated with a command button
▶ Add a combo box to a form
▶ Modify properties of a combo box
▶ Use a combo box
▶ Create a switchboard
▶ Modify switchboard pages
▶ Modify switchboard items
▶ Use a switchboard

Project 6

CREATION *and* CULTURES *by Design*

Four days the dark cloud rested at the summit of the peak, until Talking God ascended the mountain to investigate. At the place where the cloud rested, he found rain softly falling and heard the cry of an infant. Beneath a rainbow, a baby girl lay on a bed of flowers. Born of Darkness, she was fathered by Dawn. Talking God named her Changing Woman, then gave her to First Man and First Woman to rear. When Changing Woman came of age, one day she awoke from a deep sleep, knowing that she would bear a child. Within four days, she gave birth to Monster Slayer, and four days after that, Child Born of Water entered the world. After seeking out their father — the Sun — these Hero Twins became the founders of the Navaho Nation.

This story about the origins of the Navaho people first became familiar to non-Navahos through the novel of

Tony Hillerman. It is but one of untold numbers of creation legends, since virtually every culture in the history of the world has conceived a story to explain its own existence.

In his landmark work, *The Historical Atlas of World Mythologies*, noted scholar Joseph Campbell illustrates the remarkable similarities between mythologies of cultures not only widely separated by distance and custom, but by centuries of time.

Genesis, the basis for Judeo-Christian beliefs, tells of Adam and Eve, who with Cain and Abel, founded the human race. A Pygmy tale from the Congo and a Bassari legend of Togo contain the story of a woman tempted to eat forbidden fruit. In Plato's *Protagoras Myth*, the gods of Greek legend gave to Epimetheus and Prometheus the task of distributing powers and characteristics to man and the beasts. In the Brahman *Upanishad*, the Universal Self divides into two — a man and a woman — then transforms into pairs of every type of animal in order to populate the earth. In the Icelandic *Prose Edda*, written by Snorre Sturlasons, a single god created heaven and earth and Adam and Eve, but two of the main heroes are named Thor and Odin. In the Japanese *Kojiki*, Izanagi and Izanami are the gods from whom the eight great islands of Japan and the Japanese people sprang.

A story of another beginning involves database creation and its associated application systems. In this project, you will use Microsoft Access to create a switchboard system, which includes adding command buttons and a combo box to carry out specific tasks with greatly enhanced performance. The improved design environment of Access provides developer-oriented features with powerful tools such as macros, Visual Basic for Applications, and the Switchboard Manager. These tools assist you in both the way you work and the speed at which you create database applications, allowing you to be productive and save valuable time.

With all that extra time, you may be able to produce a personal database to chronicle your own family origins.

Project 6

Microsoft

Access 97

Case Perspective

The management of Pilotech Services is pleased with the tables, forms, and reports that you have created thus far. They have two additional requests, however. First, they would like some improvements to the Client Update Form, which would include placing buttons on the form for moving to the next record, moving to the previous record, adding a record, deleting a record, and closing the form. Then, they want a simple way of searching for a client given the client's name. They also require an easier way to access the various tables, forms, and reports merely by clicking a button or two to open any form or table, preview any report, or print any report. They believe this will increase employee productivity at the organization if employees do not have to remember all the steps required to perform any of these tasks.

Creating an Application System Using Macros, VBA, and the Switchboard Manager

Introduction

In previous projects, you created tables, forms, and reports. Each time you want to use any of these, you must follow the correct series of steps. To open the Client Update Form in a maximized window, for example, first you must click the Forms tab in the Database window, and then right-click the correct form. Then, you will click Open on the shortcut menu and finally, click the Maximize button for the window containing the form.

All these steps are unnecessary if you create your own switchboard system, such as the one shown in Figures 6-1a and 6-1b. A **switchboard** is a form that includes buttons to perform a variety of actions. In this system, you just click a button — View Form, View Table, View Report, Print Report, or Exit Application — to indicate the action you wish to take. Other than Exit Application, clicking a button leads to another switchboard. For example, clicking the View Form button leads to the View Form switchboard as shown in Figures 6-1a and 6-1b. You then click the button that identifies the form you want to view. Similarly, clicking the View Table button would lead to a switchboard on which you would click a button to indicate the table you want to view. Thus, viewing any form, table, or report, or printing any report requires clicking only two buttons.

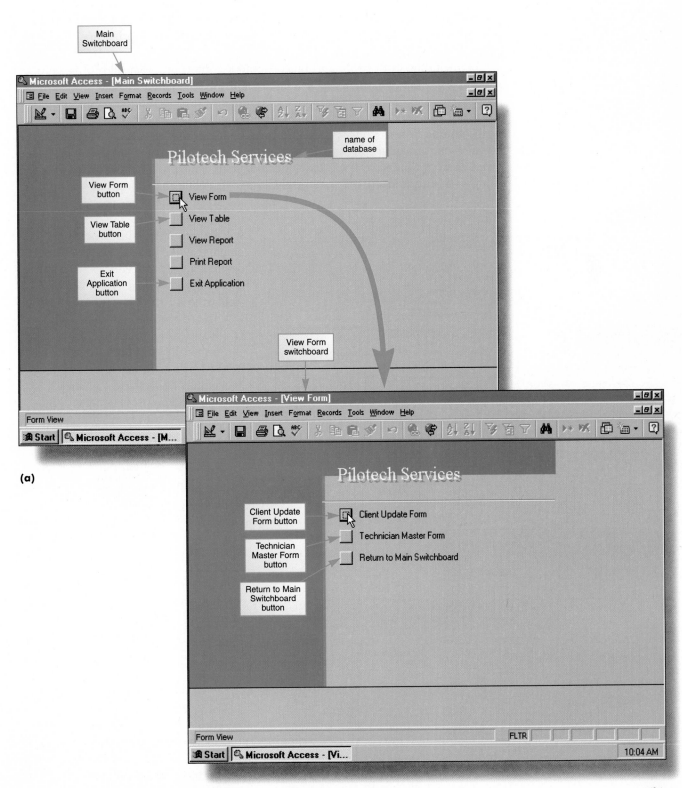

FIGURE 6-1

More *About*
Switchboards

An application system is simply an easy-to-use collection of forms, reports, and/or queries designed to satisfy the needs of some specific user or groups of users, like the users at Pilotech Services. A switchboard system is one type of application system that is very popular in the Windows environment.

In this project, you will create the switchboard system represented in Figures 6-1a and 6-1b. You will begin by creating **macros**, which are collections of actions designed to carry out specific tasks, such as opening a form and maximizing the window containing the form. You can run the macros directly from the Database window. When you do, Access will execute the various steps, called **actions**, in the macro. You also can use the macros in the switchboard system. Clicking certain buttons in the switchboard system you create will cause appropriate macros to be run.

By including both command buttons and a combo box that allows users to search for clients by name, you will enhance the Client Update Form you created earlier (Figure 6-2). When you add the command buttons and the combo box to the form, you will use appropriate Access wizards. The **wizards** create the button or the combo box to your specifications and place it on the form. They also create an event procedure for the button or the combo box. An **event procedure** is a series of steps that Access will carry out when an event, such as the clicking of a command button, occurs. For example, when you click the Delete Record button, the steps in the event procedure created for the Delete Record button will be executed. This procedure actually will cause the record to be deleted. Event procedures are written in a language called **Visual Basic for Applications**, or **VBA**. This language is a standard throughout Microsoft applications.

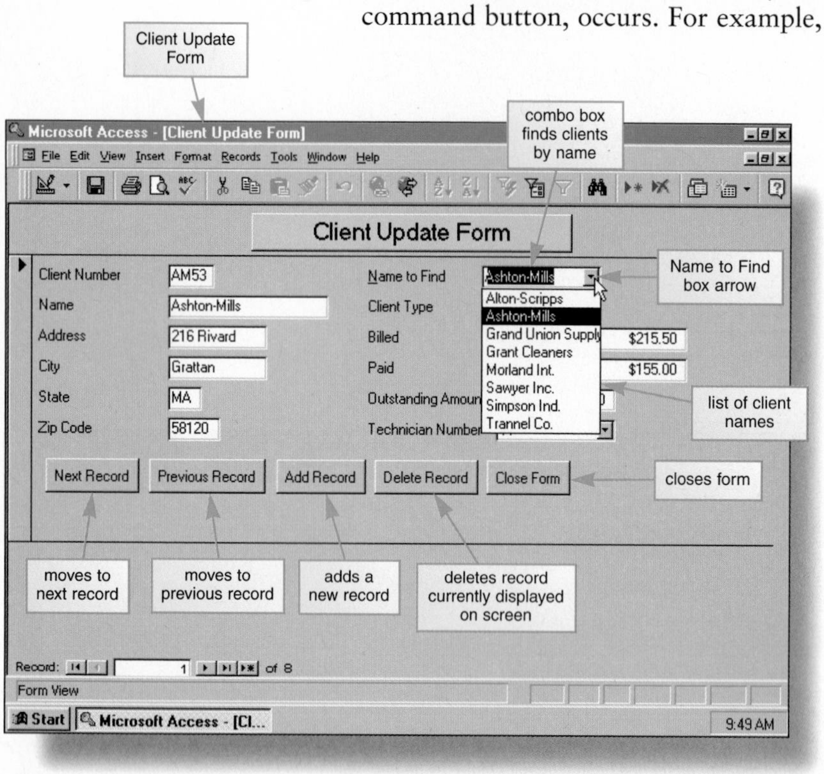

Generally, you do not even need to be aware that these event procedures exist. Access creates and uses them automatically. Occasionally, however, you may wish to make changes to an event procedure. Without making changes, for example, clicking the Add Record button blanks out the fields on the form so you can enter a new record. Yet, it would not produce an insertion point in the Client Number field. It would require you to take special action, such as clicking the Client Number field, before you could begin entering data. You can rectify this by making a change to the event procedure for the Add Record button.

FIGURE 6-2

Project Six – Creating an Application System for Pilotech Services

Before creating the switchboard system required by the management of Pilotech Services, first you must create and test the macros that will be used in the system. In addition, you must add the necessary buttons to the Client Update Form. Then, you must add the combo box that allows users to find a client given the client's name. Finally, you must create the switchboard system that will allow users to access any form, table, or report simply by clicking the appropriate buttons.

Overview of Project Steps

The project steps create the macros necessary to implement the switchboard system in Figures 6-1a and 6-1b on page A 6.5. They add the command buttons and combo box to the Client Update Form in Figure 6-2. Finally, they create the switchboard system in Figures 6-1a and 6-1b. The following tasks will be completed in this project.

1. Start Access.
2. Create the macros needed for the switchboard system.
3. Place command buttons on the Client Update Form.
4. Modify the VBA code for the Add Record button.
5. Place a combo box on the Client Update Form.
6. Modify the properties of the combo box.
7. Create a switchboard.
8. Create the switchboard pages.
9. Create the switchboard items.

The following pages contain a detailed explanation of these steps.

Opening the Database

Before creating the macros, modifying the form, or creating the switchboard system, first you must open the database. Perform the following steps to complete this task.

TO OPEN A DATABASE

Step 1: Click the Start button on the taskbar.
Step 2: Click Open Office Document on the Start menu, and then click 3½ Floppy (A:) in the Look in list box. If necessary, double-click the Access folder. Make sure the Pilotech Services database is selected.
Step 3: Click the Open button.

The database opens and the Pilotech Services : Database window displays.

Creating and Using Macros

A **macro** consists of a series of actions that Access will perform when the macro is run; therefore, you will need to specify the actions when you create the macro. The actions are entered in a special window called a **Macro window**. Once a macro is created, you can run it from the Database window by right-clicking it and then clicking Run on the shortcut menu. Macros also can be associated with items on switchboards. When you click the corresponding button on the switchboard, Access will run the macro. Whether a macro is run from the Database window or from a switchboard, the effect is the same. Access will execute the actions in the macro in the order in which they are entered.

In this project, you will create macros to open forms and maximize the windows; open tables in Datasheet view; open reports in preview windows; and print reports. As you enter actions, you will select them from a list box. The names of the actions are self-explanatory. The action to open a form, for example, is OpenForm. Thus, it is not necessary to memorize the specific actions that are available.

More *About*
Macros

The actions in a macro are executed when a particular *event* occurs. The event simply could be a user clicking Run on the macro's shortcut menu. It also could be the clicking of a button on a form or switchboard, provided the macro is associated with the button.

To create a macro, perform the following steps to begin the process.

Steps To Create a Macro

1 **Click the Macros tab and point to the New button.**

The list of previously created macros displays (Figure 6-3). Currently, no macros exist.

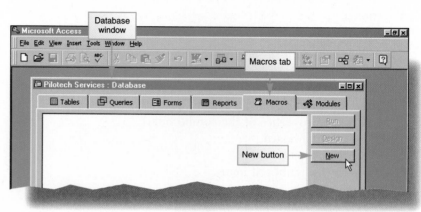

FIGURE 6-3

2 **Click the New button.**

The Macro1: Macro window displays (Figure 6-4).

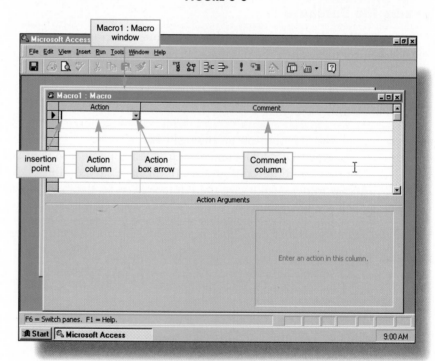

FIGURE 6-4

The Macro Window

The first column in the Macro window is the **Action column**. You enter the **actions** you want the macro to perform in this column (Figure 6-4). To enter an action, click the arrow in the Action column and select the action from the list that displays. Many actions require additional information, called the **arguments** of the action. If you select such an action, the arguments will display in the lower portion of the Macro window and you can make any necessary changes to them.

The second column in the Macro window is the **Comment column**. In this column, you enter **comments**, which are brief descriptions of the purpose of the corresponding action. The actions, the arguments requiring changes, and the comments for the first macro you will create are shown in Table 6-1.

Table 6-1			
ACTION	ARGUMENT TO CHANGE	NEW VALUE FOR ARGUMENT	COMMENT
Echo	Echo On	No	Turn echo off to avoid screen flicker
Hourglass			Turn on hourglass
OpenForm	Form Name	Client Update Form	Open Client Update Form
Hourglass	Hourglass On	No	Turn off hourglass
Echo			Turn echo on

The macro begins by turning off the echo. This will eliminate the screen flicker that can be present when a form is being opened. The second action changes the shape of the mouse pointer to an hourglass to indicate that some process currently is taking place. The third action opens the form called Client Update Form. The fourth turns off the hourglass and the fifth turns the echo back on so the Client Update Form will display.

Adding Actions to a Macro

Turning on and off the echo and the hourglass are not absolutely necessary. On computers with faster processors, you might not notice a difference between running a macro that included these actions and one that did not. For slower processors, however, they can make a noticeable difference and that is why they are included here.

To create this macro, enter the actions. For each action, fill in the action and comment, and then make the necessary changes to any arguments. Once the actions have been entered, close the macro, click the Yes button to save the changes, and assign the macro a name. Perform the following steps to create, add actions to, and save the macro.

Steps To Add Actions to a Macro

1 **Click the box arrow in the first row of the Action column. Point to Echo.**

The list of available actions displays (Figure 6-5).

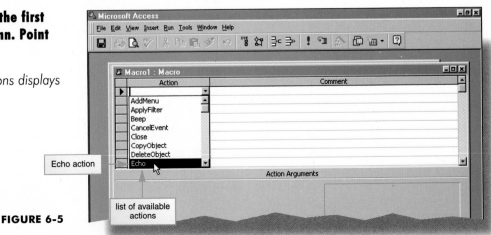

Echo action

list of available actions

FIGURE 6-5

2 **Click Echo. Press the F6 key to move to the Action Arguments for the Echo action. Click the Echo On box arrow. Point to No.**

The arguments for the Echo action display (Figure 6-6). The list of values for the Echo On argument displays. Pressing the F6 key switches panes.

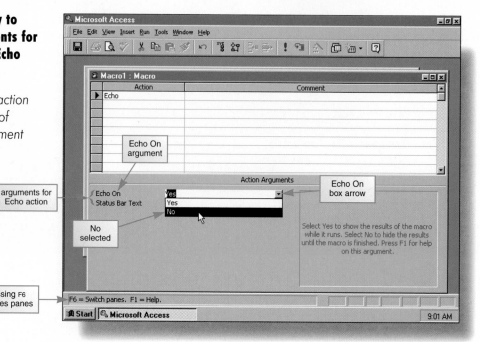

FIGURE 6-6

3 **Click No. Press the F6 key to move back to Echo in the Action column. Press the TAB key. Type** Turn echo off to avoid screen flicker **in the Comment column and then press the TAB key.**

The first action and comment are entered (Figure 6-7).

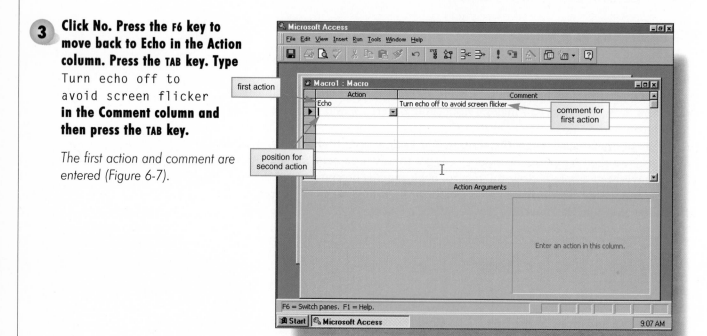

FIGURE 6-7

4 Select Hourglass as the action on the second row. Press the TAB key and then type Turn on hourglass as the comment on the second row. Press the TAB key and then select OpenForm as the third action. Press the F6 key to move to the Action Arguments and then click the Form Name box arrow. Point to Client Update Form.

A list of available forms displays (Figure 6-8).

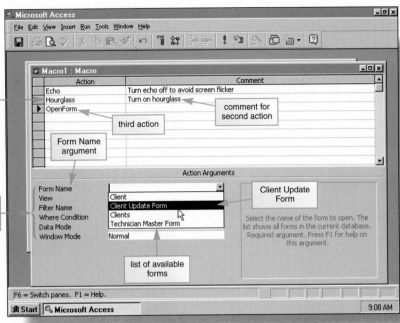

FIGURE 6-8

5 Click Client Update Form, press the F6 key, press the TAB key, and type Open Client Update Form as the comment.

6 Select Hourglass as the fourth action. Change the Hourglass On argument to No and then type Turn off hourglass as the comment.

7 Select Echo as the fifth action. Type Turn echo on as the comment.

The actions and comments are entered (Figure 6-9).

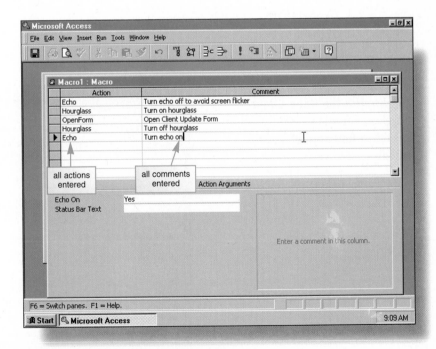

FIGURE 6-9

8 Click the Close button to close the macro, click the Yes button to save the macro, type Open Client Update Form as the name of the macro, and then point to the OK button.

The Save As dialog box displays (Figure 6-10).

9 Click the OK button.

The macro is created and saved.

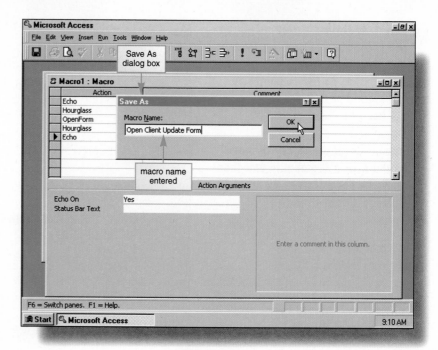

FIGURE 6-10

Running a Macro

To **run a macro**, click the Macros tab in the Database window, right-click the macro, and then click Run on the shortcut menu. The actions in the macro then will be executed. Perform the following steps to run the macro you just created.

Steps To Run a Macro

1 Right-click the Open Client Update Form macro and then point to Run on the shortcut menu.

The shortcut menu displays (Figure 6-11).

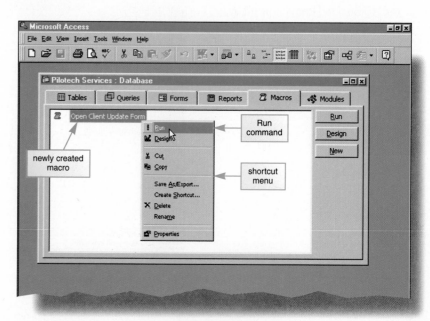

FIGURE 6-11

2 Click Run on the shortcut menu.

The macro runs and the Client Update Form displays (Figure 6-12). The window containing the form is not maximized.

3 Close the Client Update Form by clicking its Close button.

The form no longer displays.

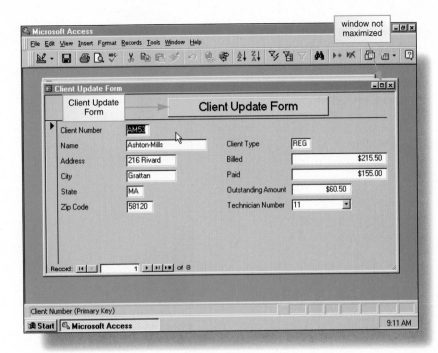

FIGURE 6-12

Other Ways
1. Click Macros tab, click macro object, click Run button
2. Click Macros tab, double-click macro object

Modifying a Macro

To **modify a macro**, right-click the macro in the Database window, click Design on the shortcut menu, and then make the necessary changes. To insert a new action, click the position for the action. If the action is to be placed between two actions, press the INSERT key to insert a new blank row. Then enter the new action, change the values for any necessary arguments, and enter a comment.

The following steps modify the macro just created, adding a new step to maximize the form automatically.

 To Modify a Macro

1 Right-click the Open Client Update Form macro and then point to Design on the shortcut menu.

The shortcut menu displays (Figure 6-13).

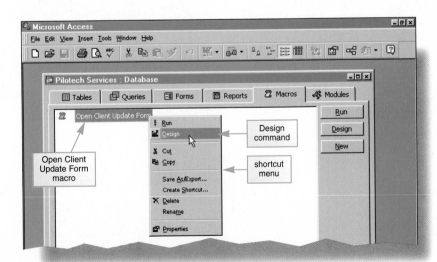

FIGURE 6-13

2 **Click Design on the shortcut menu. Point to the row selector in the fourth row, which is directly to the left of the second Hourglass action.**

The Open Client Update Form : Macro window displays (Figure 6-14).

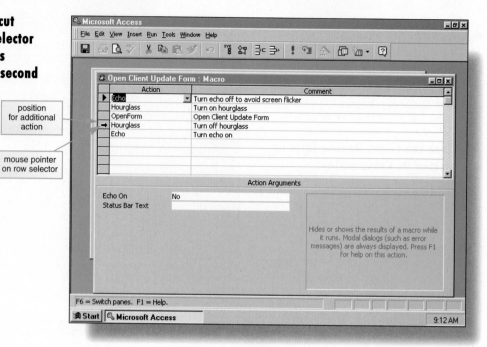

FIGURE 6-14

3 **Click the row selector to select the row, and then press the INSERT key to insert a new row. Click the Action column on the new row, select Maximize as the action, and type** Maximize the window **as the comment.**

The new action is entered (Figure 6-15).

4 **Click the Close button, and then click the Yes button to save the changes.**

The macro has been changed.

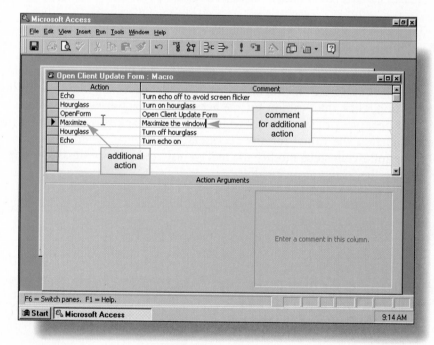

FIGURE 6-15

Other Ways

1. Click Macros tab, click macro object, click Design button

The next time the macro is run, the form not only will be opened, but the window containing the form also will be maximized.

Errors in Macros

Macros can contain **errors**. For example, if you typed the name of the form in the Form Name argument of the OpenForm action instead of selecting it from the list, you might type it incorrectly. Access then would be unable to execute the desired action. In that case, a Microsoft Access dialog box would display, indicating the error and solution (Figure 6-16).

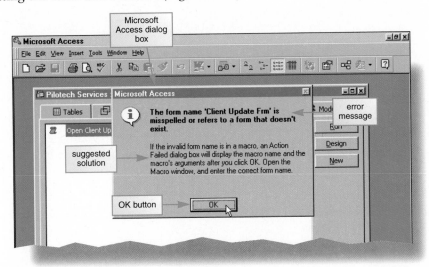

FIGURE 6-16

If such a dialog box displays, click the OK button. The Action Failed dialog box then displays (Figure 6-17). It indicates the macro that was being run, the action that Access was attempting to execute, and the arguments for the action. This information tells you which action needs to be corrected. To make the correction, click the Halt button, and then modify the design of the macro.

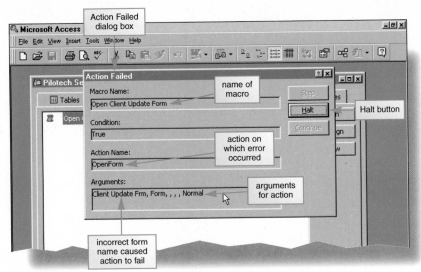

FIGURE 6-17

Creating Additional Macros

The additional macros to be created are shown in Table 6-2 on the next page. The first column gives the name of the macro and the second indicates the actions for the macro. The third contains the values of the arguments that need to be changed and the fourth contains the comments.

Table 6-2

MACRO NAME	ACTION	ARGUMENT(S)	COMMENT
Open Technician Master Form	Echo	Echo on: No	Turn echo off to avoid screen flicker
	Hourglass	Hourglass On: Yes	Turn on hourglass
	OpenForm	Form Name: Technician Master Form	Open Technician Master Form
	Maximize		Maximize the window
	Hourglass	Hourglass On: No	Turn off hourglass
	Echo	Echo on: Yes	Turn echo on
Open Client Table	OpenTable	Table Name: Client View: Datasheet	Open Client Table
	Maximize		Maximize the window
Open Technician Table	OpenTable	Table Name: Technician View: Datasheet	Open Technician Table
	Maximize		Maximize the window
Preview Billing Summary Report	OpenReport	Report Name: Billing Summary Report View: Print Preview	Preview Billing Summary Report
	Maximize		Maximize the window
Print Billing Summary Report	OpenReport	Report Name: Billing Summary Report View: Print	Print Billing Summary Report
Preview Client Amount Report	OpenReport	Report Name: Client Amount Report View: Print Preview	Preview Client Amount Report
	Maximize		Maximize the window
Print Client Amount Report	OpenReport	Report Name: Client Amount Report View: Print	Print Client Amount Report
Preview Clients by Technician	OpenReport	Report Name: Clients by Technician View: Print Preview	Preview Clients by Technician
	Maximize		Maximize the window
Print Clients by Technician	OpenReport	Report Name: Clients by Technician View: Print	Print Clients by Technician

Some macros require a change to more than one argument. For example, the action being entered in Figure 6-18 requires changes to both the Report Name argument and the View argument.

You can create additional macros using the same steps you used to create the first macro. Perform the following step to create the additional macros shown in Table 6-2.

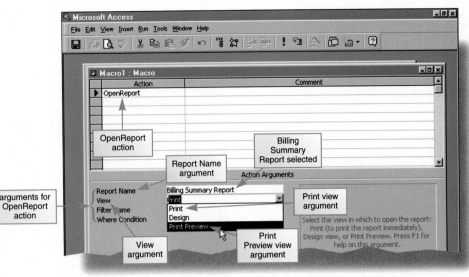

FIGURE 6-18

TO CREATE ADDITIONAL MACROS

Step 1: Using the same techniques you used to create the Open Client Update Form macro (page A 6.9), create each of the other macros in Table 6-2.

Running the Other Macros

To run any of the other macros, right-click the appropriate macro in the Database window and then click Run on the shortcut menu, just as you ran the first macro. The appropriate actions then are carried out. Running the Preview Billing Summary Report macro, for example, would display the Billing Summary Report in a maximized preview window.

Creating and Using Command Buttons

A **command button** executes a command when clicked. For example, after creating the Next Record command button, clicking it will move to the next record; clicking the Delete Record command button will delete the record currently on the screen; and clicking the Close Form command button will close the form.

Adding Command Buttons to a Form

To add command buttons, you will use the **Control Wizards button** and Command Button button in the toolbox. Using the series of **Command Button Wizard dialog boxes**, you must provide the action that should be taken when the button is clicked. Several categories of actions are available.

In the **Record Navigation category**, you will select the action Go to Next Record for one of the buttons. From the same category, you will select Go to Previous Record for another. Other buttons will use the Add New Record and the Delete Record actions from the **Record Operations category**. The Close Form button will use the Close Form action from the **Form Operations category**.

Perform the steps on the next page to add command buttons to move to the next record, move to the previous record, add a record, delete a record, and close the form.

◆ **More** *About*
Creating
Additional Macros

To create a macro that is identical to an existing macro, highlight the existing macro in the database window, click the Copy button on the toolbar, click the Paste button on the toolbar, and type a name for the new macro. You then can edit the new macro.

◆ **More** *About*
Control Wizards

There are wizards associated with many of the controls. The wizards lead you through screens that assist you in creating the control. To use the wizards, the Control Wizards button must be recessed. If not, you will need to specify all the details of the control without any assistance.

Steps To Add Command Buttons to a Form

1 **Click the Forms tab, right-click Client Update Form, and point to Design on the shortcut menu.**

The shortcut menu displays (Figure 6-19).

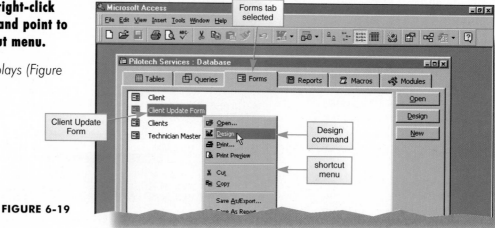

FIGURE 6-19

2 **Click Design on the shortcut menu, and then, if necessary, maximize the window. Be sure the toolbox displays and is docked at the bottom of the screen. (If it does not display, click the Toolbox button on the toolbar. If it is not docked at the bottom of the screen, drag it to the bottom of the screen to dock it there.) Make sure the Control Wizards button is recessed, and then point to the Command Button button in the toolbox.**

The design of the form displays in a maximized window (Figure 6-20).

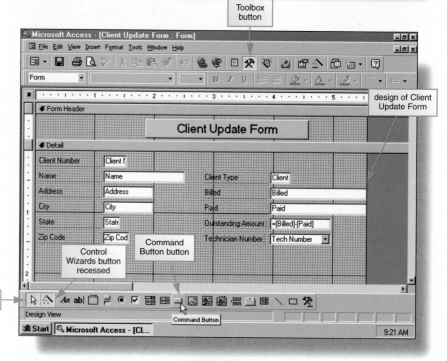

FIGURE 6-20

3 **Click the Command Button button and move the mouse pointer, whose shape has changed to a plus sign with a picture of a button, to the position shown in Figure 6-21.**

FIGURE 6-21

4 **Click the position shown in Figure 6-21. With Record Navigation selected in the Categories list box, click Go to Next Record in the Actions list box. Point to the Next button.**

The Command Button Wizard dialog box displays (Figure 6-22). Go to Next Record is selected as the action. A sample of the button displays in the Sample box.

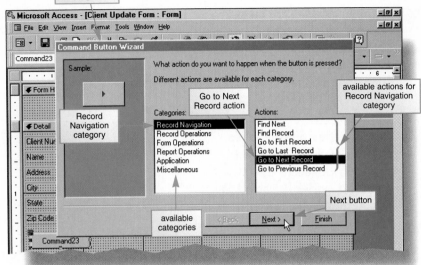

FIGURE 6-22

5 **Click the Next button. Point to the Text option button.**

The next Command Button Wizard dialog box displays, asking what to display on the button (Figure 6-23). The button can contain either text or a picture.

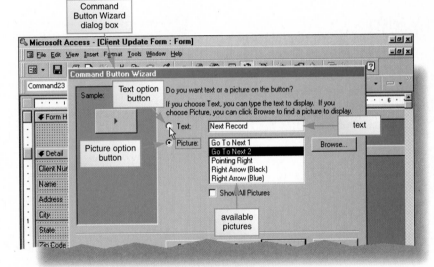

FIGURE 6-23

6 **Click Text. Next Record is the desired text and does not need to be changed. Click the Next button, and then type Next Record as the name of the button. Point to the Finish button.**

The name of the button displays in the text box (Figure 6-24).

7 **Click the Finish button.**

The button displays on the form.

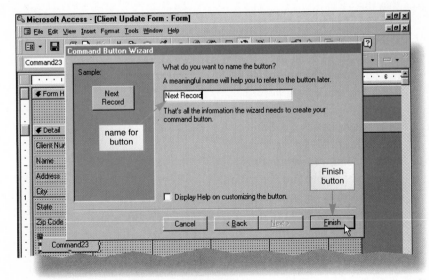

FIGURE 6-24

8 Use the techniques in Steps 3 through 7 to place the Previous Record button directly to the right of the Next Record button. Click Go to Previous Record in the Actions list box.

9 Place a button directly to the right of the Previous Record button. Click Record Operations in the Categories list box. Add New Record is the desired action. Point to the Next button.

The Command Button Wizard dialog box displays with the selections (Figure 6-25).

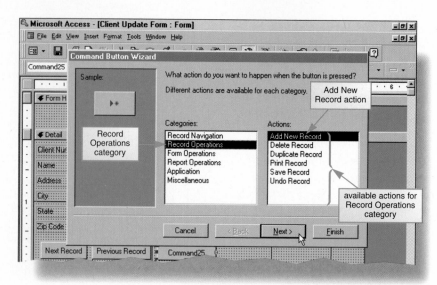

FIGURE 6-25

10 Click the Next button, and then click Text to indicate that the button is to contain text (Figure 6-26). Add Record is the desired text. Click the Next button, type Add Record as the name of the button, and then click the Finish button.

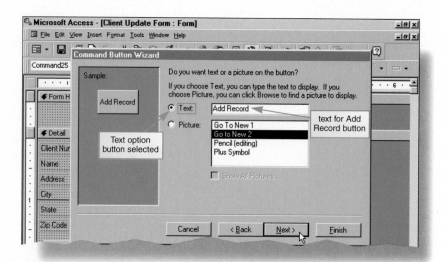

FIGURE 6-26

11 Use the techniques in Steps 3 through 7 to place the Delete Record and Close Form buttons in the positions shown in Figure 6-27. For the Delete Record button, the category is Record Operations and the action is Delete Record. For the Close Form button, the category is Form Operations and the action is Close Form. (If your buttons are not aligned properly, you can drag them to the correct positions.) Point to the View button on the toolbar.

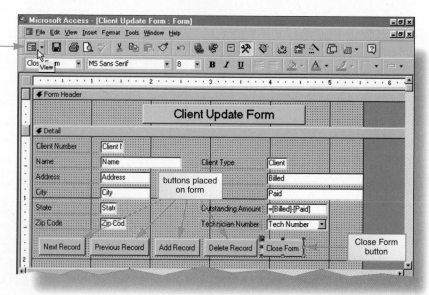

FIGURE 6-27

12 **Click the View button.**

The form displays with the added buttons (Figure 6-28).

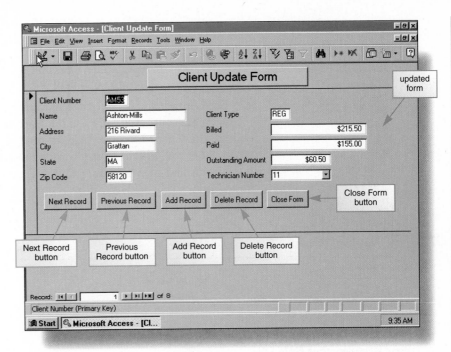

FIGURE 6-28

After creating the command buttons, you will use them. You also may need to modify them.

Using the Buttons

To move around on the form, you can **use the buttons** to perform the actions you specify. To move to the next record, click the Next Record button. Click the Previous Record button to move to the previous record. Clicking the Delete Record button will delete the record currently on the screen. You will get a message requesting you to verify the deletion before the record actually is deleted. Clicking the Close Form button will remove the form from the screen.

Clicking the Add Record button will clear the contents of the form so you can add a new record (Figure 6-29). Notice on the form in Figure 6-29, however, that an insertion point does not display. Therefore, to begin entering a record, you will have to click the Client Number field before you can start typing. To ensure that an insertion point displays in the field text box when you click the Add Record button, you must change the focus. **Focus** is the capability to receive user input through mouse or keyboard actions. The Add Record button needs to update the focus to the Client Number field.

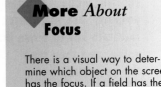

More *About* **Focus**

There is a visual way to determine which object on the screen has the focus. If a field has the focus, an insertion point will display in the field. If a button has the focus, a small rectangle will appear inside the button.

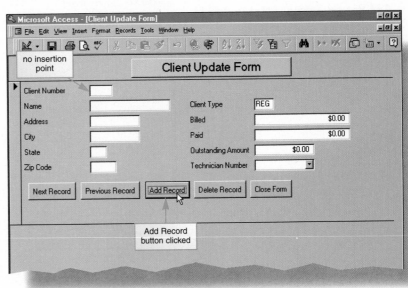

FIGURE 6-29

Modifying the Add Record Button

To display an insertion point automatically when you click the Add Record button, two steps are necessary using **Visual Basic for Applications (VBA)**. First, you must change the name of the control for the Client Number field to a name that does not contain spaces. Next, you must add a command to the VBA code that Access creates automatically for the button. The added command will move the focus to the Client Number field as soon as the button is clicked.

Perform the following steps to change the name of the Client Number control to ClNumb and then add an additional command to the VBA code that will set the focus to ClNumb.

Steps **To Modify the Add Record Button**

1 **Click the View button on the toolbar to return to the design grid. Right-click the control for the Client Number field (the white space, not the label), and then click Properties on the shortcut menu. Click the Name property, use the DELETE or BACKSPACE key to erase the current value, and then type** ClNumb **as the new name.**

The name is changed (Figure 6-30).

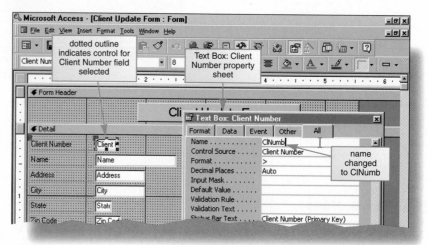

FIGURE 6-30

2 **Click the Close button to close the Text Box: Client Number property sheet. Right-click the Add Record button. Point to Build Event on the shortcut menu.**

The shortcut menu displays (Figure 6-31).

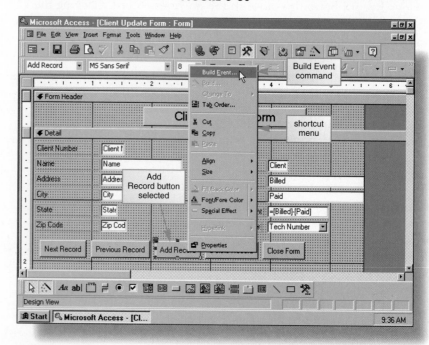

FIGURE 6-31

3 **Click Build Event on the shortcut menu.**

The VBA code for the Add Record button displays (Figure 6-32). The important line in this code is DoCmd, which stands for Do Command. Following DoCmd, is the command, formally called a method, that will be executed; in this case GoToRecord. Following GoToRecord are the arguments, which are items that provide information that will be used by the method. The only argument necessary in this case is acNewRec. This is a code that indicates that Access is to move to the new record at the end of the table; that is, the position where the new record will be added. This command will not set the focus to any particular field automatically, however, so an insertion point still will not be produced.

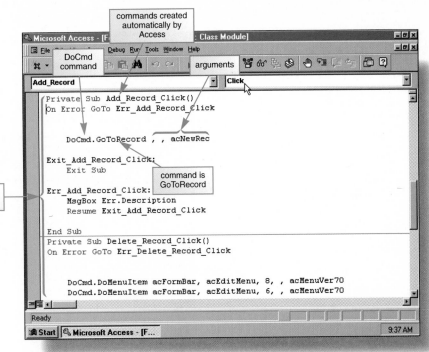

FIGURE 6-32

4 **Press the down arrow key four times, press the TAB key, and type ClNumb.SetFocus as the additional command. Press the ENTER key.**

The command is entered (Figure 6-33). While typing, a list box may display indicating selections for the command. You may ignore this list. This command will set the focus in the control named ClNumb as soon as the previous command (GoToRecord) is executed.

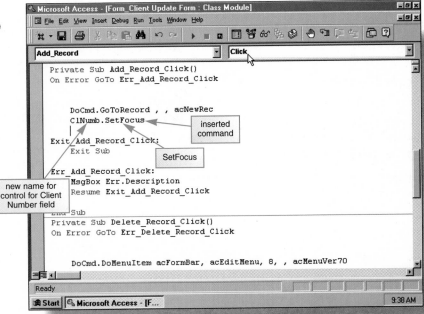

FIGURE 6-33

5 Close the window containing the VBA code. Click the View button on the toolbar and then click the Add Record button.

An insertion point displays in the Client Number field (Figure 6-34).

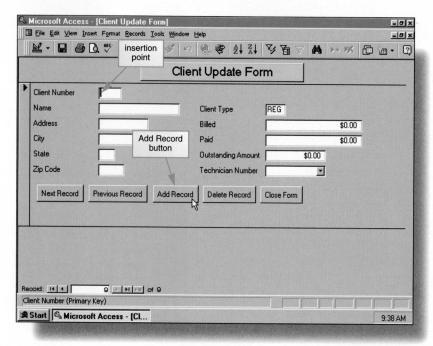

FIGURE 6-34

Creating and Using Combo Boxes

A **combo box**, such as the one shown in Figure 6-2 on page A 6.6, combines the properties of a **text box**, a box into which you can type an entry, and a **list box**, a box you can use to display a list. You could type the client's name directly into the box. Alternatively, you can click the Name to Find box arrow, and Access will display a list of client names. To select a name from the list, simply click the name.

Creating a Combo Box

To create a combo box, use the **Combo Box button** in the toolbox. The **Combo Box Wizard** then will guide you through the steps in adding the combo box. Perform the following steps to place a combo box for names on the form.

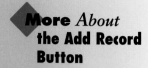

More *About* the Add Record Button

If your spelling was not consistent, you will get an error message when you click the Add Record button. To correct the problem, return to the form design. Check to make sure the name you gave to the Client Number control and the name in the SetFocus command are both the same (ClNumb).

Steps To Create a Combo Box

1 **Click the View button on the toolbar to return to the design grid. Make sure the Control Wizards button is recessed, and then point to the Combo Box button in the toolbox (Figure 6-35).**

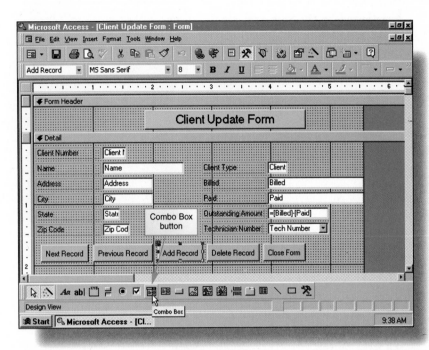

FIGURE 6-35

2 **Click the Combo Box button and then move the mouse pointer, whose shape has changed to a small plus sign with a combo box, to the position shown in Figure 6-36.**

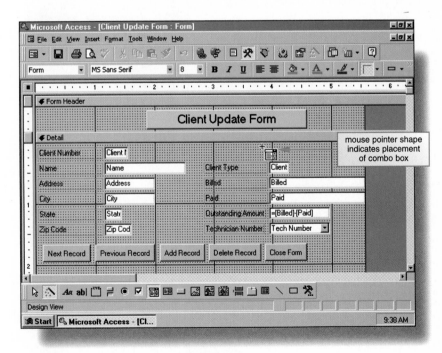

FIGURE 6-36

3 Click the position shown in Figure 6-36 to place a combo box. Click **Find a record on my form based on the value selected in the combo box.** Point to the Next button.

The Combo Box Wizard dialog box displays, instructing you to indicate how the combo box is to obtain values for the list (Figure 6-37).

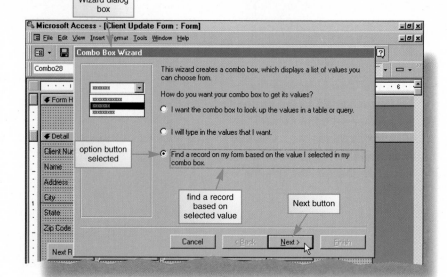

FIGURE 6-37

4 Click the Next button, click the Name field, and click the Add Field button to add Name as a field in the combo box. Point to the Next button.

The Name field is selected (Figure 6-38).

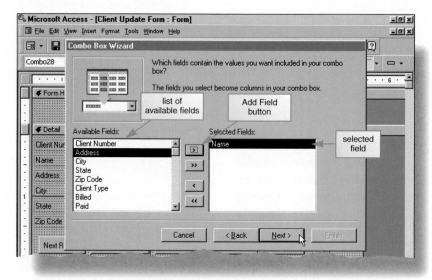

FIGURE 6-38

5 Click the Next button.

The Combo Box Wizard dialog box displays (Figure 6-39), giving you an opportunity to resize the columns in the combo box.

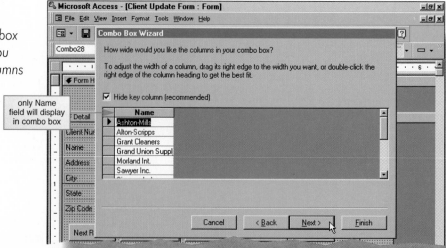

FIGURE 6-39

6 Click the Next button, and then type &Name to Find as the label for the combo box. Point to the Finish button.

The label is entered (Figure 6-40). The ampersand (&) in front of the letter N indicates that users can select the combo box by pressing the ALT+N keys.

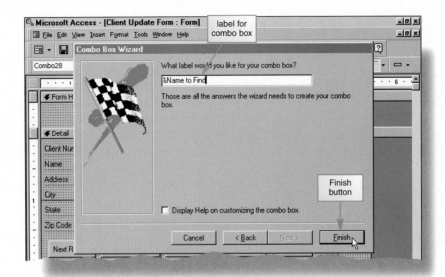

FIGURE 6-40

7 Click the Finish button. Click the label for the combo box. Point to the sizing handle on the right edge of the label.

The shape of the mouse pointer changes to a two-headed horizontal arrow, indicating that you can drag the right edge (Figure 6-41).

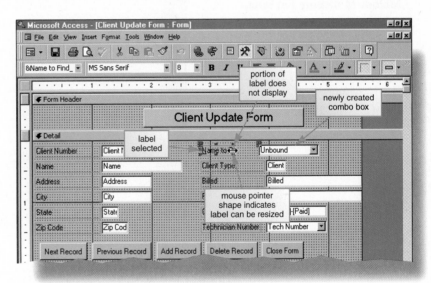

FIGURE 6-41

8 Double-click the handle so the entire label displays. Point to the View button on the toolbar.

The combo box is added and the label has been resized (Figure 6-42). The N in Name is underlined indicating that you can press the ALT+N keys to select the combo box.

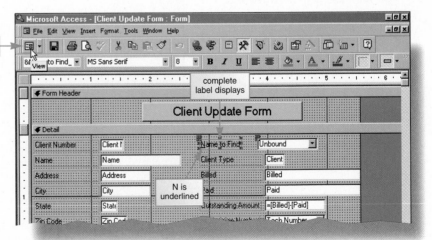

FIGURE 6-42

Using the Combo Box

Using the combo box, you can search for a client in two ways. First, you can click the combo box arrow to display a list of client names, and then select the name from the list by clicking it. Alternatively, you can begin typing the name. As you type, Access will display automatically the name that begins with the letters you have typed. Once the correct name is displayed, select the name by pressing the TAB key. Regardless of the method you use, the data for the selected client displays in the form once the selection is made.

The following steps first locate the client whose name is Morland Int., and then use the Next Record button to move to the next client.

Steps To Use the Combo Box

1 **Click the View button on the toolbar to display the form.**

The form displays (Figure 6-43).

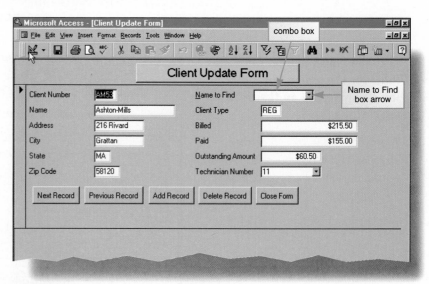

FIGURE 6-43

2 **Click the Name to Find box arrow and then point to Morland Int.**

The list of names displays (Figure 6-44).

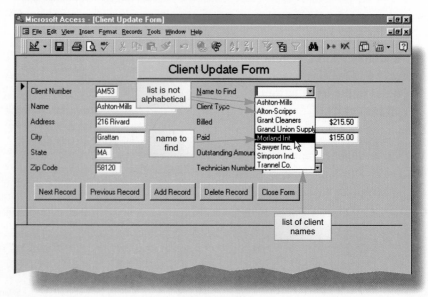

FIGURE 6-44

3 Click Morland Int.

The data for the client whose name is Morland Int. displays in the form (Figure 6-45).

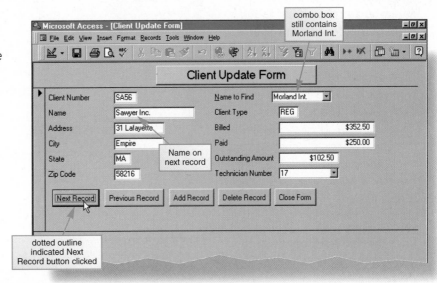

FIGURE 6-45

4 Click the Next Record button.

The data for the client whose name is Sawyer Inc. displays in the form (Figure 6-46). The combo box still contains Morland Int.

FIGURE 6-46

Issues with the Combo Box

Consider the following **issues with the combo box**. First, if you examine the list of names in Figure 6-44, you will see that they are not in alphabetical order. Second, when you move to a record without using the combo box, the name in the combo box does not change to reflect the name of the client currently on the screen. Third, pressing the TAB key should not move to the combo box.

Modifying the Combo Box

The steps on the next page modify the query that Access has created for the combo box so that first the data is sorted by name and then by the **On Current property** of the entire form. The modification to the On Current property will ensure that the combo box is kept current with the rest of the form; that is, it contains the name of the client whose number currently displays in the Client Number field. The final step changes the Tab Stop property for the combo box from Yes to No.

Perform the following steps to modify the combo box.

Steps To Modify the Combo Box

1 Click the View button on the toolbar to return to the design grid. Right-click the Name to Find combo box (the white space, not the label), and then click Properties on the shortcut menu. Note the number of your combo box, which may be different from the one shown in Figure 6-47, because it will be important later. Click the Row Source property, and then point to the Build button for the Row Source property.

The Combo Box: Combo28 property sheet displays (Figure 6-47). The combo box number is 28 (Combo28). The Row Source property is selected. Depending on where you clicked the Row Source property, the value may or may not be highlighted.

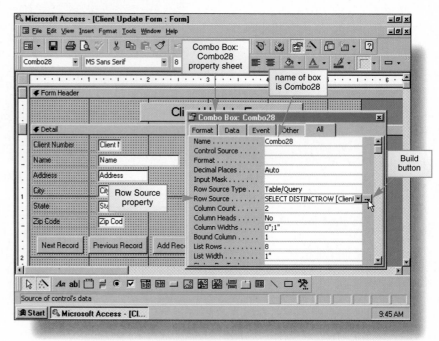

FIGURE 6-47

2 Click the Build button. Point to the Sort row under the Name field.

The SQL Statement : Query Builder window displays (Figure 6-48). This screen allows you to make changes just as you did when you created queries.

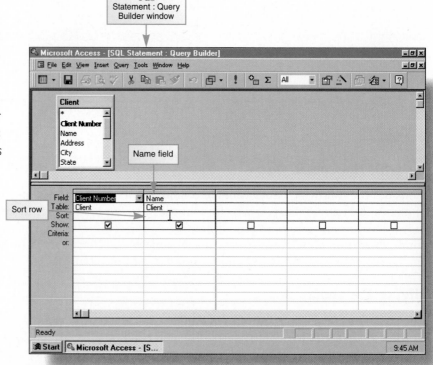

FIGURE 6-48

3 Click the Sort row in the Name field, click the box arrow that displays, and click Ascending. Point to the Close button for the SQL Statement : Query Builder window.

The sort order is changed to Ascending (Figure 6-49).

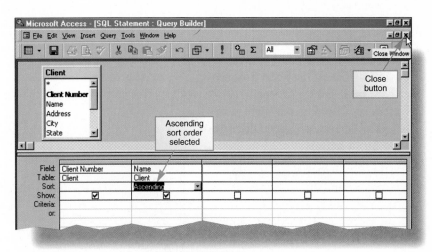

FIGURE 6-49

4 Close the SQL Statement : Query Builder window by clicking its Close button. Point to the Yes button.

The Microsoft Access dialog box displays (Figure 6-50).

5 Click the Yes button to change the property, and then close the Combo Box: Combo28 property sheet.

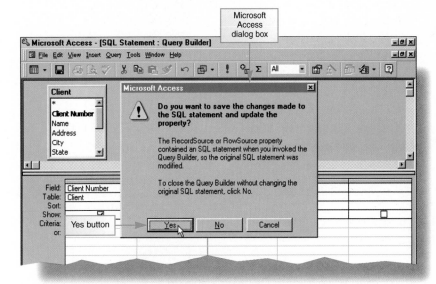

FIGURE 6-50

6 Point to the form selector, the box in the upper-left corner of the form (Figure 6-51).

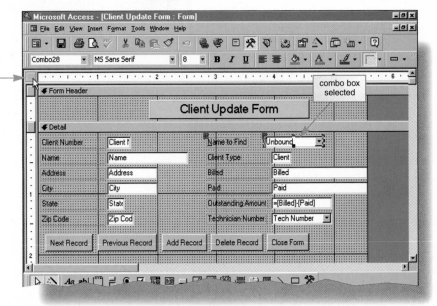

FIGURE 6-51

7 Right-click the form selector, and then click Properties on the shortcut menu. Click the down scroll arrow on the Form property sheet until the On Current property displays, and then click the On Current property. Point to the Build button.

The Form property sheet displays (Figure 6-52).

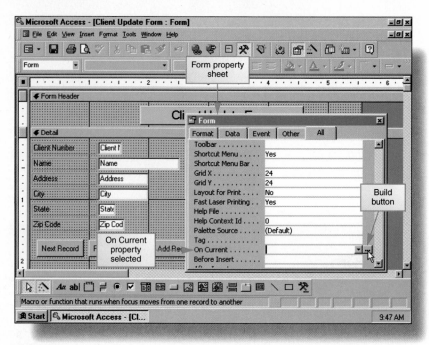

FIGURE 6-52

8 Click the Build button, click Code Builder, and point to the OK button.

The Choose Builder dialog box displays (Figure 6-53). Code Builder is selected.

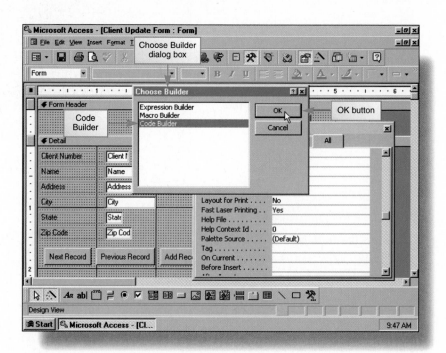

FIGURE 6-53

9 Click the OK button.

The code generated by Access for the form displays (Figure 6-54).

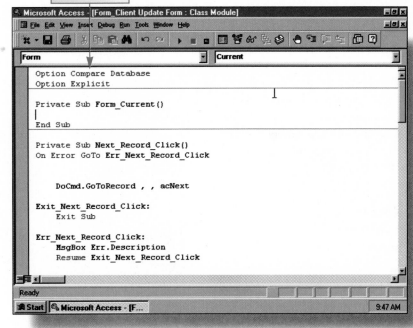

FIGURE 6-54

10 Type Combo28 = C1Numb ' Update the combo box **in the position shown in Figure 6-55, and then point to the Close button.**

This command assumes your combo box is Combo28. If yours has a different number, use your number in the command instead of 28. This command will update the contents of the combo box using the client number currently in the ClNumb control. The portion of the command following the apostrophe is called a **comment**. *It describes the purpose of the command.*

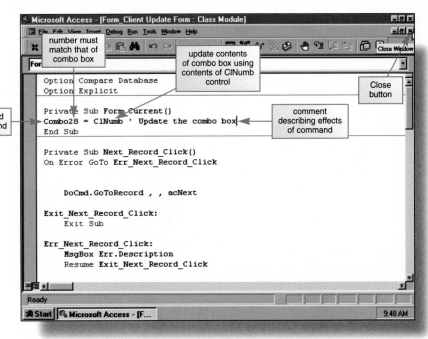

FIGURE 6-55

11 Click the Close button, and then close the Form property sheet. Right-click the combo box, and then click Properties on the shortcut menu. Click the down scroll arrow until the Tab Stop property displays, click the Tab Stop property, click the Tab Stop box arrow, and point to No (Figure 6-56).

12 Click No, and then close the Combo Box: Combo28 property sheet.

The modifications to the combo box are complete.

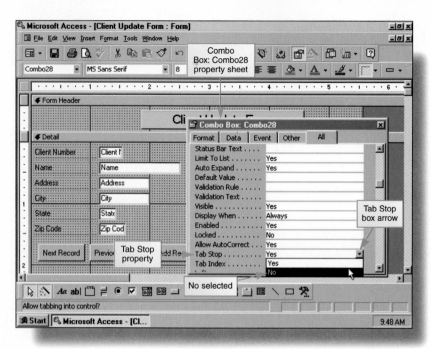

FIGURE 6-56

Using the Modified Combo Box

The problems with the combo box now are corrected. The search conducted in the following steps first search for the client whose name is Morland Int., and then move to the next record in the table to verify that the combo box also will be updated. Perform the following steps to search for a client.

 Steps To Use the Combo Box to Search for a Client

1 Click the View button on the toolbar to display the Client Update Form, and then click the Name to Find box arrow.

A list of names displays (Figure 6-57).

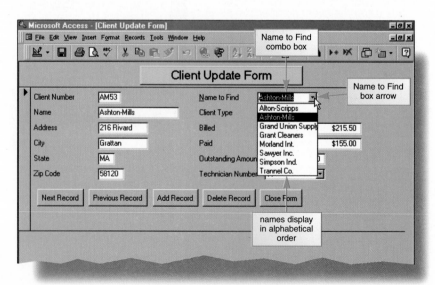

FIGURE 6-57

2 Click Morland Int., and then point to the Next Record button.

Client MI26 displays in the form (Figure 6-58).

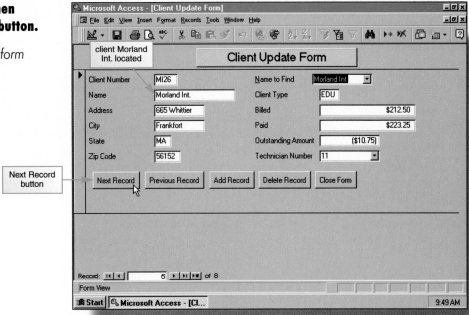

FIGURE 6-58

3 Click the Next Record button.

Client SA56 displays on the form (Figure 6-59). The client's name also displays in the combo box.

4 Close the form by clicking its Close button, and then click the Yes button to save the changes.

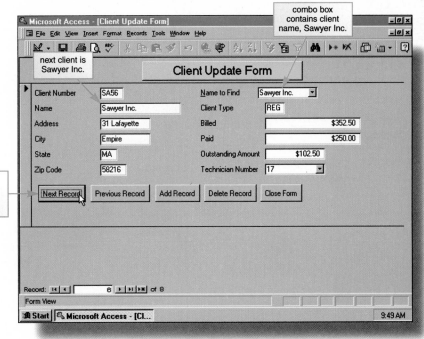

FIGURE 6-59

More *About* Switchboards

A switchboard is considered a form and is run like any other form. There is a special tool to create it, however, called the Switchboard Manager. Although you could modify the design of the form by clicking Design on its shortcut menu, it is easier to use the Switchboard Manager for modifications.

Creating and Using a Switchboard

A **switchboard** (see Figures 6-1a and 6-1b on page A 6.5) is a special type of form. It contains buttons you can click to perform a variety of actions. Buttons on the main switchboard can lead to other switchboards. Clicking the View Form button, for example, causes Access to display the View Form switchboard. Buttons can be used to open forms or tables. Clicking the Client Update Form button on the View Form switchboard opens the Client Update Form. Still other buttons cause reports to be displayed in a preview window. Other buttons print reports.

Creating a Switchboard

To create a switchboard, you use the Add-Ins command on the Tools menu and then click **Switchboard Manager**. If you have not previously created a switchboard, you will be asked if you want to create one. Clicking the Yes button causes Access to create the switchboard. Perform the following steps to create a switchboard for the Pilotech Services database.

Steps **To Create a Switchboard**

① **With the Database window displaying, click Tools on the menu bar, point to Add-Ins, and then point to Switchboard Manager.**

The Tools menu displays (Figure 6-60). The Add-Ins submenu displays. (The menu you see may be different.)

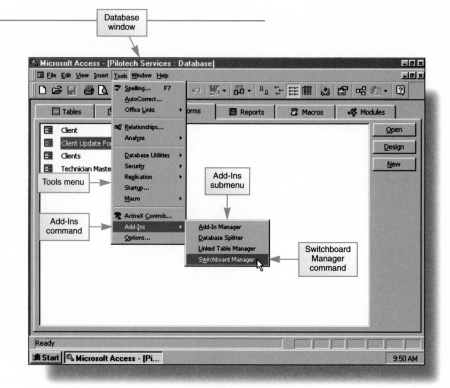

FIGURE 6-60

2 Click Switchboard Manager and then point to the Yes button.

The Switchboard Manager dialog box displays (Figure 6-61). The message indicates that no switchboard currently exists for this database.

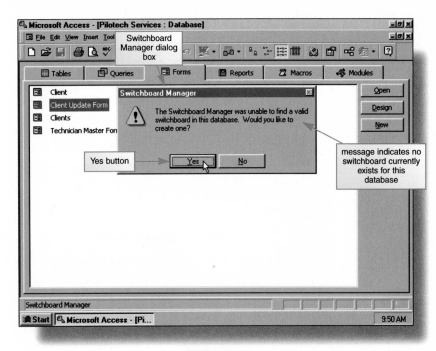

FIGURE 6-61

3 Click the Yes button to create a new switchboard. Point to the New button.

The Switchboard Manager dialog box displays (Figure 6-62).

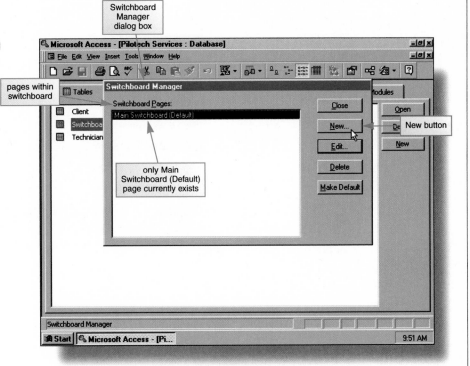

FIGURE 6-62

Creating Switchboard Pages

The next step in creating the switchboard system is to create the individual switchboards within the system. These are called the **switchboard pages**. The switchboard pages to be created are listed in the first column of Table 6-3. You do not have to create the Main Switchboard page, because Access has created it automatically. To create each of the other pages, click the New button in the Switchboard Manager dialog box, and then type the name of the page.

Table 6-3

SWITCHBOARD PAGE	SWITCHBOARD ITEM	COMMAND	ARGUMENT
Main Switchboard	View Form	Go to Switchboard	Switchboard: View Form
	View Table	Go to Switchboard	Switchboard: View Table
	View Report	Go to Switchboard	Switchboard: View Report
	Print Report	Go to Switchboard	Switchboard: Print Report
	Exit Application	Exit Application	none
View Form	Client Update Form	Run Macro	Macro: Open Client Update Form
	Technician Master Form	Run Macro	Macro: Open Technician Master Form
	Return to Main Switchboard	Go to Switchboard	Switchboard: Main Switchboard
View Table	Client Table	Run Macro	Macro: Open Client Table
	Technician Table	Run Macro	Macro: Open Technician Table
	Return to Main Switchboard	Go to Switchboard	Switchboard: Main Switchboard
View Report	View Billing Summary Report	Run Macro	Macro: Preview Billing Summary Report
	View Client Amount Report	Run Macro	Macro: Preview Client Amount Report
	View Clients by Technician	Run Macro	Macro: Preview Clients by Technician
	Return to Main Switchboard	Go to Switchboard	Switchboard: Main Switchboard
Print Report	Print Billing Summary Report	Run Macro	Macro: Print Billing Summary Report
	Print Client Amount Report	Run Macro	Macro: Print Client Amount Report
	Print Clients by Technician	Run Macro	Macro: Print Clients by Technician
	Return to Main Switchboard	Go to Switchboard	Switchboard: Main Switchboard

Perform the following steps to create the switchboard pages.

Steps To Create Switchboard Pages

1 **Click the New button in the Switchboard Manager dialog box. Type** View Form **as the name of the new switchboard page. Point to the OK button.**

The Create New dialog box displays (Figure 6-63). The name of the new page displays.

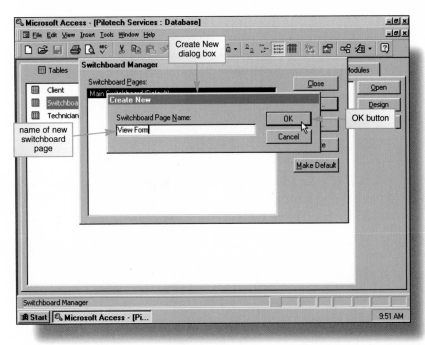

FIGURE 6-63

2 **Click the OK button to create the View Form switchboard page. Use the same technique to create the View Table, View Report, and Print Report switchboard pages.**

The newly created switchboard pages display in the Switchboard Manager dialog box in alphabetical order (Figure 6-64).

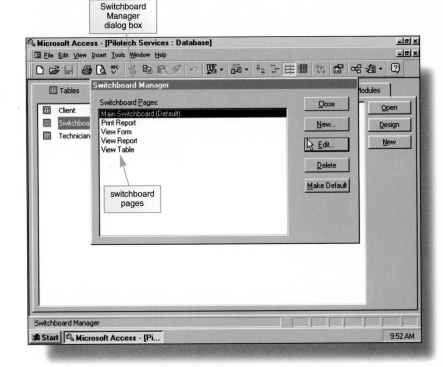

FIGURE 6-64

Modifying Switchboard Pages

To **modify a switchboard page**, after selecting the page in the Switchboard Manager dialog box, you click the **Edit button**. You can add new items to the page, move existing items to a different position in the list of items, or delete items. For each item, you can indicate the command to be executed when the item is selected.

Perform the following steps to modify the Main Switchboard page.

Steps To Modify the Main Switchboard Page

1 With the Main Switchboard (Default) page selected, point to the Edit button (Figure 6-65).

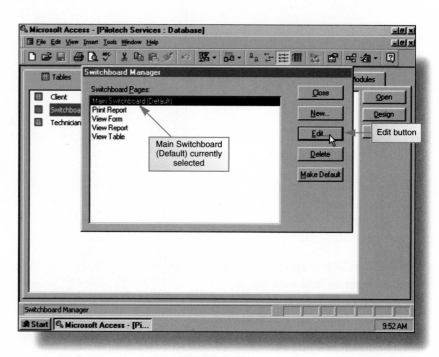

FIGURE 6-65

2 Click the Edit button, and then point to the New button in the Edit Switchboard Page dialog box.

The Edit Switchboard Page dialog box displays (Figure 6-66).

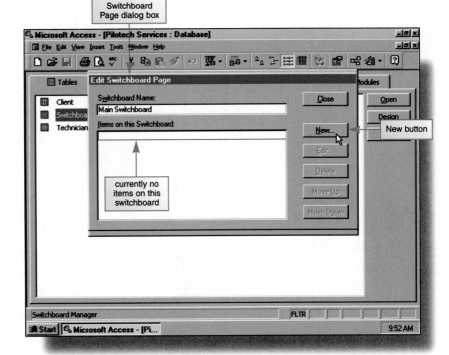

FIGURE 6-66

3 Click the New button, type View Form as the text, click the Switchboard box arrow, and then point to View Form.

The Edit Switchboard Item dialog box displays (Figure 6-67). The text is entered, the command is Go to Switchboard, and the list of available switchboards displays.

4 Click View Form, and then click the OK button to add the item to the switchboard.

5 Using the techniques in Steps 3 and 4, add the View Table, View Report, and Print Report items to the Main Switchboard page. In each case the command is Go to Switchboard. The names of the switchboards are the same as the name of the items. For example, the switchboard for the View Table item is called View Table.

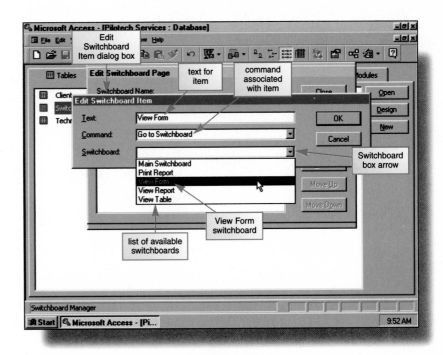

FIGURE 6-67

6 **Click the New button, type** Exit Application **as the text, click the Command box arrow, and then point to Exit Application.**

The Edit Switchboard Item dialog box displays (Figure 6-68). The text is entered, and the list of available commands displays.

7 **Click Exit Application, and then click the OK button to add the item to the switchboard. Click the Close button in the Edit Switchboard Page dialog box to indicate you are finished editing the Main Switchboard.**

The Main Switchboard page now is complete. The Edit Switchboard Page dialog box closes, and the Switchboard Manager dialog box displays.

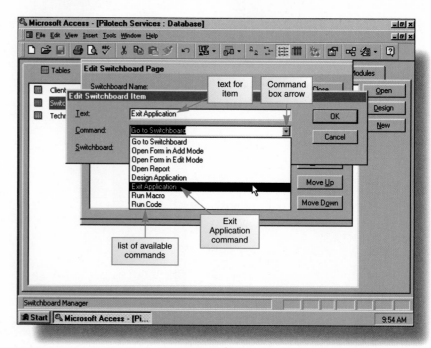

FIGURE 6-68

Modifying the Other Switchboard Pages

The other switchboard pages from Table 6-3 on page A 6.38 are modified in exactly the same manner you modified the Main Switchboard page. Perform the following steps to modify the other switchboard pages.

Steps To Modify the Other Switchboard Pages

1 **Click the View Form switchboard page, and then point to the Edit button.**

The View Form page is selected (Figure 6-69).

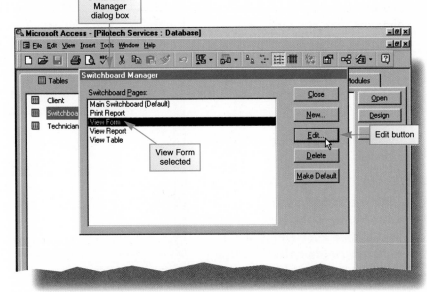

FIGURE 6-69

2 **Click the Edit button, click the New button to add a new item, type** Client Update Form **as the text, click the Command box arrow, and then click Run Macro. Click the Macro box arrow, and then point to Open Client Update Form.**

The Edit Switchboard Item dialog box displays (Figure 6-70). The text is entered, and the command has been selected. The list of available macros displays.

3 **Click Open Client Update Form, and then click the OK button.**

The Open Client Update Form item is added to the View Form switchboard.

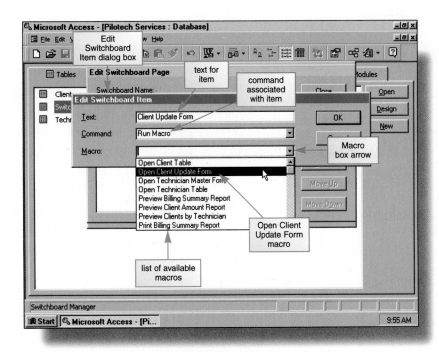

FIGURE 6-70

4 **Click the New button, type** Technician Master Form **as the text, click the Command box arrow, and then click Run Macro. Click the Macro box arrow, click Open Technician Master Form, and then click the OK button.**

5 Click the New button, type
Return to Main
Switchboard as the text, click
the Command box arrow, and
then click Go to Switchboard.
Click the Switchboard box arrow,
and then click Main Switchboard.
Point to the OK button.

*The text is entered (Figure 6-71).
The command and switchboard are
selected.*

6 Click the OK button. Click the
Close button in the Edit
Switchboard Page dialog box to
indicate you are finished editing
the View Form switchboard.

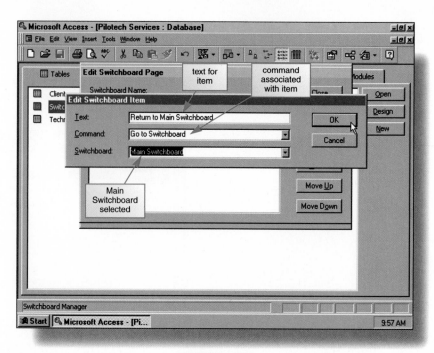

FIGURE 6-71

7 Use the techniques in Steps 1
through 6 to add the items
indicated in Table 6-3 on page
A 6.38 to the other switchboards.
When you have finished, point to
the Close button in the
Switchboard Manager dialog box
(Figure 6-72).

8 Click the Close button.

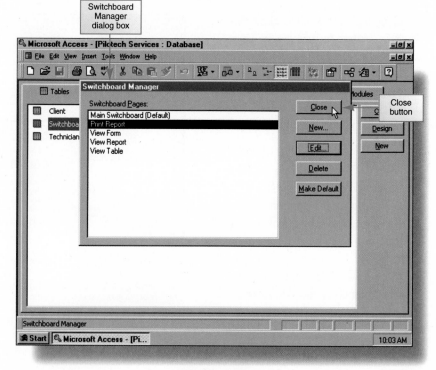

FIGURE 6-72

The switchboard is complete and ready for use. Access has created a form called Switchboard that you will run to use the switchboard. It also has created a table called Switchboard Items. *Do not modify this table.* It is used by the Switchboard Manager to keep track of the various switchboard pages and items.

Using a Switchboard

To use the switchboard, click the Forms tab, right-click the switchboard, and then click Run on the shortcut menu. The main switchboard then will display. To take any action, click the appropriate buttons. When you have finished, click the Exit Application button. The switchboard will be removed from the screen, and the database will be closed. The following steps illustrate the use of the switchboard system.

More *About*
Displaying a
Switchboard

It is possible to have the switchboard display automatically when the database is opened. To do so, click Tools on the menu bar and click Startup. Click the Display Form box arrow, select the Switchboard form, and click the OK button.

Steps To Use a Switchboard

1 **Click the Forms tab, and then right-click Switchboard. Point to Open on the shortcut menu.**

The shortcut menu for Switchboard displays (Figure 6-73).

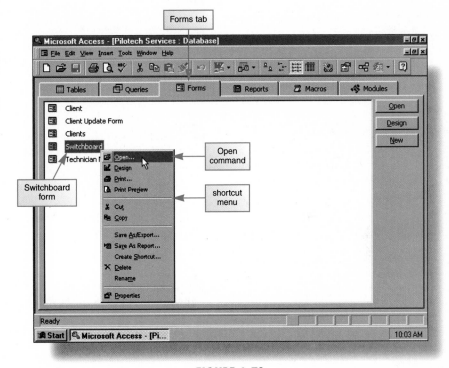

FIGURE 6-73

2 **Click Open.**

The Main Switchboard displays (Figure 6-74).

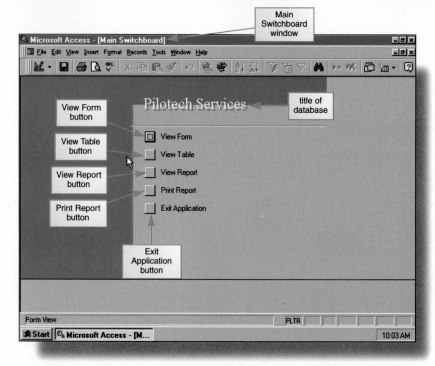

FIGURE 6-74

Click the View Form button to display the View Form switchboard page. Click the View Table button to display the View Table switchboard page. Click the View Report button to display the View Report switchboard page. Click the Print Report button to display the Print Report switchboard page. On each of the other switchboard pages, click the button for the form, table, or report you wish to view, or the report you wish to print. To return from one of the other switchboard pages to the Main Switchboard, click the Return to Main Switchboard button. To leave the switchboard system, click the Exit Application button.

If you discover a problem with the switchboard, click Tools on the menu bar, click Add-Ins, and click Switchboard Manager. You then can modify the switchboard system using the same techniques you used to create it.

Closing the Switchboard and Database

To close the switchboard and the database, click the Exit Application button. Perform the following step to close the switchboard.

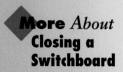

TO CLOSE THE SWITCHBOARD AND DATABASE

Step 1: Click the Exit Application button.

The switchboard is removed from the screen. The database also closes.

Project Summary

Project 6 introduced you to creating a complete switchboard system. To create the system required at Pilotech Services, you created and used several macros. In addition, you modified the Client Update Form to make it more functional for the users at Pilotech Services. You incorporated several command buttons to make it easier for the users to perform certain tasks. Then, you added a combo box to allow users to search for a client either by typing the client's name or selecting the name from a list. Using Switchboard Manager, you created the switchboard, the switchboard pages, and the switchboard items. You also used the Switchboard Manager to assign actions to the buttons on the switchboard pages.

What You Should Know

Having completed this project, you now should be able to perform the following tasks:

▶ Add Actions to a Macro *(A 6.9)*
▶ Add Command Buttons to a Form *(A 6.18)*
▶ Close the Switchboard and Database *(A 6.46)*
▶ Create a Combo Box *(A 6.25)*
▶ Create a Macro *(A 6.8)*
▶ Create Additional Macros *(A 6.17)*
▶ Create a Switchboard *(A 6.36)*
▶ Create Switchboard Pages *(A 6.39)*
▶ Modify a Macro *(A 6.13)*
▶ Modify the Add Record Button *(A 6.22)*

▶ Modify the Combo Box *(A 6.30)*
▶ Modify the Main Switchboard Page *(A 6.40)*
▶ Modify the Other Switchboard Pages *(A 6.43)*
▶ Open a Database *(A 6.7)*
▶ Run a Macro *(A 6.12)*
▶ Use the Combo Box *(A 6.28)*
▶ Use the Combo Box to Search for a Client *(A 6.34)*
▶ Use a Switchboard *(A 6.45)*

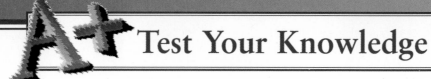

Test Your Knowledge

1 True/False

Instructions: Circle T if the statement is true or F if the statement is false.

T F 1. Macros are collections of actions designed to carry out some specific task.

T F 2. To create a macro, click the Macros tab in the Database window, and then click the Create button.

T F 3. Many actions that you enter in the Macro window require additional information called the parameters of the action.

T F 4. Setting the Hourglass action to No eliminates screen flicker.

T F 5. To run a macro, click the Macros tab in the Database window, right-click the macro, and then click Run on the shortcut menu.

T F 6. When you create a command button, you can specify only the text that appears on the button.

T F 7. A combo box combines the properties of a text box and a list box.

T F 8. To sort entries in a combo box, right-click the combo box, click Properties on the shortcut menu, and then click the Row Arrange property.

T F 9. A switchboard is a special type of form.

T F 10. To create a switchboard, click Insert on the menu bar, click Add-Ins, and then click Switchboard Manager.

2 Multiple Choice

Instructions: Circle the correct response.

1. In Access, a(n) _____ is a collection of actions designed to carry out some specific task.
   a. script
   b. button
   c. option group
   d. macro

2. Many actions require additional information called the _____ of the action.
   a. parameters
   b. properties
   c. arguments
   d. options

3. To run a macro, click the Macros tab in the Database window, right-click the macro, and then click _____ on the shortcut menu.
   a. Execute
   b. Run
   c. Do
   d. Perform

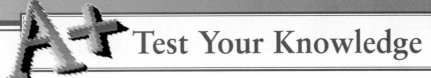 Test Your Knowledge

4. To insert a new macro action between two existing actions, select the row below where you want to insert the action, and press the _____ key(s).
   a. CTRL+N
   b. CTRL+I
   c. CTRL+INSERT
   d. INSERT

5. To sort entries in a combo box, right-click the combo box, click Properties on the shortcut menu, and click the _____ property.
   a. Row Arrange
   b. Row Source
   c. Row Sort
   d. Sort

6. A switchboard is a special type of _____.
   a. report
   b. table
   c. module
   d. form

7. To create a switchboard, click _____ on the menu bar, click Add-Ins, and then click Switchboard Manager.
   a. Edit
   b. View
   c. Insert
   d. Tools

8. Individual switchboards within a switchboard system are referred to as switchboard _____.
   a. pages
   b. frames
   c. boxes
   d. buttons

9. To move between the Action column and the Action Arguments in the Macro window, press the _____ key.
   a. F5
   b. F6
   c. F7
   d. F8

10. To keep a combo box current with the rest of a form, modify the _____ property of the entire form.
    a. On Target
    b. On Record
    c. On Current
    d. On Focus

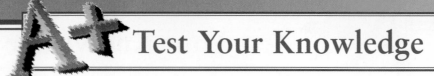

Test Your Knowledge

3 Understanding Macros

Instructions: In Figure 6-75, arrows point to various items in the Macro window. Identify these items in the spaces provided and use this figure to answer the following questions on your own paper.

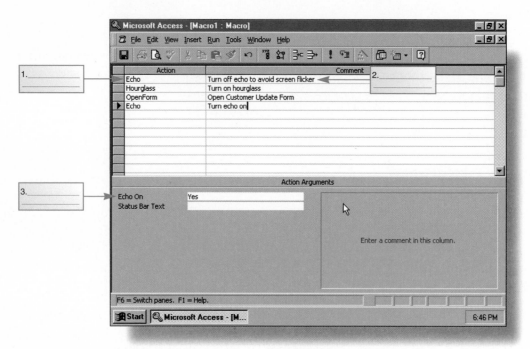

FIGURE 6-75

1. The Hourglass action to turn off the hourglass should be inserted between the OpenForm and Echo action. How can you insert a new action?
2. What value would you assign to the argument for this new action?
3. How can you maximize the form when it is opened?
4. How do you execute a macro?

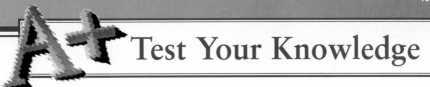

4 Understanding Combo Boxes

Instructions: Figure 6-76 shows the design grid for the Customer Update Form. The properties for the Name to Find combo box display in the window. Use this figure to answer the following questions on your own paper.

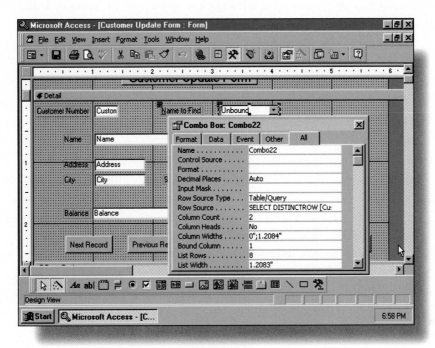

FIGURE 6-76

1. When do you place a combo box on a form?
2. What is the purpose of the Row Source property?
3. What is the purpose of the Tab Stop property?
4. What is the purpose of the On Current property?

Use Help

1 Reviewing Project Activities

Instructions: Perform the following tasks using a computer.

1. Start Access.
2. If the Office Assistant is on your screen, then click it to display its balloon. If the Office Assistant is not on your screen, click the Office Assistant button on the toolbar.
3. Type switchboard in the What would you like to do? text box. Click the Search button. Click Create and manage a switchboard form.
4. When the Help information displays, read it. Click the Create a switchboard form using the Switchboard Manager link. Read the information. Next, right-click within the box, and then click Print Topic. Hand the printout in to your instructor. Click the Help Topics button to return to the Help Topics: Microsoft Access 97 dialog box.
5. Click the Index tab. Type command bu in the top text box labeled 1 and then double-click Command Button Wizard in the middle list box labeled 2. Double-click Create a command button in the Topics Found dialog box. When the Help information displays, read it, ready the printer, right-click, and click Print Topic. Hand the printout in to your instructor. Click the Help Topics button to return to the Help Topics: Microsoft Access 97 dialog box.
6. Click the Find tab. Type combo in the top text box labeled 1. Click Combo in the middle list box labeled 2. Double-click Combo boxes: What they are and how they work in the lower list box labeled 3. When the Help information displays, read it, ready the printer, right-click, and click Print Topic. Hand the printout in to your instructor.

2 Expanding the Basics

Instructions: Use Access Help to learn about the topics listed below. If you are unable to print the Help information, then answer the questions on your own paper.

1. Using the Office Assistant, answer the following questions:
   a. How can you save a copy of a macro under a different name?
   b. How can you delete a macro?
   c. How can you rename a macro?

2. Using the keywords, command bu, and the Index sheet in the Help Topics: Microsoft Access 97 dialog box, display and print information on adding a picture to a command button. Then, answer the following questions:
   a. How can you add a picture and a caption to a command button?
   b. How do you add a picture if you are not sure of the path and file name?

3. Use the Find sheet in the Help Topics: Microsoft Access 97 dialog box to display and then print information about deleting a switchboard.

4. Use the Office Assistant to display and print information on when you should use a macro versus when you should use Visual Basic. Then, answer the following questions:
   a. When must you use a macro instead of Visual Basic?
   b. Why does using Visual Basic instead of macros make your database easier to maintain?

Apply Your Knowledge

1 Creating and Using Macros in the Green Thumb Database

Instructions: Start Access. Open the Green Thumb database from the Access folder on the Data Disk that accompanies this book. Perform the following tasks.

1. Create a macro to open the Customer Update Form you created in Project 4. The macro should maximize the form automatically when it is opened.
2. Save the macro as Open Customer Update Form.
3. Create a macro to print the Customers by Intern report you created in Project 4.
4. Save the macro as Print Customers by Intern.
5. Run the Print Customers by Intern macro and print the report.
6. Modify the Customer Update Form you created in Project 4 to create the form shown in Figure 6-77. The form includes command buttons and a combo box to search for the customer's name.

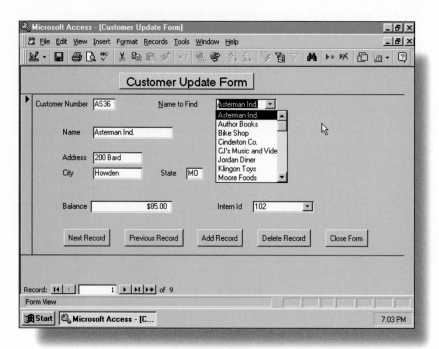

FIGURE 6-77

7. Print the form. To print the form, open the form, click File on the menu bar and then click Print. Click Selected Record(s) as the Print Range. Click the OK button.

1 Creating an Application System for the Museum Mercantile Database

Problem: The Museum Mercantile volunteers are pleased with the tables, forms, and reports you have created. They have two additional requests, however. First, they require some improvements to the Product Update Form. They would like to have buttons placed on the form for moving to the next record, moving to the previous record, adding a record, deleting a record, and closing the form. Then, they want a simple way of searching for a product given the product's description. They also would like an easy way to access the various tables, forms, and reports simply by clicking a button or two. This would make it much easier to train the volunteers that maintain and update the database.

Instructions: Open the Museum Mercantile database from the Access folder on the Data Disk that accompanies this book. Perform the following tasks.

1. Create macros that will perform the following tasks:
   a. Open the Product Update Form
   b. Open the Vendor Master Form
   c. Open the Product Table
   d. Open the Vendor Table
   e. Preview the Inventory Report
   f. Preview the Products by Vendor
   g. Preview the On Hand Value Report
   h. Print the Inventory Report
   i. Print the Products by Vendor
   j. Print the On Hand Value Report
2. Modify the Product Update Form to create the form shown in Figure 6-78. The form includes command buttons and a combo box to search for products by description.
3. Save and print the form. To print the form, open the form, click File on the menu bar and then click Print. Click Selected Record(s) as the Print Range. Click the OK button.

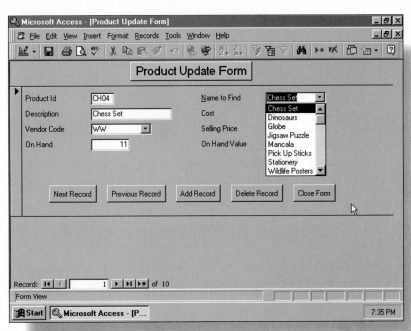

FIGURE 6-78

(continued)

In the Lab

Creating an Application System for the Museum Mercantile Database *(continued)*

4. Create the switchboard for the Museum Mercantile database shown in Figure 6-79. Use the same design for your switchboard pages as that shown in this project. For example, the View Form switchboard page should have three choices: Open Product Update Form, Open Vendor Master Form, and Return to Main Switchboard. Include all the forms, tables, and reports for which you created macros in Step 1 on the previous page.

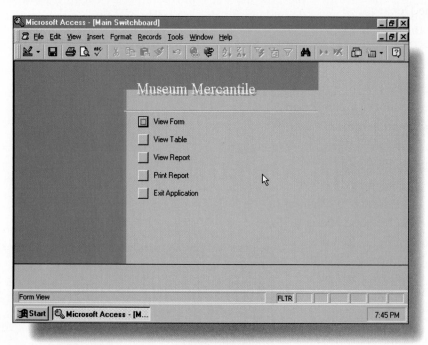

FIGURE 6-79

5. Run the switchboard and correct any errors.

2 Creating an Application System for the City Telephone System Database

Problem: The telephone manager is pleased with the tables, forms, and reports you have created. She has two additional requests, however. First, she requires some improvements to the User Update Form. She would like to have buttons placed on the form for moving to the next record, moving to the previous record, adding a record, deleting a record, and closing the form. Then, she wants a simple way of searching for a user given the user's last name. She also would like an easy way to access the various tables, forms, and reports simply by clicking a button or two. She feels that this would make the employees much more productive than if they have to remember all the steps required to perform any of these tasks.

In the Lab

Instructions: Open the City Telephone System database from the Access folder on the Data Disk that accompanies this book. Perform the following tasks.

1. Create macros that will perform the following tasks:
   a. Open the User Update Form
   b. Open the Department Master Form
   c. Open the User Table
   d. Open the Department Table
   e. Preview the Telephone List
   f. Preview the Users by Department
   g. Preview the Total Charges Report
   h. Print the Telephone List
   i. Print the Users by Department
   j. Print the Total Charges Report

2. Modify the User Update Form to create the form shown in Figure 6-80. The form includes command buttons and a combo box to search for users by the user's last name.

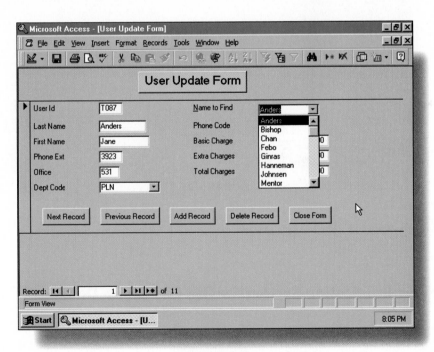

FIGURE 6-80

3. Save and print the form. To print the form, open the form, click File on the menu bar and then click Print. Click Selected Record(s) as the Print Range. Click the OK button.

(continued)

In the Lab

Creating an Application System for the City Telephone System Database *(continued)*

4. Create the switchboard for the City Telephone System database shown in Figure 6-81. Use the same design for your switchboard pages as that shown in this project. For example, the View Form switchboard page should have three choices: Open User Update Form, Open Department Master Form, and Return to Main Switchboard. Include all the forms, tables, and reports for which you created macros in Step 1 on the previous page.

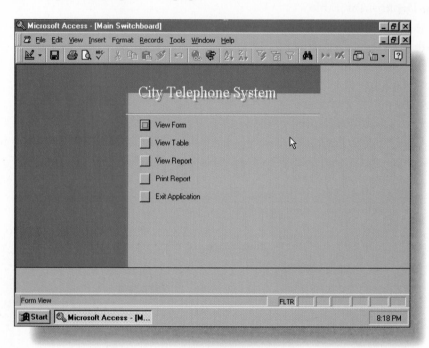

FIGURE 6-81

5. Run the switchboard and correct any errors.

3 Creating an Application System for the City Scene Database

Problem: The managing editor is pleased with the tables, forms, and reports that you have created. He has two additional requests, however. First, he requires some improvements to the Advertiser Update Form. He would like to have buttons placed on the form for moving to the next record, moving to the previous record, adding a record, deleting a record, and closing the form. He also would like a simple way of searching for an advertiser given the advertiser's name. Then, he wants an easy way to access the various tables, forms, and reports simply by clicking a button or two. He feels that this would make the employees much more productive than if they have to remember all the steps required to perform any of these tasks.

In the Lab

Instructions: Open the City Scene database from the Access folder on the Data Disk that accompanies this book. Perform the following tasks.

1. Create macros that will perform the following tasks:
   a. Open the Advertiser Update Form
   b. Open the Ad Rep Master Form
   c. Open the Advertiser Table
   d. Open the Ad Rep Table
   e. Preview the Status Report
   f. Preview the Advertisers by Ad Rep
   g. Preview the Advertising Income Report
   h. Print the Status Report
   i. Print the Advertisers by Ad Rep
   j. Print the Advertising Income Report

2. Modify the Advertiser Update Form to create the form shown in Figure 6-82. The form includes command buttons and a combo box to search for accounts by the account name.

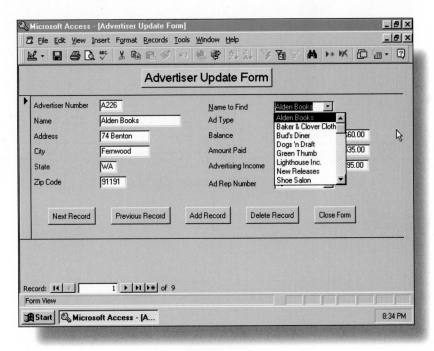

FIGURE 6-82

3. Save and print the form. To print the form, open the form, click File on the menu bar and then click Print. Click Selected Record(s) as the Print Range. Click the OK button.

(continued)

In the Lab

Creating an Application System for the City Scene Database *(continued)*

4. Create the switchboard for the City Scene database shown in Figure 6-83. Use the same design for your switchboard pages as that shown in this project. For example, the View Form switchboard page should have three choices: Open Advertiser Update Form, Open Ad Rep Master Form, and Return to Main Switchboard. Include all the forms, tables, and reports for which you created macros in Step 1 on the previous page.

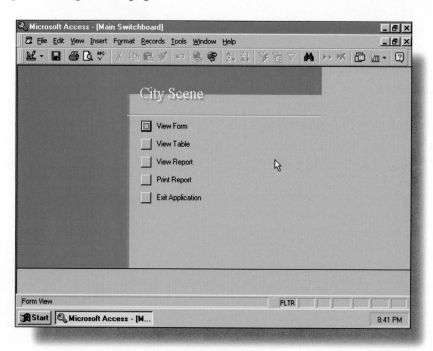

FIGURE 6-83

5. Run the switchboard and correct any errors.

Cases and Places

The difficulty of these case studies varies: ❿ are the least difficult; ❿❿ are more difficult; and ❿❿❿ are the most difficult.

1 ❿ Use the golf lesson database modified in Case Study 1 of the Cases and Places section of Project 5 for this assignment. Create macros to (a) open the Class Update and Pro Master Forms, (b) open the Lesson Revenue and Pro Tables, (c) preview the Lesson Revenue and Classes By Pro Reports, and (d) print the Lesson Revenue and Classes By Pro Reports. Also, create and run a switchboard for the golf lesson database.

2 ❿ Modify the Class Update Form created in Case Study 3 of the Cases and Places section of Project 4 to include command buttons and a combo box to search for classes by description. Save and print the form.

3 ❿❿ Use the textbook database modified in Case Study 5 of the Cases and Places section of Project 5 for this assignment. Create macros to (a) open the book form, (b) open the book table and maximize the window, (c) preview the Textbook Exchange Report, and (d) print the Textbook Exchange Report. Also, create and run a switchboard that includes these four macros.

4 ❿❿ Use the restaurant database modified in Case Study 4 of the Cases and Places section of Project 5 for this assignment. Modify the restaurant form to include command buttons. Also, create a combo box to search for restaurant names. Save and print the form.

5 ❿❿ Use the movie database modified in Case Study 3 of the Cases and Places section of Project 5 for this assignment. Create macros to (a) open the table and maximize the window, (b) open a movie report in a preview window, and (c) print the movie report. Also, create and run a switchboard that includes these three macros.

6 ❿❿❿ Use the campus directory database modified in Case Study 6 of the Cases and Places section of Project 5 for this assignment. Modify the information form to include command buttons. Also, create a combo box to serch for faculty, administration, coaches, and other key names. Save and print the form.

Cases and Places

7 ▶▶▶ Use the financial institutions database modified in Case Study 7 of the Cases and Places section of Project 5 for this assignment. Create macros to (a) open the investment table and maximize the window, (b) preview the Investment Future Value Report, and (c) print the Investment Future Value Report. Also, create and run a switchboard that includes these three macros.

Linking Excel Worksheets to an Access Database

INTEGRATION FEATURE

Case Perspective

Lamatec Industries has been using Excel to automate a variety of tasks for several years. Lamatec has maintained data on its departments and employees in an Excel worksheet, but recently, the management decided to convert this data to an Access database. After performing the conversion, they intended to discontinue using Excel for the employee data, relying instead on Access exclusively.

As the management at Lamatec reviewed its uses of the data, however, it appeared that some operations existed for which it might be better to maintain the data in an Excel workbook rather than convert the data to Access. The management at Lamatec is keenly interested in being able to use the Query, Form, and Report features of Access. Fortunately, they found that by linking the worksheets to an Access database, they could have the best of both. They can use Excel to store and manipulate the data and use Access for queries, forms, and reports.

They decided to try the approach using both Excel and Access first. They intended to analyze their usage of Excel over the next year. If later they found they were no longer realizing any benefit from it, then they would convert the data to Access and no longer rely on Excel.

Introduction

It is possible to **link** data stored in a variety of formats to Access databases. The available formats include several other database management systems (for example, dBASE, FoxPro, and Paradox). They also include a variety of non-database formats, including Excel worksheets.

When an external table or worksheet is imported, or converted, into an Access database, a copy of the data is placed as a table in the database. The original data still exists, just as it did before, but no further connection is maintained between it and the data in the database. Changes to the original data do not affect the data in the database. Likewise, changes in the database do not affect the original data.

With **linking**, the connection is retained. When an Excel worksheet is linked, for example, the worksheet is not stored in the database. Instead, Access simply establishes a connection to the worksheet so you can view or edit the data in either Access or Excel.

Figures 1a through 1d on the next page illustrate the linking process. The type of worksheet that can be linked is one where the data is stored as a **list**, which is a labeled series of rows, with each row containing the same type of data. For example, in the worksheets shown in Figures 1a and 1b, the first rows contain the labels, which are entries indicating the type of data found in the column. The entry in the first column of the Department worksheet, for example, is Dept Code, indicating that all the other values in the column are department codes. The entry in the second column is Name, indicating that all the other values in the column are department names. Other than the first row, which contains the labels, all the rows contain precisely the same type of data: a department code in the first column, a name in the second column, a location in the third column, and so on.

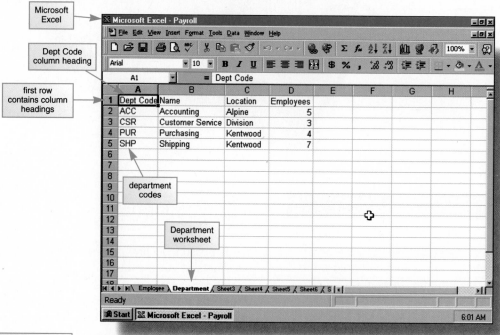

FIGURE 1a

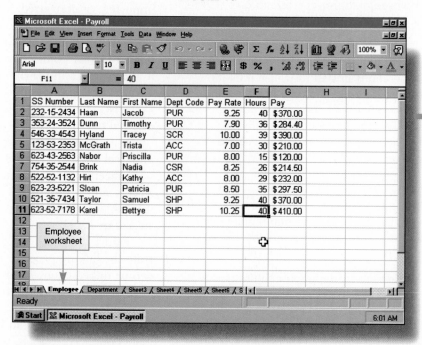

FIGURE 1b

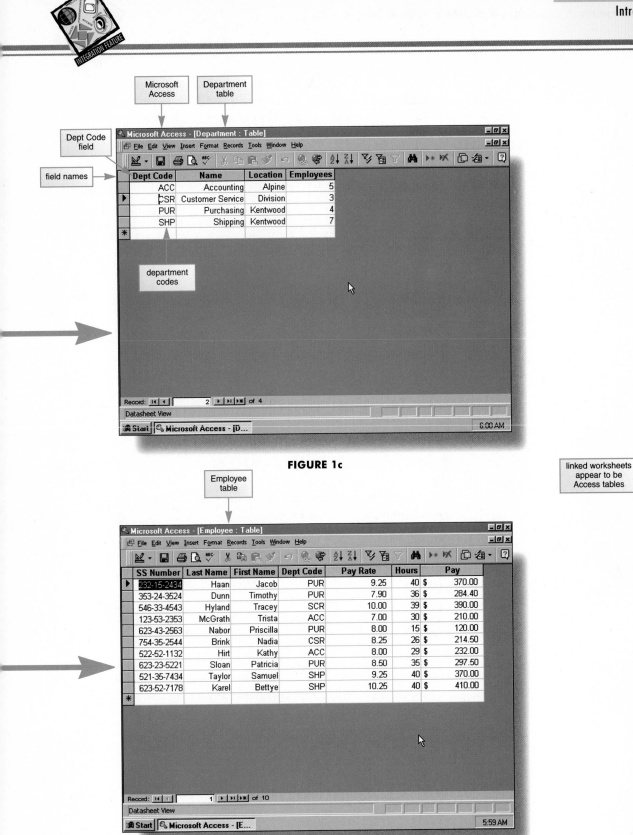

FIGURE 1c

FIGURE 1d

More *About* Linking Data: Spreadsheets

By selecting the TransferSpreadsheet action, you can use a macro to link spreadsheet data. Select Link for the Transfer Type argument, select the spreadsheet type (for example, Microsoft Excel 5-7) for the Spreadsheet Type argument, enter the name of the Access table, and the file name of the spreadsheet.

More *About* Linking Data: Databases

By selecting the TransferDatabase action, you can use a macro to link data from an external database. Select Link for the Transfer Type argument, select the database type (for example, dBASE IV), enter the name of the source table, and the name of the destination table.

More *About* Linking Data: Text Data

By selecting the TransferText action, you can use a macro to link text data. Select the appropriate file type as the value for the Transfer Type argument, enter the name of the Access table and the name of the file containing the data.

As Figures 1a and 1b on page AI 2.2 illustrate, the worksheets are linked to the database and then can be displayed as typical database tables, as shown in Figures 1c and 1d on the previous page. The columns in the worksheet become the *fields*. The column headings in the first row of the worksheets become the *field names*. The rows of the worksheets, other than the first rows, which contain the labels, become the *records* in the table. In the process, each field will be assigned the data type that seems the most reasonable, given the data currently in the worksheet.

Creating the Database

Before linking the data, you must start Access. If the database already exists, you must open it. If not, you must create it. Perform the following steps to start Access and create a new database called Payroll. The data will be linked to this database.

TO START ACCESS AND CREATE A DATABASE

Step 1: Click the Start button on the taskbar.
Step 2: Click New Office Document on the Start menu. If the General tab is not selected, click the General tab.
Step 3: Make sure the Blank Database icon is selected, and then click the OK button.
Step 4: Click 3½ Floppy (A:) in the Save in list box. Type Payroll in the File name text box.
Step 5: Click the Create button.

The Payroll database is created and the Database window displays.

Linking the Data

To **link the data**, you will use the **Get External Data command** on the File menu, and then click **Link Tables**. After selecting the desired type of linked file (Microsoft Excel, in this case), then you select the workbook containing the worksheets to be linked. Next, you will select the specific worksheet to be linked and also indicate that the first row contains the column headings. These column headings become the field names in the Access table. Perform the following steps to link the Employee and Department worksheets to the Access database.

Steps To Link Worksheets to an Access Database

1 **Click File on the menu bar, point to Get External Data, and then click Link Tables.**

The Link dialog box displays. You can use this dialog box to select the file that is to be linked.

2 **Click the Files of type box arrow and then point to Microsoft Excel.**

The list of available file types displays (Figure 2).

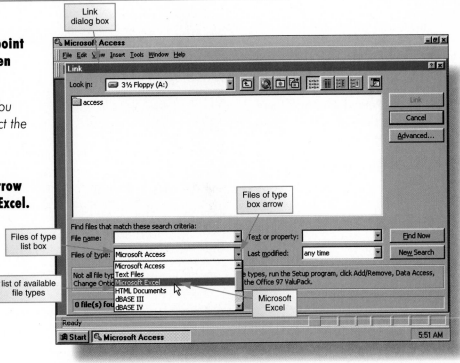

FIGURE 2

3 **Click Microsoft Excel. If the Access folder does not display in the Look in list box, point to the Access folder (Figure 3).**

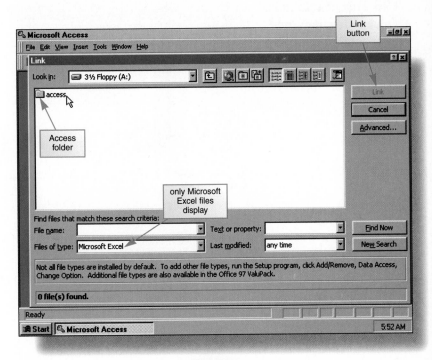

FIGURE 3

4 If necessary, click the Access folder.

The list of available Excel workbooks in the Access folder displays.

5 Click the Payroll workbook, and then click the Link button. Point to the Next button.

The Link Spreadsheet Wizard dialog box displays (Figure 4). You can use this dialog box to select the worksheet to be linked.

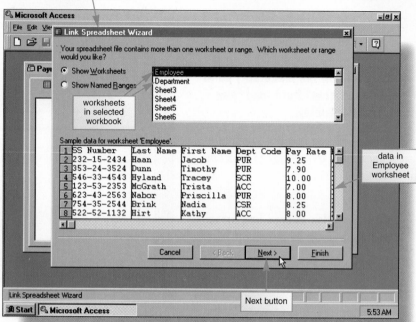

FIGURE 4

6 With the Employee worksheet selected, click the Next button. Click First Row Contains Column Headings, and then point to the Next button.

The Link Spreadsheet Wizard dialog box displays (Figure 5). You can use this dialog box to indicate that the first row contains the field names.

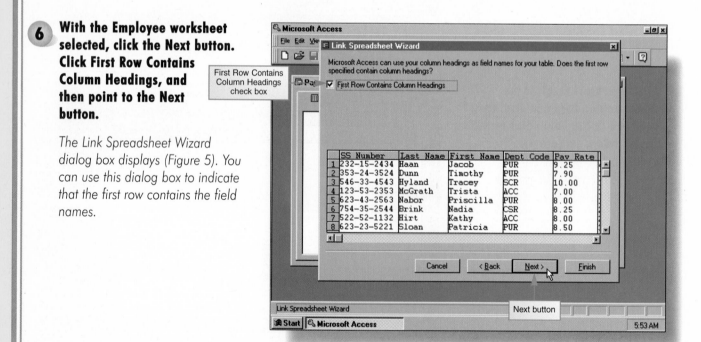

FIGURE 5

7 Click the Next button. Make sure the Linked Table Name is Employee, and then point to the Finish button.

The Link Spreadsheet Wizard dialog box displays (Figure 6). The name of the linked table will be Employee.

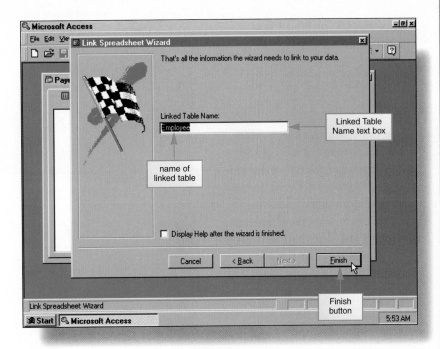

FIGURE 6

8 Click the Finish button.

The Microsoft Access dialog box displays when the process is complete (Figure 7). The name of the linked table displays in the Database window. The arrow in front of the name indicates that it is a linked object rather than a true Access table.

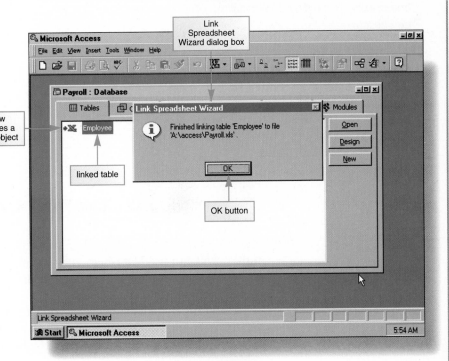

FIGURE 7

9 **Click the OK button in the Microsoft Access dialog box.**

The worksheet is linked to the database.

10 **Use the techniques in Steps 1 through 9 to link the Department worksheet in the Payroll workbook to the Payroll database. Click the Department worksheet before clicking the Next button in Step 6. Be sure the name of the linked table is Department.**

The Microsoft Access dialog box displays when the process is complete (Figure 8). The worksheets are linked to the database and display as tables in the Payroll database.

11 **Click the OK button. Close the Database window by clicking its Close button, and then quit Access.**

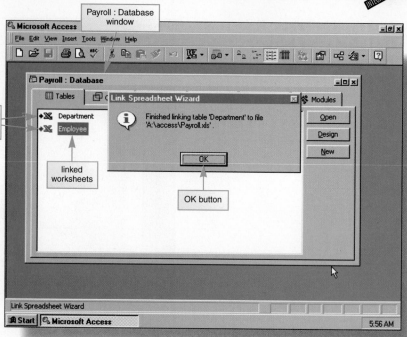

FIGURE 8

Using the Linked Worksheets

Generally, you can use the linked worksheets just as if they were regular Access tables. You can use Datasheet view or Form view to change the data. When you do, you actually are changing data within the Excel worksheets. You also can use Excel to change the data directly.

Using the linked worksheets, you can create queries such as the one shown in Figure 9. In addition, you can use the worksheets in forms and reports. The one operation you cannot perform with the linked worksheets that you can with tables is to alter their design.

When you run a query, the query will be executed using the current data in the linked worksheets. Running the query shown in Figure 9, for example, would produce the results shown in Figure 10.

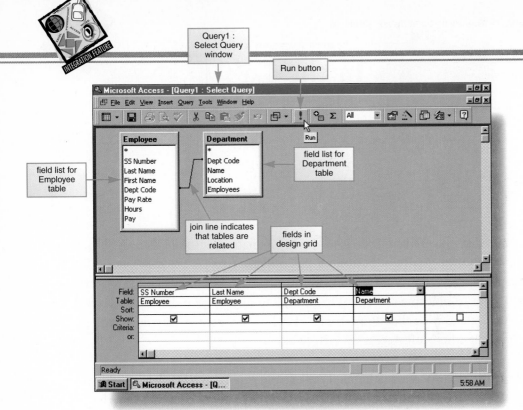

Query1 : Select Query window

Run button

field list for Employee table

field list for Department table

join line indicates that tables are related

fields in design grid

FIGURE 9

Summary

The Integration Feature covered the process of linking worksheets in an Excel workbook to an Access database. To link a worksheet to an Access database, you learned to use the Link Spreadsheet Wizard. Working with the wizard, you first identified the specific worksheet to be linked, identified that the first row of the worksheet contained the column headings, and then assigned a name to the linked worksheet. The wizard linked the worksheet to the database, enabling you to manipulate the worksheet from within Access just as you would a table.

data from Employee worksheet

data from Department worksheet

SS Number	Last Name	Dept Code	Name
522-52-1132	Hirt	ACC	Accounting
123-53-2353	McGrath	ACC	Accounting
754-35-2544	Brink	CSR	Customer Service
623-23-5221	Sloan	PUR	Purchasing
623-43-2563	Nabor	PUR	Purchasing
353-24-3524	Dunn	PUR	Purchasing
232-15-2434	Haan	PUR	Purchasing
623-52-7178	Karel	SHP	Shipping
521-35-7434	Taylor	SHP	Shipping

results of query

FIGURE 10

What You Should Know

Having completed this Integration Feature, you now should be able to perform the following tasks:

▶ Link Worksheets to an Access Database *(AI 2.5)*

▶ Start Access and Create a Database *(AI 2.4)*

In the Lab

1 Use Help

Instructions: Perform the following tasks using a computer.

1. Start Access.
2. If the Office Assistant is on your screen, click it to display its balloon. If the Office Assistant is not on your screen, click the Office Assistant button on the toolbar.
3. Type linking spreadsheets in the What would you like to do? text box. Click the Search button. Click Import or link data from a spreadsheet. When the Help information displays, read it. Next, right-click within the box and then click Print Topic. Hand the printout in to your instructor. When you are finished, close the Microsoft Access 97 Help window.
4. Start Excel.
5. Click the Office Assistant to display its balloon. Type naming cells in the What would you like to do? text box. Click the Search button. Click Name cells in a workbook. When the Help information displays, read it and then click the Name a cell or range of cells link. Read the Help information, right-click within the box and then click Print Topic. Hand the printout in to your instructor.

2 Linking Excel Worksheets to the Sales Database

Problem: Midwest Computer Supply has been using Excel to automate a variety of tasks and recently converted some of its data to an Access database. As Midwest reviewed its uses of the data, however, it decided that some financial operations are better performed in Excel. The management of Midwest would like to be able to use the Query, Form, and Report features of Access while maintaining the data in Excel worksheets.

Instructions: Perform the following tasks.

1. Create a new database in which to store all the objects related to the sales data. Use Sales as the name of the database.
2. Link the Customer and Sales Representative worksheets shown in Figures 11a and 11b to the Sales database. The worksheets are in the Sales workbook in the Access folder on the Data Disk that accompanies this book.
3. Open and print the tables in Access.

In the Lab

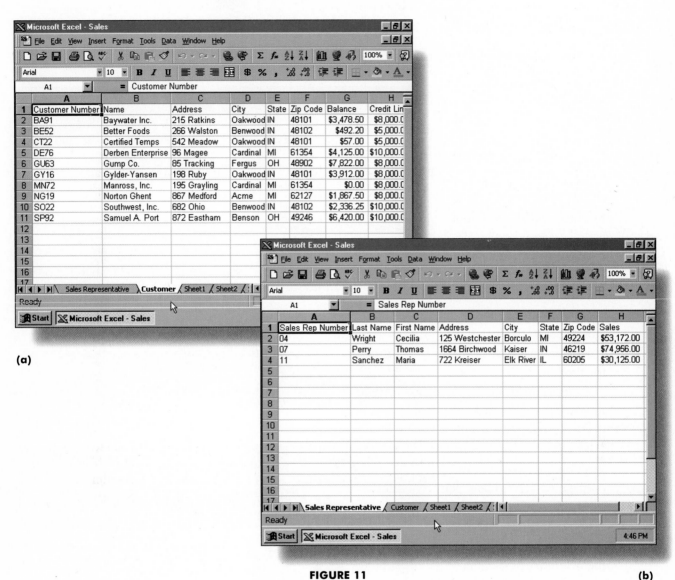

FIGURE 11

(a)

(b)

3 Linking Excel Worksheets to the Inventory Stock Database

Problem: Tennis Is Everything has been using Excel to automate a variety of tasks and recently converted some of its data to an Access database. As Tennis Is Everything reviewed its uses of the data, however, it decided that some financial operations are better performed in Excel. The management of Tennis Is Everything would like to be able to use the Query, Form, and Report features of Access while maintaining the data in Excel worksheets.

(continued)

In the Lab

Linking Excel Worksheets to the Inventory Stock Database (*continued*)

Instructions: Perform the following tasks.

1. Create a new database in which to store all the objects related to the inventory data. Use Inventory Stock as the name of the database.

2. The Product worksheet shown in Figure 12a in the Inventory Stock workbook includes formulas that do not need to be linked to the Inventory Stock database. Link only the named range, inv_data, in the Product worksheet to the Inventory Stock database. Use Product for the Linked Table Name. The worksheet is in the Inventory Stock workbook in the Access folder on the Data Disk that accompanies this book. (*Hint*: Use Help on page AI 2.10 to help you solve this problem.)

3. Link the Vendor worksheet shown in Figure 12b to the Inventory Stock database. The worksheet is in the Inventory Stock workbook in the Access folder on the Data Disk that accompanies this book.

4. Open and print the tables in Access.

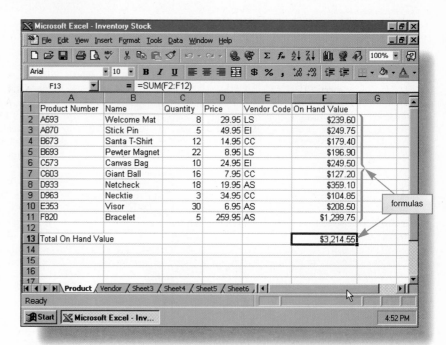

Figure 12a

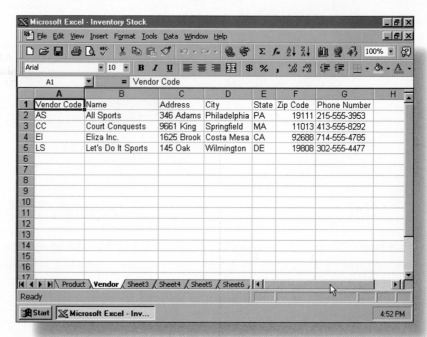

FIGURE 12b

Index

NOTE TO READER: This index contains references for Projects 1 through 6 and the Integration Features of the book, *Microsoft Access 97: Complete Concepts and Techniques*. The same references can be used for Access Projects 1 through 3 and Integration Feature 1 in the book, *Microsoft Office 97: Introductory Concepts and Techniques*, and Access Projects 4 through 6 and Integration Feature 2 in the book, *Microsoft Office 97: Advanced Concepts and Techniques*.

Microsoft **Access 97**